QuickBooks® in the Classroom

Instructor's Resource Guide

Intuit Education Program

Copyright

First printing: January 2004

Intuit Inc.

P.O. Box 7850

Mountain View, CA 94039-7850

ISBN 1-57338-102-0

Trademarks

Other attributes

Important

Terms, conditions, features, service offerings, prices, and hours referenced in this document are subject to change without notice. We at Intuit are committed to bringing you great online services through QuickBooks. Occasionally, we may decide to update our selection and change our service offerings, so please check **www.quickbooks.com** for the latest information, including pricing and availability, on our products and services.

Table of contents

Lesson 9: Analyzing financial data, 175

Lesson 10: Setting up inventory, 211

Lesson 11: Tracking and paying sales tax, 235

Introduction

This guide introduces you to QuickBooks—Intuit's easy-to-use, powerful accounting systems for small businesses. The guide contains 15 lessons in addition to this chapter.

Many of the lessons in this guide can be performed with any QuickBooks Financial Software 2004 Edition. When a lesson or exercise requires QuickBooks: Pro or QuickBooks: Premier, that requirement is stated at the beginning of the lesson or exercise.

Most of the step-by-step instructions and screen captures in this guide were created with QuickBooks Financial Software: Pro Edition 2004. Your screens may differ, and some instructions may vary slightly, if you are using QuickBooks: Basic or QuickBooks: Premier Editions instead of QuickBooks: Pro. Screen captures for features available only in Premier Editions were created with QuickBooks Financial Software: Premier Edition 2004.

Course objectives

After performing the exercises in this guide, your students should be able to do the following:

- Create a new QuickBooks company.
- Modify the preset chart of accounts to suit your needs.
- Add information to company lists, or edit information in company lists.
- Open and use registers for any QuickBooks balance sheet accounts.
- Reconcile a QuickBooks checking account.
- Track credit card transactions.
- Invoice customers.
- Create sales orders.
- Generate customer statements.
- Receive payments from customers and make bank deposits.
- Write QuickBooks checks and assign amounts to specific expense accounts.
- Work with asset and liability accounts in QuickBooks.
- Enter bills into QuickBooks accounts payable.
- Pay bills.
- Create and customize QuickBooks reports and graphs.
- Save reports and forms as Portable Document Format (PDF) files.
- Export QuickBooks reports to Microsoft® Excel.
- Set up inventory and build finished goods.
- Track and pay sales tax.
- Understand QuickBooks payroll features.

- Create estimates and do progress invoicing.
- Track time and mileage.
- Pay nonemployees for time worked.
- Customize QuickBooks sales forms.
- Write letters in Microsoft® Word using QuickBooks data.

Hardware and software requirements

For all QuickBooks: Basic, Pro, and Premier 2004 products

To use the 2004 version of any QuickBooks: Basic, Pro, or Premier product, you need the following equipment and software:

- 200 MHz IBM compatible Pentium computer (350 MHz or higher recommended).
- A minimum of 64 MB (megabytes) of RAM (random access memory); 96 MB is recommended.
- Hard disk with the following amounts of free disk space:

Installation component	Basic	Pro	Premier
QuickBooks Financial Software	230 MB	250 MB	400 MB
Microsoft Internet Explorer 6.0	70 MB	70 MB	70 MB
Additional for Timer	N/A	9 MB	9 MB

- 2x CD-ROM drive (double speed) or higher.
- 8-bit or 16-bit sound card if you want to use the sound features.
- 256-color VGA monitor, SVGA monitor, or better is recommended (minimum resolution of 800 x 600 using Small Fonts in your Windows Control Display settings).
- Either Windows 98, Me, 2000, or XP.
- Internet access (with a connection speed of 56 Kbps or higher) is required for Payroll and all online features/services.
- QuickBooks for Windows installation CD-ROM.
- Printer supported by Windows 98, Me, 2000, or XP.

For QuickBooks: Pro and Premier only

- Microsoft® Word 97, 2000, 2002, or 2003 if you plan to use the QuickBooks Letters feature.
- Microsoft® Excel 97, 2000, 2002, or 2003 if you plan to use the features in QuickBooks: Pro and QuickBooks: Premier that integrate with Microsoft Excel.
- Either Microsoft® Outlook (version 97, 98, or 2000), Symantec® ACT! version 3.0.8, 4.0.2, OR Interact® 2000 if you want to synchronize with contact management software.

Network requirements

QuickBooks 2004 network requirements are the same whether you are sharing a company file or printing to a network printer:

- Windows 2000 Server or Windows Server 2003 client-server networks.

  OR

- Peer-to-peer network using Windows 98, 2000, Me, or XP.

Important: Intuit recommends you have the latest update for your operating system or network software. If you are uncertain whether you have the latest update, contact Microsoft or your network administrator.

About the exercise file

An exercise file is included with this training guide. Install the file on the CD-ROM to your computer's hard disk as described below. You'll use a copy of this file to complete the lessons in this guide.

We recommend that you make a copy of the exercise file and store it in a safe place in case the original becomes damaged.

Using the exercise file in each lesson

For each lesson in this guide, except for lessons 1 and 2, you'll restore a copy of the exercise file **qblesson.qbb**, and use that file to complete the lesson. The qblesson.qbb file you copy into the QBtrain directory on your hard disk is a QuickBooks backup file. This means that at the start of each lesson, you'll be restoring a new qblesson file. Instructions on how to restore the file are given at the beginning of each lesson.

Installing the exercise file

To install the exercise file on your hard disk:

1. Insert the CD into your computer's CD-ROM drive.
2. From the Windows Start menu, choose Run.
3. Type ***Explorer***, and then click OK.
4. From Windows Explorer, select your hard disk (usually c:).
5. From the File menu, choose New, and then choose Folder.
6. Type ***QBtrain***, and then press Enter.
7. Select your CD-ROM drive containing the exercise file (usually d: or e:).
8. Select qblesson.qbb.
9. Drag qblesson.qbb to the QBtrain folder on your hard disk.
10. Remove the CD-ROM from your CD-ROM drive.

Your exercise file is now installed in the QBtrain folder on your hard drive.

Exercise transaction dates

The exercise file for use with this training guide was created in QuickBooks: Pro and QuickBooks: Premier 2004 with the date set to 12/15/2007. When you open the exercise file in QuickBooks, QuickBooks automatically sets the sample data file date to 12/15/2007. When you close the exercise file, use your own QuickBooks company file, or exit QuickBooks, your system and QuickBooks dates will return to the current date.

Teaching methodology and methods

This course is divided into 15 lessons and combines lectures with hands-on student participation. We encourage you to pick and choose lessons to fit the needs of your students, or to fit your own teaching objectives.

Each lesson begins with a list of student objectives, handout materials needed, and instructor preparation. Appendix B, includes a brief demonstration of QuickBooks to be presented by the instructor. The demo introduces students to QuickBooks and provides them with a road map of what they will learn in the course.

Most lessons in this course include one or more handouts. We encourage you to use the handouts provided with a lesson; they summarize or illustrate the main points of your lecture, and are helpful for students to refer to later. If you choose not to distribute a copy of each handout to all your students, you can display the handouts on an overhead projector as you explain the basic concepts.

A copy of each handout is bound into the back of this guide and we've included an electronic copy on the CD-ROM that accompanies this guide so that you can edit and print the handouts as desired. See Appendix C for copies of the handouts.

To maximize hands-on practice with QuickBooks, a computer lab with one computer per student is ideal. If this is unavailable, you can teach the course with up to three students sharing a computer. However, sharing computers lengthens the course and reduces the effectiveness of student learning.

Each lesson contains special notes that help you present the material. These notes are printed *in italics* and appear at key places in the lessons.

Finally, you'll find a brief student test and review section at the end of each lesson. The text for each section is available electronic format file on the CD-ROM that accompanies this guide.

Instructor preparation

If you are new to the latest version of QuickBooks and want to see a list of new features, search the onscreen Help index for *new features.* (From the QuickBooks Help menu, choose Help Index.) Or see the summary of new features in Appendix A. To gain a quick overview of what will be presented in the course, you may want to run through the QuickBooks demonstration in Appendix B.

An important supplement to this instructor's manual is *QuickBooks Fundamentals,* which provides conceptual explanations of QuickBooks features. You can look up common business situations and find suggestions on how to handle those situations in QuickBooks. We suggest you have a guide available for reference during the course.

Student prerequisites

No knowledge of finances or accounting is needed to use QuickBooks. Students should however, have a basic knowledge of the computer operating system and know how to move files around, create folders or directories, copy files to and from disks, and run applications.

Evaluating the guide

We are interested in your evaluation of the course guide. What would you like to see changed, added, or deleted?

We are particularly interested in the following:

- The type of course you're teaching.
- The number of days or hours the course takes (i.e., five weeks, one day).
- Do you give quizzes or tests?
- What other material do you use when teaching this course?

There is a form in the back of this guide for you to complete and mail or fax to us.

LESSON 1 Getting started

Lesson objectives

- To gain an overview of the course and the topics to be covered
- To know how QuickBooks works and how you can get around in QuickBooks
- To learn common business terms used by QuickBooks
- To see how to exit QuickBooks

Instructor preparation

- Make sure you've read the sections called "Teaching methodology and methods" and "Instructor preparation" in the introduction to this guide.
- Install QuickBooks: Pro onto your computer's hard disk.
- Copy the qblesson.qbb file from the QuickBooks in the Classroom CD-ROM onto your computer's hard disk. (See "Installing the exercise file" on page 5.)
- Run through the content in the instructor demonstration available in Appendix B to make sure you're familiar with the material.

Course introduction

This course is an introduction to QuickBooks. Its main objective is to introduce you to the basic features in QuickBooks and give you an opportunity for hands-on practice. You'll learn about the types of information you need to track in your business, and you'll see how to enter that information and track it in QuickBooks. By the time you complete the course, you'll have a good idea of all that QuickBooks offers, you'll be familiar with the most common tasks, and you'll know where to find information about more advanced features.

Depending on the size of your class, you may want to spend a little time inquiring about your students' backgrounds—whether they own a business or are the bookkeeper for a small business, for example, or whether any of them have experience with accounting. This information can help you gear the course towards your students' particular needs.

Introducing QuickBooks

Before you begin your demonstration of QuickBooks (see Appendix B), students may find it helpful to hear an introduction to the basic features in QuickBooks.

Although most small business owners are worried about revenue, running a business involves a lot of other tasks. Depending on the type of business, you need to invoice customers, record payments from customers, pay your own bills to outside vendors, manage inventory, and analyze your financial data to see where you need to focus your next efforts. QuickBooks is a tool you can use to automate the tasks you're already performing as a business owner or to set up a new business.

Tell your students that they will see a demonstration of how QuickBooks works in a few minutes so they can get an overall view of the program. But first, here's an overview of some of the basic features they'll be seeing in the demo.

When you're working in QuickBooks, you'll spend most of your time using a form, a list, or a register. Since these are so basic to QuickBooks, we're going to spend a few minutes introducing them.

Using forms

You record most of your daily business transactions on a QuickBooks form, which looks just like a paper form. Here's an example of the form you use when you want to record a bill from and write a check to one of your vendors.

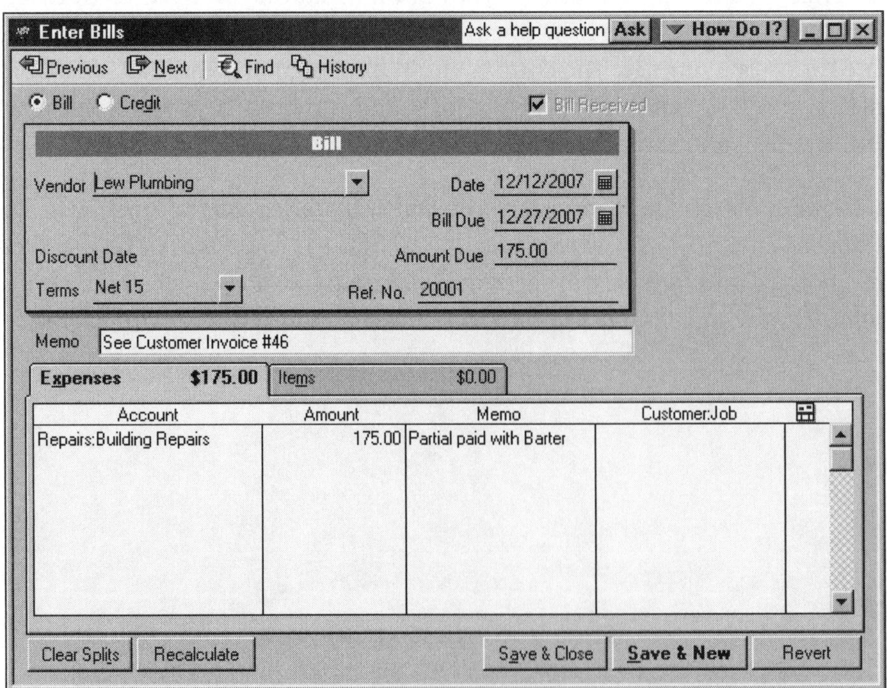

The form is intuitive—you already know how to fill out a form. But after you provide the information on a QuickBooks form, QuickBooks does the accounting for you in the background. For example, when you record a bill and then write a check (using the Pay Bills window) to pay for the business expense, QuickBooks enters transactions in your accounts payable register to show the expense you incurred and the payment you made. (*Accounts payable* is the money owed by your business to vendors.) It also records the check in your checking account, keeping your records up to date, and providing a running balance of what you owe at any time.

Using lists

The list is another basic QuickBooks feature. You fill out most QuickBooks forms by selecting entries from a list.

You may want to point out that in the Enter Bills window above, the information in the Vendor, Terms, Account, and Customer:Job fields is pulled from lists.

QuickBooks has lists where you can store information about customers, vendors, employees, items or services you sell, and so on. Lists save you time and help you enter information consistently and correctly.

When you're filling out an invoice form and you select a customer name from the Customer:Job list, QuickBooks not only fills in the name but also fills in the address, the payment terms, and the customer's sales tax, based on the information previously entered about that customer.

Here's an example of the Customer:Job list.

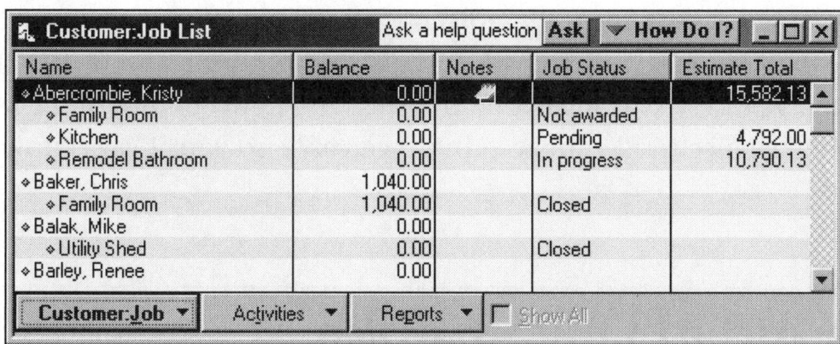

QuickBooks lets you complete a variety of activities from lists, using the menu buttons located at the bottom of each list. For example, to fill out an invoice for a customer, first select the customer from the Customer:Job list, and then choose Create Invoices from the Activities menu button.

Using registers

In addition to forms and lists, you'll also work with registers in QuickBooks. Just as you use your paper checkbook register to see a record of all the transactions in your checking account—checks you've written, other withdrawals you've made from your account, and deposits—a QuickBooks register contains a record of all the activity in one account. Almost every QuickBooks account has its own register.

You may want to explain to students that accounts receivable is the record of money owed to a business, that is, the outstanding invoices for which a business has not received payment.

Here's an example of the register for an accounts receivable account.

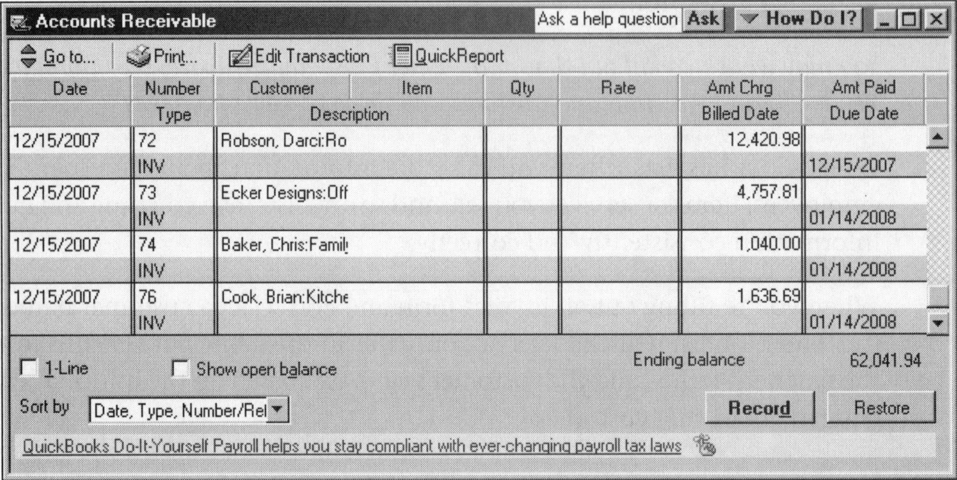

The register shows information about invoices written to customers—the date of the invoice, the date it's due, the name of the customer, and the amount. It also shows payments you've received against your invoices. The right column of the register gives you a running balance of all your accounts receivable, so you always know how much you're owed.

Getting around in QuickBooks

QuickBooks maximizes your work space and gives you quick access to the features and reports that you use most. In this section you'll learn how to do the following:

- Find information to help you get started using QuickBooks
- Manage your open windows
- Compare windows side by side
- Customize navigation features

Finding information to help you get started

If you're **new to QuickBooks**, the Getting Started window displays when you open a company file. This window guides you through the steps you need to complete after you've set up your company file. To display the Getting Started window, choose Getting Started from the Help menu.

If you're **upgrading from a previous version**, QuickBooks displays the New Features window. This window contains information about new features and explains how to find what you need to start working with the latest version. To display the New Features window, choose New Features from the Help menu.

Managing your open windows

To give you more room to work on the task at hand, QuickBooks displays one window at a time. When you open a window, it appears in front of other windows that you previously opened.

The Open Window list keeps track of the windows that are open. Use the Open Window list to switch between windows while you work. To switch to another open window, just click the title of the window that you want to display.

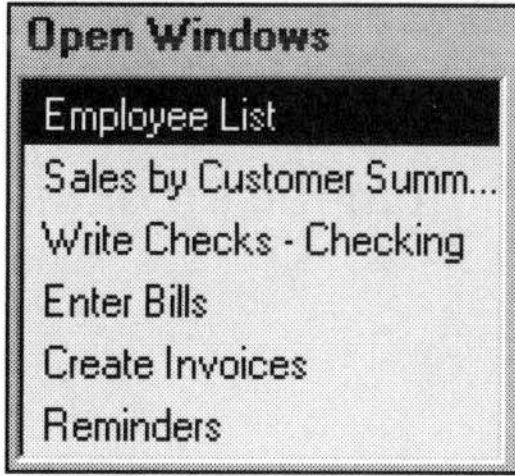

To show or hide the Open Window list:

- From the View menu, choose Open Window List.

  If the list is currently displayed, a checkmark appears to the left of the menu item.

For comparison purposes, you may wish to display more than one window at a time. You can easily switch between viewing one window at a time and viewing multiple windows. When you choose Multiple Windows from the View menu, QuickBooks tiles the windows in the main area. You can then move and resize the windows as needed.

To view multiple windows:

- From the View menu, choose Multiple Windows.

Using the menu bar

You can find all of the QuickBooks commands on the menu bar.

Many commands available on the menu bar can be added to the Icon Bar.

Using the Icon Bar

Another feature that makes it easy to get around in QuickBooks is the Icon Bar. It comes preset with shortcuts to several windows, such as Create Invoices and Enter Bills. By including the features and reports you use most, you can manage your business more quickly than ever.

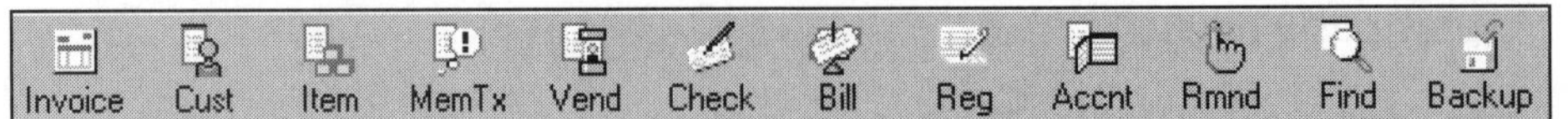

In addition to deciding which features to add to the Icon Bar, you can add or remove icons, change the order in which the icons display, insert spaces between icons, and edit icons by changing the icon text, graphic, or tooltip.

For instructions on how to customize the Icon Bar, search the onscreen Help index for *Icon Bar,* and then choose "Customizing the Icon Bar" from the list of topics that displays.

Using the Shortcut list

The QuickBooks Shortcut list groups together related lists and forms in an easy-to-follow format that helps you work more efficiently. The Shortcut list displays vertically and is an alternative to the Icon Bar.

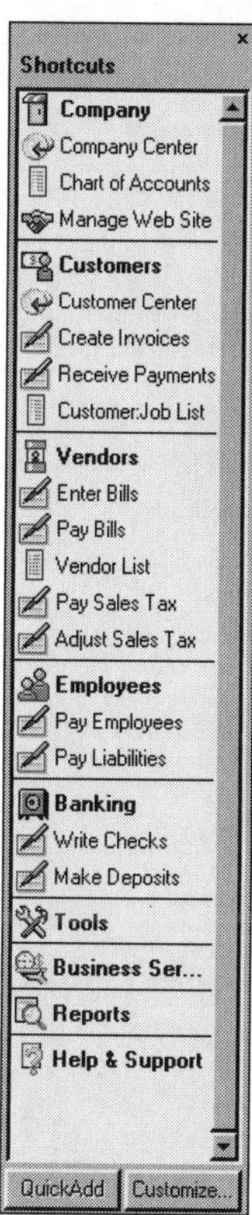

QuickBooks is preset to display the Icon Bar, but you can display the Shortcut list instead of, or in addition to, the Icon Bar.

To show or hide the Shortcut list:

- From the View menu, choose Shortcut List.

Like the Icon Bar, the Shortcut list can be customized, so you can add the forms, lists, and registers that you use frequently, and remove those that you don't use.

For instructions on how to customize the Shortcut list, search the onscreen Help for *shortcuts, Shortcut list*. Then, double-click the topic "Customizing the Shortcut list."

Making navigators your starting point

QuickBooks navigators provide a graphical representation of the workflow for a particular area of the product. For example, the Customers Navigator window has icons for important activities that are common to working with customers and making sales (such as, creating invoices, receiving payments, and making deposits). It looks like the following.

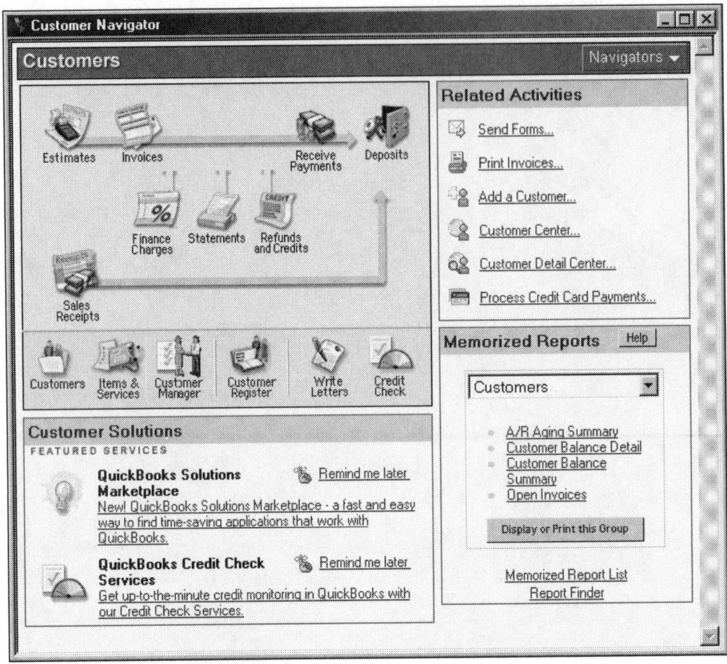

The navigators let you access features, reports, and solutions for the major areas of QuickBooks.

- Flow charts guide you in performing tasks in the correct order.
- Related Activities and Memorized Reports let you analyze your data and take action.
- Customer Solutions help you find features and services that you can use to manage your business.

To display a navigator, select its name from the Navigator list.

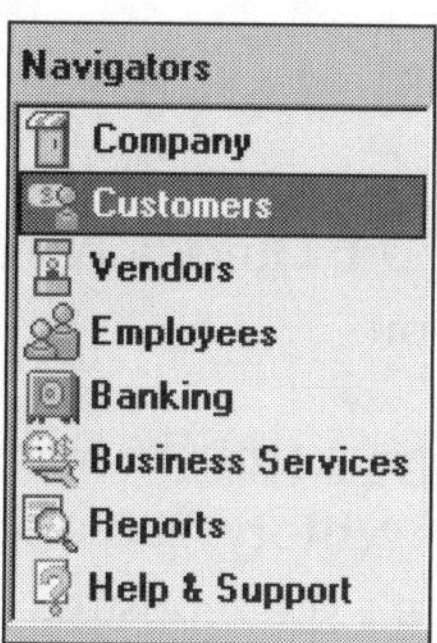

All the accounting you need to know

QuickBooks doesn't require users to learn or understand accounting jargon. However, it does use some common business terms.

The chart of accounts

When you keep books for a company, you want to track where your income comes from, where you put it, what your expenses are for, and what you use to pay them. You track this flow of money through a list of accounts called the chart of accounts.

To display the chart of accounts:

1 From the Lists menu, choose Chart of Accounts.

QuickBooks displays the chart of accounts for Rock Castle Construction Company.

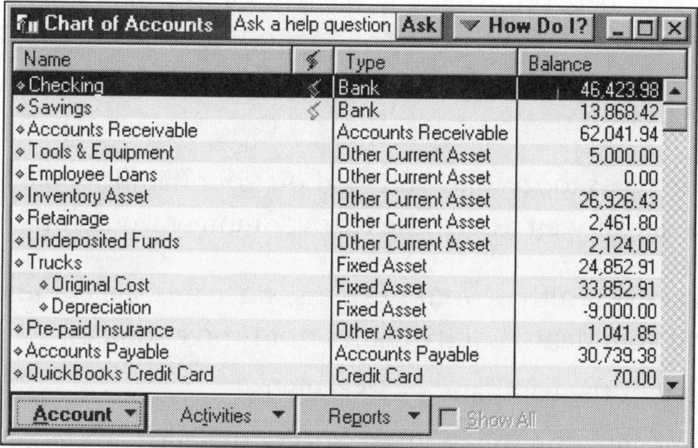
Chart of Accounts — Ask a help question — Ask — How Do I?

Name	Type	Balance
Checking	Bank	46,423.98
Savings	Bank	13,868.42
Accounts Receivable	Accounts Receivable	62,041.94
Tools & Equipment	Other Current Asset	5,000.00
Employee Loans	Other Current Asset	0.00
Inventory Asset	Other Current Asset	26,926.43
Retainage	Other Current Asset	2,461.80
Undeposited Funds	Other Current Asset	2,124.00
Trucks	Fixed Asset	24,852.91
Original Cost	Fixed Asset	33,852.91
Depreciation	Fixed Asset	-9,000.00
Pre-paid Insurance	Other Asset	1,041.85
Accounts Payable	Accounts Payable	30,739.38
QuickBooks Credit Card	Credit Card	70.00

Account — Activities — Reports — Show All

2 Scroll through the Rock Castle Construction chart of accounts. Notice that the list displays balance sheet accounts first, followed by income accounts and expense accounts.

About assets, liabilities, and equity

Assets

Assets include both what you have and what other people owe you. The money people owe you is called your accounts receivable, or A/R for short. QuickBooks uses an accounts receivable account to track the money owed you.

The rest of your company's assets may include checking accounts, savings accounts, petty cash, fixed assets (such as equipment or trucks), inventory, and undeposited funds (money you've received from customers but haven't yet deposited in the bank).

When setting up your company file in QuickBooks, please note that even though checking, savings, and petty cash are all company assets, you'll set them up as "bank" type accounts in QuickBooks.

Liabilities

Liabilities are what your company owes to other people. The money you owe for unpaid bills is your accounts payable, or A/P for short. QuickBooks uses an accounts payable account to track the money you owe different people for bills.

A liability can be a formal loan, an unpaid bill, or sales and payroll taxes you owe to the government.

When setting up your company file in QuickBooks, please note that even though unpaid bills are liabilities, you'll set them up as accounts payable type accounts in QuickBooks.

Equity

Equity is the difference between what you have (your assets) and what you owe (your liabilities):

Equity = Assets – Liabilities

If you sold all your assets today, and you paid off your liabilities using the money received from the sale of your assets, the leftover money would be your equity.

Your equity reflects the health of your business, since it is the amount of money left after you satisfy all your debts. Equity comes from three sources:

- Money invested in the company by its owners
- Net profit from operating the business during the current accounting period
- Retained earnings, or net profits from earlier periods that haven't been distributed to the owners

Of course, the owner can also take money out of the business. Such withdrawals, called owner's draws, reduce the business equity.

If you have a sole proprietorship (where the existence of the business depends solely on your efforts), you can check the value of your owner's equity by creating a QuickBooks balance sheet.

Cash versus accrual bookkeeping

When you begin your business, you should decide which bookkeeping method to use. The bookkeeping method determines how you report income and expenses on your tax forms. Check with your tax advisor or the Internal Revenue Service (IRS) before choosing a bookkeeping method for tax purposes.

Cash basis

Many small businesses record income when they receive the money and expenses when they pay the bills. This method is known as bookkeeping on a cash basis. If you've been recording deposits of your customers' payments but haven't been including the money customers owe you as part of your income, you've been using cash basis. Similarly, if you've been tracking expenses at the time you pay them, rather than at the time you first receive the bills, you've been using cash basis.

Accrual basis

In accrual-basis bookkeeping, you record income at the time of the sale, not at the time you receive the payment. Similarly, you enter expenses when you receive the bill, not when you pay it.

Most accountants feel that the accrual method gives you a truer picture of your business finances.

How your bookkeeping method affects QuickBooks

Whether you use the cash or accrual method, you enter transactions the same way in QuickBooks.

QuickBooks is set up to do your reports on an accrual basis. For example, it shows income on a profit and loss statement for invoices as soon as you record them, even if you haven't yet received payment. It shows expenses as soon as you record bills, even if they're unpaid.

You can see any report (except transaction reports) on a cash basis by changing the reporting preference. (From the Edit menu, choose Preferences. In the Preferences window, click Reports & Graphs in the left scroll box, and then click the Company Preferences tab.)

Important: When you create reports in QuickBooks, you can switch between cash and accrual reports at any time, regardless of which bookkeeping method you have chosen for tax purposes.

Measuring business profitability

Two of the most important reports for measuring the profitability of your business are the balance sheet and the profit and loss statement (also called an income statement). These are the reports most often requested by CPAs and financial officers. (For example, banks request both documents when you apply for a loan.)

If you had not planned to include hands-on student participation in this first lesson, complete these steps on your own computer while the students observe.

The balance sheet

A balance sheet is a financial snapshot of your company on one date. It shows:

- What you have (assets)
- What people owe you (accounts receivable)
- What your business owes to other people (liabilities and accounts payable)
- The net worth of your business (equity)

To see an example of a balance sheet:

1. From the Reports menu, choose Company & Financial.
2. From the submenu, choose Balance Sheet Standard.

The profit and loss statement

A profit and loss statement, also called an income statement, shows income, expenses, and net profit or loss (equal to income minus expenses). The QuickBooks profit and loss statement summarizes the revenue and expenses of a business by category (first income, then expenses).

To see a profit and loss report:

1. From the Reports menu, choose Report Finder.
2. From the "Select a type of report" drop-down list, choose Company & Financial.
3. In the "Select a report" list, click Profit & Loss Standard.
4. Click Display.
5. Scroll the report window to see all parts of the report.

The statement of cash flows

Another report that your accountant may be interested in is the statement of cash flows report. A statement of cash flows shows your receipts and payments during a specific accounting period.

To see a sample statement of cash flows report:

1. From the Reports menu, choose Report Finder.
2. From the Select a type of report drop-down list, choose Company & Financial.
3. In the Select a report list, click Statement of Cash Flows.
4. Click Display.

Exiting QuickBooks

Unlike most other Windows programs, QuickBooks doesn't require you to save your data before exiting. It does an automatic save while you're working with QuickBooks and every time you leave the program.

To exit QuickBooks:

- From the File menu, choose Exit.

If no other applications are open, QuickBooks returns you to the Windows desktop.

To prevent or minimize data loss, you should make regular backup copies of your QuickBooks company data. In the event of a data loss you can restore your data from the backup copy.

To make a backup copy of a data file:

- From the File menu, choose Back Up.

For more information about the recommended backup routine, see Chapter 5, "Protecting your data," in *QuickBooks Fundamentals*.

Moving between company files

If you work with several companies, you'll be working with multiple QuickBooks company files. You can change from one company file to another at any time, but you can have only one company file open at a time.

QuickBooks provides an easy way to find and open a company file that you've worked with before.

To open a previously opened file:

1 From the File menu, choose Open Previous Company.

2 From the submenu, choose the company file you want to open.

You can increase the number of company files that QuickBooks will display in the submenu.

To increase the number of company files displayed:

1 From the File menu, choose Open Previous Company.

2 Choose "Set number of previous companies."

3 Enter the number of company files you want QuickBooks to display (up to 20).

4 Click OK.

Student test and review

1 List the three main ways you enter data in QuickBooks.

Forms, lists, registers

2 List three ways to access features in QuickBooks.

Menu bar, Icon Bar, Shortcut list, Navigators

3 What bookkeeping method does QuickBooks use to create most reports?

Accrual, but you can see any report (except transaction reports) on a cash basis by changing the reporting preference.

LESSON 2 Setting up QuickBooks

Lesson objectives

- To discuss some of the decisions you need to make before using QuickBooks, such as your QuickBooks start date and the number of QuickBooks companies you should create
- To create a new QuickBooks company using the EasyStep Interview
- To set QuickBooks preferences in the Interview
- To record the opening balance for a checking account
- To practice using the QuickBooks Help tools

Instructor preparation

- Review this lesson, including the examples, to make sure you're familiar with the material.
- Ensure that all students have a copy of qblesson.qbb on their computer's hard disk.

Creating a QuickBooks company

A QuickBooks company contains all the financial records for a single business. Before you can use QuickBooks, you need to tell QuickBooks about your business so that it can set up your company file.

Explain to students that if they've been using Quicken or an older version of QuickBooks to keep their company's financial records, they don't need to create a new company; QuickBooks can convert their data for them. However, in this lesson, you'll be showing them how to create a new QuickBooks company.

How many companies should you set up?

If you operate a business enterprise, the IRS expects you to clearly show all sources of income and to document any business expenses you claim as deductions. For tax purposes, therefore, it's usually best to set up a separate QuickBooks company for each business enterprise you report on your tax forms.

About the EasyStep Interview

The EasyStep Interview walks you through the process of setting up your entire business on QuickBooks. The Interview is broken down into sections. You must complete the required General section first. If you are not sure how to answer a question, you can always go back and change your answer later. A few questions ask you to make a decision that's not easily reversed. When this is the case, you'll see this symbol.

The EasyStep Interview has five sections:

General—Lets you enter company information, choose a chart of accounts appropriate for your business, decide on QuickBooks preferences, and specify a business start date.

Income & Expenses—Lets you review the income and expense accounts on your business's chart of accounts, and lets you enter new accounts.

Income Details—Lets you specify whether your business income is from services and/or products you sell. Based on the information provided, QuickBooks determines which parts of the income and accounts receivable features you will be using.

Opening Balances—Lets you enter information about the customers who owe you money as of your start date, vendors to whom you owe money as of your start date, and balances in your balance sheet accounts as of your start date.

What's Next—This section describes some common tasks in QuickBooks that you may want to complete after you've gone through the other sections of the Interview.

Each major section of the Interview is divided into topics that are displayed as tabs at the top of the EasyStep Interview window. After you complete a topic or section, QuickBooks displays a checkmark on that tab.

Tip: **Most small business owners do better with QuickBooks setup if they break the job into manageable chunks.** Here's a suggested schedule for completion:

1. Choose the QuickBooks start date.
2. Gather the necessary business information and documents.
3. Set up the company file using the EasyStep Interview.
4. Fine-tune the chart of accounts.
5. Enter any historical transactions.
6. Complete customer and vendor information.
7. Complete the Item list.
8. Enter any optional adjustments.

Navigating through the Interview

- Click Next to display the next window in the Interview.
- Click Prev to display the previous window in the Interview.
- When a window has a More button (in the lower right corner), click it to see more detailed information about the question being asked in the Interview. After you read the detailed information, you can click OK to return to the Interview.
- Click Leave to leave the Interview and return to QuickBooks. You can return to the Interview later by opening your company file and then choosing EasyStep Interview from the File menu. QuickBooks remembers the information you have already entered and returns you to the Interview tab where you left off.

Tip: **Set aside a block of uninterrupted time to work on the EasyStep Interview.** Don't try to complete the Interview while you're in the middle of a busy workday. If you schedule your time before or after work hours, or on the weekend, the Interview should take a few hours.

Your goal while setting up is to provide as much information as necessary to get going, but not to provide all the details at once. For example, you should enter data for only one or two customers while you are completing the Interview. You can enter the rest of your customer data as you begin working in QuickBooks. (Or, if you have an especially large customer base, you may wish to hire a data entry clerk to complete this task for you.)

Starting the EasyStep Interview

To begin adding a new company:

1 Start QuickBooks.

2 Select "Create a new company" or choose New Company from the File menu.
QuickBooks displays the EasyStep Interview window.

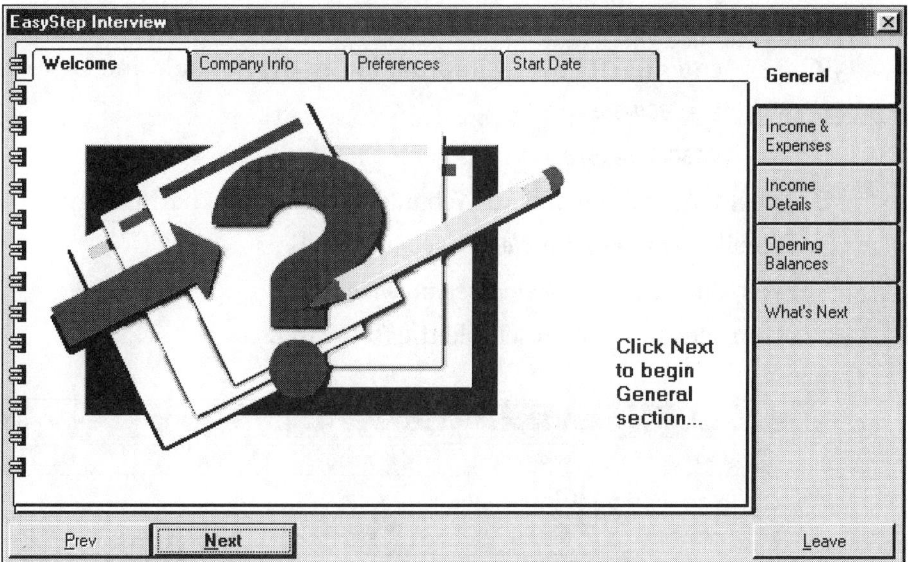

Entering company info

When you use the EasyStep Interview to create a new QuickBooks company, QuickBooks asks you questions about the type of business you own. It uses your answers to get you started quickly, by setting up the appropriate accounts and lists.

In this lesson, you'll create a new QuickBooks company for a business named Lockhart Design. Margaret Lockhart is the sole proprietor of this interior design firm. Most of her income comes from consulting services, but she also sells products such as fabrics and room accessories to clients.

To create a new QuickBooks company file:

1 At the first Welcome window for the Interview, click Next to begin.

2 Keep clicking Next, reading the information presented on the Welcome windows, until you have completed the Welcome section.
When you finish the section, QuickBooks places a checkmark on the Welcome tab.

3 Click Next until you come to the "Your company name" screen on the Company Info tab.

4 In the Company Name field, type ***Lockhart Design*** and press Tab.
When you press Tab, QuickBooks automatically enters the same name you typed into the Legal Name field. QuickBooks uses the company name on all reports.

5 Click Next.

6 Type the following information in the Your company information window.

1239 Bayshore Road

Middlefield, CA 94432

QuickBooks prints this company address on checks, invoices, and other forms.

7 Now enter the following information in the Phone # and FAX # fields:

Phone #: ***650-555-1234***

Fax #: ***650-555-5678***

8 Next enter the email and Web addresses for Lockhart Design.

Email: ***margaret@samplename.com***

Web Site: ***lockhart_design@samplename.com***

Your screen should resemble the following.

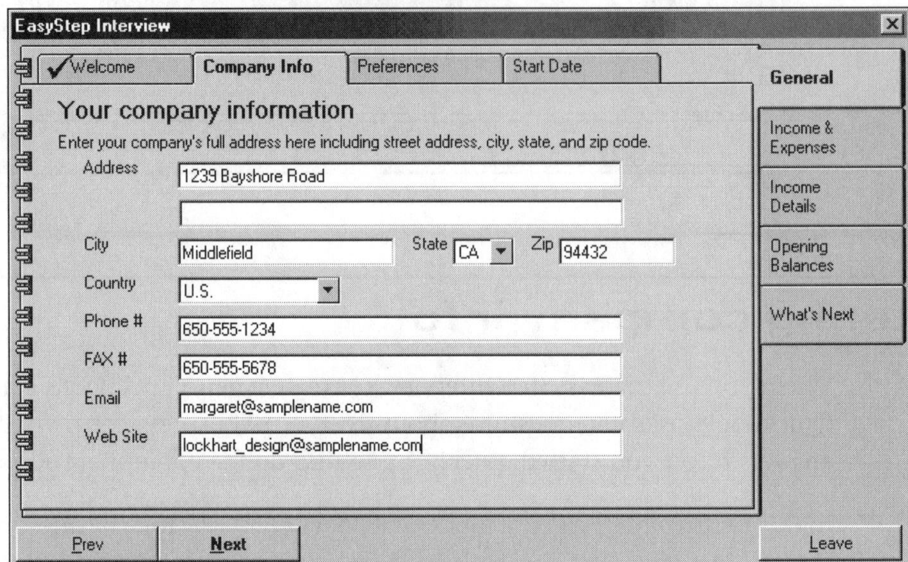

9 Click Next.

10 In the "Other company information" screen, enter the following information:

- Tax identification number: ***94-1234567***
- Make sure January is selected for the first month of the income tax year and first month of the fiscal year.

Your screen should match the following.

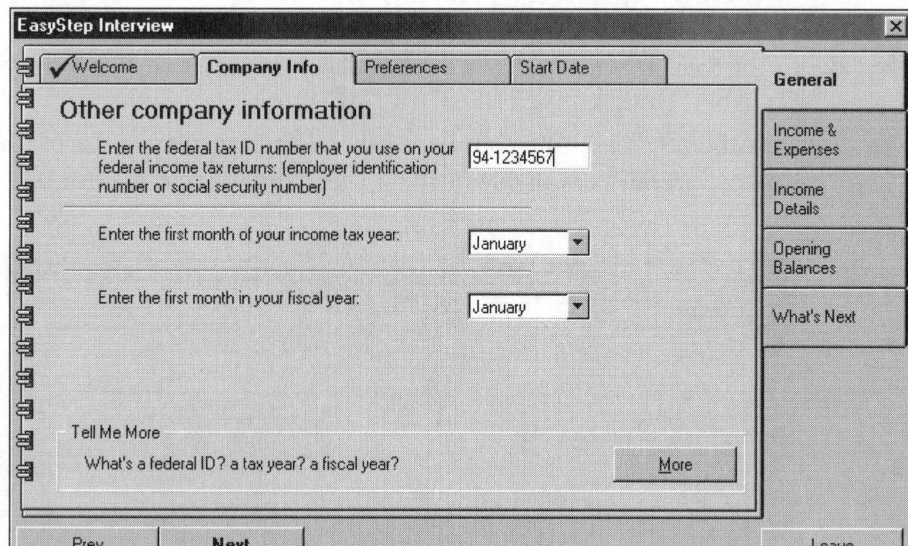

11 Click Next.

QuickBooks uses the financial year you choose to create year-to-date reports.

12 In the "Your company income tax form" screen, select Form 1040 (Sole Proprietor) from the drop-down list.

13 Click Next to display the next screen, where you select the type of business you are in. Your choice in this window affects the chart of accounts that QuickBooks sets up.

Using a preset chart of accounts

As you learned in Lesson 1 of this guide, the chart of accounts lists balance sheet accounts, income accounts, and expense accounts. When you create a new QuickBooks company, you can select a company type that most closely matches your type of business, and QuickBooks sets up a chart of accounts for you. It also sets up other lists that are appropriate for your type of company, such as payment methods, customer and vendor types, and payment terms.

Even if you own a type of company that isn't specifically listed, you should select the one that's closest and get a head start on creating your own chart of accounts. Once QuickBooks creates a chart of accounts for you, you can modify it however you want.

To create a chart of accounts:

1 In the "Select your type of business" screen, select Retail:General from the Industry list.

Although Lockhart Design receives most of its income from consulting, not from retail sales, the Retail company type will give us most of the accounts we need. We'll need to modify the chart of accounts later to include an income account for Consulting Income.

2 Click Next three more times to get to the Save As window.

3 Make sure that QuickBooks is set to save the file in the QBtrain folder you set up in the introduction to this guide.

4 In the Save As window, click Save to accept the default filename of "Lockhart Design."

QuickBooks creates the company file and then displays a list of the income and expense accounts available in the preset chart of accounts for retail businesses.

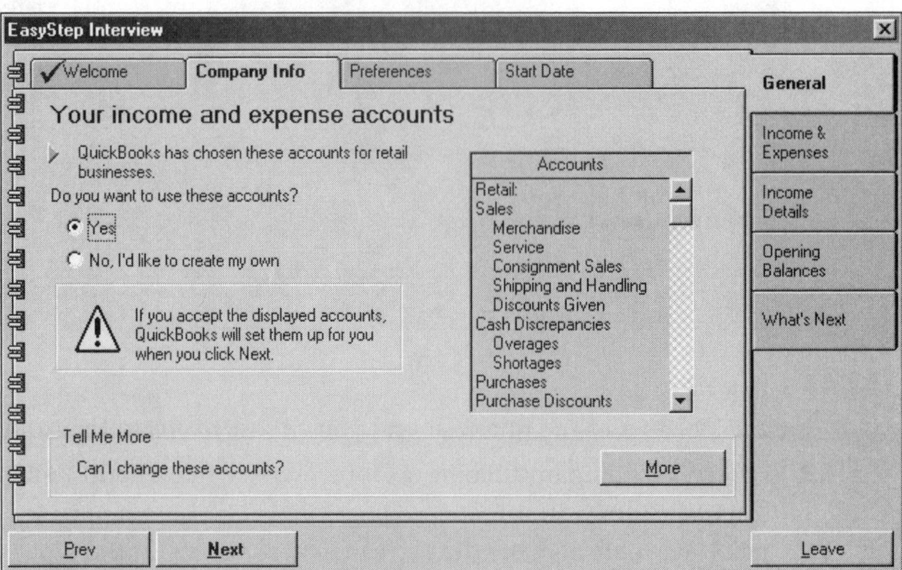

5 Scroll through the preset income and expense accounts to get an idea of what is included, and then click Yes (that you want to use these accounts).

6 Click Next to go to the next window.

7 In the "Accessing your company" screen, leave the number of people (other than you) who need to have access to the QuickBooks files at 0 and click Next.

Margaret Lockhart is the only one who needs access to the company file.

8 You don't need to create one for the purposes of this exercise, so click No when QuickBooks asks if you want to enter a password for this file.

9 Click Next until you move from the Company Info section to the Preferences section.

Setting up QuickBooks preferences

The Preferences section of the EasyStep Interview is where you indicate whether you want to use certain features of the QuickBooks program. From the Interview you can choose to use:

- Inventory (whether turned on)

  Turning on inventory from the EasyStep Interview is not available for all industries. When this is the case for your industry, you can turn it on from the Preferences window. (From the Edit menu, choose Preferences. Click Purchases & Vendors in the left scroll box. Click the Company Preferences tab, and then click the "Inventory and purchase orders are active" checkbox.)
- Sales tax
- The invoice format you want to use
- Payroll (whether turned on)
- Estimates (Pro and Premier only)
- Progress invoicing (Pro and Premier only)
- Sales orders (Premier only)
- Time tracking (Pro and Premier only)
- Classes
- How you want to enter bills: by entering checks directly or by entering bills first, and then payments
- Reminders (whether to turn on)
- Whether you want accrual- or cash-basis reports

Entering sales tax information

This part of the Preferences section asks whether you charge sales tax. You should turn the sales tax preference off only if you *never* charge sales tax. Margaret Lockhart typically charges sales tax, so we'll turn on sales tax in her company file.

To set up QuickBooks to track sales tax:

1. Click Next to move to the Sales tax screen in the Preferences section of the Interview.
2. At the Sales Tax window, click Yes for the question, "Do you collect sales tax from your customers?" Then click Next.
3. Select "I collect single tax rate paid to a single tax agency."

   Margaret Lockhart collects one sales tax for one tax district, paid to only one tax agency. If your customers are from different states, you should click "I collect multiple tax rates or have multiple tax agencies."

4 Click Next.

QuickBooks automatically creates a current liability account, called Sales Tax Payable, that keeps track of the sales tax you collect in your business.

5 Fill out the Sales Tax Information window as shown below.

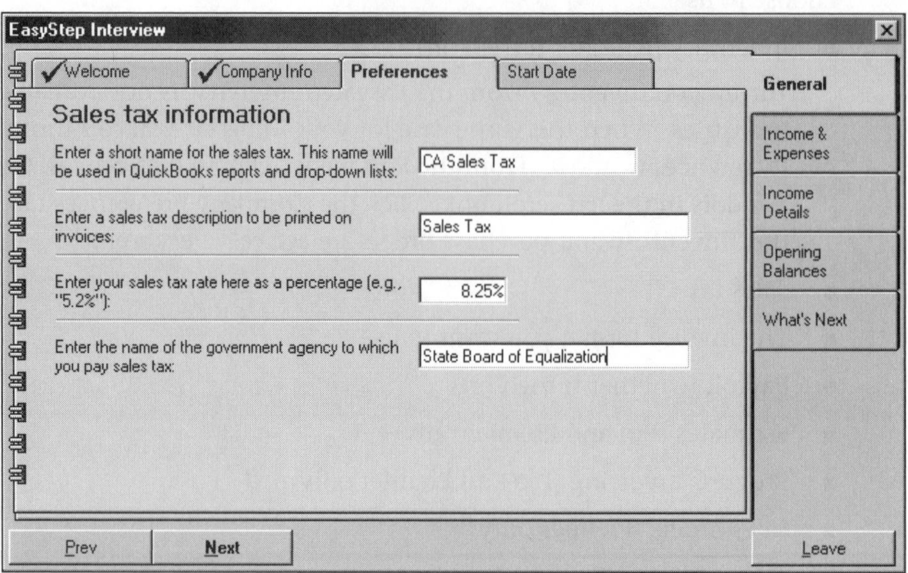

6 Click Next.

Choosing an invoice format

QuickBooks offers four different formats for invoices: Product, Professional, Service, and Custom. The type you choose affects the look of your invoices.

- The **Product invoice** is for businesses that sell parts or products and need fields relevant for shipping (for example, a retail store).
- The **Professional invoice** is for businesses that sell services and need a lot of room for descriptions of their services (for example, a public relations consultant).
- The **Service invoice** is for businesses that primarily provide services, but that also sell some goods (for example, an interior design firm).
- The **Custom invoice** is for businesses that want to create their own invoice format.

You can also customize any of these formats to suit your needs. You'll see how to do that in Lesson 15 of this guide. For Lockhart Design, which primarily sells consulting services, but also sells the occasional product, we'll choose the Service invoice format.

To select the invoice format for Lockhart Design:

- In the Interview window leave Service selected, and then click Next.

Tracking sales orders

If you use a QuickBooks: Premier Edition product, QuickBooks asks if you want to track sales orders. If you do, click Yes, and then click Next.

If you are using QuickBooks: Basic or Pro, you will not see this preference.

Choosing remaining preferences

The rest of the Preferences section is a series of "yes or no" questions. Simply click Yes or No, then click Next to move forward in the Interview. For Lockhart Design, complete the preferences by giving the following responses:

For this item...	Do this...
Payroll	Click Yes.
Estimates (QuickBooks: Pro and Premier only)	Click Yes.
Progress invoicing (QuickBooks: Pro and Premier only)	Click Yes.
Time tracking (QuickBooks: Pro and Premier only)	Click Yes.
Classes	Click Yes.
How to deal with bills and payments	Select "Enter the bills first and then enter the payments later"
How often would you like to see your Reminders list	Select "At start up"
Type of reports you want to create	Select "Accrual-based reports"

This completes the Preferences portion of the EasyStep Interview. All that remains of the General section is to specify a start date.

Choosing a start date

Before you start entering your company's financial data, you need to choose a QuickBooks start date. This is the starting point you want to use for all your QuickBooks accounts. The start date is the date for which you give QuickBooks a financial snapshot of your company assets and liabilities.

Once you decide on a start date, you enter all your company's transactions *since* that date. That's why you should choose a start date that's not too far back in the past for you to handle. Many business owners like to use the last day of a financial period as their start date, such as the end of last fiscal year, last quarter, or last month. You need to enter all historical transactions from the day after your start date up through today.

For example, if you decide on a start date of March 31, you'd enter your historical transactions from April 1 up through today.

Continue clicking Next as you move through the Start Date section of the Interview. When you get to the "Choose your company start date" window, select "I want to start entering detailed transactions as of 1/1/2003," and then click Next.

Tip: **When choosing the start date you want to use for your own QuickBooks company file, consider this question: Is having a lot of historical data important to you?** If it is, you'll want to choose a start date as close to the beginning of your fiscal year as possible.

If historical data is not very important to you, you can make setup easier by choosing a start date as close to today as possible. (You only have to enter historical data between your start date and today.)

Setting up income and expense accounts

Because you chose an industry from the list earlier in the Interview, QuickBooks has already created income and expense accounts for your company. The Income & Expenses section of the EasyStep Interview lets you view the preset income and expense accounts and add new income or expense accounts from within the Interview.

To streamline the Interview process, you won't add income or expense accounts in this lesson. You'll see how to add new accounts to the chart of accounts in Lesson 3, "Working with lists."

For now, move through this portion of the Interview by answering "No" to the following questions:

- Do you want to add an income account now?
- Would you like a more detailed explanation of expense accounts and subaccounts?
- Do you want to add an expense account now?

Click Next until you get to the Income Details section.

Providing details about your income

The Income Details section of the EasyStep Interview is where you specify whether you track accounts receivable, set up QuickBooks items to track the services you provide or products you sell, and set up inventory items if you plan to track inventory in QuickBooks.

You should complete the Introduction tab of the Income Details section because that tells QuickBooks whether you need the accounts receivable feature and whether you need statement charges (for businesses that send regular monthly statements showing past due, current balance, and so on).

To complete the Income Details section:

1 In the Income Details Introduction window, click Next two times.

2 For the question, "Do you receive full payment at the time (or before) you provide a service or sell a product?" make sure "Sometimes" is selected and then click Next.

3 For "Statement charges," select No, and then click Next two more times.

4 In the Items section, click No when asked if you want to set up service items, non-inventory part items, or other charge items.

   You'll see how to set up a new service item in Lesson 6, "Entering sales and invoices."

5 Click Next two times.

6 Select "Skip inventory items" to complete the Inventory tab.

Entering opening balances

The Opening Balances section of the EasyStep Interview is where you enter the amounts currently owed you by customers as of your start date, the amounts you currently owe vendors as of your start date, and the balances in your balance sheet accounts as of your start date. We recommend that you provide the opening balances from within the Interview; that makes it easier when you're ready to use QuickBooks for your daily business transactions.

The balance sheet accounts in the QuickBooks chart of accounts start with an opening balance of zero. Before you begin working in QuickBooks, you need to enter an opening balance for each balance sheet account as of your start date.

The opening balance is important because QuickBooks can't give you an accurate balance sheet (what your company owns and what it owes) without it. An accurate balance sheet gives you a true picture of your company's finances. Also, if you start with an accurate balance as of a specific date, you can reconcile your QuickBooks bank accounts with your bank statements, and your QuickBooks checking accounts will show the actual amount of money you have in the bank.

The easiest way to determine an account's opening balance is to work from an accurate balance sheet. If you have a balance sheet as of your start date, you can take the opening balance from there.

Let's assume Margaret Lockhart wants to enter an opening balance for her checking account. The opening balance for a QuickBooks bank account is the dollar amount in the bank on the start date. This amount can be determined two ways: using the ending balance on the last bank statement on or immediately prior to the start date, or using the bank account balance from a balance sheet prepared by an accountant. Margaret has a recent bank statement for this account, so we'll use that method.

To enter the checking account opening balance:

1 Click the Accounts tab in the Opening Balances section of the Interview and click Next. (Skip the Customers and Vendors tabs.)

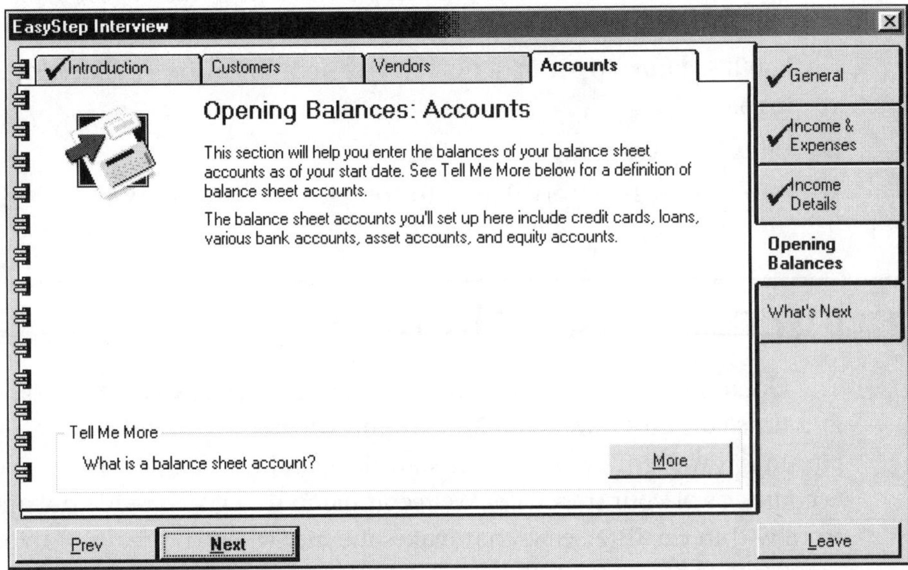

2 Click No when QuickBooks asks if you want to set up credit card accounts, lines of credit, and liability accounts.

3 For "Would you like to set up a bank account?", make sure Yes is selected and then click Next.

4 Type ***Checking*** as the name of the account and then click Next.

5 For Statement Ending Date, enter the same date you used for Lockhart Design's start date (1/1/2003).

6 In the Statement Ending Balance field, type ***8359.00*** and then click Next.

7 When QuickBooks asks if you want to add another bank account, click No. Then click Next.

8 When QuickBooks asks if you print checks or deposit slips from QuickBooks, click No, and then click Next.

The rest of the Opening Balances section lets you add asset and equity accounts. In the interest of time, we won't be adding any other accounts from within the Interview. We will add more accounts in Lessons 4 and 5.

Finishing the Interview

The final section in the EasyStep Interview is What's Next. This is not an essential item for initial setup, so we will not cover it in this lesson.

- To leave the EasyStep Interview and save your changes, click Leave.

After you have completed the EasyStep Interview, Intuit recommends that you not use the Interview to make changes to your company file. Instead, use the information in the help options described in the next section of this chapter to help you make changes and adjustments to your company file.

Completing the company setup process

When you are setting up your own company in QuickBooks, you may want to use the Getting Started window to help you finish setting up your own company file. The information provided there will guide you through the rest of the setup process and help you get started using QuickBooks. To display the Getting Started window, choose Getting Started from the Help menu.

If you have upgraded from an earlier version of QuickBooks, choose New Features from the Help menu.

For more information, choose Help & Support from the Help menu.

Tip: **If your QuickBooks start date is before today's date, you also need to enter past transactions so that you have complete financial records from the start date forward.** It is important to enter historical transactions in this order:

1. All sales (sales receipts, invoices, or statement charges)
2. Customer payments received for outstanding invoices after the start date
3. Bills received since the start date
4. Bills paid since the start date
5. Deposits made to any of the accounts since the start date
6. Any other checks written (other than bills) since the start date

Getting help while using QuickBooks

QuickBooks provides extensive help in various formats. When you have questions, QuickBooks provides:

- Step-by-step instructions. These are available from the onscreen Help and How Do I menu.

- A search engine that provides you with a list of topics related to the word or phrase you enter in the Ask field.
- Conceptual explanations of how to apply QuickBooks to your particular business situation.

Finding a topic in the onscreen Help Index

Suppose you want to find out how to add a new customer. You can type what you're looking for in the Help Index, and QuickBooks displays a list of topics.

To find a topic in onscreen Help:

1. From the Help menu, choose Help Index.
2. Type ***customers***.

   QuickBooks selects the first occurrence of the word "customers" in the index. You can see there is a topic for "customers, adding new."
3. Double-click "customers, adding new."

   QuickBooks displays the topic in the screen to the right.

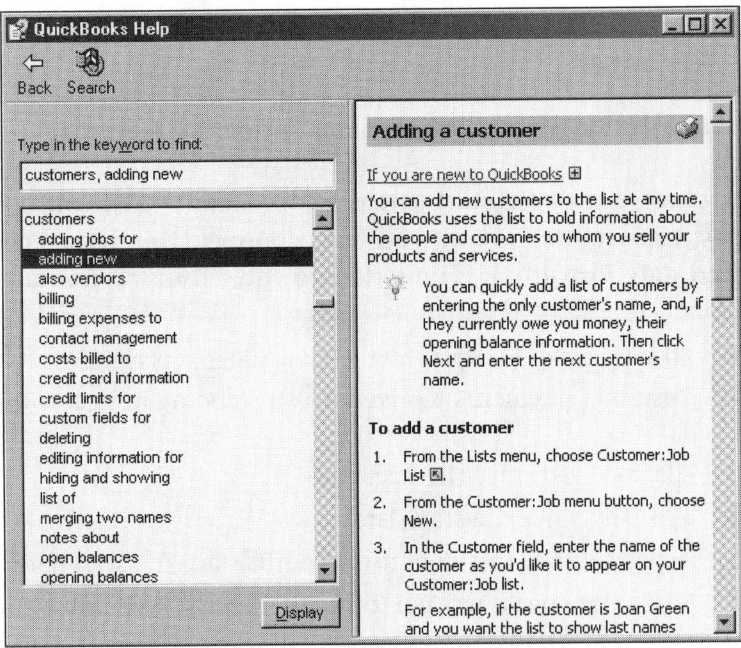

4. Close the Help window.

Finding answers from the How Do I menu

Throughout QuickBooks, you'll find windows with a drop-down menu called How Do I. This menu provides quick access to information and instructions for the current window.

To use the How Do I menu:

1 From the Customers menu, choose Create Invoices.

QuickBooks displays the Create Invoices window.

2 From the How Do I menu, choose "Reformat and print invoices." Then choose "Add my logo."

QuickBooks displays a Help window on how to add a company logo to an invoice form.

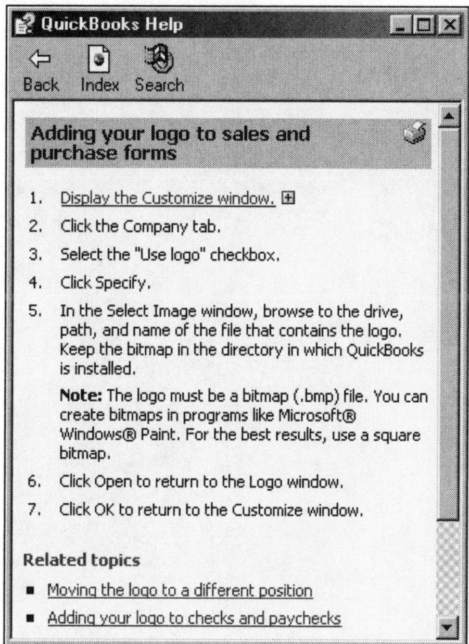

3 Close the Help window and the invoice.

Student test and review

1 The ________________ section of the EasyStep Interview is where you indicate whether you want to use certain QuickBooks features.

Preferences

2 Search the onscreen Help index for information on how to turn on the inventory feature in QuickBooks.

LESSON 3 Working with lists

Lesson objectives

- To edit the company chart of accounts
- To add a new customer to the Customer:Job list
- To add a new vendor to the Vendor list
- To learn about custom fields, and to practice adding custom fields
- To see how to manage lists in QuickBooks

Handout materials

- Handout 1: Balance sheet accounts
- Handout 2: Accounts created automatically

Instructor preparation

- Review this lesson, including the examples, to make sure you're familiar with the material.
- Ensure that all students have a copy of qblesson.qbb on their computer's hard disk.
- Have Handouts 1 and 2 ready for distribution.

To start this lesson

Before you perform the following steps, make sure you have installed the exercise file (qblesson.qbb) on your hard disk. See "Installing the exercise file" in the Introduction to this guide if you haven't installed it.

The following steps restore the exercise file to its original state so that the data in the file matches what you see on the screen as you proceed through each lesson.

To restore the exercise file (qblesson.qbb):

1. From the File menu in QuickBooks, choose Restore.
   QuickBooks displays the Restore Company Backup window.
2. In the "Get Company Backup From" section of the window, click Browse and select your c:\QBtrain directory.
3. Select the qblesson.qbb file, and then click Open.
4. In the "Restore Company Backup To" section of the window, click Browse and select your c:\QBtrain directory.

5 In the File name field of the Restore To window, type ***lesson 3*** and then click Save.

6 Click Restore.

Using QuickBooks lists

QuickBooks lists organize a wide variety of information, including data on customers, vendors, inventory items, and more. Lists save you time by helping you enter information consistently and correctly. When you store information on a list, you enter it once and never need to retype it. Think about how much information you use more than once in your business:

- Names, addresses, and other information about customers who purchase from you on a regular basis
- Contact information for vendors from whom you purchase your supplies
- Descriptions and prices for products or services you sell again and again

Simply enter repetitive information into a list once, and then use it over and over on checks, on invoice forms, and other daily transactions. You don't have to enter all the information for your company lists before you begin working with QuickBooks. You can add information to lists as you go along.

Editing the chart of accounts

The chart of accounts is your most important list because it shows how much your business has, how much it owes, how much money you have coming in, and how much you're spending. When you set up your own company in QuickBooks, the EasyStep Interview lets you choose a chart of accounts designed especially for your type of business. However, not every business has the same needs; you'll want to make a few changes to the list.

To display the chart of accounts:

1 From the Lists menu, choose Chart of Accounts.

QuickBooks displays the chart of accounts for Rock Castle Construction.

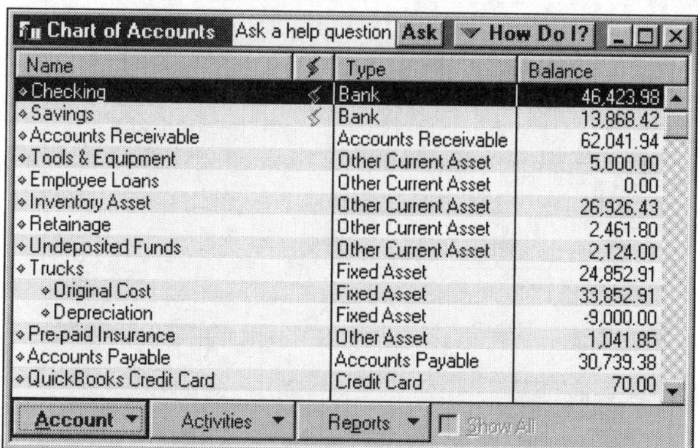

2 Scroll through the list. The chart of accounts displays balance sheet accounts first, followed by income and expense accounts.

Tip: **Before you modify the preset chart of accounts, we recommend that you have your accountant or QuickBooks ProAdvisor review the chart of accounts that QuickBooks has set up for you.** You may need to add income and expense accounts, add subaccounts, delete accounts, or move accounts. It is important to decide on an account structure before you begin entering transactions.

Refer to Handout 1, "Balance sheet accounts" as you explain each account type and the kinds of transactions you use each type for.

Editing an account

If any of the accounts don't suit your needs, you can edit or delete them. In the next exercise, you'll edit Rock Castle Construction's Checking account to provide the account number.

To edit an account:

1 In the chart of accounts, select Checking.

2 Click the Account menu button (at the bottom of the window), and then select Edit.

QuickBooks displays the Edit Account window.

3 In the Description field, type ***Great Statewide Bank.***

4 In the Bank Acct. field, type ***555-333-2222***.

Your window should look like this.

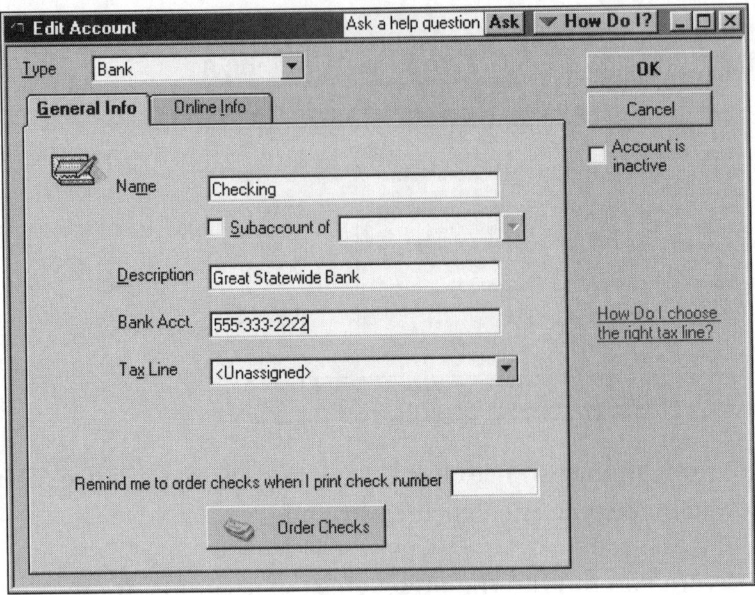

5 Click OK.

Adding subaccounts

The Dues and Subscriptions expense account has one subaccount called Union Dues. Rock Castle Construction wants to add a second subaccount for trade publications.

To add a subaccount:

1 In the chart of accounts, click the Account menu button and then choose New.

QuickBooks displays the New Account window.

2 In the Type field, select Expense from the drop-down list.

3 In the Name field, type ***Trade Pubs***.

4 Select the "Subaccount of" checkbox, and then select Dues and Subscriptions in the drop-down list.

5 In the Description field, type ***Trade Publications***.

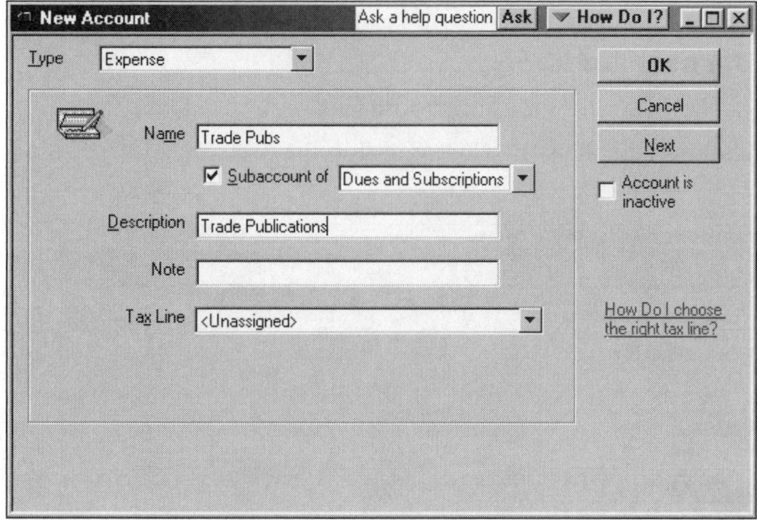

6 Click OK.

QuickBooks displays the new subaccount in the chart of accounts list.

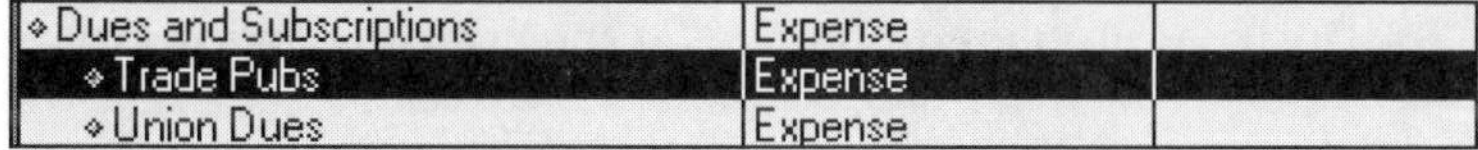

7 Close the chart of accounts.

Explain to students that in addition to the accounts that QuickBooks sets up by default based on the industry they select during the EasyStep Interview, QuickBooks also creates certain accounts as needed based on the features used in the program. For a list of these accounts, refer to Handout 2, "Accounts created automatically."

Working with the Customer:Job list

The Customer:Job list stores names, addresses, and other information about your customers. It also holds information about the jobs or projects you may want to track for each customer.

Adding new customers

In this exercise, you'll add a new customer to the Customer:Job list.

To add a new customer:

1 From the Customers menu, choose Customer:Job List.

QuickBooks displays the Customer:Job list.

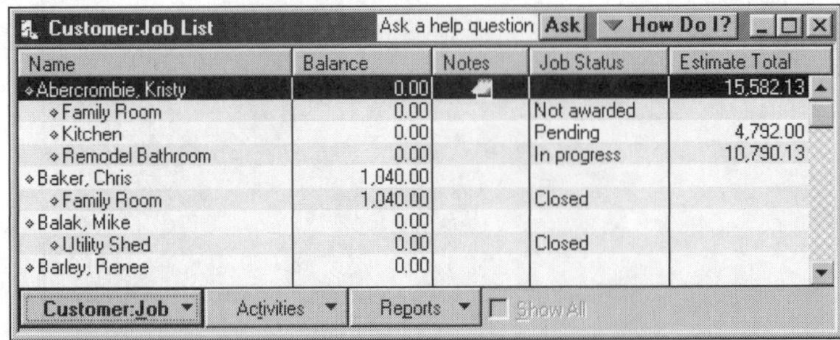

The Customer:Job list lets you add, edit, and get reports on your customers. Each customer in the list can have multiple jobs (you may call them projects or accounts). Notice that this Customer:Job list already has quite a few entries.

2 Click the Customer:Job menu button (at the bottom of the list window), and select New.

QuickBooks displays the New Customer window.

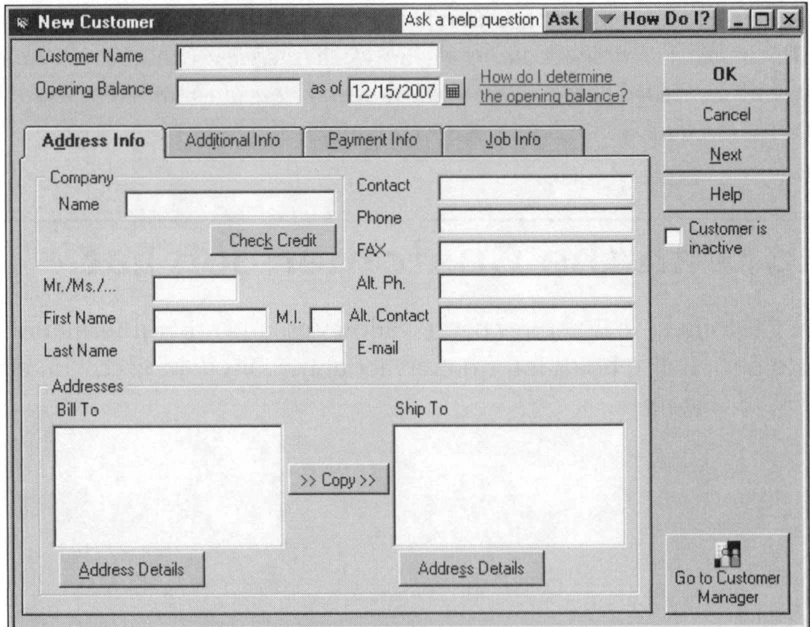

The New Customer window is where you enter all the information about a new customer, including billing and shipping addresses, contacts, credit limit, and payment terms. QuickBooks uses the information you enter to complete invoices, bills, and receipts. When you're setting up your company file, you use this window to record customers' opening balances.

3 In the Name field in the Company section, type ***Godwin Manufacturing,*** and then press Tab.

Notice that QuickBooks fills in the Customer Name field and the first line of the Bill To field with the information you typed in the Company Name field.

QuickBooks displays the name listed in the Customer Name field in the Customer:Job list. By default, QuickBooks sorts the list alphabetically.

If you are entering individual names, you may want to use last name, first name in the Customer Name field so that your Customer:Job list displays the names with the last name first. This is useful for alphabetical sorting of lists and reports.

4 In the Bill To field, click at the end of the line below the company name and press Enters.

5 Type ***376 Pine Street,*** and then press Enter.

Notice that you press Tab to move between fields, but you press Enter to move from one line to the next within a field.

6 On the next line of the Bill To field, type ***Bayside, OR 64326.***

7 Click Copy to have QuickBooks copy the billing address to the Ship To field.

8 Continue filling out the customer information by providing the following information:

- Contact: ***John Godwin***
- Phone: ***325-555-9841***
- Fax: ***325-555-0012***
- Alt Contact: ***Tracy Heldt***

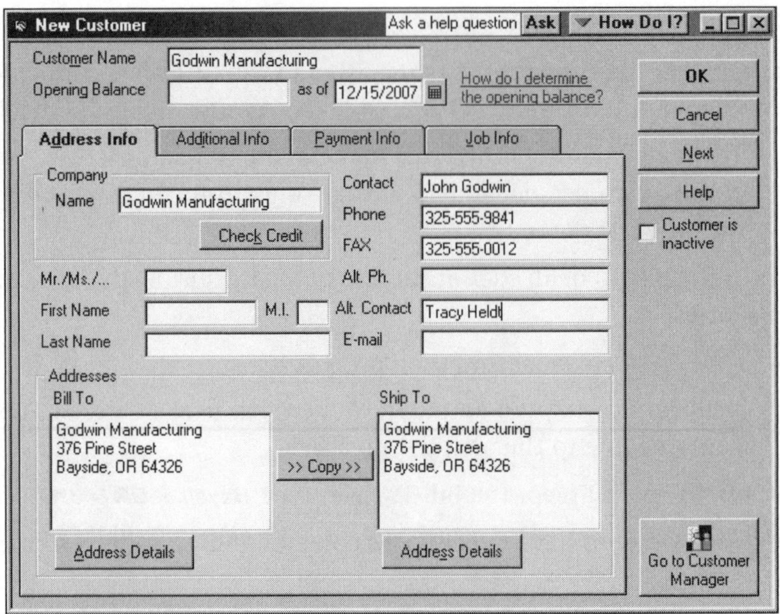

Note: **If you use plan to e-mail invoices or statements to customers using the Send Forms feature, use this window to enter your customers' e-mail addresses.**

Providing additional customer information

You've just completed the Address Info tab for a new customer. The Additional Info tab is where you can provide other important information, such as customer type (if you want to categorize your customers in some way), payment terms, and sales tax information.

To add additional information to a customer record:

1 Click the Additional Info tab.

QuickBooks displays the Additional Info tab of the New Customer window.

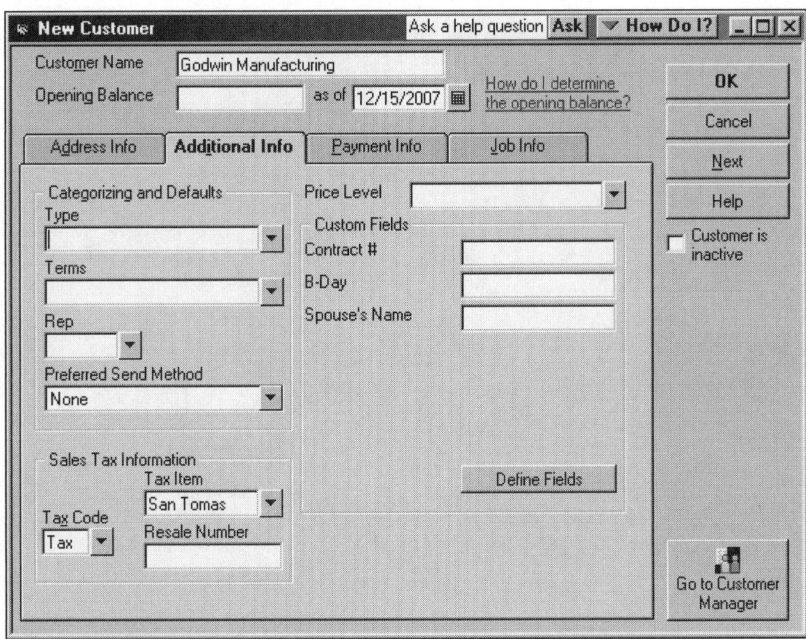

2 In the Type field, type ***Industrial***.

The Type field lets you track customers in any way that is meaningful for your business. For example, if you run ads on television, radio, and in print, and you want to know which advertising method brings you the most customers, you can assign customers a "type" (TV, Radio, or Print) and run reports that tell you which referral source is most effective. Rock Castle Construction uses the Type field to categorize customers by the type of service provided.

3 Press Tab.

QuickBooks tells you that "Industrial" is not currently on the Customer Type list and asks if you wish to add it.

4 Click the Quick Add button to add the customer type to the list.

Quick Add lets you set up the item with a minimum amount of data. If you click Set Up, you can enter more detailed information, but that interrupts the process of creating a new customer.

5 In the Terms field, type ***Net 30***.

6 In the Tax Code field, select Non from the drop-down list.

7 In the Tax Item drop-down list, select Out of State.

Your screen should now look like this.

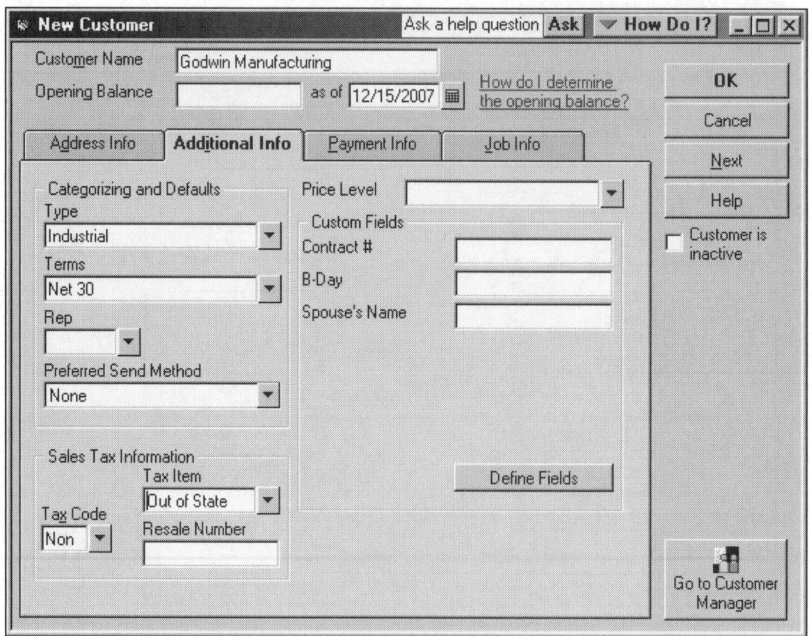

Providing customer payment information

The Payment Info tab is where you enter customer account numbers and credit limits. QuickBooks remembers each customer's credit limit and warns you when a customer is about to exceed it. You can also record information about each customer's preferred payment method. For customers who pay by credit card, you can enter credit card numbers and expiration dates.

To add payment and credit information to a customer record:

1 Click Payment Info.

2 In the Credit Limit field, type ***2000***.

3 In the Preferred Payment Method drop-down list, choose Check.

When you finish, your window should look like this.

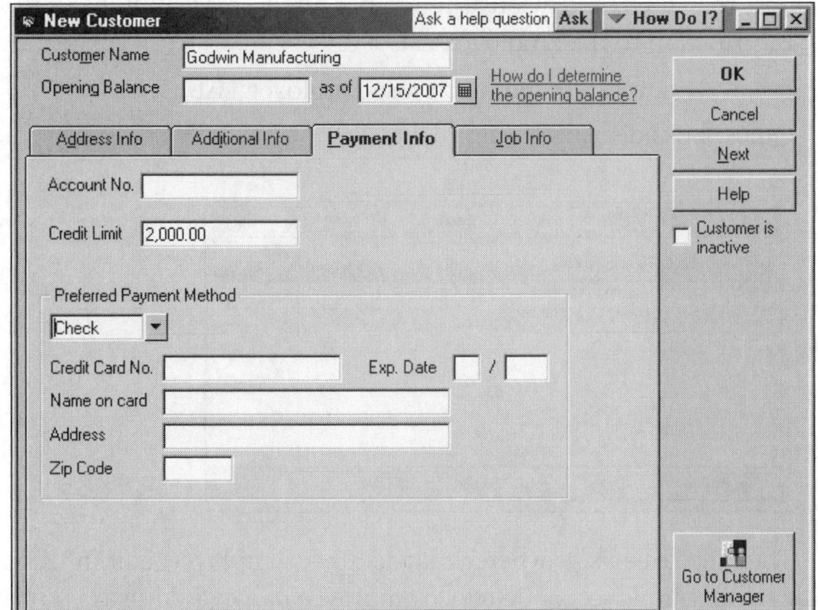

4 Click OK to add the customer and close the New Customer window.

QuickBooks displays the Customer:Job list with Godwin Manufacturing added.

5 Close the Customer:Job list.

Tip: **QuickBooks has several preset reports related to customers.** Some reports you may find useful are the sales by customer summary and the sales by customer detail reports (under the Sales submenu in the Reports menu).

You may also find the A/R aging summary, A/R aging detail, customer balance summary, customer balance detail, and open invoices reports useful. You'll find them under the Customers & Receivables submenu in the Reports menu.

Working with the Employee list

The Employee list stores information about your employees such as name, address, and social security number. It also stores information QuickBooks needs to calculate employee paychecks (if you are using QuickBooks for payroll). You'll learn how to enter employee payroll information later in this course. For now, enter only the basic employee information.

QuickBooks uses the information you enter in the Employee list to track sales and fill in information on checks and other forms.

Adding new employees

Suppose that Rock Castle Construction has hired a new employee and you want to add her information to the Employee list.

1 From the Employees menu, choose Employee List.

QuickBooks displays the Employee list.

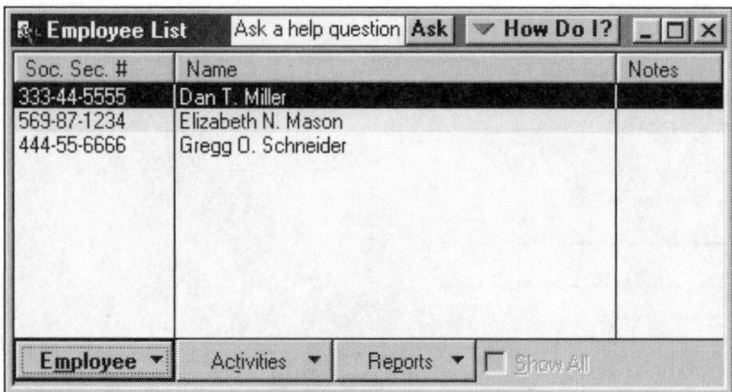

The Employee list is where you add a new employee, edit information for an existing employee, or delete an employee name (as long as you have not used the employee name in any transactions).

2 Click the Employee menu button and choose New.

QuickBooks displays the New Employee window.

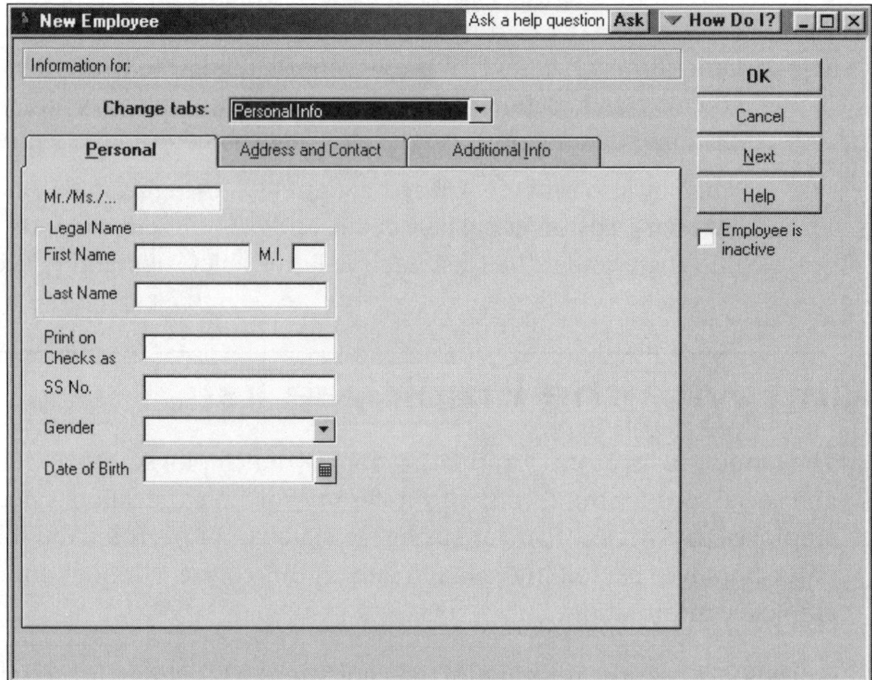

The Personal tab is where you enter basic information about the employee, such as name, Social Security Number, and date of birth.

3 In the First Name field, type ***Marlene***.

4 In the Last Name field, type ***Duncalf***.

Notice that QuickBooks fills in the Print on Check as field with the information you entered in the name fields. You can enter a different name if you wish.

5 In the Social SS No. field type ***123-45-6789***.

6 In the Gender field, select Female from the drop-down list.

7 In the Date of Birth field, type ***7/18/82***.

The Personal tab should look like this.

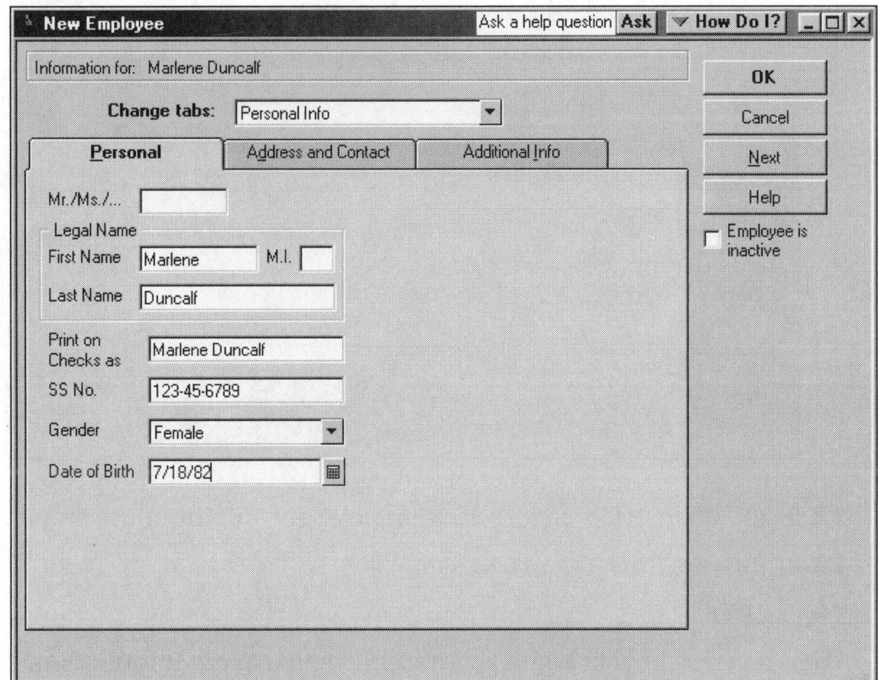

8 Click the Address and Contact tab.

9 In the Address field, type ***195 Spruce Avenue, #202***.

10 For the City, State, and Zip fields, type ***Bayshore, CA 94326***.

11 In the Phone field, type ***415-555-1111***.

When you finish, the window should look like this.

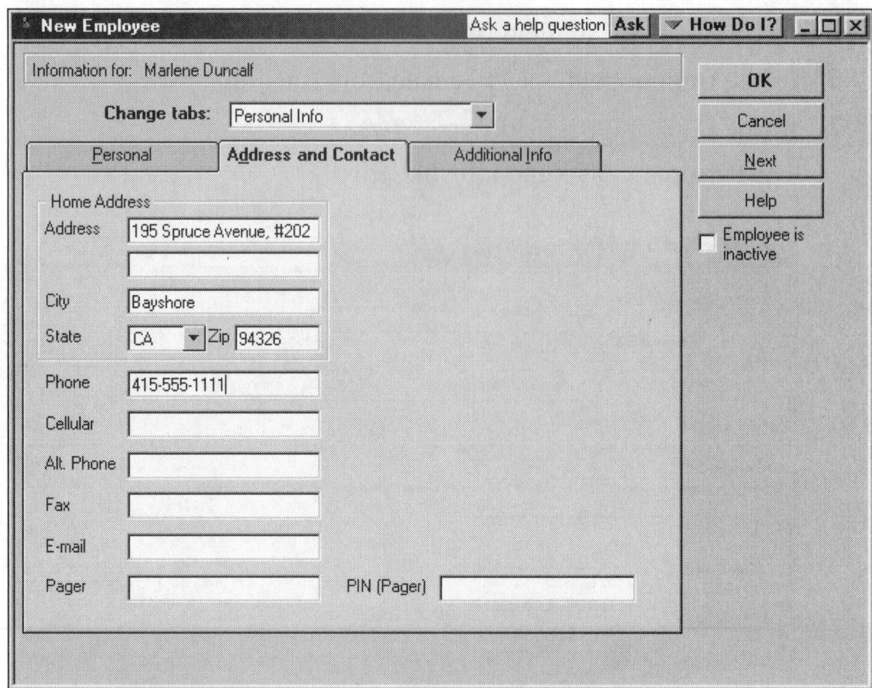

12 In the Change tabs field, select Employment Info from the drop-down list.

13 In the Hire Date, type ***11/26/2007***.

14 Click OK.

15 When QuickBooks asks if you want to set up payroll information, click Leave As Is.

You learn how to set up payroll in Le sson12.

16 QuickBooks updates and displays the Employee list with the new employee's name added.

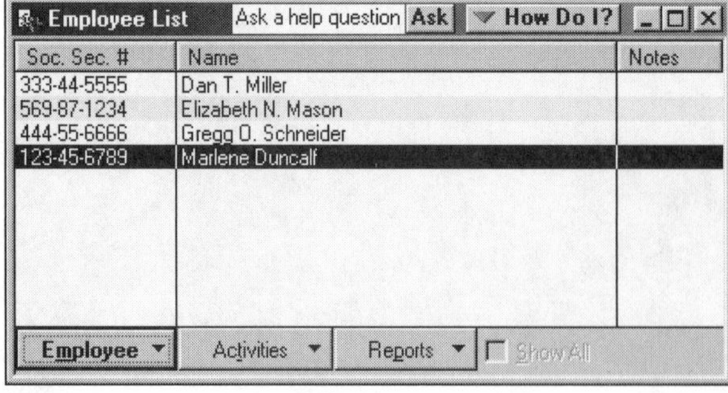

17 Close the Employee list.

Working with the Vendor list

The Vendor list is where you record information about the companies or people from whom you buy goods or services. QuickBooks uses the data in the Vendor list to fill in purchase orders, receipts, bills, and checks as you receive and pay for goods and services.

Adding new vendors

In this exercise, you'll add a new vendor to the Vendor list. Suppose Rock Castle Construction is working with a new subcontractor, and it needs to add information about the new vendor to its QuickBooks Vendor list.

1 From the Vendors menu, choose Vendor List.

QuickBooks displays the Vendor list.

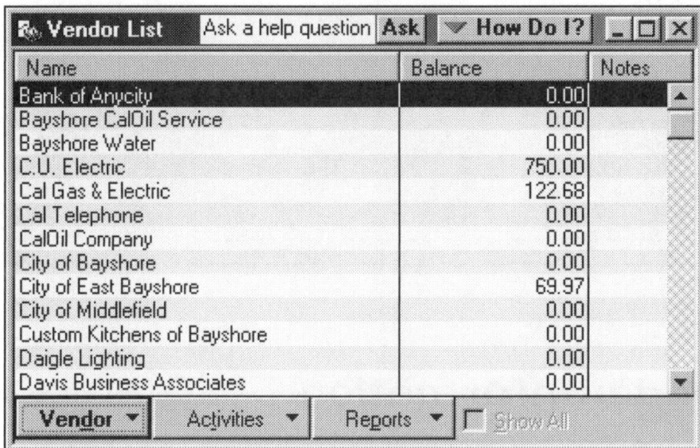

2 Click the Vendor menu button, and then choose New.

QuickBooks displays the New Vendor window.

The New Vendor window is where you enter all of the information regarding a new vendor, such as name, phone, contact, address, and opening balance. Just as when you add a new customer, you start by providing basic information on the Address Info tab.

3 In the Vendor Name field, type ***Hughes Electric.***

This is the name QuickBooks displays for this vendor in the Vendor list. If the vendor is an individual, you may wish to enter the last name first, then the first name.

4 In the Company Name field, type ***Hughes Electric.***

5 Click in the Address field, below the company name displayed on the first line.

Notice that QuickBooks displays the company name on the first line of the Address field.

6 On the second line of the Address field, type ***P.O. Box 2316.***

7 Press Enter to move to the next line.

8 Type ***Middlefield, CA 94432.***

9 In the Contact field, type ***David Hughes***.

10 In the Phone field, type ***510-555-6666***.

11 In the FAX field, type ***510-555-6667***.

When you finish, your window should look like this.

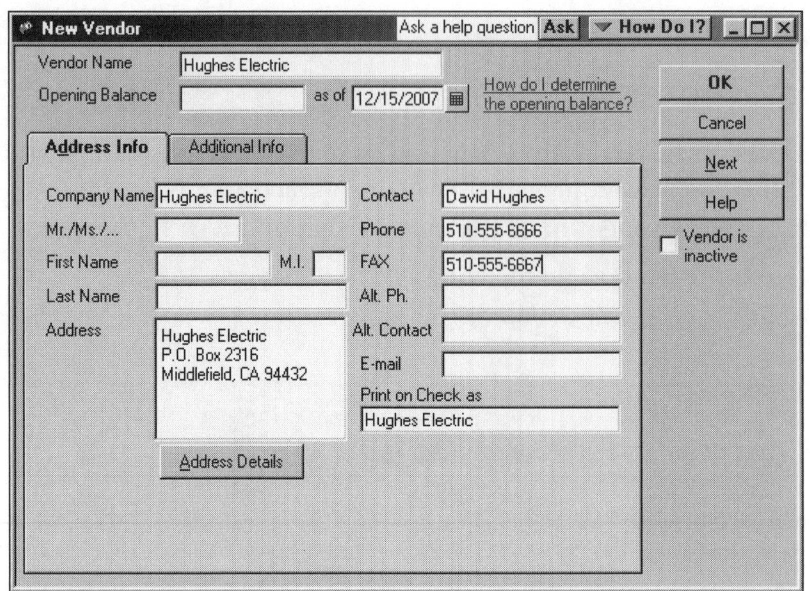

Providing additional vendor information

The Additional Info tab in the New Vendor window is where you can enter a vendor type (if you want to categorize your vendors), payment terms, your credit limit, the vendor's tax identification number, whether this vendor is eligible for a 1099 form, and your opening balance. You'll add this information now for Hughes Electric.

To add information to a vendor record:

1 Click the Additional Info tab.

QuickBooks displays the Additional Info tab of the New Vendor window.

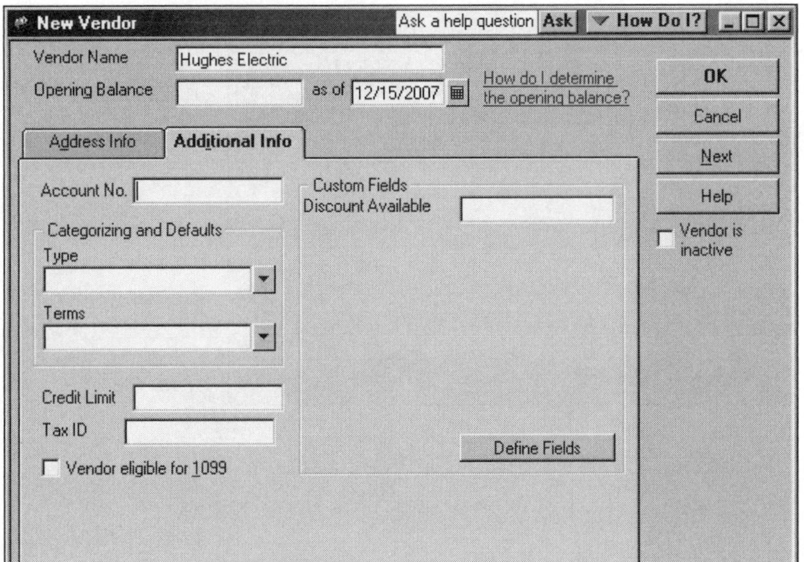

2 In the Account No. field, type ***123-445***.

3 In the Type field, type ***Subcontractors***.

Notice that when you type “sub,” QuickBooks fills in the rest of the word.

4 In the Terms field, choose 2% 10 Net 30 from the drop-down list.

5 In the Credit Limit field, type ***2000*** and press Tab.

Your New Vendor window should resemble the figure below.

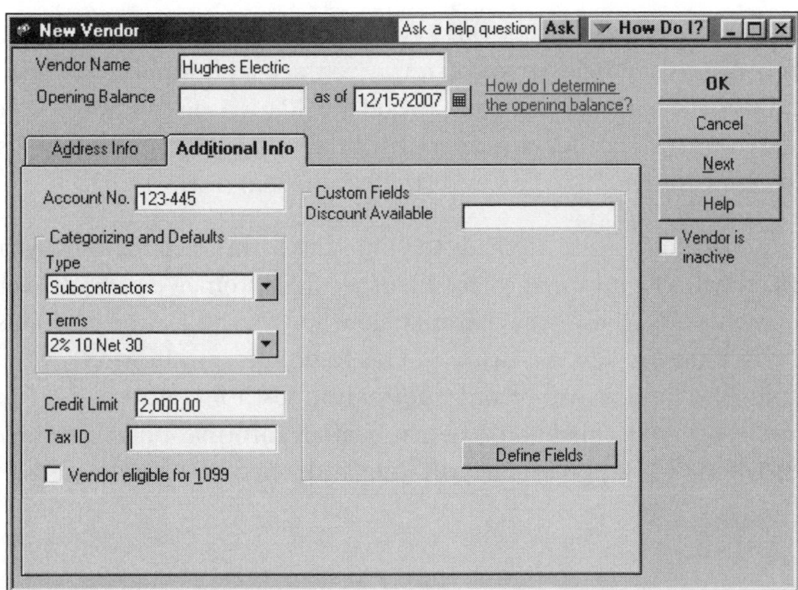

6 Click OK.

QuickBooks adds the vendor and displays the updated Vendor list.

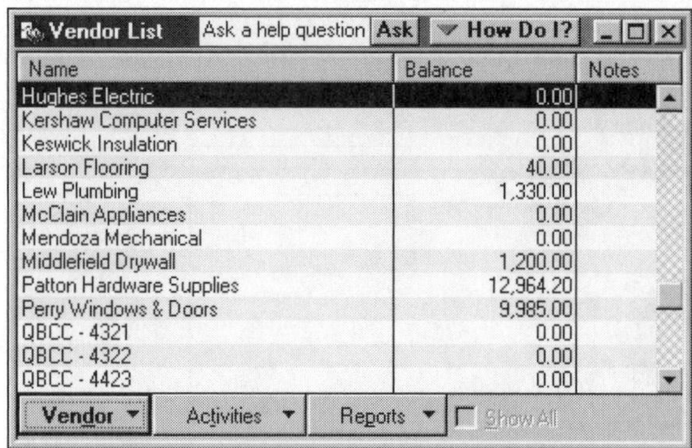

Notice that Hughes Electric has been added to the list.

7 Close the Vendor list.

Tip: **QuickBooks has several preset reports related to vendors.** Some reports you may find useful are the purchases by vendor summary and detail reports (under the Purchases submenu in the Reports menu).

You may also find the A/P aging summary, the A/P aging detail, unpaid bills, and the vendor balance summary reports useful. You'll find them under the Vendors & Payables submenu in the Reports menu.

Adding custom fields

QuickBooks lets you add custom fields to the Customer:Job, Vendor, Employee, and Item lists. Custom fields give you a way to track additional information specific to your business. For example, you can add a field for pager numbers to your Vendor and Employee lists, a field for customers' birthdays to your Customer:Job list, and fields for units of measurement, color, and size to your Item list.

When you add the custom fields to your sales forms or purchase orders, the fields are prefilled with the information for that specific customer, employee, vendor, or item (if you specified a value for the custom field when you added the customer, for example). You don't have to add the custom fields to your forms, however; you can also use custom fields as a way to record information just for your use, such as a credit rating for each customer. QuickBooks remembers the information you entered in the custom fields when you import and export data and when you memorize transactions.

For each of the names lists (customer, vendor, and employee), you can add up to seven custom fields, including fields that are on more than one list. For example, if you add a custom "Birthday" field for customers and vendors, QuickBooks counts it as one field used for each—for a total of two custom fields. You can add up to five custom fields for the Item list. (Custom fields for the Item list are tracked separately from custom fields for the customer, vendor, and employee lists.)

After you add custom fields, you can use them on invoices, credit memos, sales receipts, purchase orders, estimates (QuickBooks: Pro and QuickBooks: Premier only), and sales orders (Premier only).

Adding custom fields for customers, vendors, and employees

You can enter information in the custom fields only through the New or Edit windows (for example, the New Customer or Edit Customer windows). You can display information from the custom fields on form as well as add custom fields to reports.

First, look at the custom fields that Rock Castle Construction has already added to its Customer:Job, Vendor, and Employee lists. Then, you'll add two new custom fields.

To add custom fields:

1 From the Customers menu, choose Customer:Job List.

QuickBooks displays the Customer:Job list.

2 In the Customer:Job list, select Cook, Brian.

3 Click the Customer:Job menu button, and then choose Edit.

QuickBooks displays the Edit Customer window.

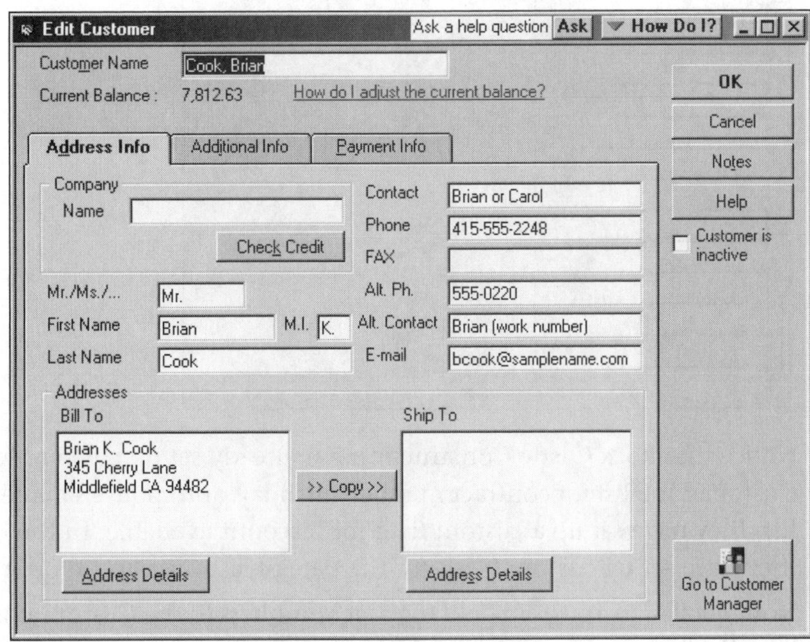

4 Click the Additional Info tab.

QuickBooks displays the Additional Info tab in the Edit Customer window.

5 Click Define Fields.

QuickBooks displays the Define Fields window.

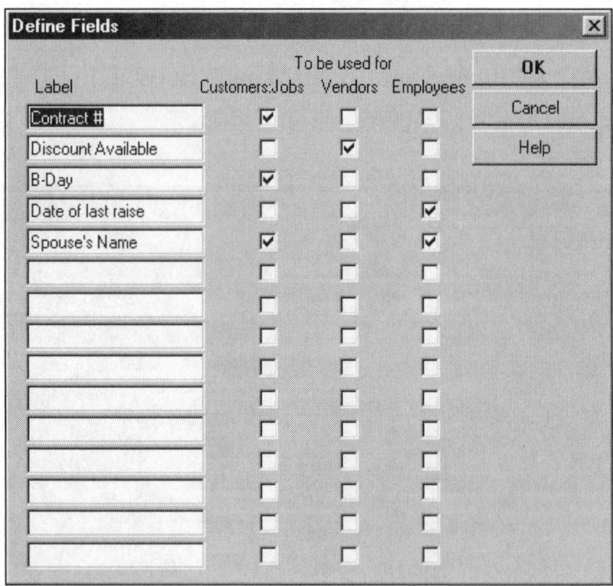

Notice that Rock Castle Construction has already set up custom fields in the Customer:Job list for contract number, birthday, and spouse's name. In the Vendor list, they have set up a custom field for discount available. In the Employee list, they have set up custom fields for the date of last raise and spouse's name.

Now, you'll add a custom field for pager numbers to the Customer:Job and Vendor lists. You'll also add a custom field to the Employee list that tracks the date of each employee's last review.

6 In the first blank Label field, type ***Pager Number***.

7 Click the Customers:Jobs checkbox to select it.

8 Click the Vendors checkbox to select it.

9 In the next blank Label field, type ***Date of last review***.

10 Click the Employees checkbox to select it.

Your Define Fields window should now look like this.

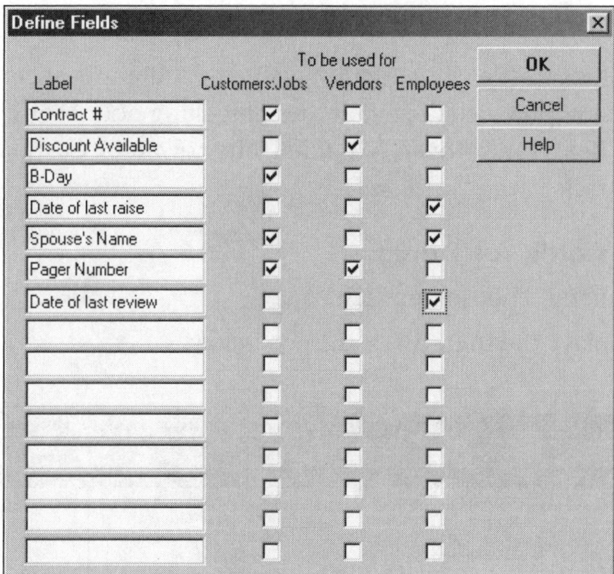

11 Click OK.

12 If you see an informational message about using the custom fields in transactions by turning them on in your custom templates, click OK.

QuickBooks has added the Pager Number field to the Edit Customer window.

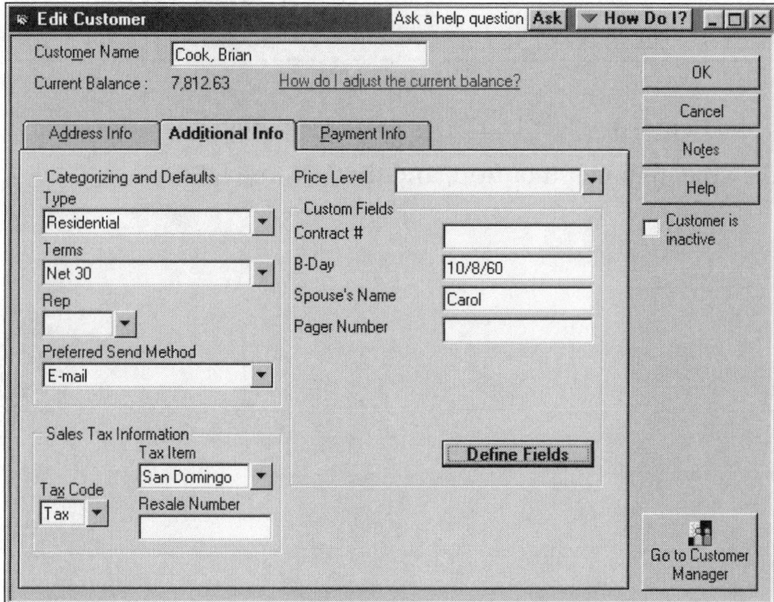

13 In the Pager Number field, type ***415-555-9876***.

If you customize your sales forms to display the Pager Number field, this number displays whenever you create a form for this customer. It also displays on reports modified to display the Pager Number column.

14 Click OK to close the Edit Customer window.

15 Close the Customer:Job list.

Adding custom fields for items

Now suppose that Rock Castle Construction wants to add another custom field to its Item list. The company purchases several types of locking doorknobs. The Item list already has custom fields for Color and Material, but now Rock Castle wants to add an additional field to track Style.

To add custom fields for items:

1 From the Lists menu, choose Item List.

QuickBooks displays the Item list, as shown below.

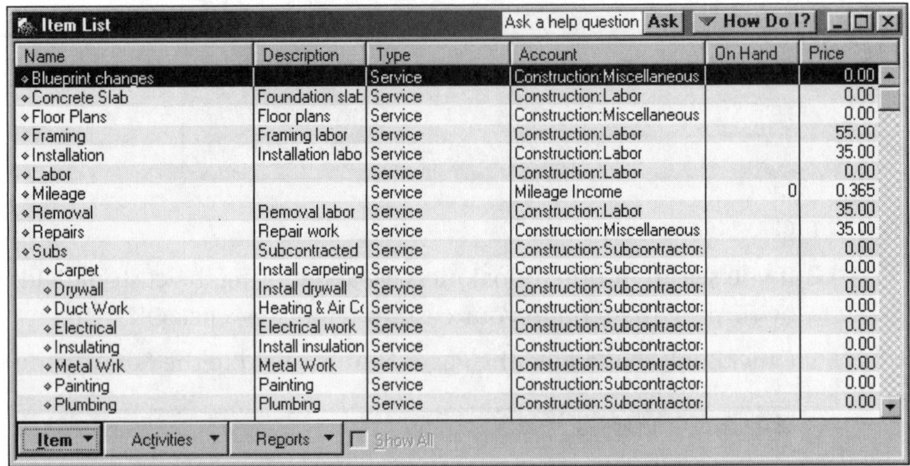

2 In the Item list, select Lk Doorknobs (a sub item of Hardware).

3 Click the Item menu button, and then choose Edit.

QuickBooks displays the Edit Item window.

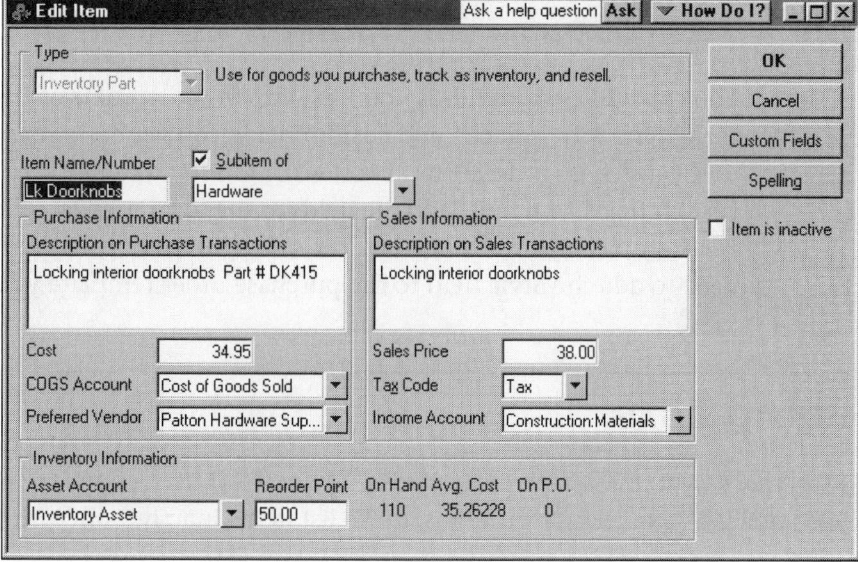

4 Click Custom Fields.

QuickBooks displays the custom fields already defined for this item.

5 Click Define Fields.

QuickBooks displays the Define Custom Fields for Items window.

6 In the "Use" column, click the first blank checkbox to select it. Then type ***Style*** in the Label field.

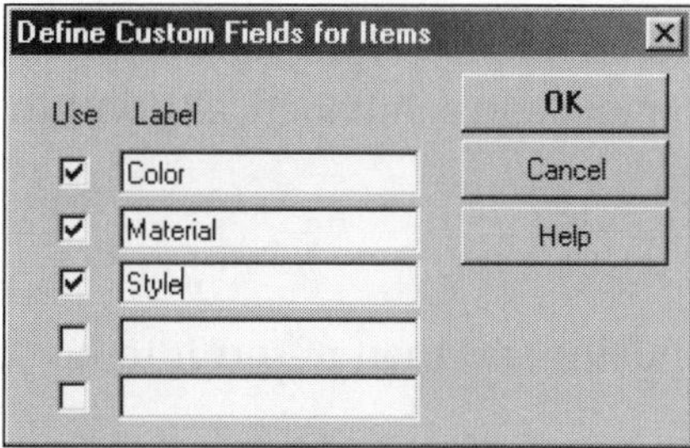

7 Click OK to close the window.

8 If you see an informational message about using the custom fields in transactions by turning them on in your custom templates, click OK.

9 In the "Custom Fields for Lk Doorknobs" window, type ***Round*** in the Style field.

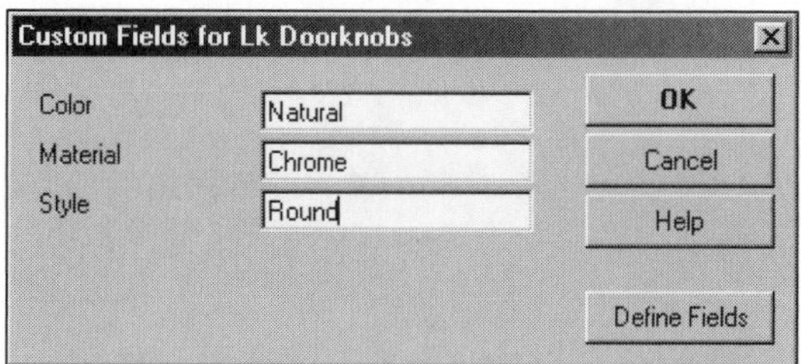

10 Click OK to close the Custom Fields for Lk Doorknobs window, and then click OK to close the Edit Item window.

11 Close the Item list.

Tip: **You can add custom fields you've set up for customers or items to any sales form.** Similarly, you can add custom fields you've set up for vendors or items to the purchase order form. If you want to filter a report based on text in a custom fields, you must add the fields to the form used to generate the report. For example, if you want to filter the open purchase orders report by style, you need to add the Style field to the purchase order template you use.

Managing lists

Lists are easy to manage in QuickBooks. You can sort lists, combine (merge) list items, rename list items, delete list items, make list items inactive, and print lists.

Sorting lists

You can sort many QuickBooks lists manually or alphabetically. To sort a list manually, simply use the mouse to drag a list item to its new location. Lists that you can sort this way are the Chart of Accounts, Customer:Job, Class, Customer Type, Vendor Type, Job Type, and Memorized Transaction lists.

If you have changed the order of a list by dragging items and then decide you'd rather have an alphabetically sorted list, QuickBooks has a Re-sort List command. In the chart of accounts, the Re-sort List command sorts alphabetically within account type; in the Item list, the Re-sort List command sorts alphabetically within item type.

Sorting lists manually

In this exercise, you'll sort a list manually, and then re-sort it to put it back in alphabetical order.

To sort a list manually:

1 From the Lists menu, choose Chart of Accounts.

QuickBooks displays the chart of accounts for Rock Castle Construction.

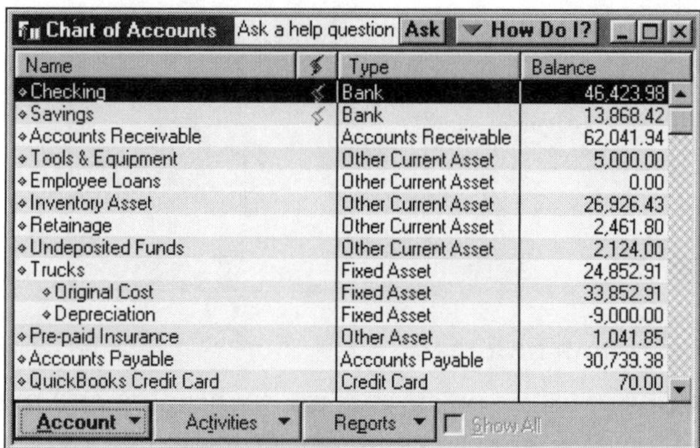

Name		Type	Balance
◆Checking	✓	Bank	46,423.98
◆Savings	✓	Bank	13,868.42
◆Accounts Receivable		Accounts Receivable	62,041.94
◆Tools & Equipment		Other Current Asset	5,000.00
◆Employee Loans		Other Current Asset	0.00
◆Inventory Asset		Other Current Asset	26,926.43
◆Retainage		Other Current Asset	2,461.80
◆Undeposited Funds		Other Current Asset	2,124.00
◆Trucks		Fixed Asset	24,852.91
◆Original Cost		Fixed Asset	33,852.91
◆Depreciation		Fixed Asset	-9,000.00
◆Pre-paid Insurance		Other Asset	1,041.85
◆Accounts Payable		Accounts Payable	30,739.38
◆QuickBooks Credit Card		Credit Card	70.00

2 Click the diamond to the left of the Owner's Draw subaccount of Owner's Equity.

The mouse pointer becomes a four-directional arrow.

3 Click and hold the mouse button, and drag the pointer upward until you see a dotted line directly below Owner's Equity.

4 Release the mouse button to drop the account in the new position.

The Owner's Draw account is now directly under the Owner's Equity account.

◆Owner's Equity	Equity	19,000.00
◆Owner's Draw	Equity	-6,000.00
◆Owner's Contribution	Equity	25,000.00

Now you can use the Re-sort List command to return the list to alphabetical order.

5 To re-sort the list alphabetically, click the Account menu button, and select Re-sort List.

QuickBooks asks you to confirm that you want to return the list to its original order.

6 Click OK.

QuickBooks re-sorts the chart of accounts alphabetically by account type.

7 Close the chart of accounts.

Sorting lists in ascending or descending order

Depending on the type of business you have, you may want to order your list entries in a certain way. For example, perhaps you'd like to see people who owe you money at the top of your Customer:Job list. In this exercise, you'll learn how to sort the Customer:Job list in descending order by customer balance.

To sort a list in descending order:

1 From the Lists menu, choose Customer:Job List.

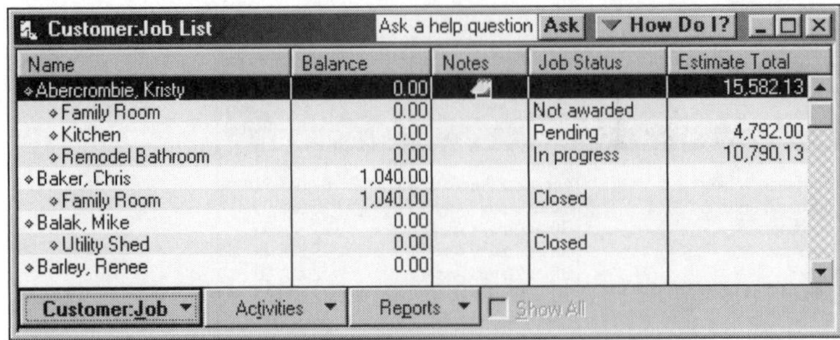

2 Click the Balance column heading.

Notice that an arrow pointing up appears on the heading and the list is sorted in ascending order by customer balance.

3 Click the column heading again.

Notice that the arrow now points down and the list is sorted in descending order with the customers with the highest balances at the top of the list.

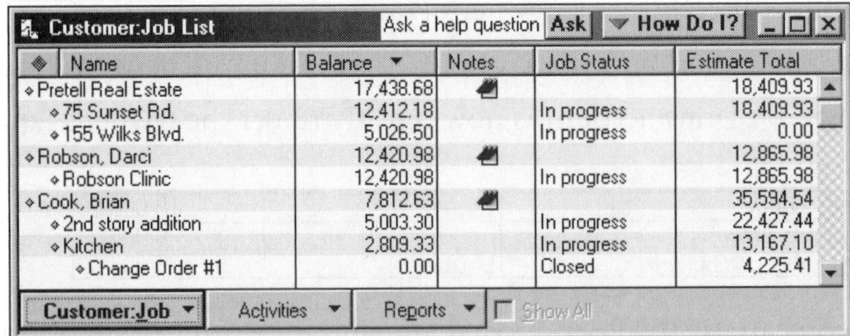

4 To return to the order you started with, click the large diamond to the left of the Name column heading.

5 Close the Customer:Job list.

Merging list items

In most lists, you can combine two list items into one. For example, you may find that you've been using two customers (because of different spellings) when you really need only one on your Customer:Job list. You can merge list items in the Chart of Accounts, Item, Customer:Job, Vendor, Employee, and Other Names lists.

Important: After you merge list items, you cannot separate them. When working in your own company file, we recommend that you back up your data before merging list items.

In this exercise, suppose you want to merge Hughes Electric (the vendor you added earlier in the lesson) with C.U. Electric. To merge them, you edit the incorrect name to match the spelling of the correct name.

To merge items on a list:

1 From the Vendors menu, choose Vendor List.

QuickBooks displays the Vendor list.

2 Double-click the entry for Hughes Electric.

QuickBooks displays the Edit Vendor window.

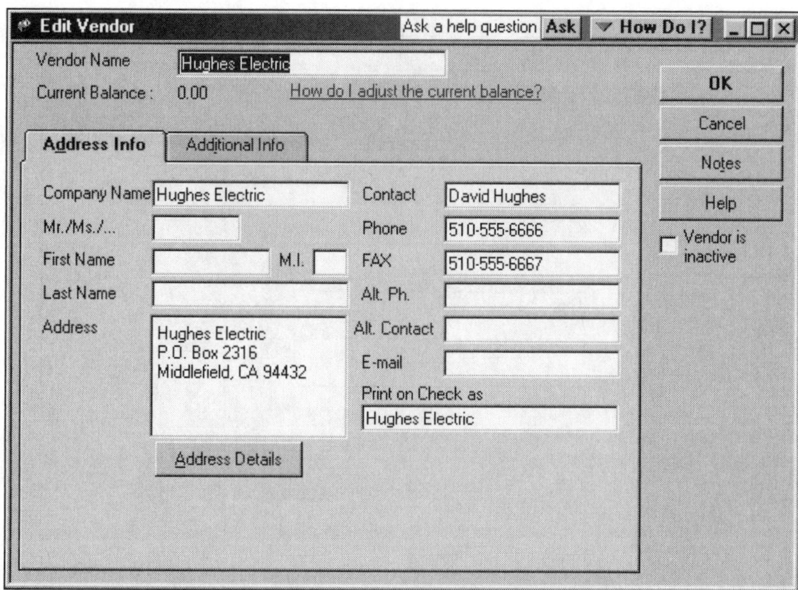

3 In the Vendor Name field, type ***C.U. Electric***. (This is the vendor name you want to merge with.)

4 Click OK.

QuickBooks asks if you would like to merge the names.

5 Click Yes.

QuickBooks merges the two names, and you now have only C.U. Electric in the Vendor list.

6 Close the Vendor list.

Note: **You cannot merge items on the Fixed Asset Item list.** In addition, if you use assembly items in QuickBooks Premier Edition products, you cannot merge them with other assembly items or with any other type of item.

Renaming list items

You can rename any list item. When you make the change, QuickBooks automatically modifies all existing transactions containing the item. If you don't want to change existing transactions, add a new name or item instead.

To rename a list item in the chart of accounts:

1. From the Lists menu, choose Chart of Accounts to display the chart of accounts for Rock Castle Construction.
2. In the chart of accounts, select Checking.
3. Click the Account menu button, and choose Edit.

   QuickBooks displays the Edit Account window.

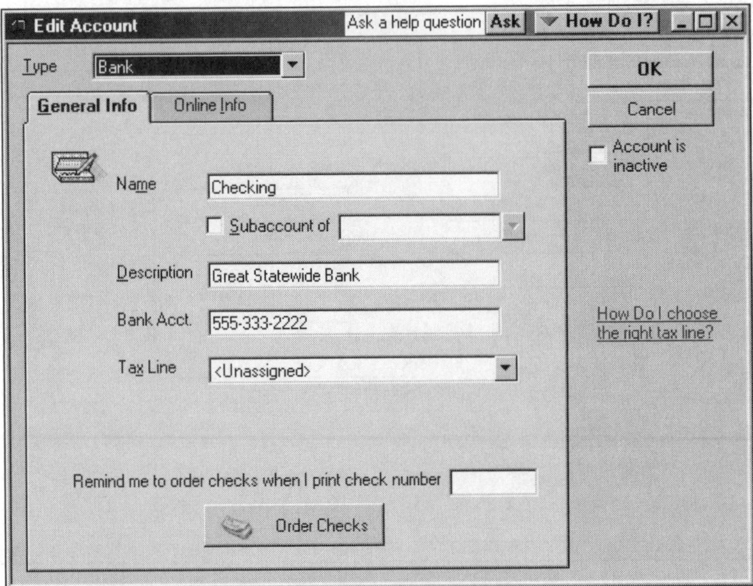

4. In the Name field, type ***Master Checking Account***.
5. Click OK.

   QuickBooks changes the account name in the chart of accounts.

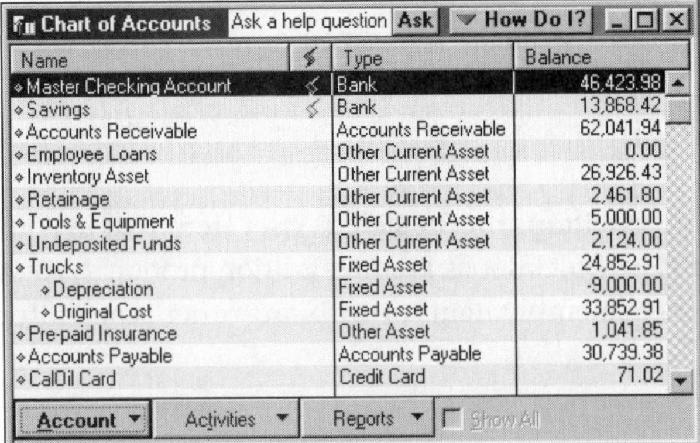

6. Close the chart of accounts.

Deleting items and making list items inactive

You can delete list items only if you have not used them in any transactions. If you try to delete a list item that is used in a transaction, QuickBooks displays a warning that the item can't be deleted. If you don't want to use a list item but you can't delete it, you can make it inactive.

To make a list item inactive:

1 From the Customers menu, choose Customer:Job List.

QuickBooks displays the Customer:Job list.

2 Select Milner, Eloyse in the list. (Select her name, not the job.)

3 Click the Customer:Job menu button, and choose Make Inactive.

Notice that Eloyse Milner (and the job for her room addition) no longer appears on the Customer:Job list. (The customer:job item is only removed from the list—transactions associated with this customer:job will still show in reports.)

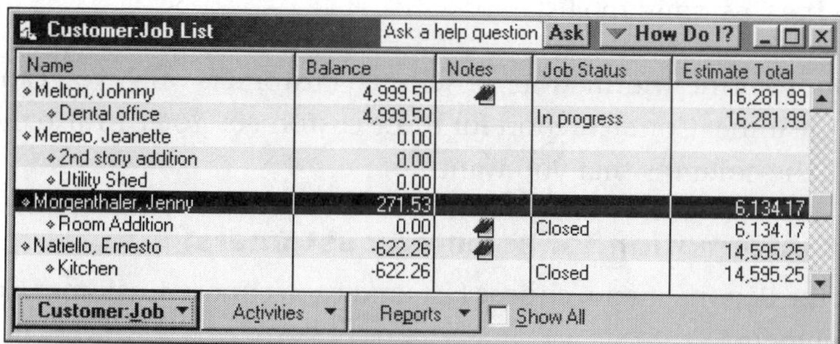

4 To see inactive list items, select the Show All checkbox in the list window.

QuickBooks displays all the list items again, but the Xs signify that this customer is still inactive. (You make the customer active again by choosing Make Active from the Customer:Job menu button.)

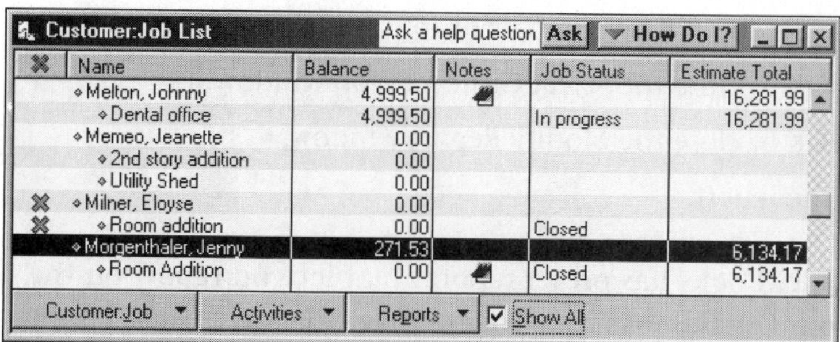

5 Leave the Customer:Job list open, you'll print it in the next exercise.

Printing a list

You can print a QuickBooks list for reference, or you may print a list to a file to use in your word processor or spreadsheet.

To print the customer:job list:

1 Click the Customer:Job menu button, and then choose Print List.

QuickBooks displays a message telling you that you can also print list information from the Reports menu.

2 Click OK to bypass the List Reports message.

QuickBooks displays the Print Lists window, which displays the name of your printer and printer port.

You can select to print to a printer or to a file.

3 Click Print.

Note: This is a fairly long list, so if you don't want to print it now, click Cancel.

4 Close the Customer:Job list.

If you want to print information for selected customers only, you can generate and filter the Customer Contact report for those customers. You can also modify the report to include the columns that you want.

To print information for selected customers:

1 From the Reports menu, choose List, and then choose Customer Contact List from the submenu.
2 Click Modify Report.
3 Click the Filters tab.
4 Select Customer in the Filters list.
5 In the Customer field, choose Selected customers/jobs.
6 Make sure Manual is selected and then click to put a checkmark next to those customers about which you want to print contact information.
7 Click OK to close the Select Customer Job window.
8 Click OK to close the Modify Report window.
9 Print the report.

Tip: **QuickBooks has preset reports that let you report on the information in your QuickBooks lists.** For example, you can create a phone list and a contact list for you customers, employees, and vendors. You can also create a price list for the items stored on your QuickBooks Item list.

To create a list report, from the Reports menu, choose List, and then choose the list report you want to generate.

Let students know that if they want to print the list to a file (so that they can use it in their word processing, spreadsheet, or database program), they can select File and select the appropriate file format from the drop-down list.

Student test and review

1 What is unique about the QuickBooks Retained Earnings account?

It doesn't have a register associated with it.

2 Add the following customer using the data below:

- Customer Name: Alla Rozenvasser
- Opening Balance: $234.00
- Company Name: Rozenvasser Advertising
- Contact: Alla Rozenvasser
- Bill to: 300 Main Street, Suite #3, Middlefield, CA 94432
- Phone: 415-555-6767
- Fax: 415-555-9090
- Alt. Contact: Shannon Stubo
- Type: Commercial
- Credit Limit: $2500
- Terms: Net 15
- Tax Item: San Domingo

3 Add a new vendor using the data below:

- Vendor: Martin Drywall
- Contact: Sean D. Martin
- Address: P.O. Box 76, Middlefield, CA 94432
- Phone: 555-5432
- Fax: 555-6565
- Account: 082-4343
- Type: Subcontractors
- Terms: Net 30
- Credit Limit: 1,000.00

LESSON 4 Working with bank accounts

Lesson objectives

- To learn how to work with the registers for QuickBooks bank accounts
- To demonstrate how to open a register
- To learn the features common to all registers
- To learn when and how to make entries directly in the register
- To demonstrate how to reconcile a QuickBooks bank account

Handout materials

- Handout 3: Registers associated with QuickBooks windows

Instructor preparation

- Review the lesson, including the examples, to make sure you're familiar with the material.
- Ensure that all students have a copy of qblesson.qbb on their computer's hard disk.
- Have Handout 3 ready for distribution

To start this lesson

Before you perform the following steps, make sure you have installed the exercise file (qblesson.qbb) on your hard disk. See "Installing the exercise file" in the Introduction to this guide if you haven't installed it.

The following steps restore the exercise file to its original state so that the data in the file matches what you see on the screen as you proceed through each lesson.

To restore the exercise file (qblesson.qbb):

1. From the File menu in QuickBooks, choose Restore.

   QuickBooks displays the Restore Company Backup window.
2. In the "Get Company Backup From" section of the window, click Browse and select your c:\QBtrain directory.
3. Select the qblesson.qbb file, and then click Open.
4. In the "Restore Company Backup To" section of the window, click Browse and select your c:\QBtrain directory.
5. In the File name field of the Restore To window, type ***lesson 4*** and then click Save.
6. Click Restore.

Writing a QuickBooks check

You can enter checks directly into the check register by using the QuickBooks Write Checks window. When you enter a check at the Write Checks window, you can see the address information and easily allocate the check between multiple accounts.

Suppose that you need to write a check to pay Rock Castle Construction's telephone bill.

To write a check:

1 From the Banking menu, choose Write Checks.

QuickBooks displays the Write Checks window.

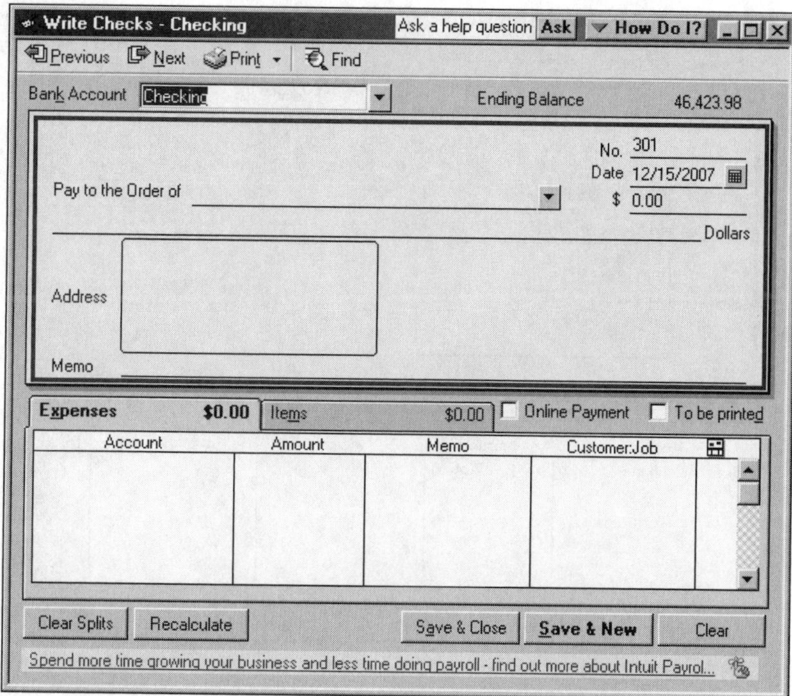

The Bank Account field shows the account from which you are writing this check. QuickBooks displays the current date in the Date field. (The sample data is set to display December 15, 2007 as the current date.) You can change either of these values if you wish, but they are fine for our example.

2 Select the "To be printed" checkbox.

QuickBooks displays a checkmark in the checkbox.

3 In the Pay to the Order of field, type ***Cal Telephone***.

4 Press Tab to move to the Amount field.

QuickBooks has an AutoRecall feature that fills in the amount from the last transaction with a payee. This is convenient when you have recurring payments of the same amount. You can turn on AutoRecall by choosing Preferences from the Edit menu. Click General, and then select the checkbox for "Automatically recall last transaction for this name" on the My Preferences tab.

5 Type ***156.91*** (the amount of the telephone bill), and then press Tab.

Notice that QuickBooks spells out the amount of the check for you on the line below the payee.

6 Click in the Account column on the Expenses tab, and then choose Utilities:Telephone from the drop-down list.

Your screen should resemble the following figure.

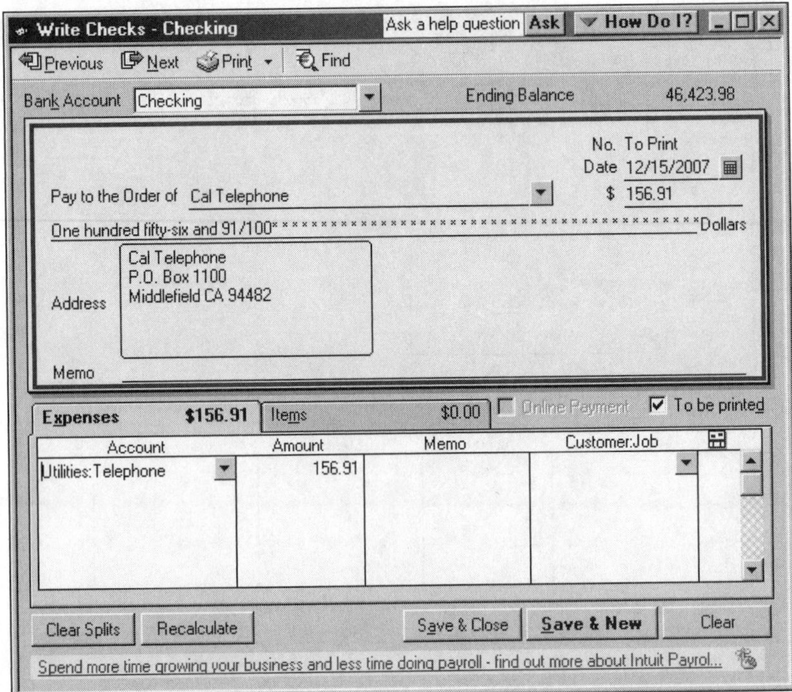

The Expenses tab is where you assign the amount of the check to one of the expense accounts on your company's chart of accounts. In this case, Rock Castle Construction assigns the check to its Utilities account and the Telephone subaccount. You use the Items tab only when purchasing items you plan to stock in inventory.

7 Click Save & Close.

8 From the Banking menu, choose Use Register.

Rock Castle Construction has more than one type of bank account, so QuickBooks displays the Use Register window and asks you to specify the account you want.

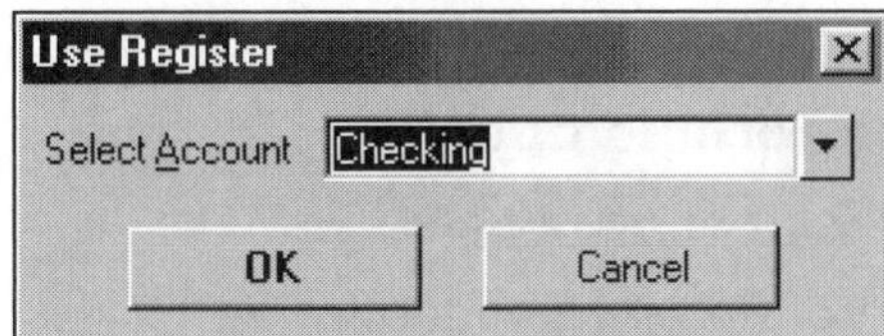

9 Click OK to accept Checking as the account whose register you want to see.

QuickBooks opens the Checking register.

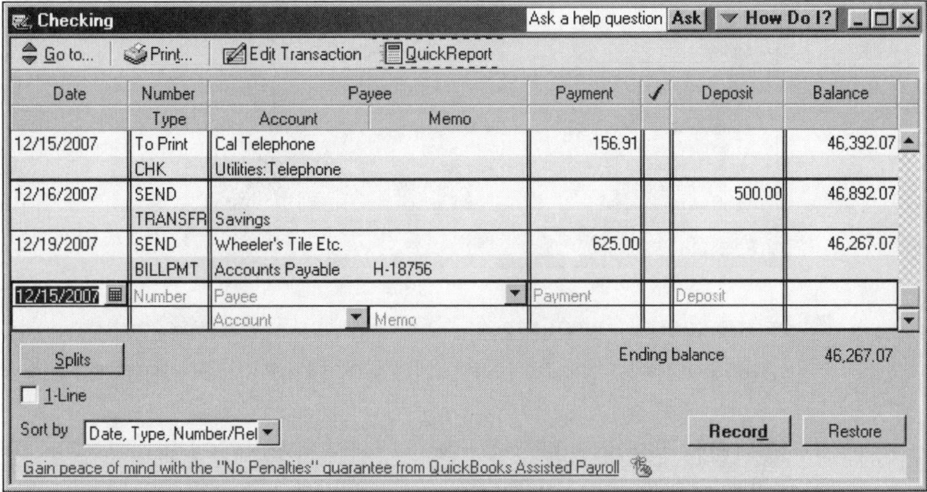

Notice that the check you just wrote is listed in the register as a check that needs to be printed.

10 Close the Checking account register.

Tip: **Do NOT use the Write Checks window if you are paying sales tax, paying payroll taxes and liabilities, or paying bills that you have entered previously (that is, you are using A/P to track them).** Instead, use the Pay Sales Tax window for a sales tax payment, the Pay Liabilities window for payroll taxes, and the Enter Bills and Pay Bills windows for paying A/P bills.

Using bank account registers

When you work in QuickBooks, you often use forms—such as a check or an invoice—to enter information. But behind the scenes, QuickBooks records your entries in the appropriate account register. Each balance sheet account listed on the chart of accounts has a register associated with it (except the Retained Earnings account).

Refer to Handout 3, "Registers associated with QuickBooks windows"

Opening a register

When you have a QuickBooks form displayed on your screen, you can view its account register by choosing Use Register from the Banking menu, or by double-clicking the account name in the chart of accounts.

To open a register (when no form is open):

1. From the Lists menu, choose Chart of Accounts.

   QuickBooks displays the Chart of Accounts window.

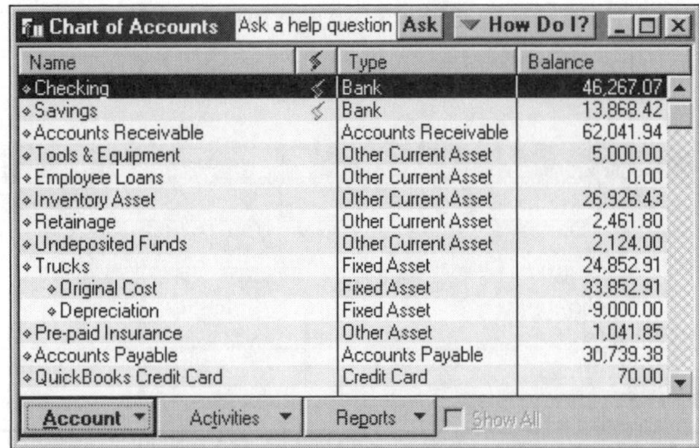

2. In the chart of accounts, double-click the Savings account.

   QuickBooks opens the register for Rock Castle Construction's Savings account.

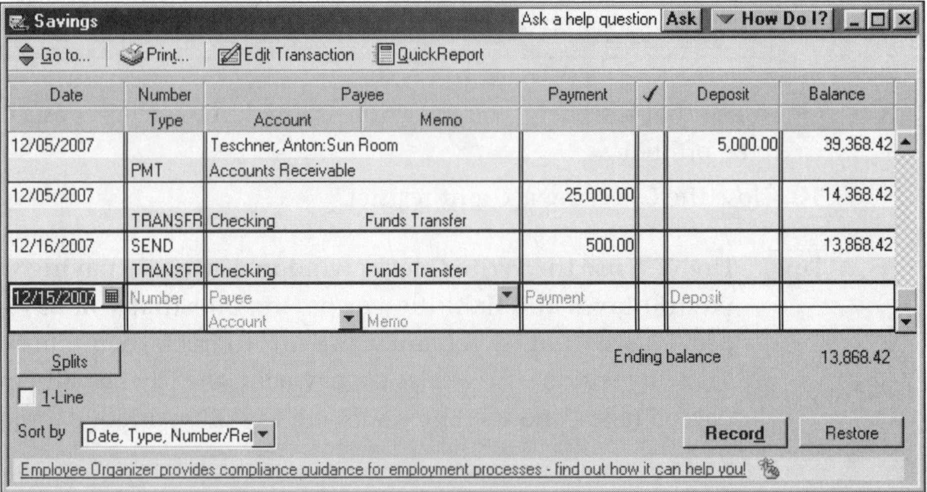

Common features of QuickBooks registers

All QuickBooks registers work the same way, regardless of the accounts with which they are associated. Here are some common features of all QuickBooks registers:

- The register shows every transaction that affects an account's balance and lists them in chronological order (though you can change the order by choosing a different option from the Sort by drop-down list). For example, in a checking account, the register shows checks you've written (either with QuickBooks or by hand), deposits to the account, and withdrawals from the account.
- The columns in the register give specific information about the transaction. The first column is the date. The second column shows a reference number (a check number or a vendor's P.O. number) and a type (to tell you whether the transaction represents a check or a bill payment, for example). The next column lists the payee, the account to which you've assigned the transaction, and any descriptive memo you choose to type. The final columns for a bank account show the transaction amount (either in the Payment or Deposit column) and whether the transaction has cleared the bank (indicated by a checkmark in the column).
- On every transaction line, QuickBooks shows the account's running balance. The bottom of the register window shows the account's ending balance—the balance takes into account all the transactions entered in the register, including checks you haven't yet printed.

To complete the exercise:

1. Close the Savings register window.
2. Close the chart of accounts.

Tip: **You can edit transactions in registers with some restrictions: You cannot edit a sales tax payment.** You can edit split amounts for checks (CHK), deposits (DEP), credit card charges (CC), credit card credits (CC CRED), bills (BILL), and vendor credits (BILLCRED) if all the amounts are assigned to expense (or other) accounts. (If any amount is assigned to an item, you must select the transaction and click Splits to edit the split amounts.) For all other kinds of transactions, only certain fields can be edited directly in the register. To edit one of these transactions without restrictions, select the transaction and click Edit Transaction to display the transaction in its complete form.

Entering a handwritten check

Sometimes you need to write a check on the spot for items you did not plan to purchase. QuickBooks lets you write the check, and then enter it later in the checking account register or on the check form.

Suppose that while picking up supplies one day, you stop at Bayshore Office Supply and find a new office chair on sale for $99.95. The sale ends today, so you write a check on the spot. You'll have to enter it in QuickBooks later.

To enter a handwritten check in the checking account register:

1. From the Banking menu, choose Use Register.

   QuickBooks displays the Use Register window.
2. Click OK to accept Checking.

   QuickBooks displays the register for the Checking account.
3. Click in the Number field in the blank transaction at the bottom of the register, then double-click to highlight the number that QuickBooks prefills.
4. Type ***1204***, and then press Tab.
5. In the Payee field, type ***Bayshore Office Supply***, and then press Tab.

   QuickBooks displays a message telling you that Bayshore Office Supply is not on the Name list.
6. Click Quick Add.

   QuickBooks displays the Select Name Type window.

   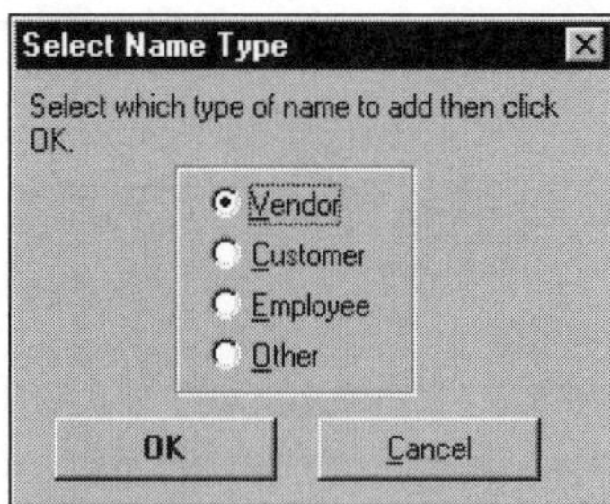

   Bayshore Office Supply is a vendor, so you can accept the displayed choice.
7. Click OK.

   QuickBooks adds the new vendor to the Vendor list.
8. In the Payment field, type ***99.95***, and then press Tab.
9. In the Account field, type ***Of***, and then press Tab.

   QuickBooks fills in Office Supplies.

10 In the Memo field, type ***Office chair.***

The Checking account register on your screen should resemble the following figure.

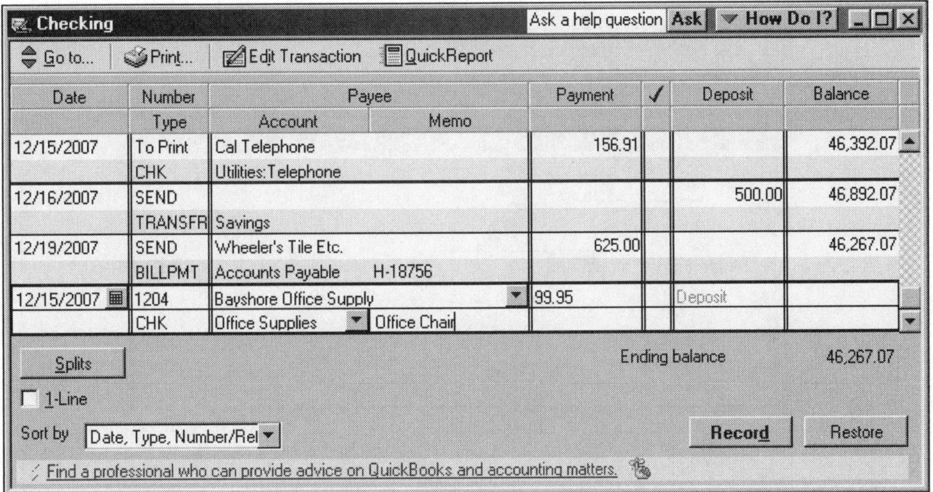

11 Click Record.

12 Close the Checking account register.

Transferring money between accounts

You can easily transfer money to different accounts using the QuickBooks Transfer Funds Between Accounts window. Rock Castle Construction wants to transfer $5,000.00 from checking to savings.

To transfer money:

1. From the Banking menu, choose Transfer Funds.

   QuickBooks displays the Transfer Funds Between Accounts window.

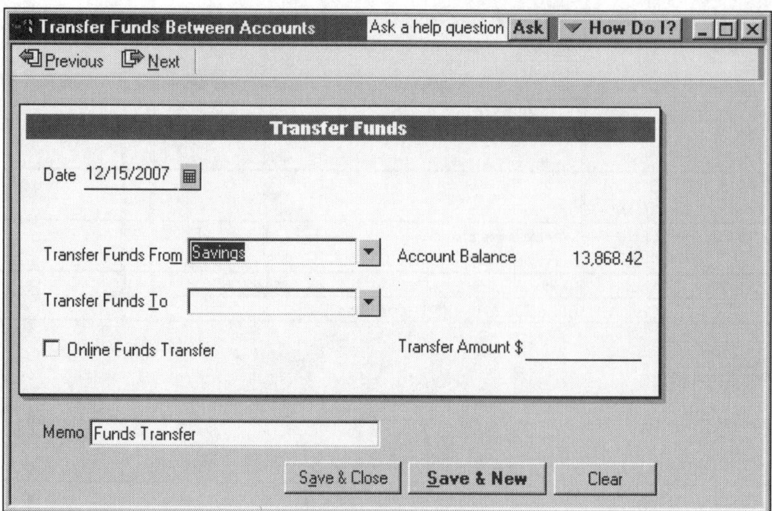

   Notice that QuickBooks displays the current balance for the Savings account.

2. In the Transfer Funds From field, choose Checking from the drop-down list.
3. In the Transfer Funds To field, choose Savings from the drop-down list.
4. In the Transfer Amount field, type ***5000***.

   Your screen should resemble the following figure.

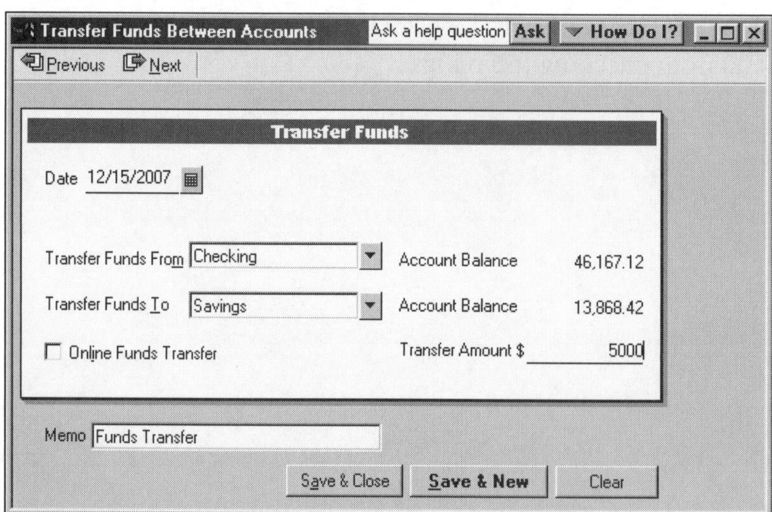

5. Click Save & Close.

QuickBooks decreases the balance in the checking account by $5,000 and increases the balance in the savings account by $5,000.

Reconciling checking accounts

Reconciling is the process of making sure that your checking account record matches the bank's record.

An overview of reconciliation

When you keep your records with QuickBooks, you don't have to worry about addition or subtraction errors like you do when you're using a paper check register. Even so, it is important to get in the habit of reconciling your QuickBooks bank accounts on a monthly basis. This helps you avoid overdraft charges for bad checks, gives you a chance to spot possible bank errors, and helps you keep more accurate financial records.

Your bank sends you a statement for each of your accounts each month. The statement shows all the activity in your account since the previous statement:

- The opening balance for your bank account (amount in your account as of the previous statement)
- The ending balance for your bank account (amount in your account as of the closing date for the statement)
- The amount of interest, if any, you've received for this statement period
- Any service charges assessed by the bank for this statement period
- Checks that have cleared the bank
- Deposits you've made to the account
- Any other transactions that affect the balance of your account (for example, automatic payments or deposits or ATM withdrawals or deposits)

When you receive a statement from your bank or from a credit card company, you need to reconcile the statement with your QuickBooks records. You can reconcile any QuickBooks bank account, including accounts for savings and money market funds. The goal of reconciling is to make sure that your QuickBooks records and the bank's statement agree about your account balance.

Marking cleared transactions

To begin reconciling an account, you need to tell QuickBooks which account you want to reconcile. Then you can provide information from the top part of your bank statement.

To reconcile your account:

1 From the Banking menu, choose Reconcile.

QuickBooks displays the Begin Reconciliation window.

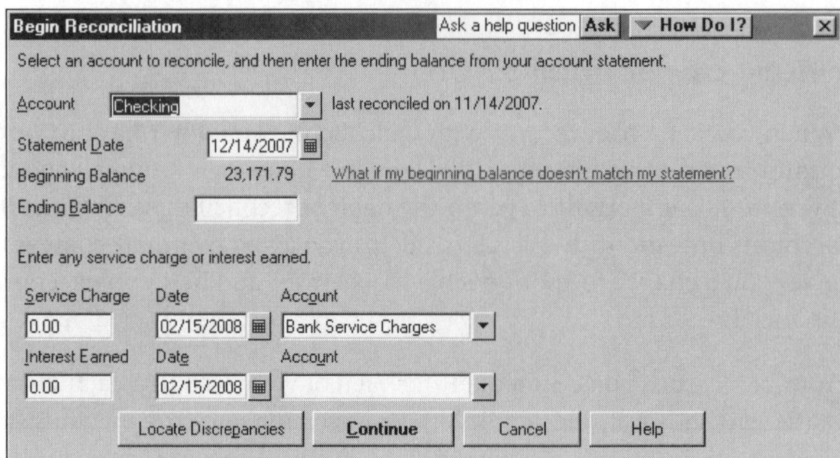

2 In the Account field, make sure Checking is selected.

3 In the Statement Date field, type ***12/15/2007***.

4 In the Ending Balance field, type ***34592.98***.

5 In the Service Charge field, type ***14.00***.

Your screen should resemble the following.

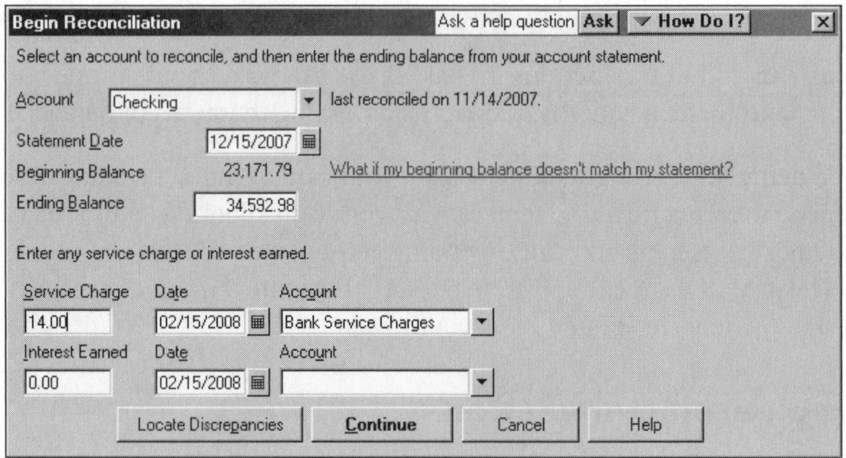

6 Click Continue.

QuickBooks displays the Reconcile - Checking window.

You can select which columns you want to display by clicking Columns to Display.

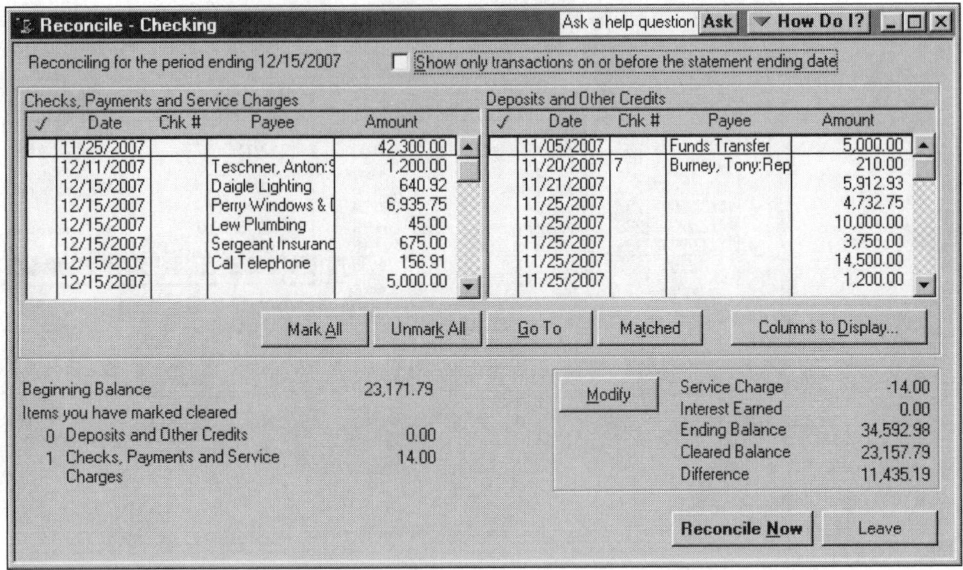

7 Select Mark All.

QuickBooks places a checkmark to the left of all items.

If you need to make a correction to a transaction before you reconcile the account, highlight the transaction, and click Go To. QuickBooks takes you to the transaction and allows you to return to the reconciliation without losing your work.

8 In the Checks, Payments and Service Charges section, click to clear the checkmarks for all items with dates later than 12/12/2007).

9 Repeat the process in the Deposits and Other Credits section—click to clear the checkmarks for all items with dates later than 12/12/2007.

Your screen should resemble the following figure.

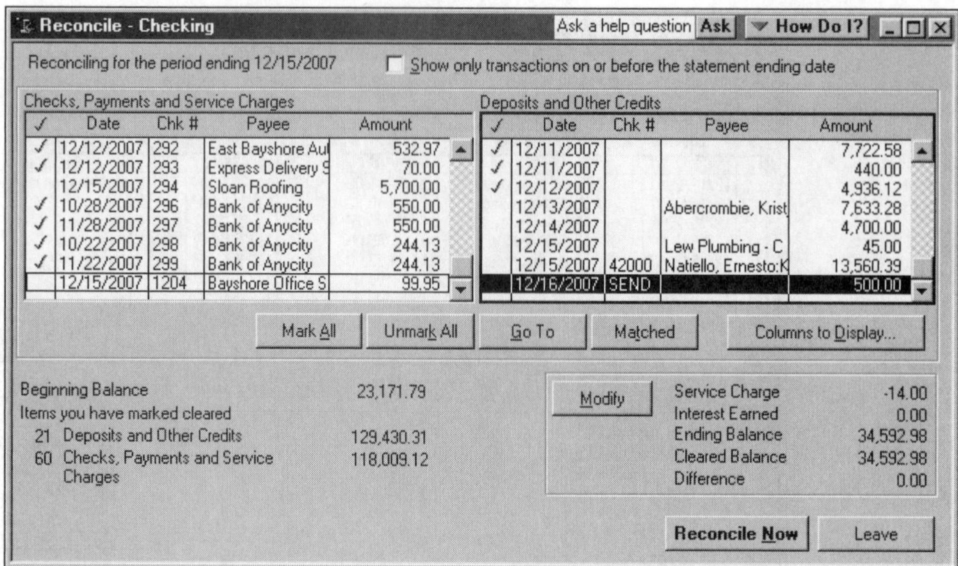

10 Click Reconcile Now.

QuickBooks displays the Select Reconciliation Report window.

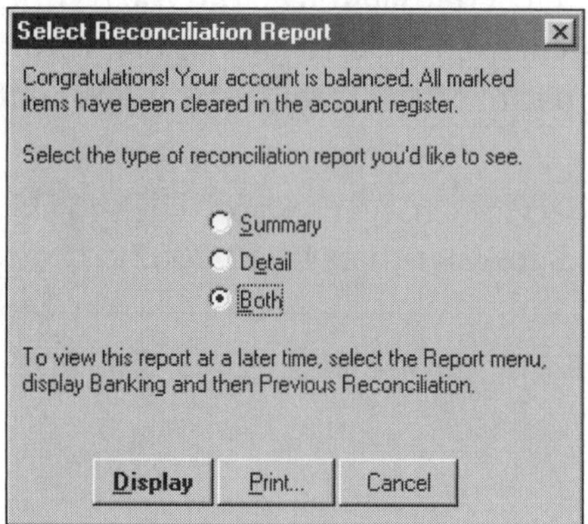

11 In the Select Reconciliation Report window, make sure "Both" is selected, and then click Display.

12 Click OK at the message that QuickBooks displays.

QuickBooks displays both the reconciliation summary and reconciliation detail reports. It's a good idea to save each reconciliation report, but for the purposes of this lesson viewing the reports is sufficient.

13 Close the report windows.

Because Basic and Pro overwrite the previous reconciliation report with data from the latest reconciliation, you may want to print a copy of the report, print the report to a file, or save the report in PDF format in case you need to reference it again. (To save a report in PDF format, with the report displayed, choose Save as PDF from the File menu.) If you're using QuickBooks: Premier, you can print the reconciliation reports for all previous reconciliations.

In addition to the summary and detail reports (which you can view as PDF files), there is an additional report option: the Reconcile Discrepancy report. The Reconcile Discrepancy report shows changes and deletions made to previously reconciled transactions, making it easier to find discrepancies. This report is useful when the beginning balance that QuickBooks shows is different than the ending balance from the bank statement for the previous period. (To generate the report, choose Reconcile from the Banking menu, click Locate Discrepancies, and then click Discrepancy Report.)

If the last reconciliation was in error, by clicking Undo Previous Reconciliation in the Locate Discrepancies window, you can undo it without having to identify and manually clear each affected transaction.

Viewing cleared checks in the register

Now you know that the balance in your QuickBooks check register is accurate as of the latest bank statement. The next time you look at the check register, you'll see a checkmark in the Cleared column next to each reconciled transaction.

Open the Checking account register to see the cleared checks.

To viewed cleared checks in the register:

1. From the Banking menu, choose Use Register.

   QuickBooks displays the Use Register window.
2. Click OK to accept Checking.

3 Scroll through the register to view the cleared items.

Your register should resemble the figure below.

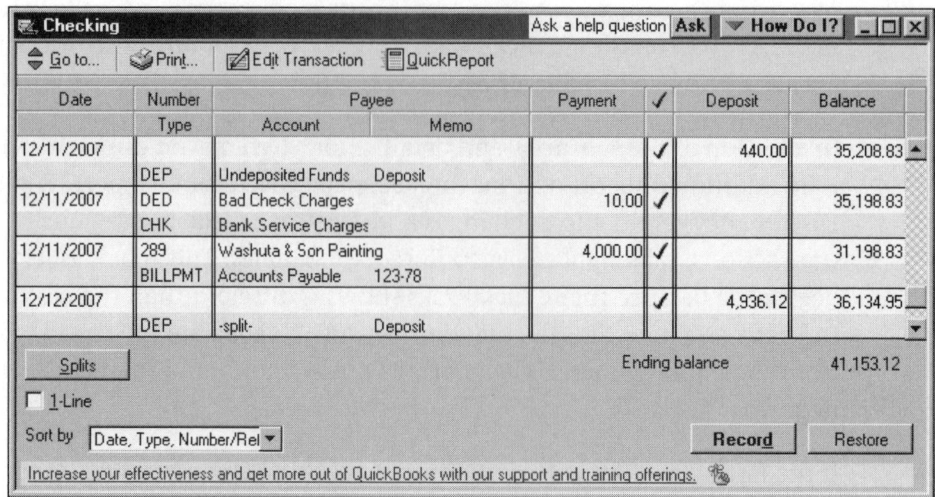

Notice that QuickBooks displays a checkmark next to all cleared items.

4 Close the Checking account register.

Tip: **You can use the QuickBooks Find command to search for specific checks you've written.** For example, suppose you want to find all checks greater than or equal to $500.00 that you wrote during the current year.

1. From the Edit menu, choose Advanced Find.
2. In the Find window, select Transaction Type in the Filters box.
3. Select Check from the list of transactions types.
4. Select Date in the Filters box, and then choose "This Calendar Year-to-date" from the list of date ranges.
5. Select Amount in the list of filters, and then click > (greater than or equal to).
6. Enter 500.00 and click Find.

Student test and review

1. Use the checking account register to enter a handwritten check for $76.95. Use the next available check number and make the check payable to Express Delivery Service, for delivery of a new sign. Assign the check to the Freight & Delivery expense account.
2. Write a QuickBooks check to Bayshore Water for $143.87 to pay this month's water bill. Assign the check to the Utilities:Water expense account.

LESSON 5 Working with other account types

Lesson objectives

- To introduce the other account types available in QuickBooks
- To learn how to track credit card transactions in QuickBooks
- To reconcile a credit card account
- To see how to make a credit card payment
- To discuss the different types of asset and liability accounts you can create and see how to track assets and liabilities in QuickBooks
- To introduce the subject of equity and QuickBooks equity accounts

Instructor preparation

- Review the lesson, including the examples, to make sure you're familiar with the material.
- Ensure that all students have a copy of qblesson.qbb on their computer's hard disk.

To start this lesson

Before you perform the following steps, make sure you have installed the exercise file (qblesson.qbb) on your hard disk. See "Installing the exercise file" in the Introduction to this guide if you haven't installed it.

The following steps restore the exercise file to its original state so that the data in the file matches what you see on the screen as you proceed through each lesson.

To restore the exercise file (qblesson.qbb):

1. From the File menu in QuickBooks, choose Restore.

   QuickBooks displays the Restore Company Backup window.
2. In the "Get Company Backup From" section of the window, click Browse and select your c:\QBtrain directory.
3. Select the qblesson.qbb file, and then click Open.
4. In the "Restore Company Backup To" section of the window, click Browse and select your c:\QBtrain directory.
5. In the File name field of the Restore To window, type ***lesson 5*** and then click Save.
6. Click Restore.

Using other account types

In this lesson, you'll learn about these types of QuickBooks accounts:

- **Credit card accounts**—Used to track transactions you pay for with a credit card.
- **Asset accounts**—Used to track both current assets (those assets you're likely to convert to cash or use up within one year, such as inventory on hand) and fixed assets (such as long-term notes receivable and depreciable assets your business owns that aren't liquid, such as equipment, furniture, or a building).
- **Liability accounts**—Used to track both current liabilities (those liabilities scheduled to be paid within one year, such as sales tax, payroll taxes, and short-term loans) and long-term liabilities (such as loans or mortgages scheduled to be paid over terms longer than one year).
- **Equity accounts**—Used to track owner's equity, including capital investment, draws, and retained earnings.

Tracking credit card transactions

Many businesses pay for expenses with a credit card rather than a check. For travel expenses especially, a credit card is invaluable because it gives a detailed listing of each charge. You can track credit card transactions in QuickBooks just as easily as you track expenses you pay for by check.

You should set up a QuickBooks credit card account for each credit card you use in your business. Like any QuickBooks account, a credit card account has its own register. The register lists all the charges and credits you've recorded, as well as payments you've made.

The way you open and scroll through a credit card register is the same way you open and scroll through any QuickBooks account register.

Entering credit card charges

QuickBooks lets you choose when you enter your credit card charges. You can enter credit card charges when you charge an item or when you receive the bill. Your choice depends on whether you like to enter information into QuickBooks incrementally or all at once. The advantage to entering charges when you charge an item is that you can keep close track of how much you owe. In addition, if the charge is for a particular job, you can keep track of how much you're spending on that job.

Suppose you have a $30 gasoline charge you want to enter into QuickBooks. The form you use is the Enter Credit Card Charges form.

To enter a credit card charge:

1 From the Banking menu, choose Record Credit Card Charges, and then choose Enter Credit Card Charges from the submenu.

QuickBooks displays the Enter Credit Card Charges window.

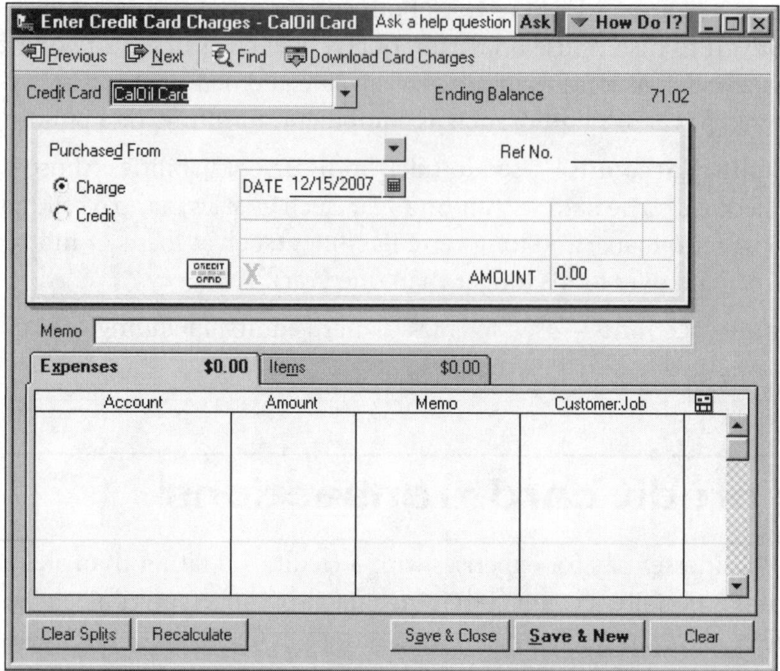

This is the window where you enter your charges. Notice that the form at the top of the window looks just like a familiar credit card charge slip.

2 In the Credit Card field, select CalOil Card from the drop-down list (if it's not already selected).

3 In the Purchased From field, select Bayshore CalOil Service from the drop-down list.

The next field is called Ref No. Most credit card receipts have some sort of transaction number near the top, which exists for identification and tracking purposes. Entering this number from a credit card receipt gives you additional information for the credit card charge, but you don't have to use it. You don't need to enter one for this example.

4 Click in the Amount field, and then double-click to select the entire amount.

5 Type ***30*** and then press Tab.

6 Click the Expenses tab.

7 In the detail area, click in the Account column and assign the charge to the Automobile:Fuel expense account, as shown in the figure below. (Automobile is the account; Fuel is the subaccount.)

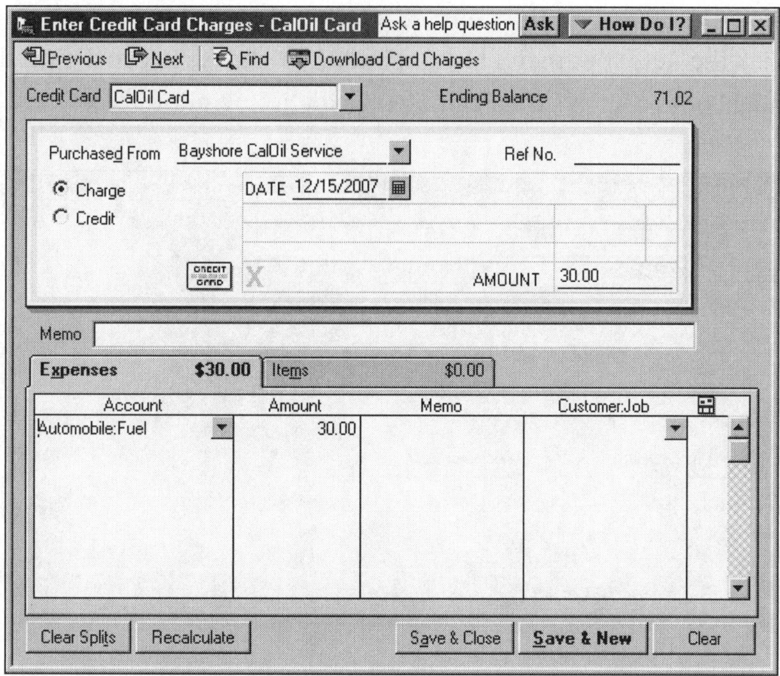

8 Click Save & Close to record the transaction and close the window.

After you record this credit card charge, QuickBooks adds a $30 transaction to the credit card account register (increasing the liability by $30). It also adds $30 to the Automobile:Fuel expense account. (You will see the increase when you create reports on their expense accounts.)

Tip: **If you used your credit card to purchase a reimbursable expense (you want to pass along the expense to a particular customer), you need to indicate this in the Enter Credit Card Charges window.**

For each expense or item you enter on the bottom part of the form, select the appropriate customer in the Customer:Job column. To indicate that this expense should be passed along to the customer, leave the invoice in the Billable column (the column headed by the small invoice icon) without an 'X' through it. This will allow the expense to be passed along when you invoice the customer.

Reconciling a credit card statement

Just as we reconciled a bank account in the previous lesson, you should compare your credit card receipts with your statement and reconcile your credit card statement. Reconciling a credit card account is almost identical to reconciling a bank account.

To reconcile a credit card statement:

1 From the Company menu, choose Chart of Accounts.

QuickBooks displays the chart of accounts.

2 Click CalOil Card in the list once to select it.

3 Click the Activities menu button, and then choose Reconcile Credit Card.

QuickBooks displays the Begin Reconciliation window.

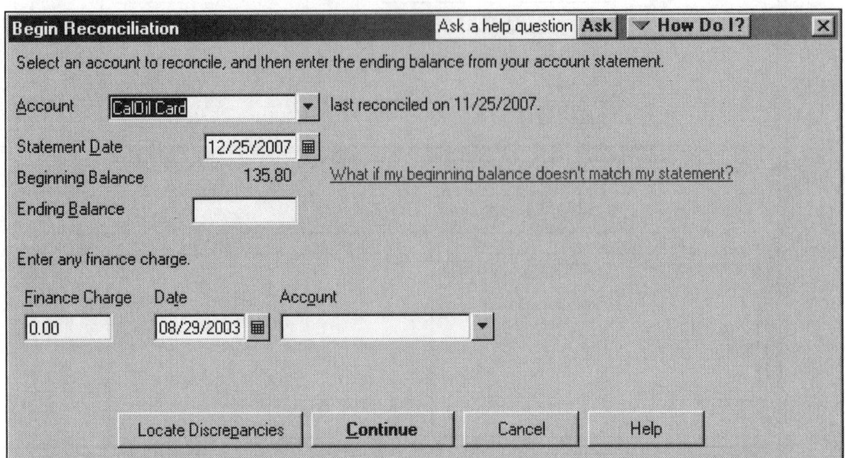

In the Opening Balance field, QuickBooks displays the balance of all cleared transactions in the credit card register. To reconcile a credit card statement, all you have to do is enter the ending balance and check off each transaction listed on your statement.

4 In the Statement Date field, enter 12/15/2007.

5 In the Ending Balance field, type ***101.02***.

Note: When the ending balance is different from the previous month's ending balance, check for cleared transactions that are now showing as uncleared.

6 Press Continue.

QuickBooks displays the Reconcile Credit Card window.

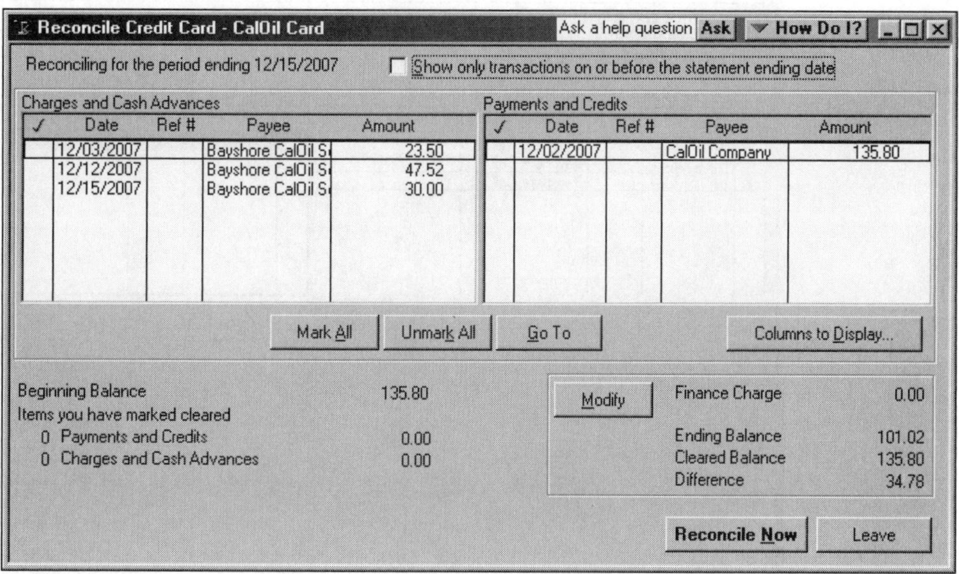

The Reconcile Credit Card window shows all the transactions for the credit card account that have not yet cleared. You'll use this window to check off the transactions listed on your statement.

Marking cleared transactions

To mark the transactions as cleared:

1 In the "Charges and Cash Advances" section of the window, select all three charges.

2 In the Payments and Credits section of the window, select the 12/02/07 payment for $135.80.

QuickBooks places a checkmark in the column to the left of each transaction you select. Your Reconcile Credit Card window should resemble the following figure.

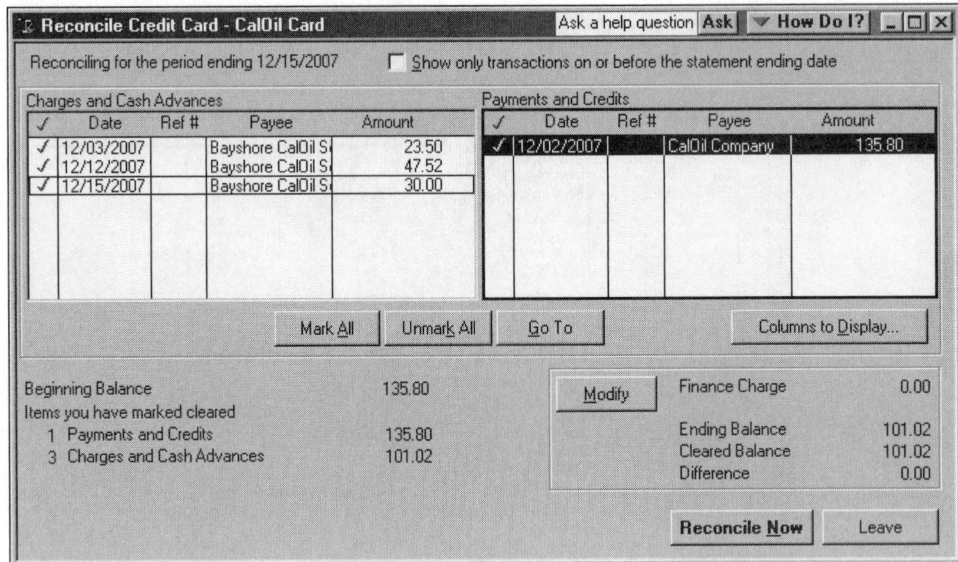

3 Click Reconcile Now.

QuickBooks displays the Make Payment window.

When you've finished reconciling a credit card account, QuickBooks gives you a chance to pay part or all of the balance due on your credit card.

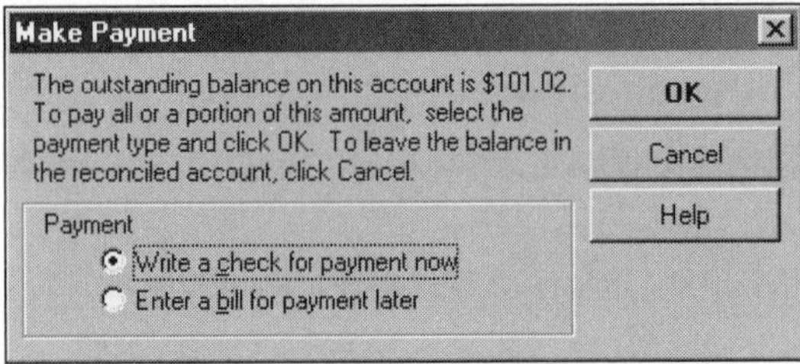

4 For this exercise, you want to write a check for payment now, so leave that option selected and click OK.

QuickBooks displays the Select Reconciliation Report window.

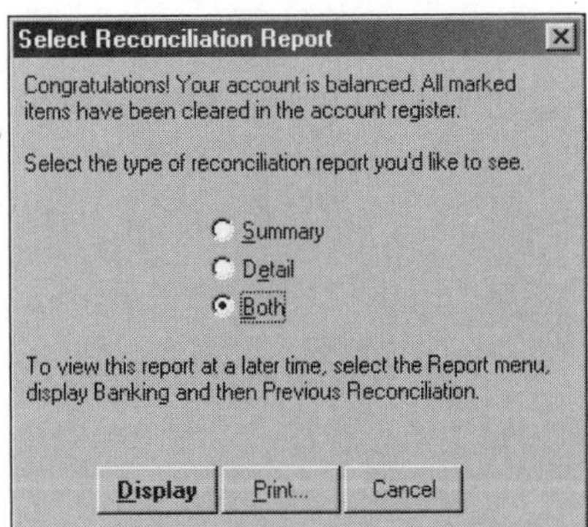

5 In the Select Reconciliation Report window, select Detail and then click Display.

You don't need to do so in this exercise, but to keep a record of the reconciliation report, you could choose Save as PDF from the File menu and save the report as a PDF file.

You could also click Print to print a hard copy of the report. You don't need to print the report for this lesson.

6 Click OK at the message that QuickBooks displays.

7 Close the report.

Paying a credit card bill

To write a check for the bill now:

1 In the Write Checks window, make sure Checking is listed as the bank account.

Notice that QuickBooks has already filled in the amount of the payment for you, and has assigned the expense to the CalOil Card account. (If you change your mind and decide you only want to make a partial payment, you can change the amount here.)

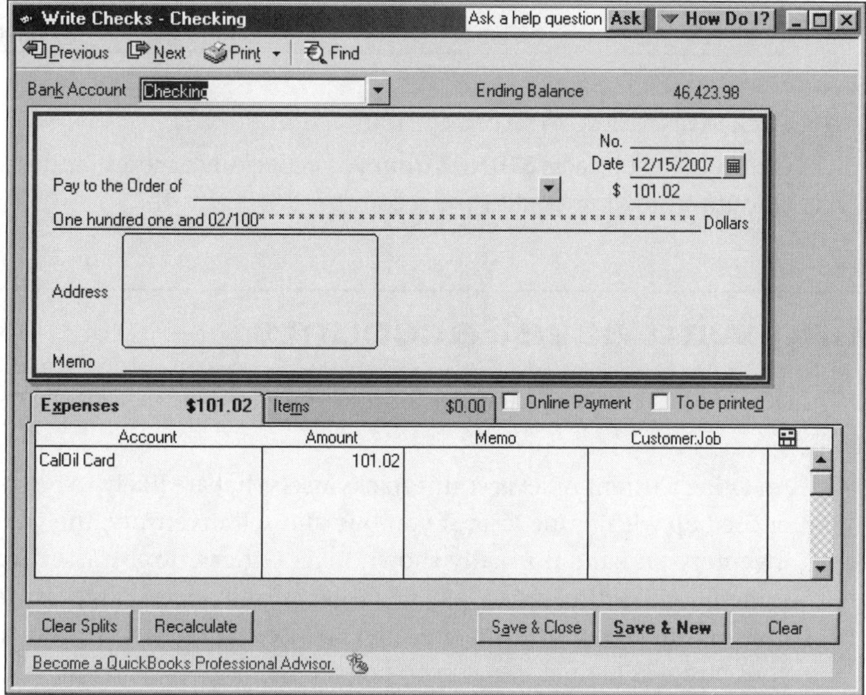

2 Click in the Pay to the Order of field and select CalOil Company as the name of the credit card company from the drop-down list.

3 Click the "To be printed" checkbox to select it.

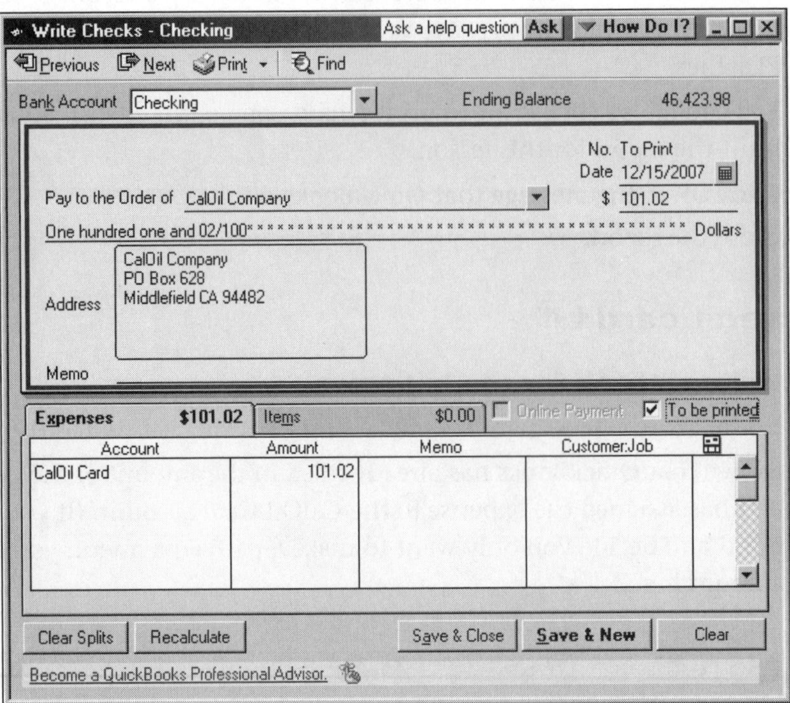

4 Click Save & Close to record the transaction.

QuickBooks subtracts $101.02 from your checking account and also subtracts that amount from your credit card account.

Working with asset accounts

QuickBooks has two account types for tracking the value of your short- and long-term assets:

- An Other Current Asset account tracks assets that are likely to be converted to cash or used up within one year. If you buy and sell inventory, the value of all your inventory on hand is usually shown in an Other Current Asset account called something like "Inventory Asset." Other current assets might include treasury bills, certificates of deposit, prepaid expenses (amounts already paid for services your business has yet to receive), prepaid deposits (which will be returned to you at a later date), reimbursable expenses, and notes receivable (if due within one year).
- A Fixed Asset account tracks assets your business owns that are *not* likely to be converted into cash within a year. A fixed asset is usually something necessary for the operation of your business, like a truck, cash register, computer, or photocopier.

Discuss with students that some additional examples of other current assets are accounts receivable, bank accounts, and cash. QuickBooks provides three types of current asset accounts for you to use as you create asset accounts for your company: **bank account** *(to track each bank account as well as petty cash),* **accounts receivable** *(to track money owed to your business), and* **other current asset**.

Setting up an Other Current Asset account

Suppose you need an Other Current Asset account to track a prepaid expense for rent. (The landlord requires a six-month advance payment.)

1 In the chart of accounts, click the Account menu button, and then choose New.

QuickBooks displays the New Account window.

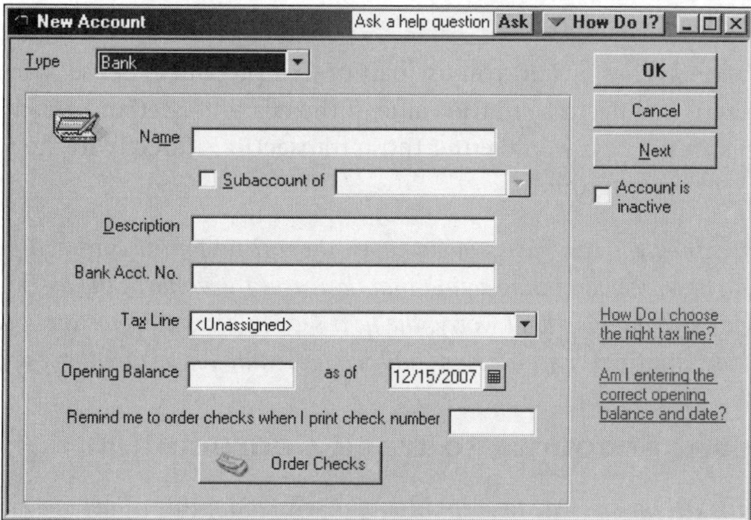

2 For the Type, choose Other Current Asset from the drop-down list.

3 In the Name field, type ***Prepaid rent***.

4 In the Opening Balance field, type ***6000***.

5 Click OK.

QuickBooks displays the new account in the chart of accounts.

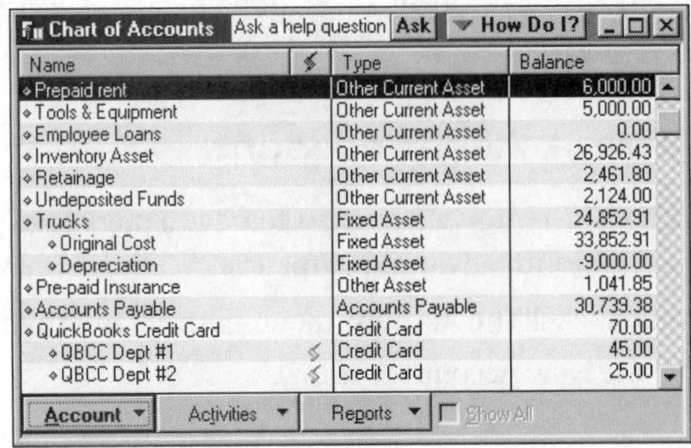

As each month goes by and you use part of that prepaid expense, you can enter each month's rent as a decrease in the value of the current asset and assign it to the rent expense account. You would enter those transactions directly in the register for the Prepaid rent asset account.

If you have time, you can have students open the register for the current asset account, and show them how to enter a transaction that decreases the value of the asset. If you don't feel you have time to do this, don't worry: the next section gives students an opportunity to enter transactions in a fixed asset account, and the procedure for a current asset is very similar.

Setting up asset accounts to track depreciation

There is more than one way to keep track of depreciation; this is just one suggested method. If you have students who are keeping track of asset depreciation in other ways, assure them that they can continue using their own method.

Fixed assets are equipment or property your business owns that are not for sale. Since they last a long time, you don't completely charge their cost to the year in which you buy them. Instead, you spread their cost over several years. But because fixed assets wear out or become obsolete, their value declines constantly from the day you purchase them. The amount of this decline in value is called *depreciation.*

To determine the estimated value of a fixed asset at any point in time, you need to subtract its accumulated depreciation (total amount of depreciation since the asset's purchase) from its original cost.

Usually, you'll want your balance sheet to show the original cost of an asset (plus any subsequent improvements) on one line, with the accumulated depreciation subtracted from the original cost on a second line, and the current value (net) on a third line. The method you'll learn in this lesson lets you see each asset's cost and its accumulated depreciation separately on your balance sheet. You set up a separate fixed asset account for each asset, and two subaccounts under each fixed asset account: one for cost and one for accumulated depreciation.

To set up asset accounts to track depreciation on a new trailer purchased by Rock Castle Construction:

1 In the chart of accounts window, click the Account menu button, and then choose New.

  QuickBooks displays the New Account window.

2 In the Type field, choose Fixed Asset from the drop-down list.

3 In the Name field, type ***Trailer***.

4 Leave the opening balance blank, and click OK.

  QuickBooks displays the new fixed asset account in the chart of accounts.

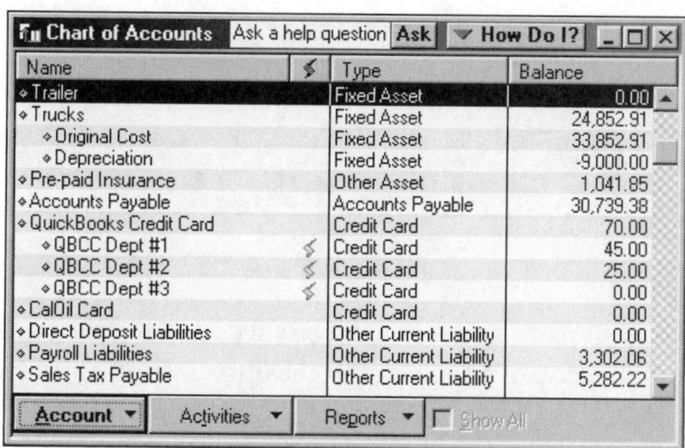

Name		Type	Balance
◆Trailer		Fixed Asset	0.00
◆Trucks		Fixed Asset	24,852.91
◆Original Cost		Fixed Asset	33,852.91
◆Depreciation		Fixed Asset	-9,000.00
◆Pre-paid Insurance		Other Asset	1,041.85
◆Accounts Payable		Accounts Payable	30,739.38
◆QuickBooks Credit Card		Credit Card	70.00
◆QBCC Dept #1	✓	Credit Card	45.00
◆QBCC Dept #2	✓	Credit Card	25.00
◆QBCC Dept #3	✓	Credit Card	0.00
◆CalOil Card		Credit Card	0.00
◆Direct Deposit Liabilities		Other Current Liability	0.00
◆Payroll Liabilities		Other Current Liability	3,302.06
◆Sales Tax Payable		Other Current Liability	5,282.22

Now you need to add two subaccounts: one for the asset's cost, and the other for depreciation.

To add subaccounts:

1 In the chart of accounts window, click the Account menu button, and then choose New.

2 In the Type field, choose Fixed Asset from the drop-down list.

3 In the Name field, type ***Cost***.

4 Select the "Subaccount of" checkbox, and then select ***Trailer*** as the parent account.

5 Leave the opening balance blank.

The opening balance is the original cost of the asset, if you purchased the asset before your QuickBooks start date. If you're buying the asset now, as the owner of Rock Castle Construction is, you leave the opening balance for the Cost account blank. When you enter information about the loan Rock Castle Construction takes out to pay for the truck (later in this lesson), you'll update the Cost account with the truck's original cost.

Your screen should resemble the following figure.

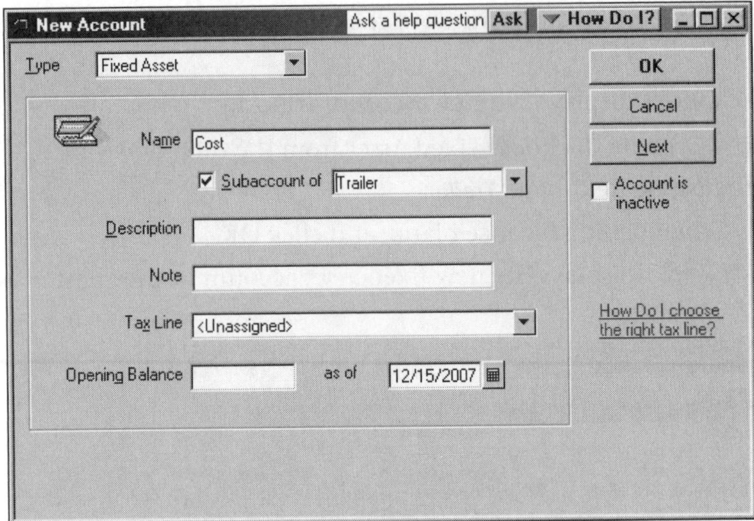

6 Click OK.

7 Repeat the previous steps to add a second subaccount to the Trailer fixed asset account. Call the subaccount "Accumulated Depreciation," and leave the opening balance blank.

The New Account window should look like this.

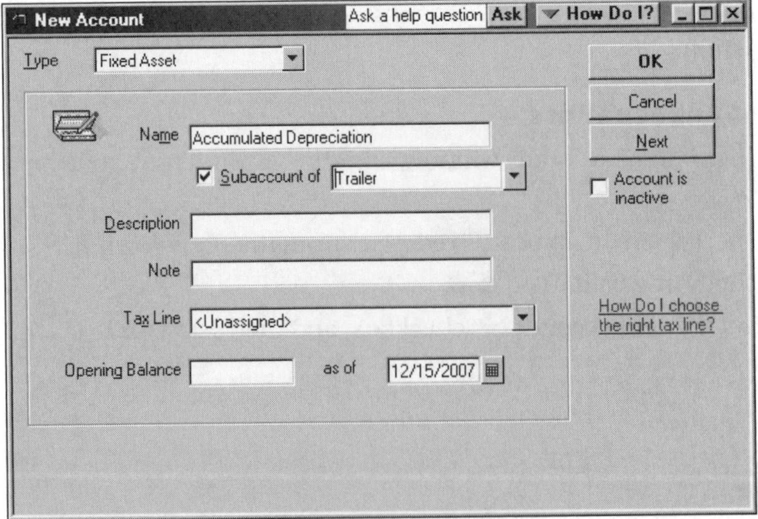

When you complete these steps, your chart of accounts should look like this.

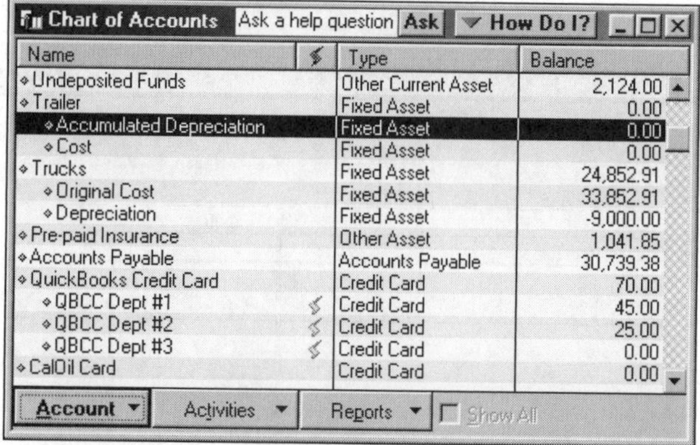

Note: **The amount you enter as the opening balance depends on whether you acquired the asset after or before your QuickBooks start date.** If you acquired the asset after your QuickBooks start date, you don't enter an opening balance. If you acquired the asset before your QuickBooks start date, you enter the accumulated depreciation of the asset as of the start date—entered as a negative number.

Entering depreciation transactions

When it's time to enter depreciation for an asset, you can use the register for the asset's accumulated depreciation account.

Determining the amount of depreciation to deduct can be a complex process, and the IRS rules on the subject change often. Students should ask a competent advisor for help in figuring actual depreciation amounts for tax purposes.

To enter a transaction for depreciation:

1. In the chart of accounts, select the Accumulated Depreciation subaccount.
2. Click the Activities menu button, and then choose Use Register.

   QuickBooks displays the register for the Trailer:Accumulated Depreciation asset account.
3. In the Decrease column, type ***1300*** and press Tab. This is the depreciation amount.

4 In the Account field, select Depreciation Expense from the drop-down list. Your register should resemble the following figure.

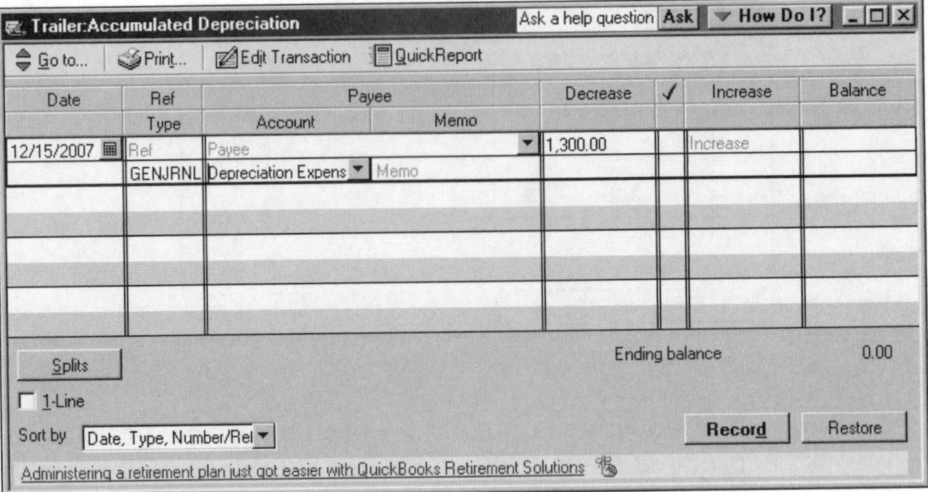

5 Click Record.

6 Close the register window.

When you record the transaction, QuickBooks does the following:

- Subtracts the depreciation amount from the current value of the asset in the asset's fixed asset account.
- Enters the depreciation amount as an increase to your company's depreciation expense in the expense account that tracks depreciation.

Tip: **When you purchase an asset and pay for it with a company check or credit card, you should enter the purchase in the Write Checks or Enter Credit Card Charges window.** Then, in the Account field, choose the account for the asset.

Working with liability accounts

QuickBooks has two account types for tracking the value of your short- and long-term liabilities:

- An Other Current Liability account tracks liabilities that your company expects to pay within a year. Other current liabilities might include short-term loans or a line of credit.
- A Long-term Liability account tracks debts that your business is *not* likely to pay off within a year. The most common long-term liabilities are loans that you expect to pay off in more than one year.

Tip: **Some additional examples of other current liabilities are accounts payable, credit card accounts, accrued sales tax, and accrued payroll.** QuickBooks provides three types of current liability accounts for you to use as you create liability accounts for your company: credit card (to track credit card charges and payments), accounts payable (to track money owed by your business), and other current liability.

Tracking a loan with a long-term liability account

You've already added an asset account to track the value of the new trailer. Because the trailer loan is not going to be paid off in a year or less, you need to add a long-term liability account.

To add a long-term liability account:

1. In the chart of accounts, click the Account menu button, and then choose New.
2. In the New Account window, select Long Term Liability in the Type drop-down list.
3. In the Name field, type ***Trailer Loan***.
4. Leave the Opening Balance field blank.

   Your screen should resemble the figure below.

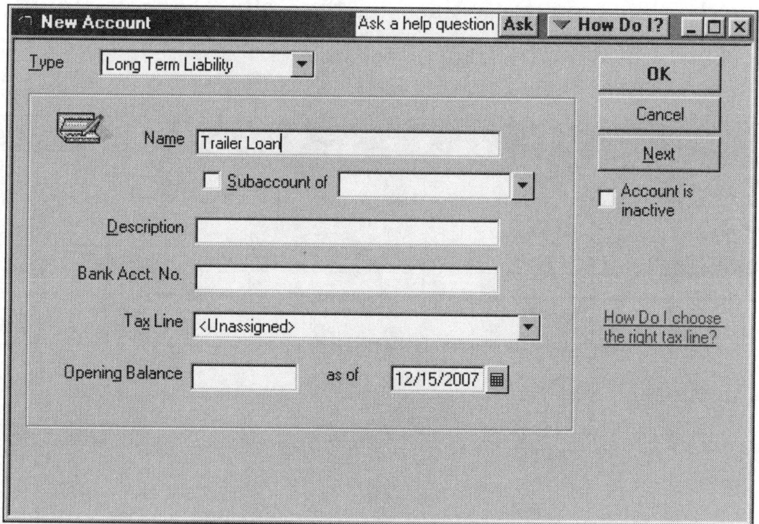

5 Click OK.

QuickBooks displays the new liability account in the chart of accounts.

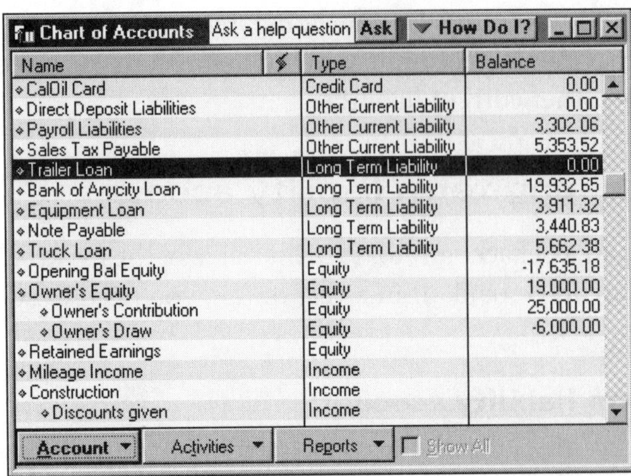

Because this is a new loan, you are either receiving money to deposit in your bank account or receiving a new asset. In this example, you received an asset (the new trailer), so you need to show an increase in the asset's Cost account.

To record an increase in the asset's Cost account:

1 In the chart of accounts, double-click the Trailer:Cost subaccount.

QuickBooks displays the Trailer:Cost register.

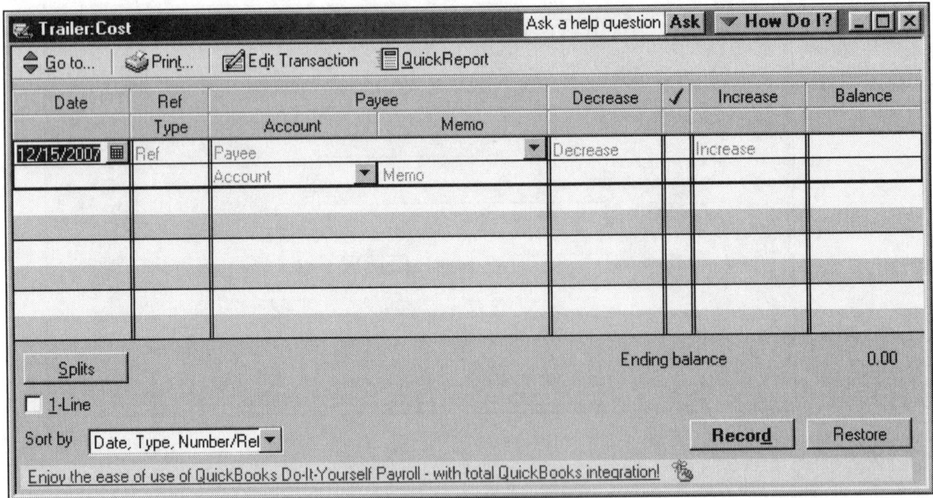

2 In the Increase field, type ***30,000***.

3 In the Account field, select the Trailer Loan liability account from the drop-down list.

Make sure that you select the Trailer Loan long-term liability account, not the Trailer fixed asset account.

Your screen should resemble the following.

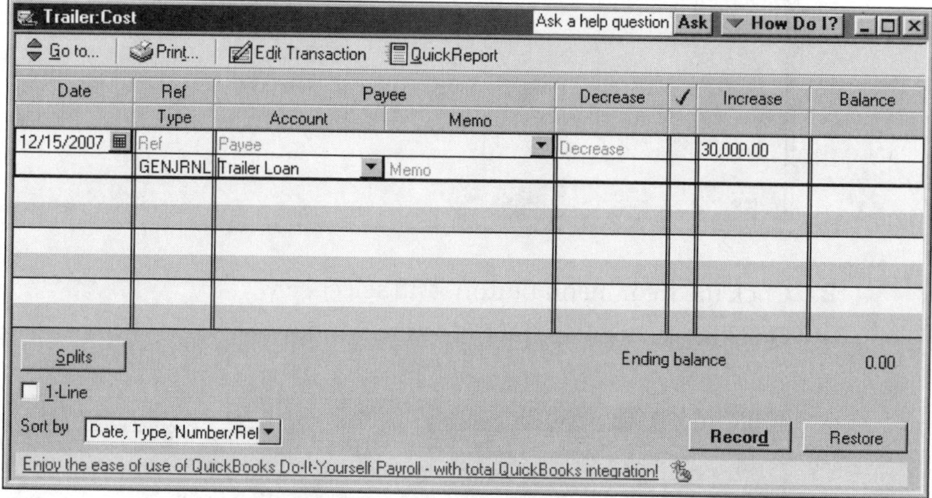

4 Click Record.

5 Close the register window.

6 Close the chart of accounts.

When you complete these steps, QuickBooks increases the value of your Cost asset account to 30,000. (This effectively sets the opening balance.) It also enters a liability of 30,000 in the liability account you use to track the loan. (Again, this sets the opening balance.)

Tracking fixed assets

If you're using QuickBooks: Pro or higher, you can enter theTrailer on the Fixed Asset Item list. Tracking fixed assets using the Fixed Asset Item list enables you to record such information about an asset as purchase date and price, whether the asset was new or used when purchased, and the asset's sale price if you decide to sell it. You can also generate customizable reports listing all your fixed assets.

The information you enter in the Fixed Asset Item list does not transfer to the chart of accounts.

Note: **You must be using QuickBooks: Pro or higher to complete the following procedure.**

To create a fixed asset item:

1 From the Lists menu, choose Fixed Asset Item List.

2 QuickBooks displays the Fixed Asset Item list.

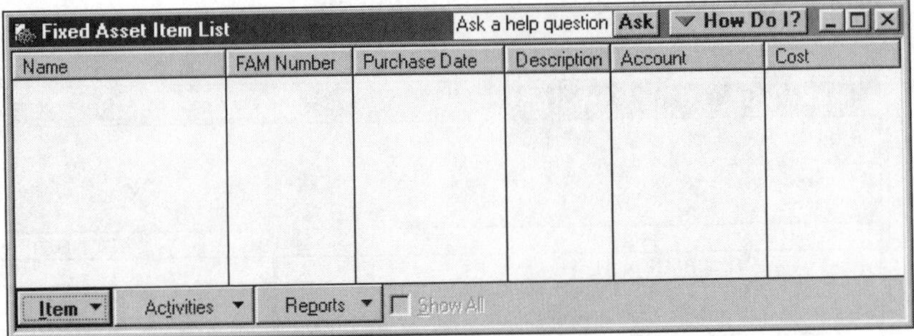

3 Click the Item menu button, and select New.

QuickBooks displays the New Item window.

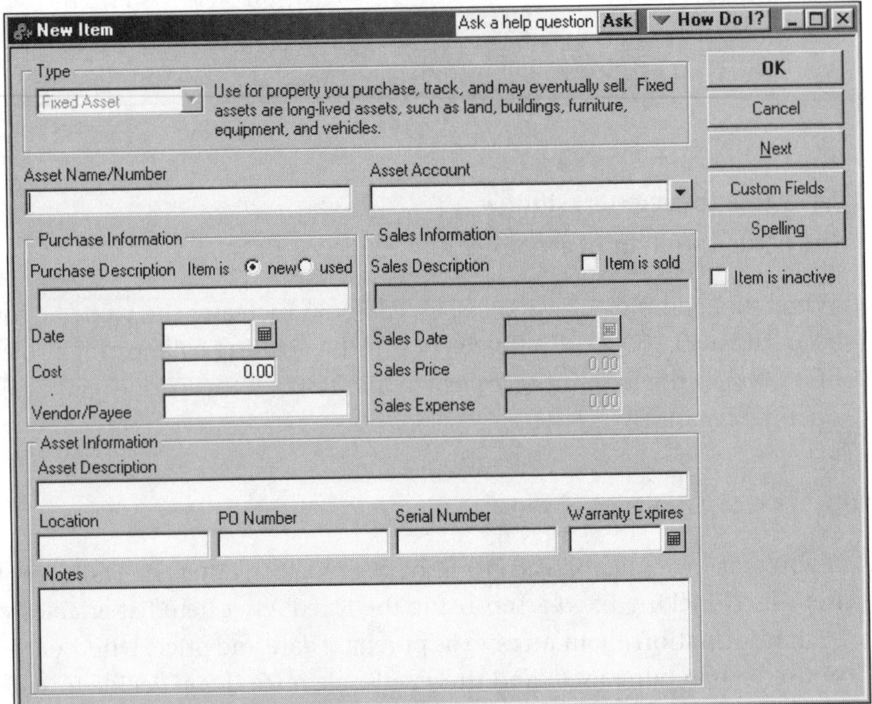

The item type is preset as Fixed Asset.

4 In the Asset Name/Number field, type ***Trailer.***

5 Enter the following information to complete the Purchase Information section:

- Item is: new
- Purchase Description: Trailer
- Date: 12/15/2007
- Cost: 30,000
- Vendor/Payee: East Bayshore Auto Mall

The New Item window should look like the following graphic.

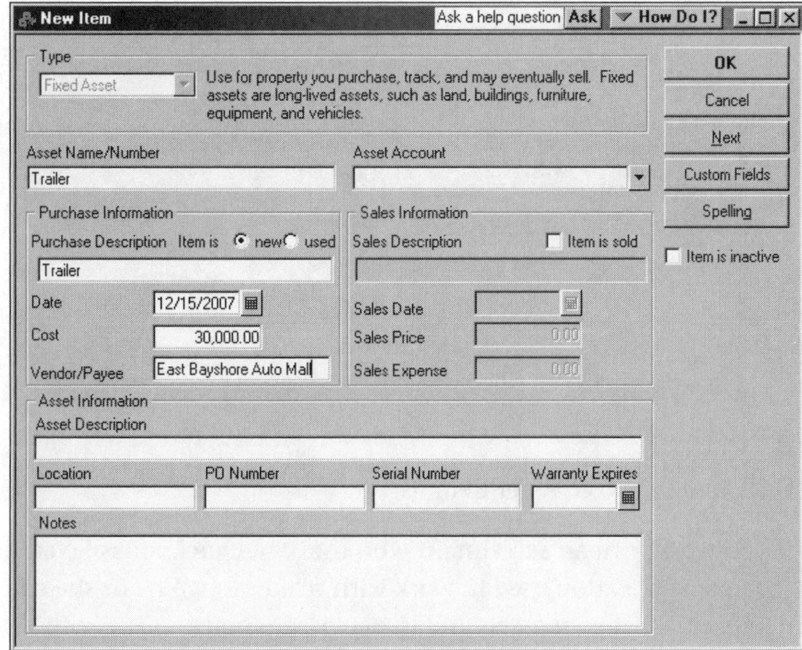

6 Enter the following information to complete the Asset Information section:

- Asset Description: White trailer with company logo
- Serial Number: 123456789
- Warranty Expires: 12/15/2010

7 From the Asset Account drop-down list, choose Trailer:Cost.
The New Item window should look like the following graphic.

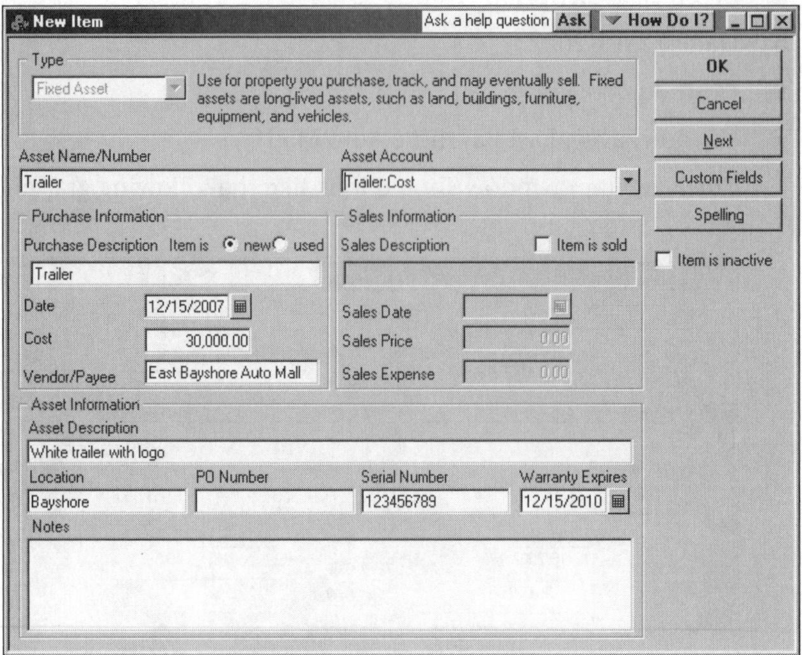

8 Click OK.
9 Close the Fixed Asset Item list.

If you work with an accountant who uses the QuickBooks Fixed Asset Manager (a separate application used to work with fixed assets), he or she can determine the depreciation of your assets and update your company file with that information. A summary of information calculated in the QuickBooks Fixed Asset Manager and sent to QuickBooks displays in the Fixed Asset Item list.

Recording a payment on a loan

When it's time to make a payment on a loan, use the Write Checks window to record a check to your lender. You'll want to assign part of the payment to a loan interest expense and the remainder to loan principal.

To record a payment on a loan:

1 From the Banking menu, choose Write Checks.
QuickBooks displays the Write Checks window.
2 In the "Pay to the Order of" field, type ***Great*** and then press Tab.
QuickBooks fills in the field with Great Statewide Bank. If QuickBooks asks whether you want to use the last transaction for this vendor, click No.
3 For the dollar amount of the check, type ***500.00***.
4 Click the Expenses tab, and then click in the Account column and choose the Interest Expense:Loan Interest expense account from the drop-down list.

5 In the Amount column highlight the amount that QuickBooks prefilled and then type ***225.00***.

6 Assign the remainder of the expense (275.00) to the Trailer Loan liability account.

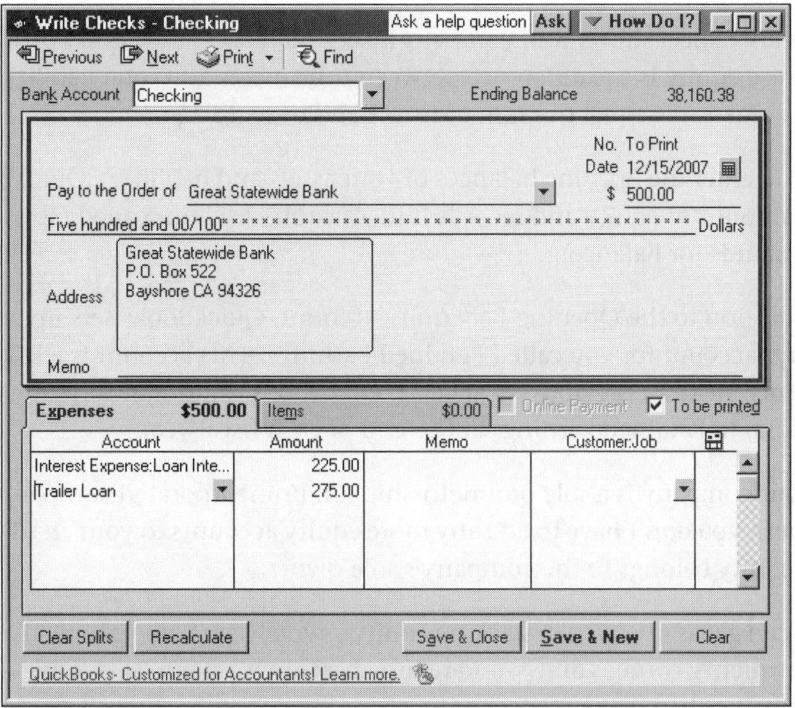

7 Click Save & Close to record the payment.

When you record the transaction, QuickBooks automatically updates the accounts affected by this transaction:

- In your checking account, QuickBooks subtracts the amount of the check from your balance.
- In the expense account that tracks interest, QuickBooks enters the interest amount as an increase to your company's interest expense.
- In the Trailer Loan liability account, QuickBooks subtracts the principal amount from the current value of the liability (reducing the amount of your debt).

Understanding equity accounts

Many students will see the equity accounts QuickBooks automatically adds for them, and wonder what equity is all about. Equity can be a complicated subject, especially for newer business owners, and a complete discussion of it is not the focus of this lesson. This section introduces the subject of equity, and helps students understand why QuickBooks creates the two default equity accounts.

If you want to teach equity in more detail, see the discussion in QuickBooks Fundamentals.

Equity is the difference between what you have (your assets) and what you owe (your liabilities). If you sold all your assets today and paid off your liabilities using the money received from the sale of your assets, the money you'd have left would be your equity.

A balance sheet shows your company assets, liabilities, and equity on a particular date. Because equity is the difference between total assets and total liabilities, it's also true that total assets equal the sum of total liabilities and equity.

As you enter the opening balances of your assets and liabilities, QuickBooks calculates the amount of equity and records it in an equity account called Opening Bal Equity (Bal stands for Balance).

In addition to the Opening Bal Equity account, QuickBooks sets up another type of equity account for you called Retained Earnings. This account tracks your company's net income from previous fiscal years. QuickBooks automatically transfers your profit (or loss) to Retained Earnings at the end of each fiscal year.

If your company is a sole proprietorship (an unincorporated company with only one owner), you don't have to add any more equity accounts to your chart of accounts. All the equity belongs to the company's sole owner.

You can get as involved in tracking equity as you wish. Some people like to track owner investments, owner's draws, and retained earnings prior to their QuickBooks start date by putting them in separate equity accounts. If your business is a partnership, you'll probably want to set up separate equity accounts for each partner.

To learn more about equity and to learn how to set up equity accounts for your business, search the onscreen Help index for *equity*.

Tip: **A common use of an equity account is to record an owner's draw (a payment you make to yourself).** To record an owner's draw, use the Write Checks window to make out a check to yourself. In the detail area of the check, assign the amount of the check to the equity account you use to record owner draws.

Student test and review

Assume that the owner of Rock Castle Construction has taken out a loan and purchased a computer system for $15,000. He wants to track the accumulated depreciation and cost of the system in two separate fixed asset accounts.

1. Create a fixed asset account called Computer System and two subaccounts—one for Cost and one for Accumulated Depreciation.
2. Create a long-term liability account to track the loan.

   Enter the amount of the loan as an increase in the asset's Cost account. Assign the transaction to the loan liability account.

LESSON 6 Entering sales and invoices

Lesson objectives

- To learn about the different formats available for sales forms
- To save sales and purchase forms in Portable Document Format (PDF)
- To practice creating a new invoice
- To learn the purpose and use of the QuickBooks Item list
- To see how QuickBooks records the information you enter on sales forms
- To memorize an invoice transaction for reuse
- To add a new item to the Item list
- To add a new price level to the Price Level list
- To associate a price level with a customer
- To generate customer statements
- To create sales orders

Handout materials

- Handout 4: QuickBooks item types

Instructor preparation

- Review this lesson, including the examples, to make sure you're familiar with the material.
- Ensure that all students have a copy of qblesson.qbb on their computer's hard disk.
- Have Handout 4 ready for distribution.

To start this lesson

Before you perform the following steps, make sure you have installed the exercise file (qblesson.qbb) on your hard disk. See "Installing the exercise file" in the Introduction to this guide if you haven't installed it.

The following steps restore the exercise file to its original state so that the data in the file matches what you see on the screen as you proceed through each lesson.

To restore the exercise file (qblesson.qbb):

1. From the File menu in QuickBooks, choose Restore.

   QuickBooks displays the Restore Company Backup window.
2. In the "Get Company Backup From" section of the window, click Browse and select your c:\QBtrain directory.
3. Select the qblesson.qbb file, and then click Open.
4. In the "Restore Company Backup To" section of the window, click Browse and select your c:\QBtrain directory.
5. In the File name field of the Restore To window, type ***lesson 6*** and then click Save.
6. Click Restore.

Using sales forms in QuickBooks

Any time you make a sale in your business, you record it in QuickBooks on a sales form. A sales form can be an invoice (when you expect payment to come later), a sales receipt (when you expect payment at the time you make the sale), or a credit memo.

You use a credit memo when a customer returns merchandise for which you've already entered a payment or a cash sale. This lesson shows students how to use invoices and sales receipts.

When to use different types of sales forms

The type of sales form you use depends on whether you expect payment in the future or at the time of the sale.

For payment in the future

If you expect to receive payment at some future date, you enter an invoice. The invoice lists the customer's name and address, along with an itemized list of how much that customer owes.

To display a completed invoice form in QuickBooks:

1 From the Customers menu, choose Create Invoices.

QuickBooks displays the Create Invoices window.

2 Click Previous to display the previously created invoice.

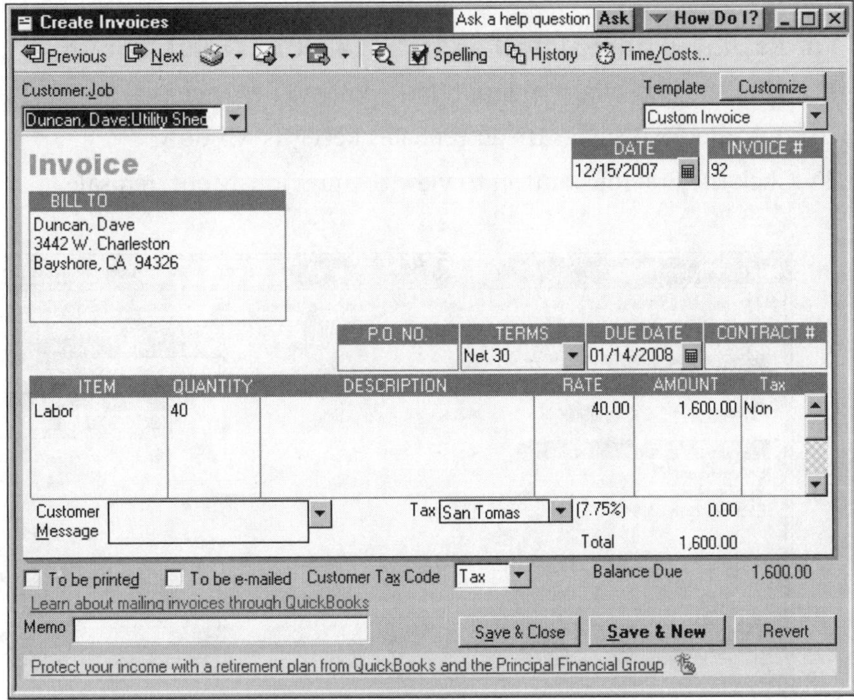

If you own a business that sells products, like Rock Castle Construction, your invoice lists the products purchased by the customer, the amount charged for each item, and any sales tax you need to apply. Notice that Rock Castle Construction's invoice charges for both products and services (such as labor).

A business that sells mainly services, such as a consulting firm, might use a different type of sales form than the one shown above. QuickBooks lets you choose from three different preset formats for your sales forms, or you can create your own customized forms.

3 Close the Create Invoices window.

For payment at the time of sale

If you receive payment at the time you make a sale—either by cash, check, or credit card—you fill out a sales receipt instead of an invoice. Like the invoice, the QuickBooks sales receipt includes information about the items or services purchased, but it also includes information about how payment was made.

To display a completed sales receipt in QuickBooks:

1 From the Customers menu, choose Enter Sales Receipts.

  QuickBooks displays the Enter Sales Receipts window.

2 Click the Previous button to view the previously entered sale.

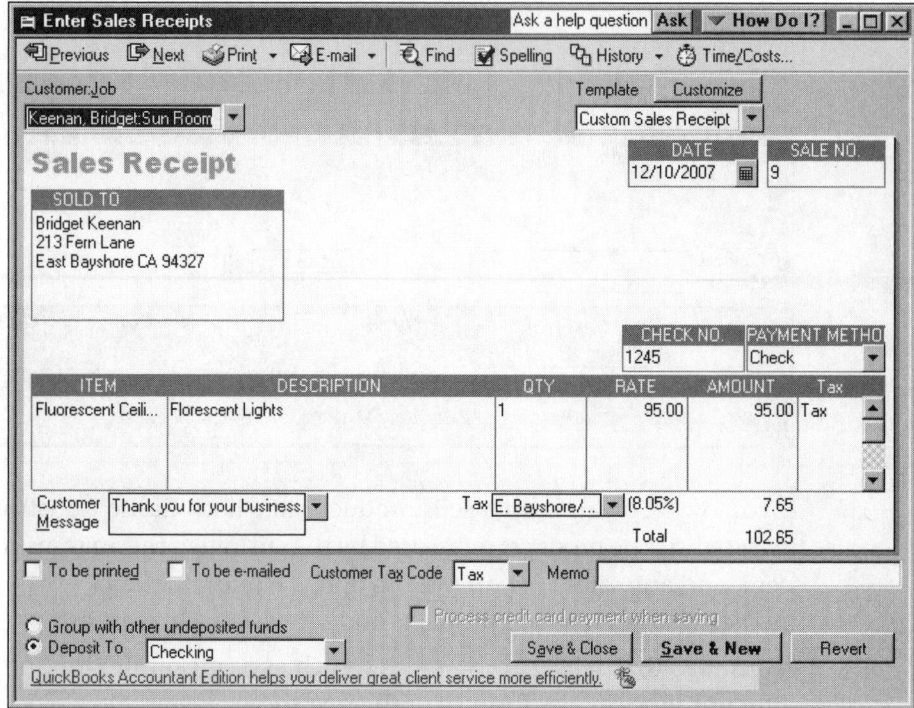

The sales receipt is similar to the invoice—both forms display customer information and describe the items and services purchased. However, because payment is made at the time of sale, the sales receipt has deposit information at the bottom of the window.

3 Close the Enter Sales Receipts window.

Choosing a format for sales forms

QuickBooks has four main formats for invoices: Service, Professional, Product, and Custom. (There are other also preset formats available for specific industries.)

- Use the Service format if you primarily sell services but occasionally sell goods.
- Use the Professional format if you sell services and need a lot of room for descriptions of your services.

- Use the Product format if you sell parts or products and need fields relevant to shipping.
- Use the Custom format if you want to tailor a form to your type of business.

Each format has an onscreen version and a printed version. This lets you record all the sales detail you need, but print only what you want customers to see. For example, if you use the Professional format, the onscreen version shows the number of hours you're billing the client as well as your hourly rate; the printed version shows only the Description and the Amount fields.

Each of the invoice templates can be customized to meet your needs. If you use pre-printed form templates available from Intuit, you are limited as to how extensively you can modify the standard forms (for example, you can't move fields or the information might not print in the correct part of the form. If you don't use pre-printed forms, you can modify the templates as necessary.

You'll learn how to customize forms in Lesso n15, "Customizing forms and writing QuickBooks Letters."

You can save all QuickBooks sales and purchase forms as portable document format (PDF) files. To save a form as a PDF file, display the form and then choose Save as PDF from the File menu.

Filling in a sales form

Suppose Rock Castle Construction wants to bill a customer for a portion of a kitchen remodeling job. Because they expect payment to be made in the future—rather than cash on the spot—they need to create an invoice.

Filling in the customer information

Filling in an invoice is just like filling in a paper form; you enter the customer information first, followed by a description of the charges.

To enter customer information on an invoice:

1. From the Customers menu, choose Create Invoices.

   Notice that the new invoice already has the current date (12/15/2007 in the sample file) entered in the Date field, and the next invoice number assigned in the Invoice # field.
2. In the Template field, select Custom Invoice from the drop-down list.
3. In the Customer:Job field, click the arrow next to the drop-down list.

   QuickBooks shows you a list of Rock Castle Construction's existing customers and jobs.
4. Choose Jacobsen, Doug:Kitchen for the customer and job.

Because this name has already been entered on the Customer:Job list, QuickBooks knows the billing name, the address, and the payment terms. It provides this information for you on the top half of the form.

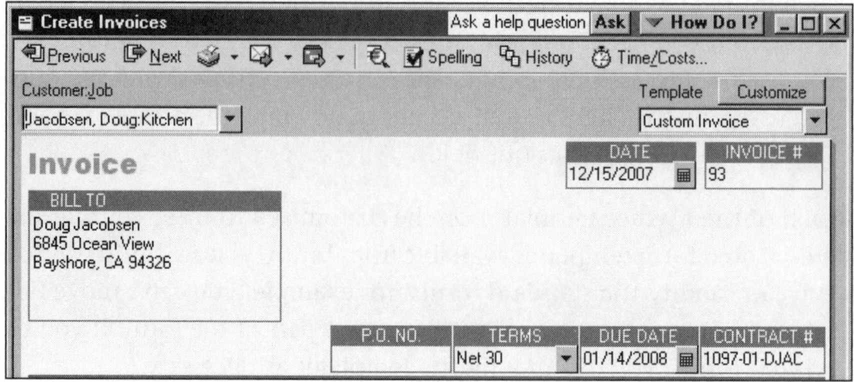

Filling in the line item area

On the bottom half of the invoice, you list each service or product you're selling on its own line, along with the amount the customer owes for that item. Because information about individual items is on separate lines, the lines are called line items.

In QuickBooks, you enter line items using the Item list, so you don't have to type and retype lines for services or products you sell frequently. For example, an architect would have one item for design and another for construction supervision.

But items are not just products you sell or services you provide to clients. Line items can be anything you might want to put in the detail area of an invoice, like a discount, a subtotal line, a markup, or a sales tax calculation.

Rock Castle Construction has already entered the items for which it bills customers on its Item list.

To complete the line item area of an invoice:

1 In the Item field, type the letters ***rem*** (for Removal).

QuickFill is an alternative to choosing from a list. Whenever you're in a field where you'll use a list item, you can start typing the first letter or two of the list item you want, and QuickBooks fills in the field with the item that matches the letters you're typing.

2 Press Tab.

When you press Tab to accept a QuickFill entry, QuickBooks fills in other information about the item, like its description and rate. In this case, QuickBooks displays "Removal labor" in the Description column and a rate of $35 per hour. All you have to do is enter the number of hours.

3 Type ***40*** in the Quantity column.

4 Press Tab to have QuickBooks update the invoice total.

ITEM	QUANTITY	DESCRIPTION	RATE	AMOUNT	Tax
Removal	40	Removal labor	35.00	1,400.00	Non

Completing the sales form

If you want to check the form before you print it, you can use the print preview feature in the Create Invoices window.

To complete and record the invoice:

1. On the Create Invoices window toolbar, click the Print drop-down arrow, and then choose Preview.

   QuickBooks displays the invoice page as it will look when printed.

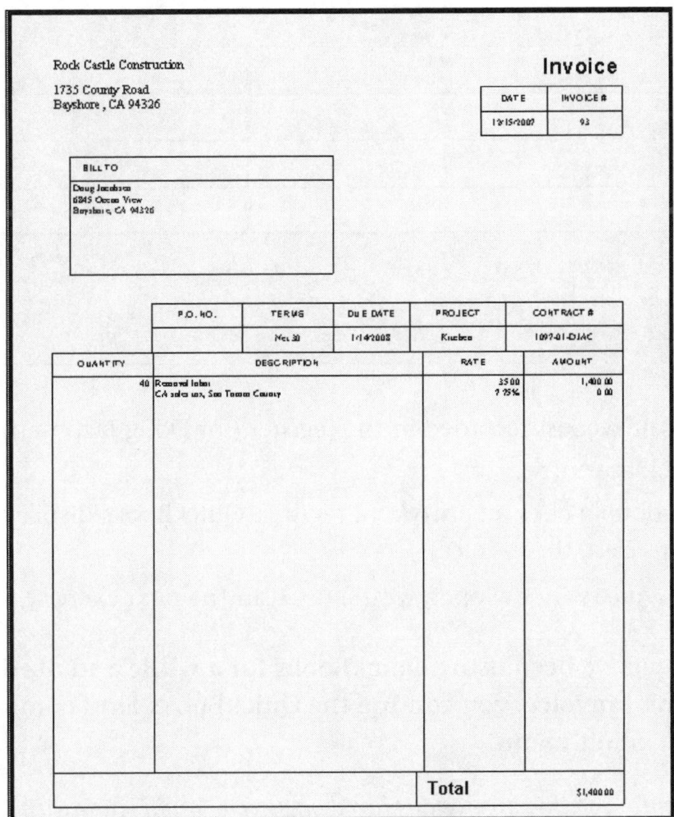

Rock Castle Construction

1735 County Road
Bayshore, CA 94326

Invoice

DATE	INVOICE #
12/15/2007	93

BILL TO

Doug Jacobsen
6845 Ocean View
Bayshore, CA 94326

P.O. NO.	TERMS	DUE DATE	PROJECT	CONTRACT #
	Net 30	1/14/2008	Kitchen	1097-01-DJAC

QUANTITY	DESCRIPTION	RATE	AMOUNT
40	Removal labor	35.00	1,400.00
	CA sales tax, San Tomas County	7.75%	0.00
		Total	$1,400.00

2. Click Zoom In and use the scroll bars to see the invoice items at greater magnification.
3. Click Close.
4. In the Create Invoices window, record the sale by clicking Save & Close.

QuickBooks records the invoice in your accounts receivable register. If this were a sales receipt, QuickBooks would record the sale in your Undeposited Funds account until you deposit the money at the bank, or record a deposit in the bank account you specified in the Enter Sales Receipts window.

The accounts receivable register keeps track of how much money your customers owe you.

To see the Accounts Receivable register:

1. From the Company menu, choose Chart of Accounts.

   QuickBooks displays the chart of accounts.
2. In the chart of accounts, double-click the Accounts Receivable account.

   QuickBooks displays the accounts receivable register.

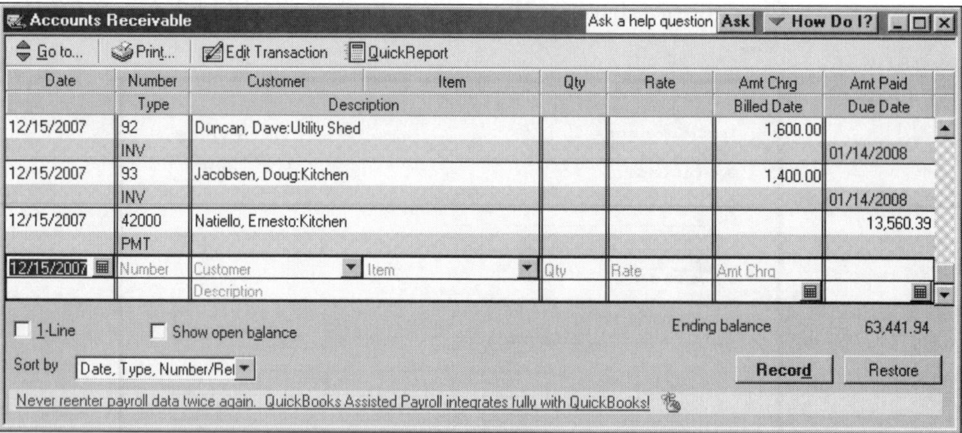

3. Select the sale we just recorded in the register (for Doug Jacobsen).
4. Double-click the entry.

   When you double-click an entry in a register, QuickBooks displays the original form (in this case, the invoice).
5. Keep the invoice window open, you'll use it in the next exercise.

Tip: **When you've been using QuickBooks for a while and need to find a particular invoice, you can use the QuickBooks Find command available from the Edit menu.**

Make sure students keep this invoice displayed on screen. You'll show then how to memorize it in the next lesson.

Memorizing a sale

Many of the sales you make in your business are ones you repeat again and again. For example, you may have a standing monthly order from a customer, or you may perform essentially the same services for more than one client. QuickBooks lets you memorize sales forms so that you don't have to retype the information.

To memorize the invoice:

1. Make sure you have the invoice you want to memorize displayed on your screen.
2. From the Edit menu, choose Memorize Invoice.

   QuickBooks displays the Memorize Transaction window.

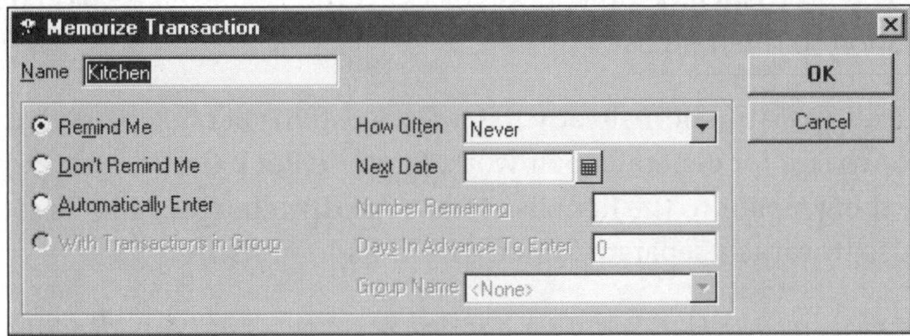

3. Type a description that helps you recognize the memorized invoice, or keep the default description QuickBooks has provided.

   You can enter any description you like. Notice that you can also have QuickBooks remind you when to use the memorized transaction (for an invoice you always send at the end of the month, for example).
4. Click OK.
5. From the Window menu, choose Close All.

When you memorize an invoice, QuickBooks adds it to the Memorized Transaction list.

To recall a memorized sale:

1. From the Lists menu, choose Memorized Transaction List.

   QuickBooks displays the Memorized Transaction List window.

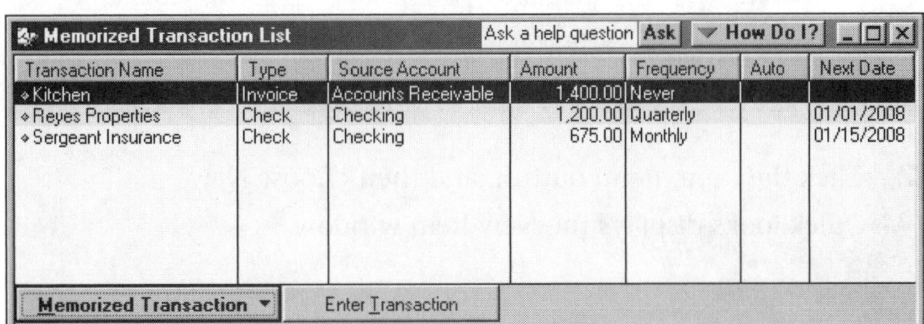

2 Double-click the transaction you just added.

QuickBooks displays the Create Invoices window, with the information you memorized displayed on the form. It gives you a new invoice number and displays the current date. You can modify the information as you wish, or just save the invoice as is.

3 Click Save & Close to record the invoice.

4 Press the Esc key to close the Memorized Transaction list.

Entering a new service item

When you begin using your own QuickBooks company file, you'll need to create your own line items to include on your invoices. In the next exercise, you'll see how to add information to the Item list.

Rock Castle Construction already has a service item called Repairs that it uses when it wants to charge for general repair work. Suppose Rock Castle wants to add a subitem for plumbing repairs to the Item list. (The company charges a higher rate for plumbing repairs, so it wants a separate item for it on its Item list.)

Have students refer to Handout 4 for a review of the types of items they can add to the Item list.

To create a new service item:

1 From the Customers menu, choose Item List.

QuickBooks displays the Item list for Rock Castle Construction.

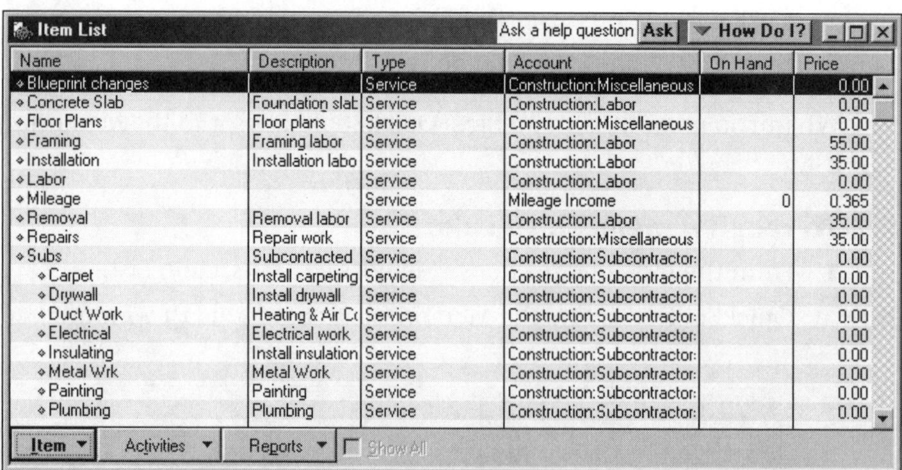

2 Click the Item menu button, and then choose New.

QuickBooks displays the New Item window.

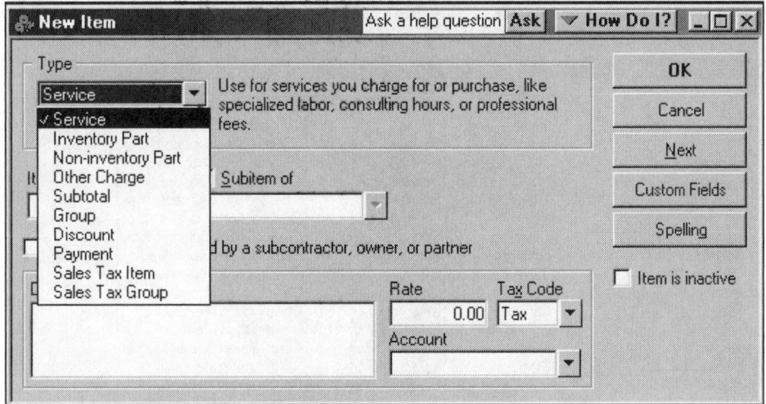

If you're using a QuickBooks Premier product, you'll also see Assembly Item listed as an item type.

3 In the Type field, select Service from the drop-down list.

4 In the Item Name/Number field, type ***Plumbing***.

5 Click the "Subitem of" checkbox to select it.

6 In the drop-down list below the "Subitem of" field, select Repairs.

7 In the Description field, type ***Plumbing repairs and maintenance*** and Press Tab.

8 In the Rate field, type ***55***.

9 In the Tax Code drop-down list, select Non.

Now you need to assign this line item to one of Rock Castle Construction's income accounts.

10 In the Account field, select Construction:Labor from the drop-down list.

Your screen should look like the following figure.

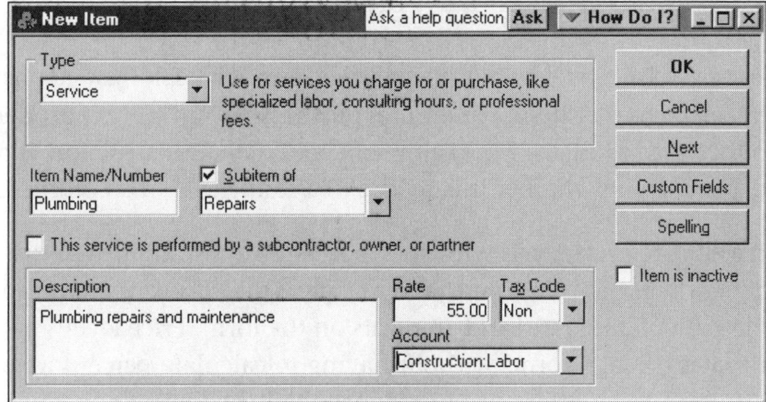

11 Click OK to add the new item to Rock Castle Construction's Item list.

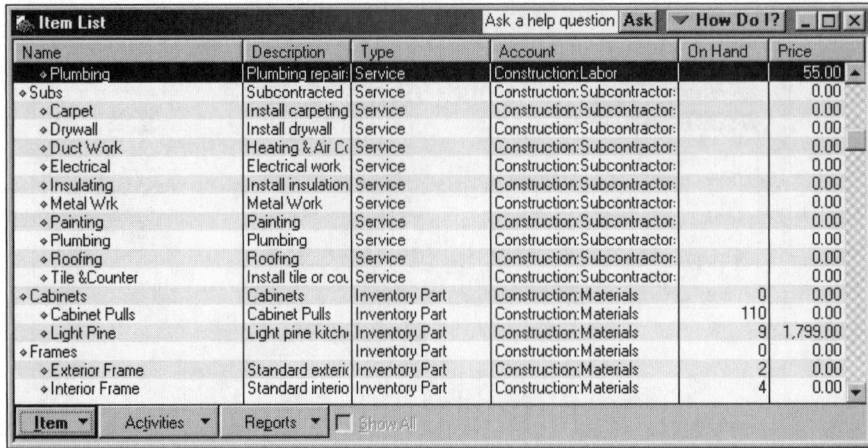

12 Close the Item list.

Now that the new item is on the Item list, Rock Castle Construction can invoice for plumbing repairs separate from its general repair work. It can also create sales reports that show sales for general repairs separate from sales for plumbing repairs.

Tip: **To offer a discount on an invoice (or other sales form) at the time of sale (for example, for a senior discount), create a "discount" type item and enter it as a line item on the form.**

If the discount is to apply to more than one item, first use a "subtotal" type item to calculate the total of the items. Then, enter the discount item beneath the subtotal.

Using multiple price levels

In the last exercise, you set up a new service item for Rock Castle construction and assigned a price to that item. Sometimes businesses want to vary an item's price based on who they are selling to. For example, Rock Castle Construction charges different prices depending on whether it is selling to a residential or a commercial customer.

You can associate price levels with specific customers so that each time you create an invoice (or other sales form) for that customer, QuickBooks uses the appropriate price level when calculating rates and amounts on the form. Price levels make it easy to use different rates on sales forms without having to calculate percentage amounts manually. Price levels affect amounts for service, inventory, non-inventory part, and inventory assembly items only. (Inventory assembly items are not available in QuickBooks: Basic or QuickBooks: Premier.)

In this section, you'll create a new price level, associate it with one of Rock Castle's customers, and then create an invoice for that customer.

Note: **The ability to create multiple price levels is not available in QuickBooks: Basic.** You must be using QuickBooks: Pro or QuickBooks: Premier to complete the rest of this lesson.

Creating new price levels

Rock Castle Construction charges its residential customers the base sales price it set up on its Item list. The company charges its commercial customers 10 percent less than the base sales price. In this exercise, you'll create a new price level for Rock Castle Construction to use to reduce the sales amount for its commercial customers.

For each price level you create, you assign a name and percentage increase or decrease to the item's base sales price. You can create up to 100 price levels to use on invoices, sales receipts, and credit memos.

To create a new price level:

1 From the Lists menu, choose Price Level List.

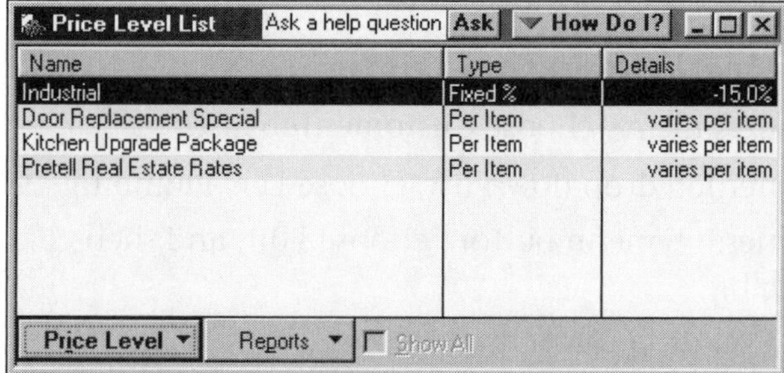

2 From the Price Level menu button, choose New.

3 In the Price Level field type ***Commercial.***

4 Leave "decrease" selected in the "This price level will" field, and then type ***10*** in the percentage field.

Always enter the percentage as a positive number.

Your window should look like the following.

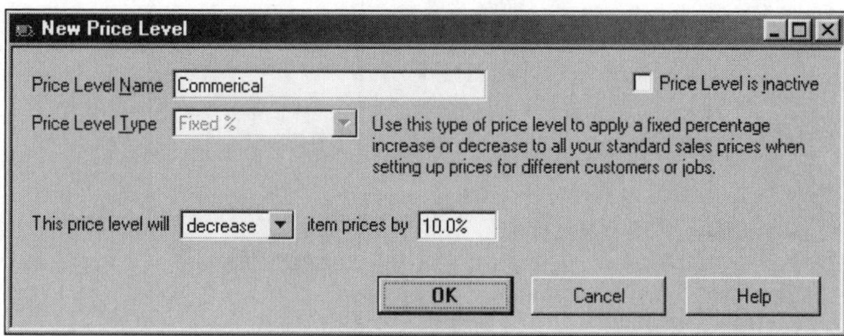

5 Click OK.

Your screen should now resemble the following.

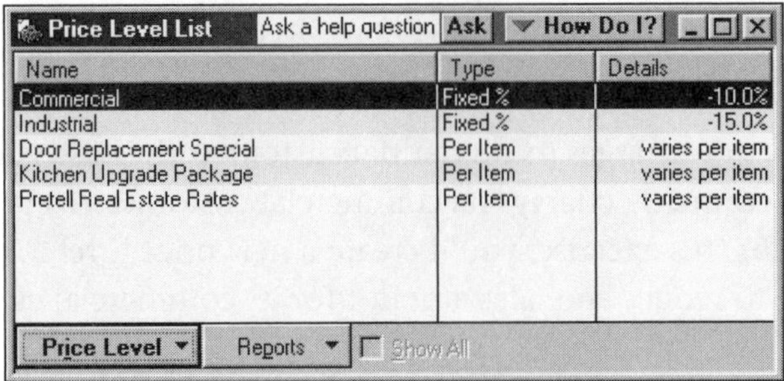

6 Close the Price Level list.

Associating price levels with customers

When you assign price levels to customers, QuickBooks calculates rates and amounts on sales forms based on the price level associated with that customer.

To associate a price level with a customer:

1 From the Customers menu, choose Customer:Job List.

2 From the Customer:Job drop-down list, choose Lew Plumbing - C.

3 From the Customer:Job menu button, choose Edit, and then click the Additional Info tab.

4 From the Price Level drop-down list, choose Commercial.

Your screen should look like this.

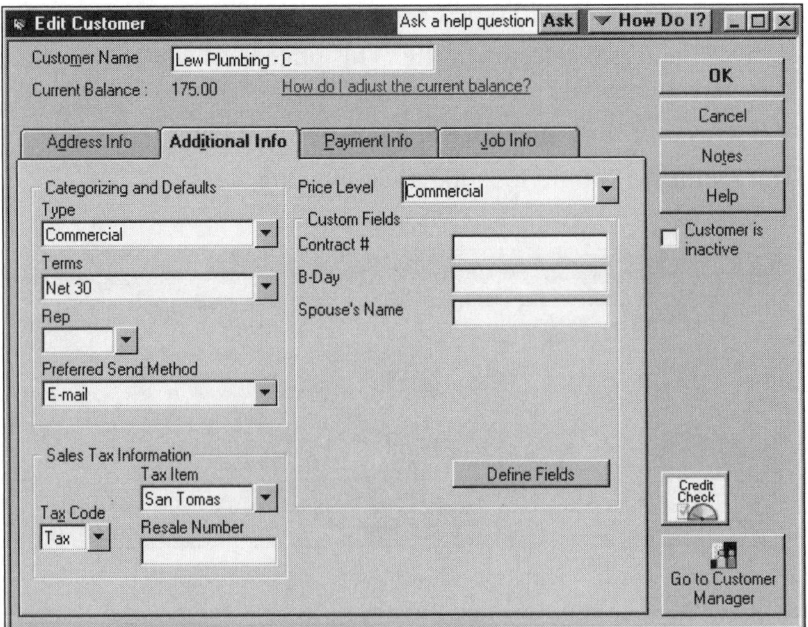

5 Click OK to close the Edit Customer window and save your changes.

6 Close the Customer:Job list.

Using price levels on sales forms

In this section, you'll create an invoice for the customer with whom you just associated the Commercial price level to see how the price level affects amounts on the form.

To use a price level associated with a customer:

1 From the Customers menu, choose Create Invoices.

2 From the Customer:Job drop-down list, choose Lew Plumbing - C.

Notice that QuickBooks displays the name of the price level associated with this Customer:Job in parentheses above the Customer:Job drop-down list. (This information will not be printed on the form.)

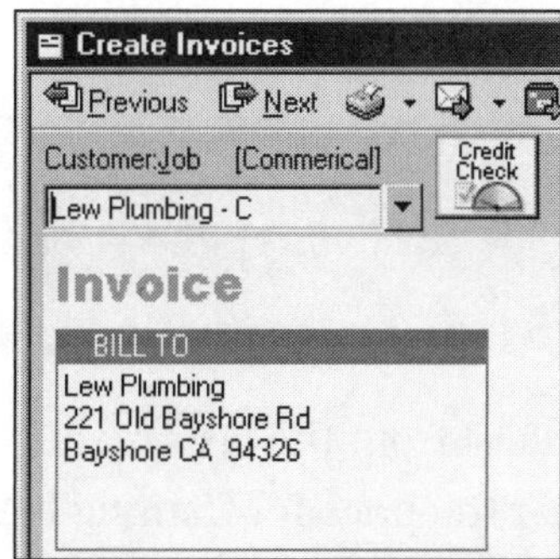

3 Click in the Item column and choose Framing from the drop-down list.

4 In the Quantity field, type ***8***.

5 Click below Framing in the Item field and choose Wood Door:Exterior from the drop-down list.

6 In the Quantity field, type ***2*** and then press Tab.

Your screen should look like this.

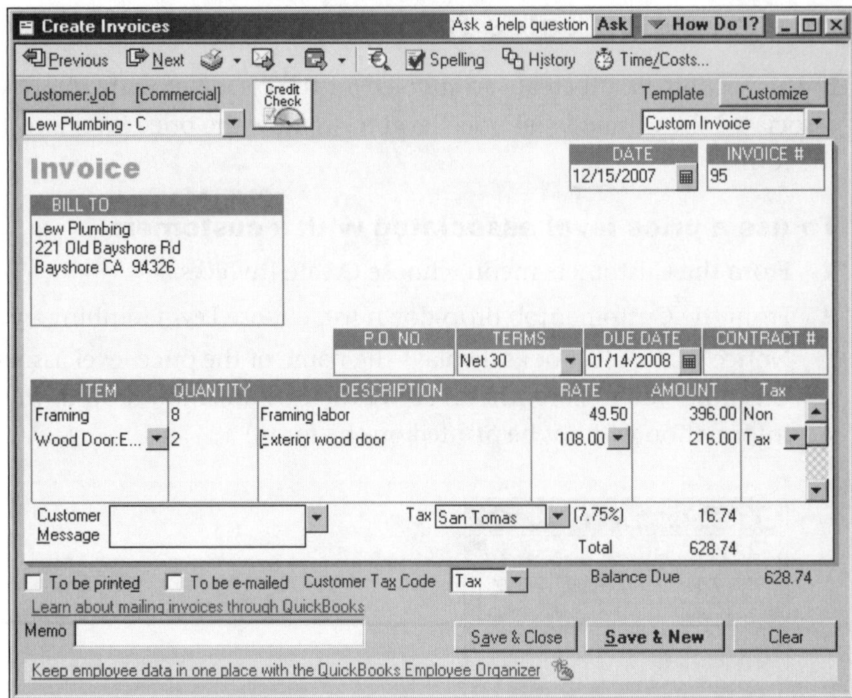

7 Keep the invoice open and choose Item List from the Lists menu.

8 In the Item list, go to Framing. Note that the price for framing is $55.00, but the rate on the invoice is $49.50—10 percent less than the base sales price. QuickBooks has automatically reduced the rate on the invoice by 10 percent.

Note: You can set up QuickBooks to round rates up to the next whole dollar. From the Edit menu, choose Preferences. Choose Sales & Customers from the scroll list and then click the Company Preferences tab. Click the "Round all sales prices up to the next whole dollar" checkbox and click OK.

9 Scroll to the Wood Door:Exterior item and note that the base sales price is $120—10 percent greater than the rate listed on the invoice using the Commercial price level.

10 Close the Item list.

11 Record the invoice by clicking Save & Close.

Assigning price levels to individual line items

In addition to associating price levels with customers, you can also use price levels on an individual basis on sales forms. The following are some examples of when you might want to do this.

- You've associated a price level with a customer, but want to charge the base sales price for an item on a sale to that customer.

- You want to use a price level for one or more items, but you don't want to assign a price level to the customer for whom you're recording the sale.

To apply a price to a single line item:

- Click in the Rate column and select the price level you want to use from the drop-down list that displays.

  When you move out of that field on the form, QuickBooks recalculates the amount and balance due.

If you use QuickBooks: Premier, you can refine your price levels even further by setting price levels for select items. For example, you could give a particular customer or group of customers an extra discount for a specific item or group of items as shown in the following graphic.

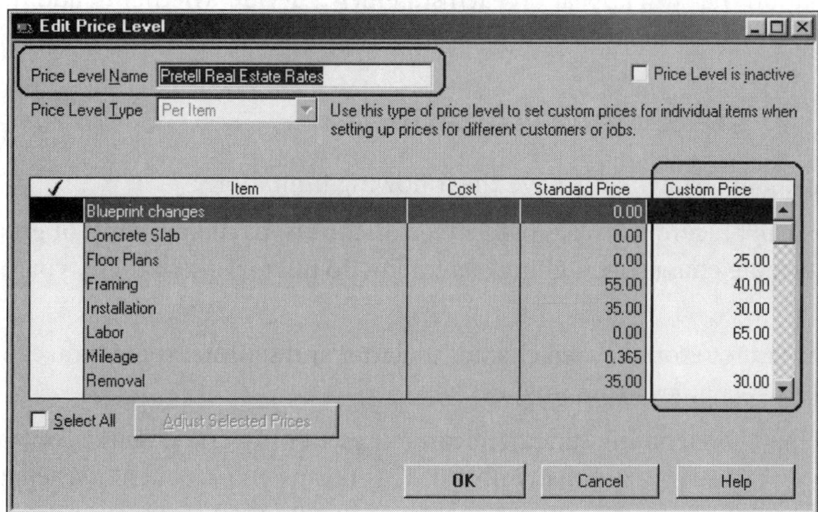

Using statements to bill customers

Another option for billing customers is to send statements. Statements are ideal if you want to accumulate charges before requesting payment, or if you assess a regular monthly charge. *Billing* statements list the charges a customer has accumulated over a period of time.

You enter statement charges one by one, as you perform services for the customer. Later, you print a billing statement that shows the previous balance, details of all new charges, payments received, and the new balance. Billing statements are appropriate if you want to send monthly statements that show the detail of new charges as well as the previous balance and payments received.

If you bill the same charge to a group of customers on a regular basis, you can set up QuickBooks to enter the charges automatically when it's time to send out your statements. Any business that bills a recurring charge on statements can use this feature. For more information, search the onscreen Help index for *memorized transactions, for statement charges*.

Reminder statements summarize a customer's account with your company by listing recent invoices, credit memos, and payments received. You use reminder statements when you bill through invoices but want to remind your customers about delinquent payments.

Reminder statements are different than other "forms" in QuickBooks such as invoices, sales receipts, or checks. Because QuickBooks already has all the information you need to create reminder statements, you don't have to fill them out. Instead, you review the information that will appear on each statement, decide whether to add finance charges, and print them.

Understanding statement limitations

In QuickBooks, statements have the following limitations:

- You can't record sales tax, percentage discounts, payment items, or group items as a separate charge on a billing statement. To bill for any of these, you must use an invoice.
- You cannot group related charges together and subtotal them (you can group and subtotal charges on an invoice).
- A charge on a billing statement can represent only one item (in contrast, an invoice can represent many items). This means you must enter a separate statement charge for each service or product you sell.
- You cannot add custom fields (for lists or items) to the statement form.

Customer statements are available in all QuickBooks editions, however, QuickBooks: Pro and QuickBooks: Premier have additional functionality. For example, in QuickBooks: Pro and QuickBooks: Premier, you can include invoice detail on statements and include all open transactions as of a certain date.

Note: **To complete the following exercises, you must be using QuickBooks: Pro or QuickBooks: Premier.**

Generating customer statements

Rock Castle uses invoices to bill its customers, but it sends reminder statements to customers with overdue invoices. In this exercise, you generate statements to send to customers with outstanding balances.

Rock Castle wants to send reminder statements to all customers who have balances more than 30 days past due.

To generate reminder statements:

1 From the Customers menu, choose Create Statements.

QuickBooks displays the Create Statements window.

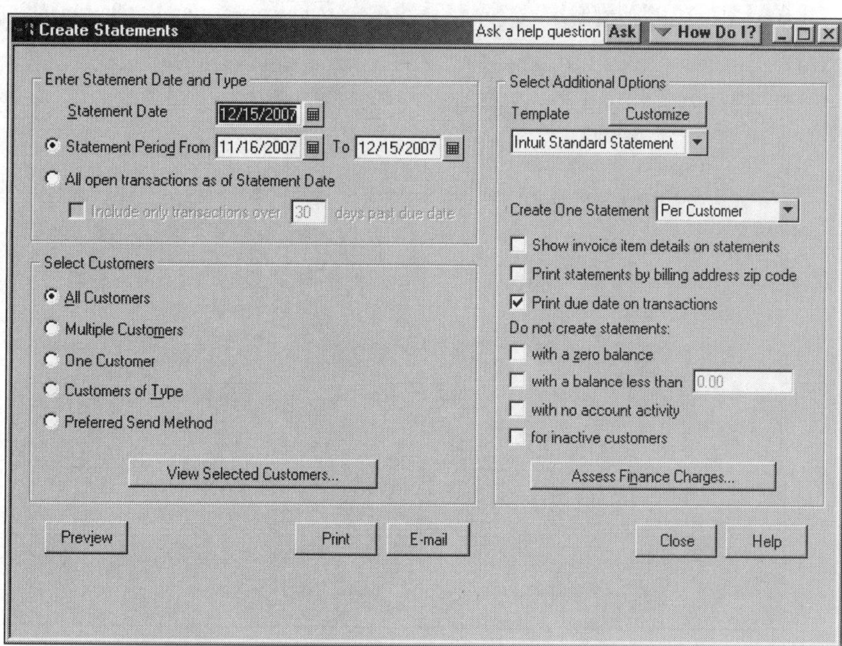

2 In the Enter Statement Date and Type section of the window, select the "All open transactions as of Statement Date" option.

3 Click to select the "Include only transactions over" checkbox.

4 Leave the number of days past due field entry at 30.

5 In the Select Customers section, leave "All Customers" selected.

6 In the Select Additional Options section, click to select the "Show invoice item details on statements" checkbox.

Your screen should look like the following graphic.

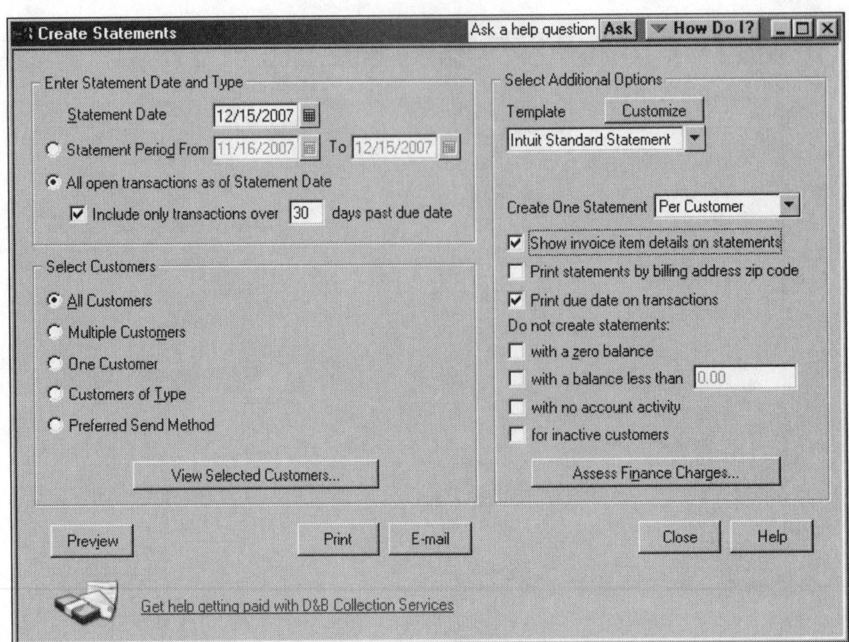

7 Click Assess Finance Charges.

QuickBooks displays the Assess Finance Charges window.

8 Click Unmark All.

9 In the Assess column, click to put a checkmark in the row for the 155 Wilks job for Pretell Real Estate.

Your screen should look like the following graphic.

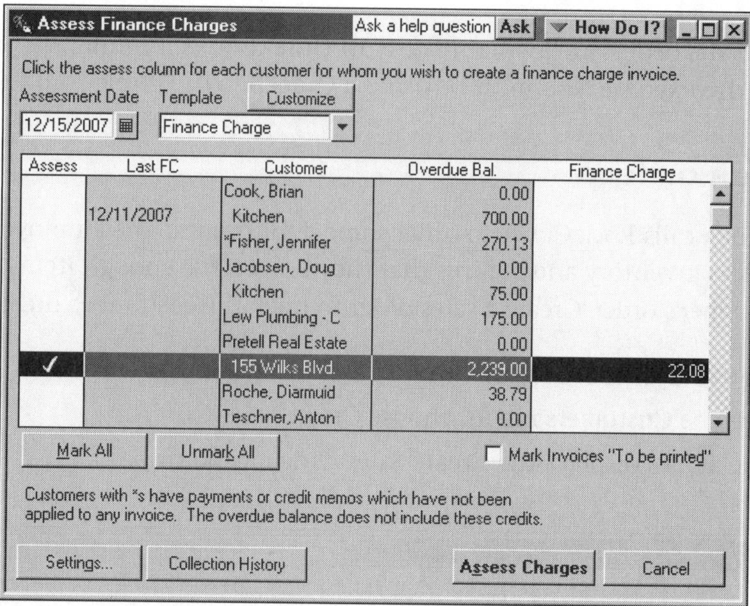

10 Click Assess Charges.

11 Answer Yes when QuickBooks displays the message telling you that finance charges have already been assessed today.

QuickBooks creates a finance charge invoice for Pretell Real Estate in the amount of $22.08. This amount does not display on the current statement, but you can send the finance charge invoice with the reminder statement.

12 Click Preview.

QuickBooks displays reminder statements for the three customers whose balances are 30 days or more past due—including the details from the original invoices.

13 Click Close.

At this point you could generate and send the reminder statements to your customers.

14 Close the Create Statements window.

Processing sales orders

The sales order feature lets you track orders from customers and "set items aside." You can also use sales orders to track back orders when a customer orders something and you are out of stock. Using this feature, you can track the orders you need to fill without affecting accounts receivable. Sales orders affect only inventory quantities—not values—until you actually sell the items.

When inventory items come in, you can create an invoice directly from the sales order. If only some of the items have come in, you can invoice for those items, and use the sales order to create invoices for the remaining items later. Once all items have been received and invoiced for, QuickBooks Premier closes the sales order.

Note: **Sales orders are available only in QuickBooks: Premier.** To proceed through this exercise, you must be using a QuickBooks: Premier product.

Creating sales orders

A customer calls Rock Castle to order some door frames. The employee who took the call checks inventory and realizes that they don't have enough items on hand to fill the customer's order. Create a sales order to track the customer's order.

To create a sales order:

1 From the Customers menu, choose Create Sales Orders.

QuickBooks displays the Create Sales Orders window.

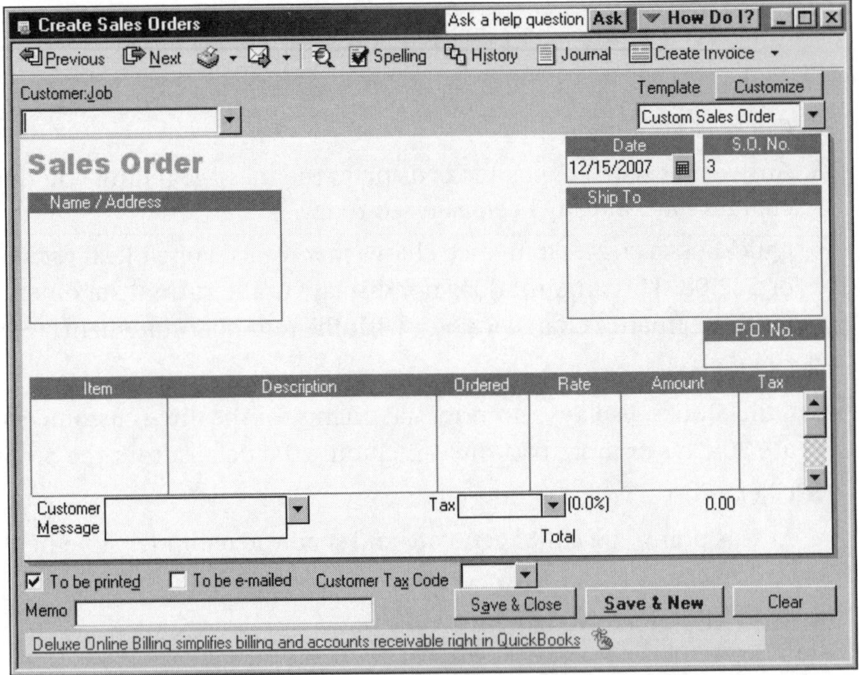

2 In the Customer:Job drop-down list, select Roche, Diarmuid:Room Addition.

3 Click in the Item column and select Frames:Exterior Frame from the drop-down list.

4 Press Tab twice to move to the Ordered column.

5 Type ***4.***

6 Press Tab, and then type ***25.00*** in the Rate column.

7 Press Tab again.

The sales order should look like the following graphic.

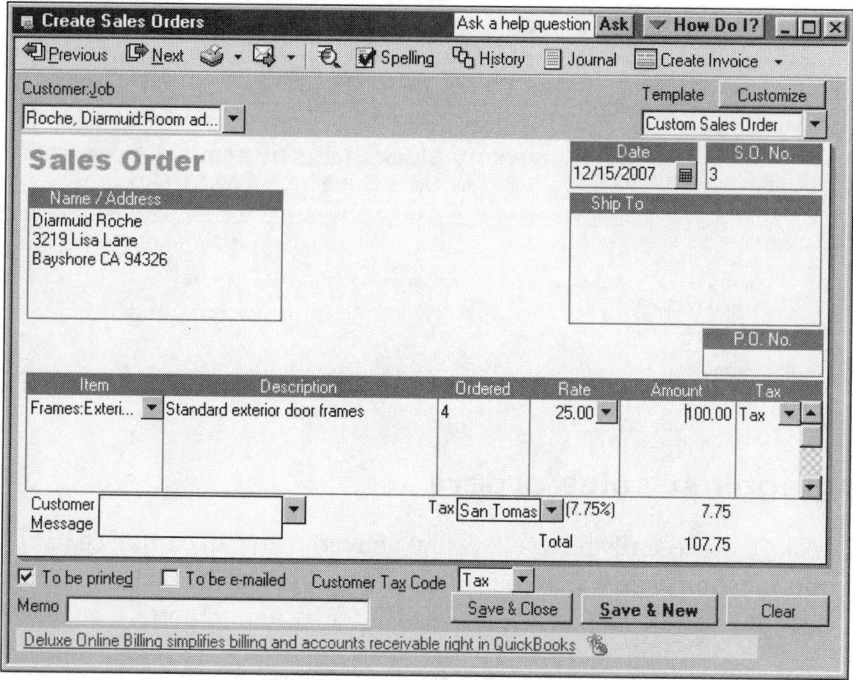

8 Click Save & Close.

If the inventory items are not already on order, create a purchase order. When the items arrive, enter them into inventory as usual, and then invoice the customer.

Checking stock status

If you want to see how sales orders affect inventory quantities, run the stock status by item report.

The following graphic shows the Frame item before the sales order for Diarmuid was created.

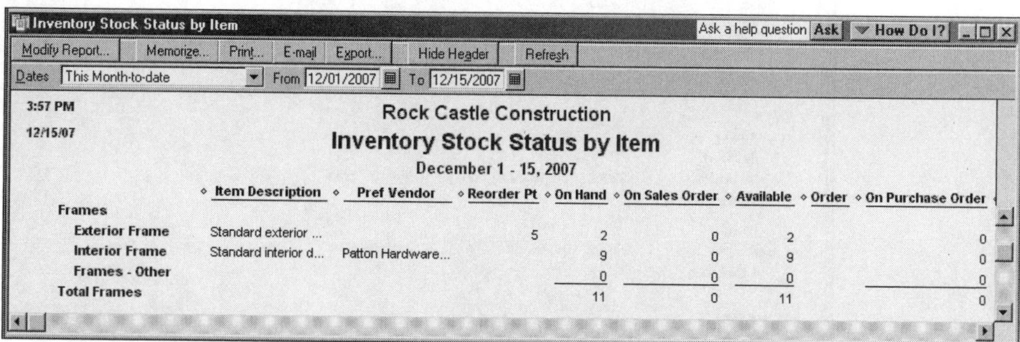

This graphic shows the Frame item after the sales order was created. Notice that QuickBooks tracks the items listed on sales orders.

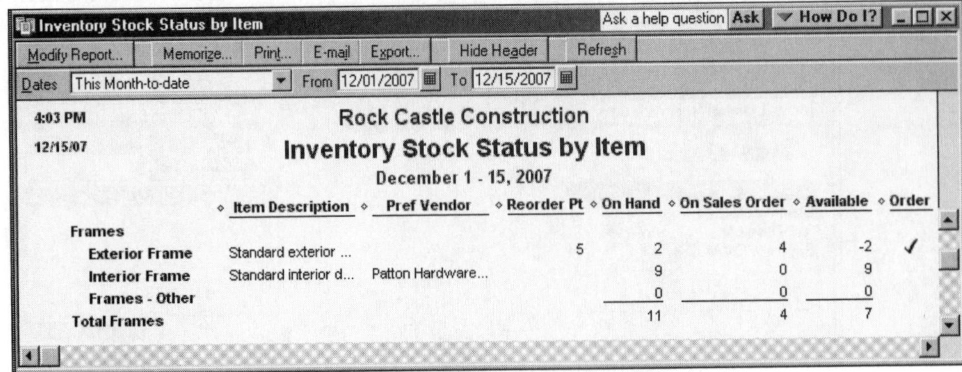

Invoicing against sales orders

Rock Castle recently received several deliveries and an employee has entered the items into inventory. He wants to find out if any of these items have been ordered for customers, so he runs the open sales order by item report.

To run the sales order by item report:

1 From the Reports menu, choose Sales.

2 Choose Open Sales Orders by Item from the submenu.

QuickBooks displays the report.

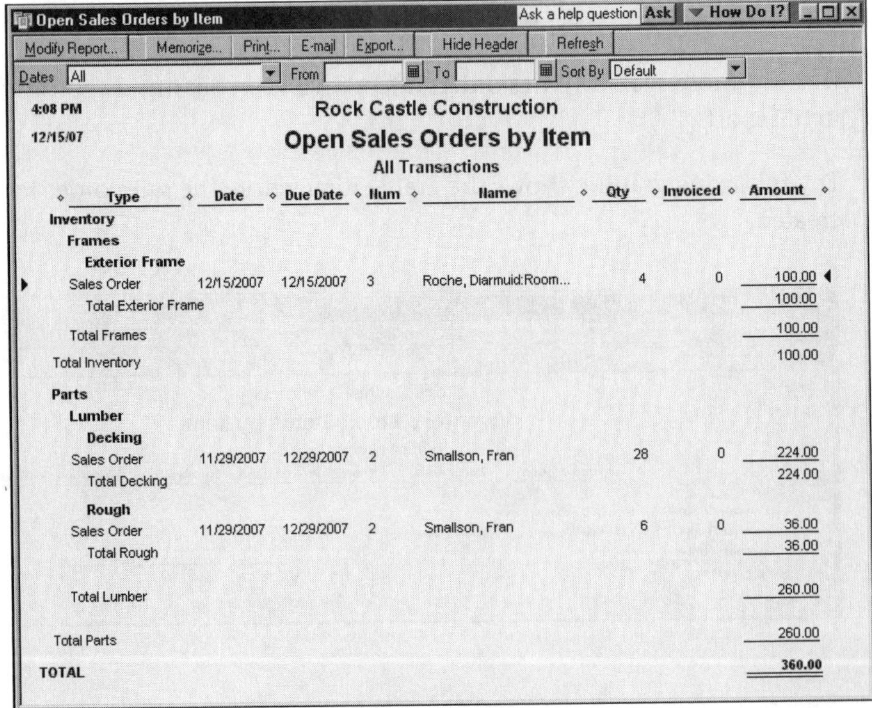

In addition to the sales order you just entered, the report shows that there is an open sales order for Exterior wood doors for Fran Smallson. Rock Castle now has sufficient quantity on hand to fill the customer's order, so you can close the sales order and invoice the customer.

In this exercise, you'll create an invoice from a sales order. If you're using a Premier product, you can also generate purchase orders directly from sales orders by clicking the down arrow on the Create Invoices button in the Create Sales Order window, and then selecting Purchase Order. You don't need to create the purchase order in this exercise.

To create an invoice and close the sales order:

1 Double-click on the line for Decking in the report window for Sales Order #2 for Fran Smallson.

QuickBooks opens the sales order.

2 In the Create Sales Orders window, click Create Invoice on the toolbar.

QuickBooks displays the Create Invoice Based On Sales Order window.

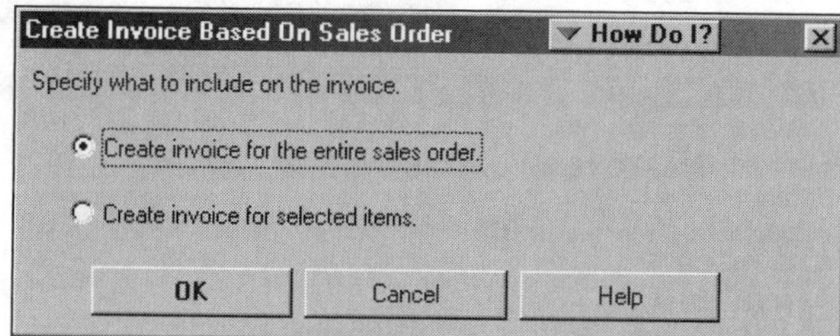

3 Leave the "Create invoice for the entire sales order" option selected, and click OK.

QuickBooks creates an invoice for the customer.

In this case, all of the items the customer order arrived, so you can close the sales order. If only some of the items had come in, you could invoice for only those items and keep the sales order open until any remaining items arrived. QuickBooks tracks which items are still open.

4 In the Create Invoices window, click Save & Close.

5 Close the report window.

Student test and review

1 From which list (or lists) does QuickBooks get the information for A, B, and C in the graphic below?

- *A: Customer:Job list*
- *B: Customer:Job list (if associated terms with the customer); Terms list*
- *C: Item list*

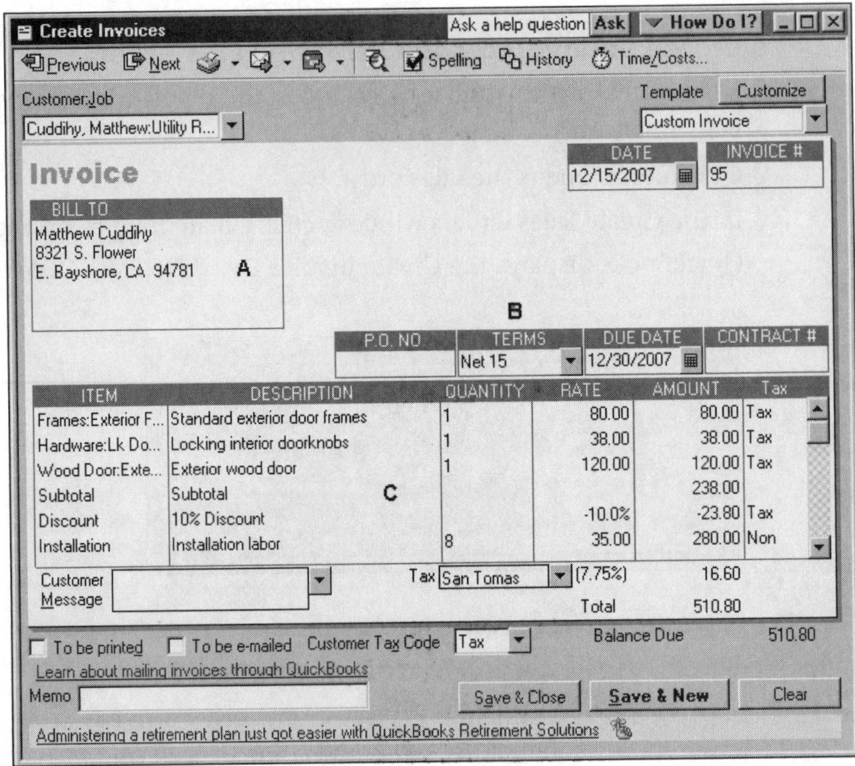

2 List the item types used in the line item area of the invoice above.

Inventory Part, Subtotal, Discount, and Service.

3 Create an invoice for Rock Castle Construction that uses the new Repairs:Plumbing line item. Create the invoice for a new customer by adding information to the Customer list "on the fly."

4 Filling out a sales receipt is similar to filling out an invoice form. Create a sales receipt for a customer of Rock Castle Construction, and select the Undeposited Funds option. After you create the sales receipt, open the Undeposited Funds account register to see the transaction QuickBooks created automatically.

LESSON 7 Receiving payments and making deposits

Lesson objectives

- To learn how to record customer payments in QuickBooks
- To learn how to handle customer discounts, partial payments, overpayments, or down payments
- To see how to record a deposit in QuickBooks, and learn how QuickBooks treats the deposit behind the scenes
- To learn how to enter cash back from a deposit in QuickBooks

Instructor preparation

- Review this lesson, including the examples, to make sure you're familiar with the material.
- Ensure that all students have a copy of qblesson.qbb on their computer's hard disk.

To start this lesson

Before you perform the following steps, make sure you have installed the exercise file (qblesson.qbb) on your hard disk. See "Installing the exercise file" in the Introduction to this guide if you haven't installed it.

The following steps restore the exercise file to its original state so that the data in the file matches what you see on the screen as you proceed through each lesson.

To restore the exercise file (qblesson.qbb):

1. From the File menu in QuickBooks, choose Restore.

   QuickBooks displays the Restore Company Backup window.
2. In the "Get Company Backup From" section of the window, click Browse and select your c:\QBtrain directory.
3. Select the qblesson.qbb file, and then click Open.
4. In the "Restore Company Backup To" section of the window, click Browse and select your c:\QBtrain directory.
5. In the File name field of the Restore To window, type ***lesson 7*** and then click Save.
6. Click Restore.

Recording customer payments

If you're receiving payment at the time of a sale, and you fill out a sales receipt, QuickBooks records a customer payment. When you invoice a customer, and you receive payment later, you enter the payment in the QuickBooks Receive Payments window.

The Receive Payments window lets you match up payments you receive with invoices you've written. You'll be working with the Receive Payments window in this lesson.

Recording a payment in full for a single job

The simplest case is when a customer has one outstanding invoice for one job and sends you a payment for the full amount. Suppose that Rock Castle Construction receives a check for $4735.73 from Mike Violette for his workshop. Here's how you'd enter the payment.

To record a payment in full:

1 From the Customers menu, choose Receive Payments.

QuickBooks displays the Receive Payments window.

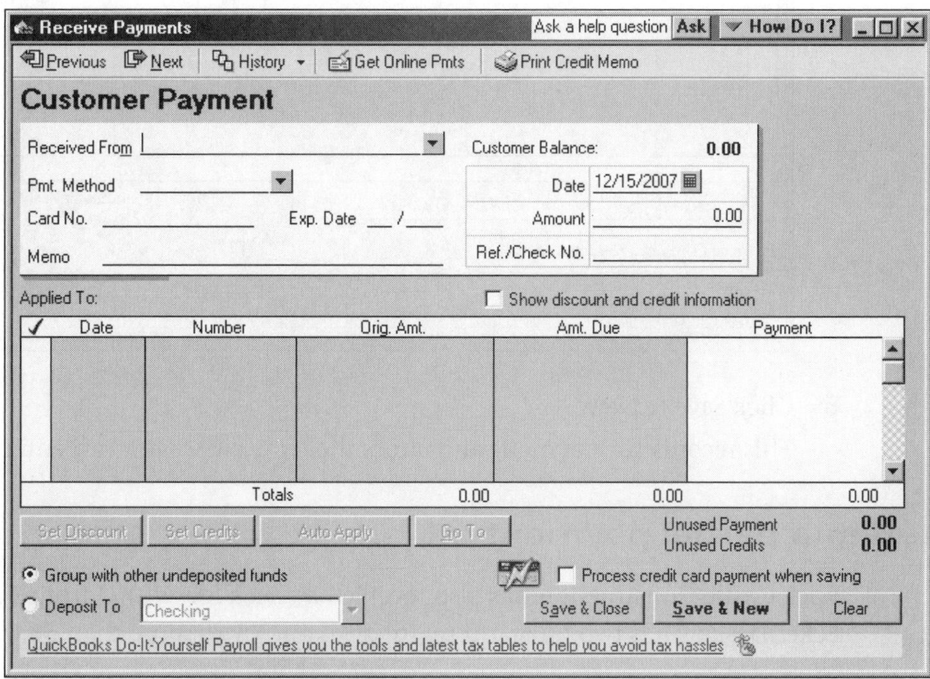

The first step is to enter the name of the customer from whom you've received a payment.

2 In the Received From field, select Violette, Mike:Workshop from the drop-down list.

QuickBooks displays the outstanding invoice for Mike Violette in the Applied To section of the window.

3 Press Tab twice to move to the Amount field.

4 In the Amount field, type ***4735.73*** and press Tab.

QuickBooks changes the Total to Apply to 4735.73, and applies the payment to the one outstanding invoice.

5 In the Ref./Check No. field, type ***6745*** and then press Tab.

6 In the Pmt. Method field, select Check from the drop-down list.

7 Click "Group with other undeposited funds" if it is not selected already.

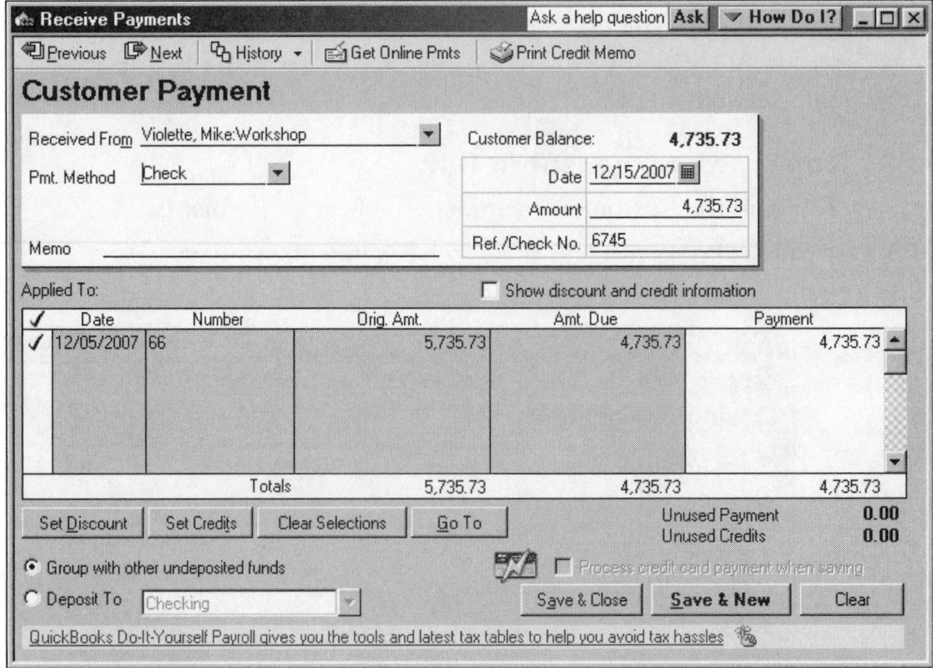

8 Click Save & New.

This records the payment and clears the window so you can enter another one.

Entering a partial payment

Rock Castle Construction has also received a check for $1,000 from Ecker Designs. Ecker Designs has two outstanding invoices and owes more than $6,000.

To enter a partial payment:

1 In the Received From field, select Ecker Designs:Office Repairs from the drop-down list.

In the middle of the window, QuickBooks shows you the invoices still outstanding for the job. In this case, there are two.

2 Press Tab twice to move to the Amount field, and then type ***1000***. Then press Tab again.

QuickBooks automatically applies the payment you've entered to Ecker Design's oldest invoice.

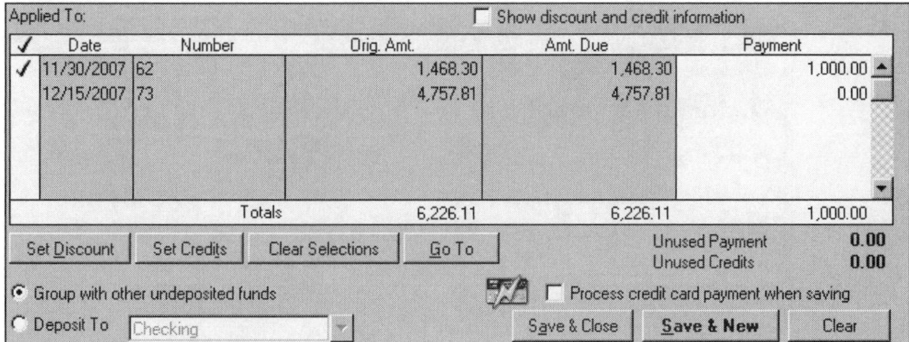

To choose which invoice a payment applies to, rather than having QuickBooks apply it to the oldest one, you can clear the selections and apply the payments as you wish.

3 Click Clear Selections.

4 In the Payment column, type ***1000*** as the amount you want to apply to the second invoice, and then press Tab.

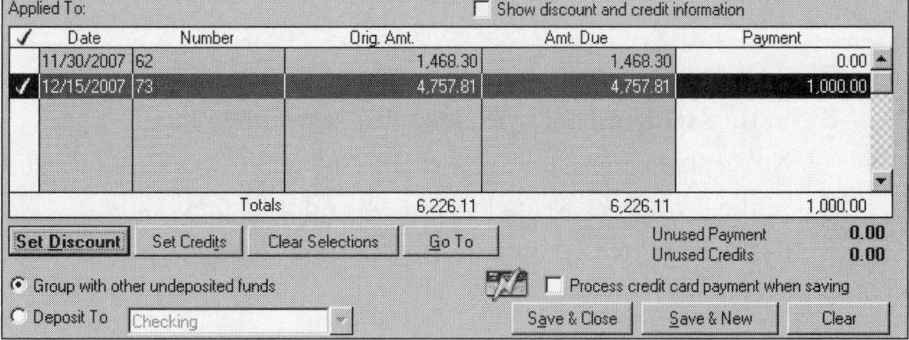

5 In the Pmt. Method field, select Check from the drop-down list.

6 Make sure that "Group with other undeposited funds" is selected.

7 Click Save & New to record the partial payment and clear the window.

Applying one payment to multiple jobs

Rock Castle Construction is working on several jobs for a customer, Brian Cook. Brian has payments outstanding for four invoices. He wants to write one check to cover all outstanding payments.

In this exercise, you'll apply this single payment to invoices for multiple jobs.

To apply one payment to multiple jobs:

1. In the Receive Payments window, select Cook, Brian from the Received From drop-down list.

   QuickBooks lists the open invoices for all of the jobs associated with Brian Cook.

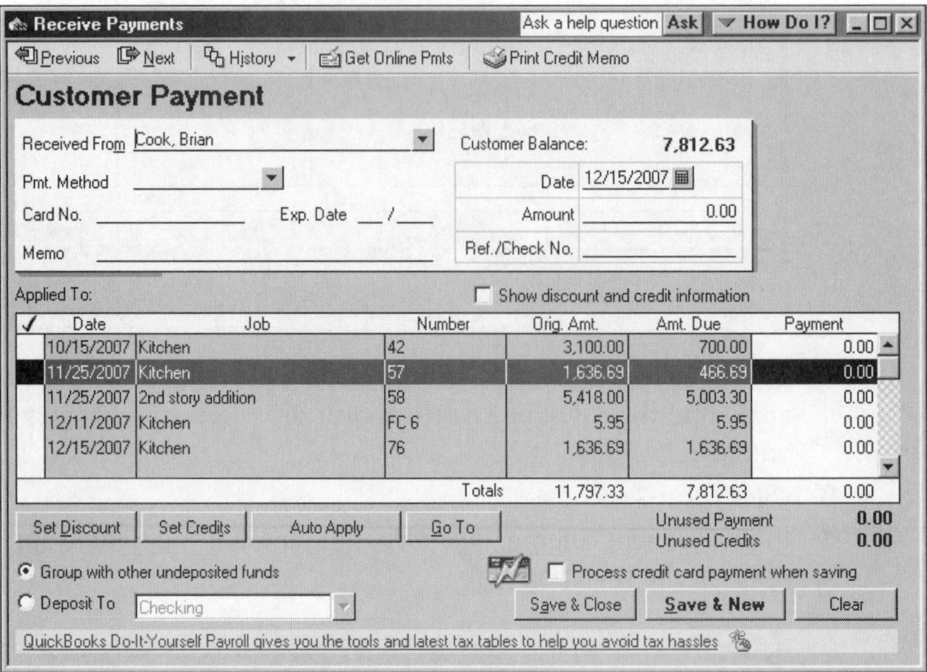

2. Press Tab twice to move to the Amount field.
3. In the Amount field, type ***7812.63*** and then press Tab.

   Notice that QuickBooks applies the payment to all outstanding invoices.

4. In the Ref./Check No. field, type ***575*** and then press Tab.
5. In the Pmt. Method drop-down list, select Check.

Your window should look like this.

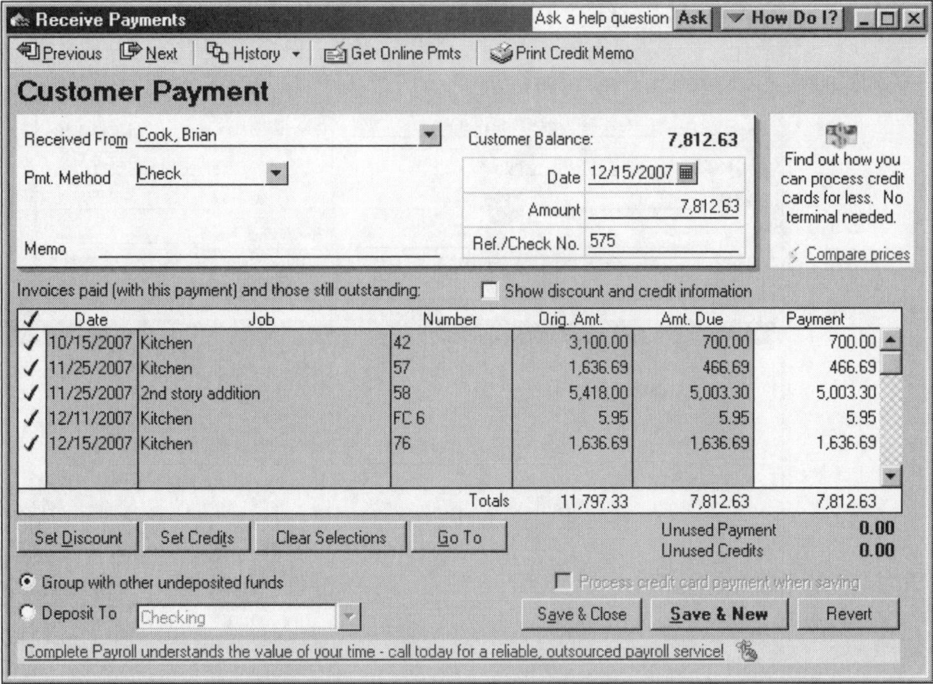

6 Make sure that "Group with other undeposited funds" is selected.

7 Click Save & New.

Entering overpayments

If a customer sends you an overpayment, you simply enter the amount in the Receive Payments window, and QuickBooks keeps track of the additional payment. When the customer has future invoices, you can apply the overpayment to those amounts.

Suppose that Rock Castle Construction has received a payment of $12,500.00 from Pretell Real Estate for the 75 Sunset Rd. job. The outstanding invoice for that job is $12,412.18.

To enter the payment:

1 In the Received From field of the Receive Payments window, select Pretell Real Estate:75 Sunset Rd. from the drop-down list.

QuickBooks displays an invoice dated 12/01/2007 for $12,412.18.

2 Press Tab twice and type ***12500*** in the Amount field.

3 Press Tab again.

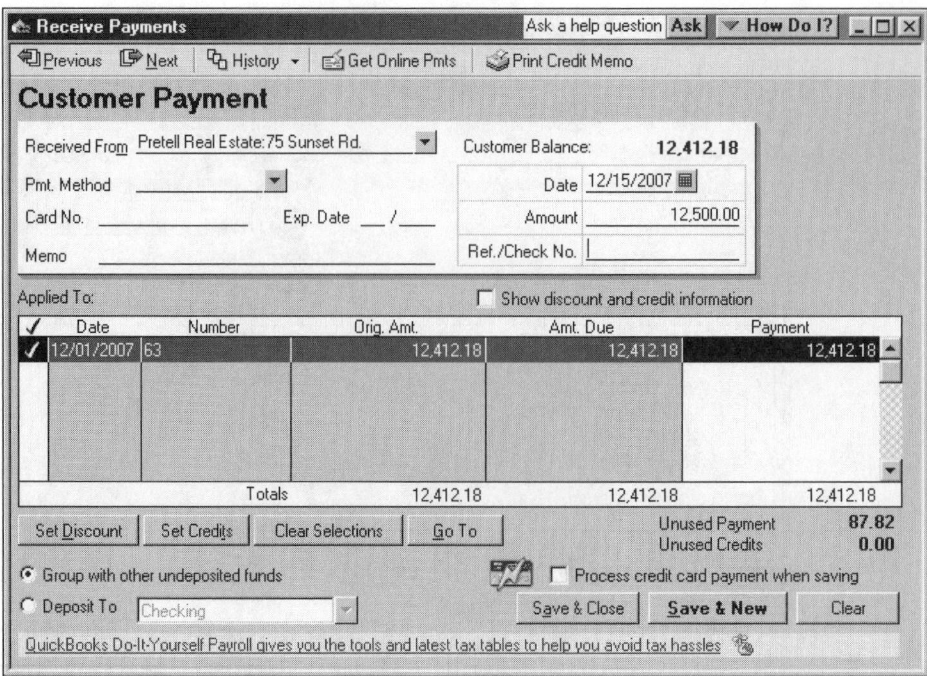

QuickBooks shows an Unused Payment amount of $87.82. QuickBooks keeps track of the overpayment amount for you, and you can apply it to any future invoices for the customer. The next time you invoice Pretell Real Estate and receive a payment, the Receive Payments window will show $87.82 in unused credits.

4 Select Check from the drop-down list in the Pmt. Method field.

5 Make sure "Group with other undeposited funds" is selected.

Tell students that to print a copy of the credit memo for the customer acknowledging the amount they owe, they can click the Print Credit Memo button at the top of the Receive Payments window.

6 Click Save & New.

7 When QuickBooks displays a message telling you that the customer will have a credit if you proceed, click OK.

Handling down payments or prepayments

If a customer makes a payment before you've invoiced him for services (for example, he may be making a down payment or paying a retainer fee), you can still record the payment at the Receive Payments window. However, because you don't have any invoices to which to apply the payment, QuickBooks records the payment as an unused payment (just like an overpayment).

QuickBooks holds the unapplied amount with the customer's name. The next time you enter that customer in the Receive Payments window, QuickBooks displays the credit amount in the Unused Credits area. The customer's balance also reflects the credit amount.

Tip: **To apply a discount for early payment for any customer whose payment terms include a discount for payment before the due date, use the Set Discount button in the Receive Payments window.**

Even if the customer has already sent you a payment for the full amount of the invoice, you can apply a discount. QuickBooks holds any credit amount in accounts receivable until you apply it to an invoice or issue a refund check.

Suppose Kristy Abercrombie wants Rock Castle Construction to do a kitchen remodeling job for her. She's sent Rock Castle Construction a check for $1,000 as an initial payment, but the company hasn't invoiced her yet.

To enter the down payment you've received:

1 In the Received From field, select Abercrombie, Kristy:Kitchen from the drop-down list.

2 In the Pmt. Method field, select Check from the drop-down list.

3 Highlight the numbers in the Amount field and type ***1000***. Then press Tab.

QuickBooks displays the payment as an Unused Payment.

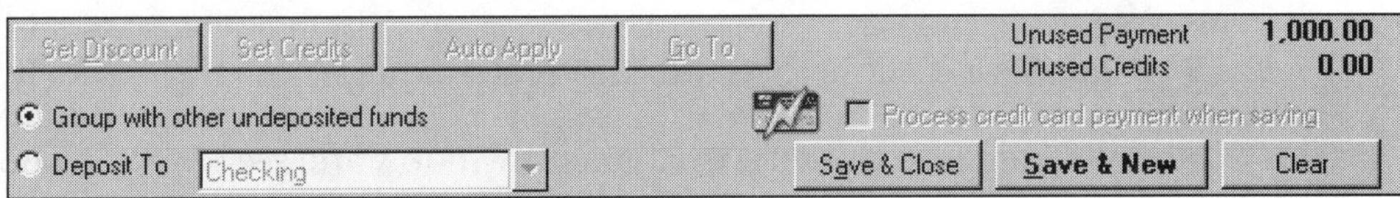

4 Click "Group with other undeposited funds" if it is not selected already.

5 Click Save & Close.

6 When QuickBooks displays a message telling you that the customer will have a credit if you proceed, click OK.

Later, Rock Castle Construction is ready to prepare its invoices and needs to invoice Kristy for the labor the workers have already completed on the job.

To create an invoice for a customer who made a down payment:

1 From the Customers menu, choose Create Invoices.

QuickBooks displays the Create Invoices window.

2 In the Customer:Job field, select Abercrombie, Kristy:Kitchen from the drop-down list.

3 If you have QuickBooks: Pro or Premier, QuickBooks displays the Available Estimates window. You don't want to create the invoice from the estimate listed, so click Cancel.

4 From the Template drop-down list, choose Custom Invoice.

5 Click in the Item column, select Removal from the Item drop-down list, and then press Tab.

6 In the Quantity column, type ***40*** and press Tab.

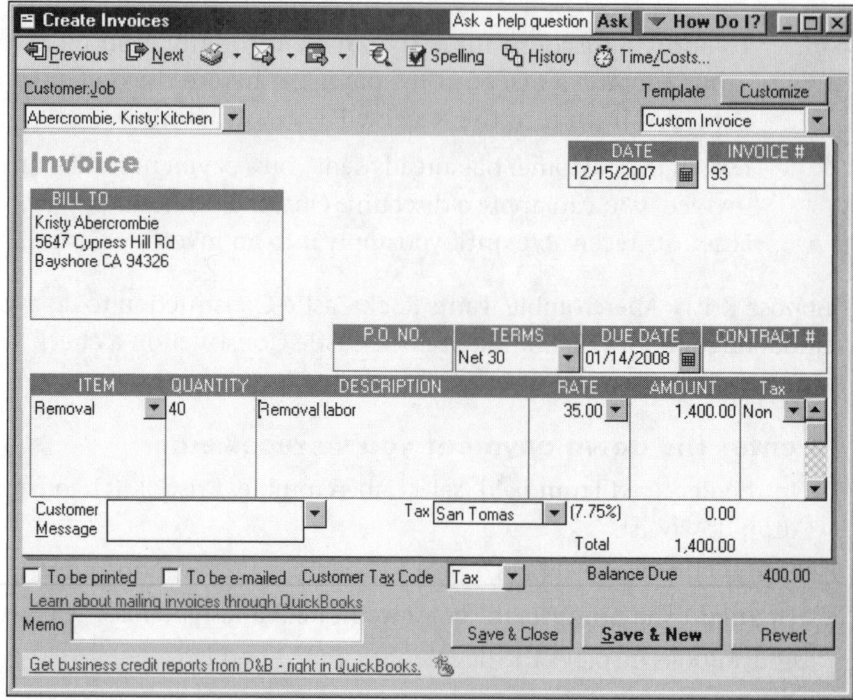

7 Click Save & Close to record the invoice and to close the Create Invoices window.

Now you can go to the Receive Payments window and see how QuickBooks applies the payment Kristy made earlier.

To view a down payment:

1 From the Customers menu, choose Receive Payments.

2 In the Received From field, select Abercrombie, Kristy:Kitchen from the drop-down list.

QuickBooks shows Unused Credits of $1,000.

3 Click in the Payment column, and then Click Set Credits.

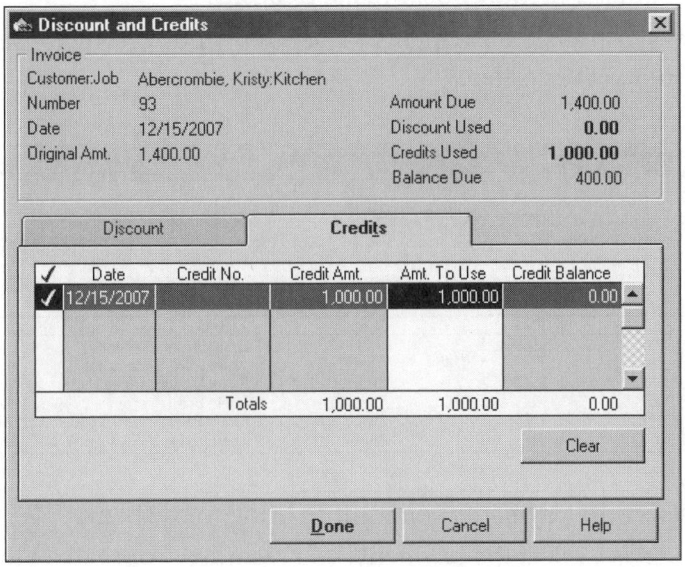

Discount and Credits

Invoice

Customer:Job Abercrombie, Kristy:Kitchen

Number 93

Date 12/15/2007

Original Amt. 1,400.00

Amount Due 1,400.00

Discount Used **0.00**

Credits Used **1,000.00**

Balance Due 400.00

Discount | **Credits**

✓	Date	Credit No.	Credit Amt.	Amt. To Use	Credit Balance
✓	12/15/2007		1,000.00	1,000.00	0.00
		Totals	1,000.00	1,000.00	0.00

Clear

Done Cancel Help

In the Discounts and Credits window, notice that QuickBooks has applied the full credit amount to the invoice, which is what you wanted. If there were other invoices to which you wanted to apply part of the credit amount, you would use this window to apply the credits to the appropriate invoices.

4 Click Done.

QuickBooks applies the existing credit to the new invoice.

5 Click Save & Close to record the payment.

Tip: **To see all the transactions related to customers, grouped by customer and job, create a customer balance detail report. (From the Reports menu, choose Customers & Receivables, then choose Customer Balance Detail.)**

Making deposits

When you use the Enter Sales Receipt window (for a sales receipt where you receive payment on the spot), the Receive Payments window (for payments on invoices), or a payment item on an invoice, QuickBooks keeps track of the money you've received until you deposit it in the bank.

Selecting payments to deposit

At your office, you might hold payments in a locked cash drawer or a cash register until you can get to the bank; QuickBooks holds the amount in an asset account called Undeposited Funds. When you're ready to take your payments to the bank, you can record the deposit in QuickBooks, print a deposit slip to bring with you, and enter cash back amounts.

To select payments to deposit:

1 From the Banking menu, choose Make Deposits.

QuickBooks displays the Payments to Deposit window, which lists the payments you have not yet deposited.

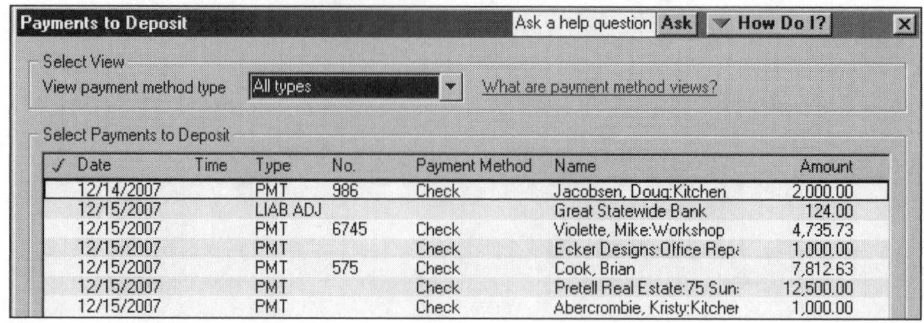

2 Click to select the payments you want to bring to the bank.

For this exercise, select the payments you recorded from Mike Violette, Ecker Designs, Brian Cook, Pretell Real Estate, and Kristy Abercrombie.

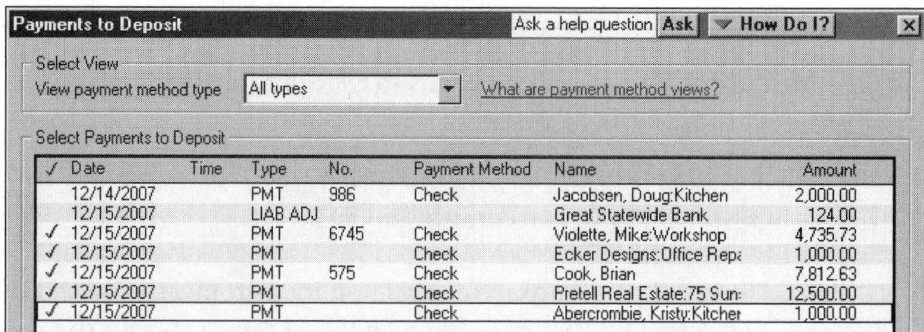

3 Click OK.

QuickBooks displays the Make Deposits window, which shows the payments you just selected.

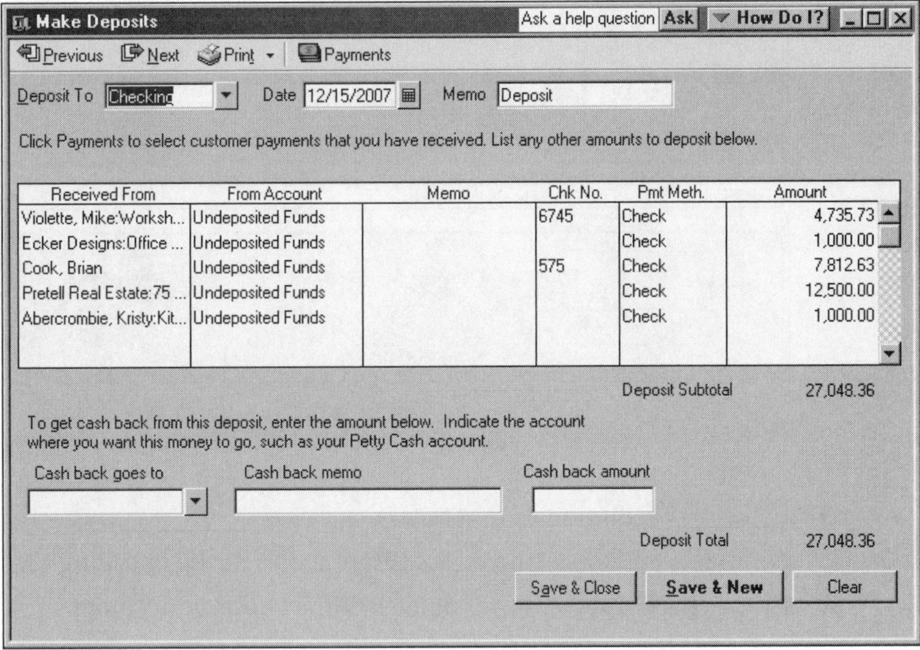

4 In the Deposit To field, make sure that Checking is selected.

Note: If you have money to deposit that is not the result of a payment you received for a sale, you can enter it in the detail area of the window. For example, if you received a premium refund from your insurance vendor, you would enter it here.

QuickBooks updates the deposit total at the bottom of the window automatically. If you wanted to print a deposit slip to take to the bank, you would click Print. The Printable Deposit Slips that you can order to work with QuickBooks work only with deposits of cash and checks.

5 Click Save & Close to record the deposit.

How QuickBooks handles the deposit

QuickBooks updates the Undeposited Funds account to show that you've made a deposit. It also adds the deposit to your checking account register.

To view the Undeposited Funds account:

1 From the Lists menu, choose Chart of Accounts.

2 In the chart of accounts, double-click the Undeposited Funds account.

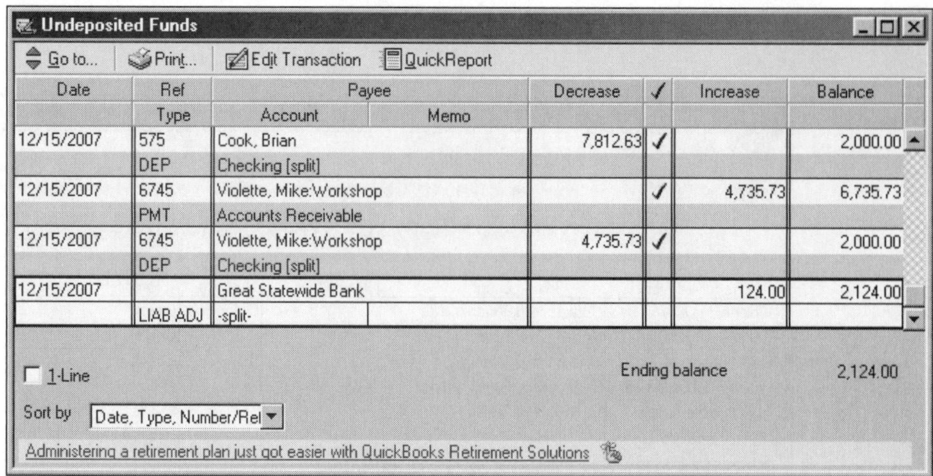

QuickBooks displays your deposits and reduces the balance in the account by the amount of the deposits.

3 Close the account register window.

Now you can look at the deposit transaction in the checking account.

4 In the chart of accounts, double-click the checking account.

12/15/2007					27,048.36	74,033.62
	DEP	-split- Deposit				

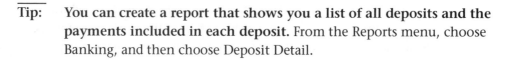

QuickBooks has entered the deposit as a transaction in the checking account register and has updated the balance of your checking account.

5 Close the checking account register and the chart of accounts.

Tip: **You can create a report that shows you a list of all deposits and the payments included in each deposit.** From the Reports menu, choose Banking, and then choose Deposit Detail.

Getting cash back from a deposit

In the Make Deposits window, you can enter information about any cash you took out of the deposit when you are recording the deposit.

To record getting cash back from a deposit:

1 From the Banking menu, choose Make Deposits.

QuickBooks displays the Payments to Deposit window. Notice that the deposits you made in the last exercise are no longer listed.

2 In the Payments to Deposit window, select the payment from Doug Jacobsen.

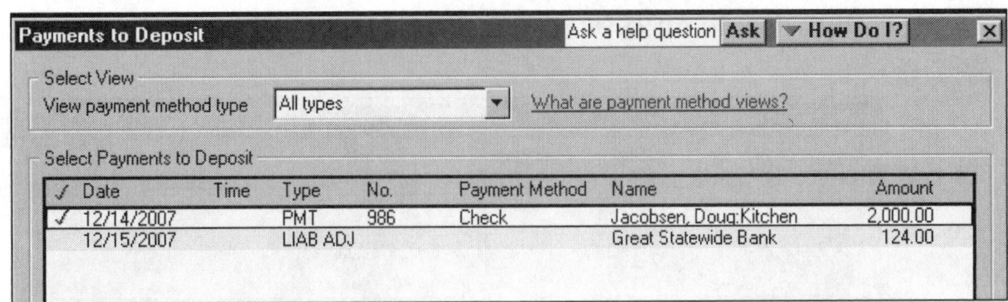

3 Click OK.

4 In the Make Deposits window, type ***Petty Cash*** in the "Cash back goes to" field and press Tab.

5 When QuickBooks displays a message telling you that Petty Cash is not on the account list, click Set up.

QuickBooks displays the New Account window with the name preset to Petty Cash.

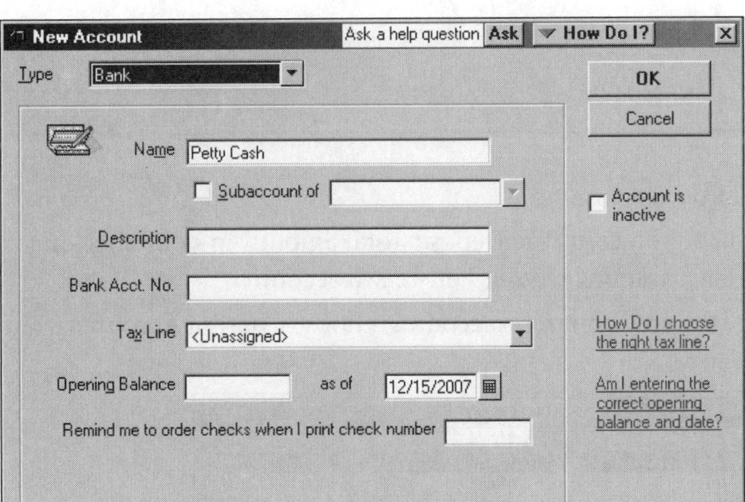

6 Make sure Bank is selected in the Type drop-down list, and then click OK to return to the Make Deposits window.

7 In the "Cash back amount" field, type ***200*** and press Tab.

QuickBooks displays the deposit subtotal amount ($2000.00) and the total less the cash back amount ($1800.00).

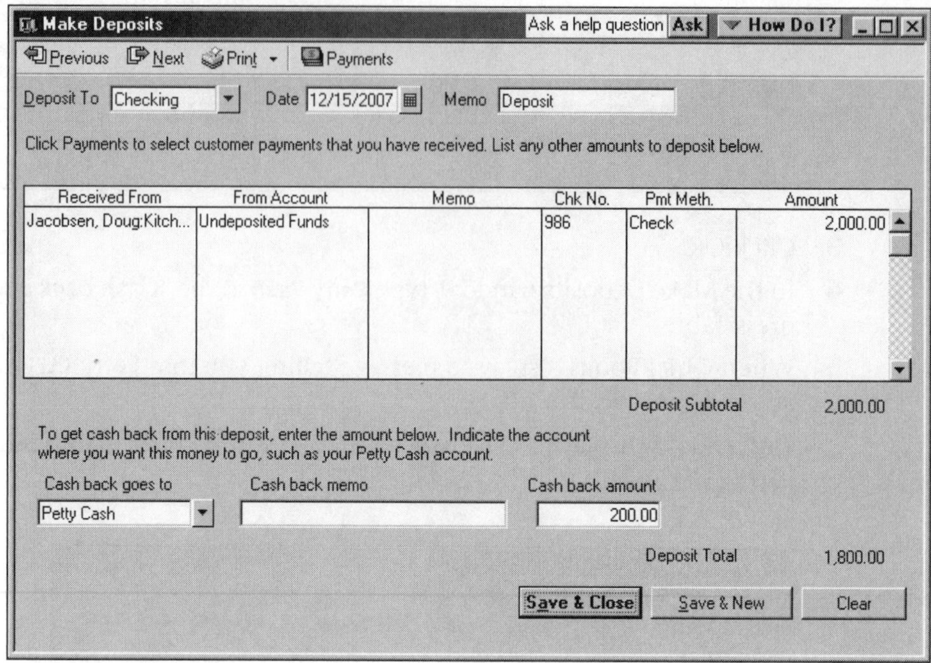

8 Click Save & Close.

QuickBooks records the Deposit Total amount in your checking account and the cash back amount in your Petty Cash account.

9 To see the effect on these accounts, choose Chart of Accounts from the Lists menu.

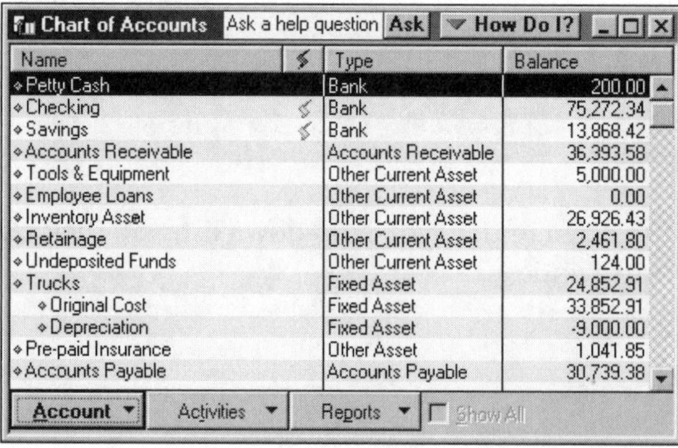

10 Close the chart of accounts.

Student test and review

1. Create an invoice for Bryan Ruff's utility shed job.

   Add items to Rock Castle Construction's Item list as needed.

2. After you invoice Bryan, record a payment from him in the Receive Payments window.

3. Record Rock Castle Construction's deposit of the payment.

LESSON 8 Entering and paying bills

Lesson objectives

- To discuss the different ways you can handle bills in QuickBooks
- To learn how to enter a bill in QuickBooks
- To use the Pay Bills window to pay a bill in QuickBooks
- To learn how to enter a discount on a bill from a vendor

Instructor preparation

- Review this lesson, including the examples, to make sure you're familiar with the material.
- Ensure that all students have a copy of qblesson.qbb on their computer's hard disk.

To start this lesson

Before you perform the following steps, make sure you have installed the exercise file (qblesson.qbb) on your hard disk. See "Installing the exercise file" in the Introduction to this guide if you haven't installed it.

The following steps restore the exercise file to its original state so that the data in the file matches what you see on the screen as you proceed through each lesson.

To restore the exercise file (qblesson.qbb):

1. From the File menu in QuickBooks, choose Restore.

   QuickBooks displays the Restore Company Backup window.
2. In the "Get Company Backup From" section of the window, click Browse and select your c:\QBtrain directory.
3. Select the qblesson.qbb file, and then click Open.
4. In the "Restore Company Backup To" section of the window, click Browse and select your c:\QBtrain directory.
5. In the File name field of the Restore To window, type ***lesson 8*** and then click Save.
6. Click Restore.

Handling bills in QuickBooks

When you have a business expense, you can handle it in one of the following ways:

- You can write a check manually and enter the information into a QuickBooks check register later. This doesn't take advantage of features in QuickBooks, but sometimes it's necessary. For example, if you purchase supplies at a retail store, they expect payment on the spot, and you may not know the amount in advance.
- You can use QuickBooks to write and print a check. When you receive a bill that you want to pay immediately, you can write a QuickBooks check more quickly and accurately than you can by hand. An additional advantage is that QuickBooks makes the entry in the checking account register for you.
- You can use the QuickBooks accounts payable feature to track the amounts you owe to vendors, track your cash flow needs, and handle bills you want to pay later.
- You can pay by credit card and enter the credit card receipt into QuickBooks later.

Lesson 4, "Working with bank accounts," shows you how to enter a handwritten check and a QuickBooks check. In Lesson 5, "Using other accounts in QuickBooks," you learn about credit card accounts. This lesson shows you how to use QuickBooks for accounts payable.

Using QuickBooks for accounts payable

Some business owners, especially if they own smaller, home-based businesses, pay their bills when they receive them. Most business owners, however, find it more convenient to pay bills less often. (They also like keeping the cash in the company for as long as possible.) If you don't plan on paying your bills right away, QuickBooks can help you keep track of what you owe and when you owe it.

The money you owe for unpaid bills is called *accounts payable*. QuickBooks uses the Accounts Payable account to track all the money you owe. Like any QuickBooks balance sheet account, the Accounts Payable account has a register where you can view all your bills at once.

To see the Accounts Payable register:

1 From the Lists menu, choose Chart of Accounts.

QuickBooks displays the chart of accounts.

2 Double-click Accounts Payable in the list to open the register.

QuickBooks displays the Accounts Payable register.

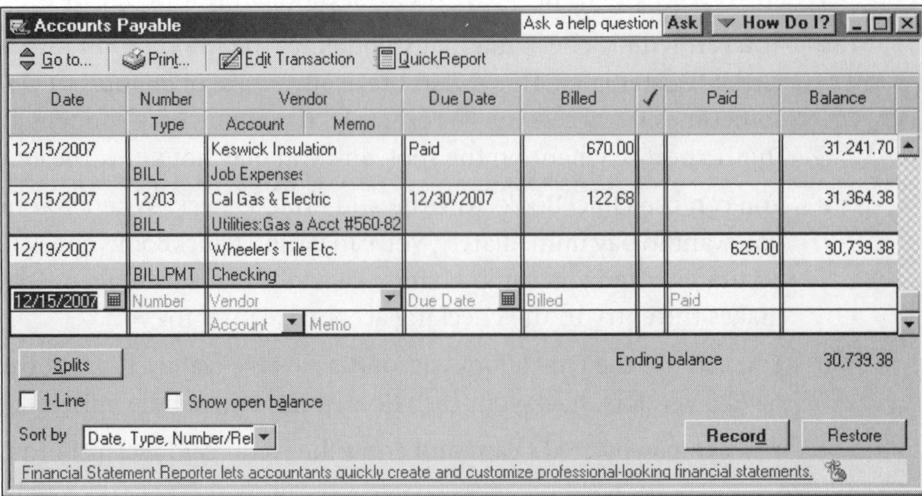

The register keeps track of each bill you have entered, shows you the due date, and keeps a running balance of all the bills you owe. As a business owner, this helps you forecast your cash flow, and the QuickBooks reminder system helps you pay your bills on time.

3 Press Esc twice to close the open windows.

Using accounts payable to pay your bills involves two steps: entering the bill and paying the bill. You'll practice both steps in this lesson.

Entering bills

When you receive a bill from a vendor, you should enter it into QuickBooks as soon as you can. This keeps your cash flow forecast reports up to date and doesn't give you the chance to set aside a bill and forget about it.

Rock Castle Construction received a bill from the company that created its new brochures. The bill includes a charge for courier delivery. Rock Castle Construction doesn't plan to pay the bill until close to its due date, but the company wants to keep an eye on the accounts payable total, so it enters the bill now.

To enter a bill:

1 From the Vendors menu, choose Enter Bills.

QuickBooks displays the Enter Bills window.

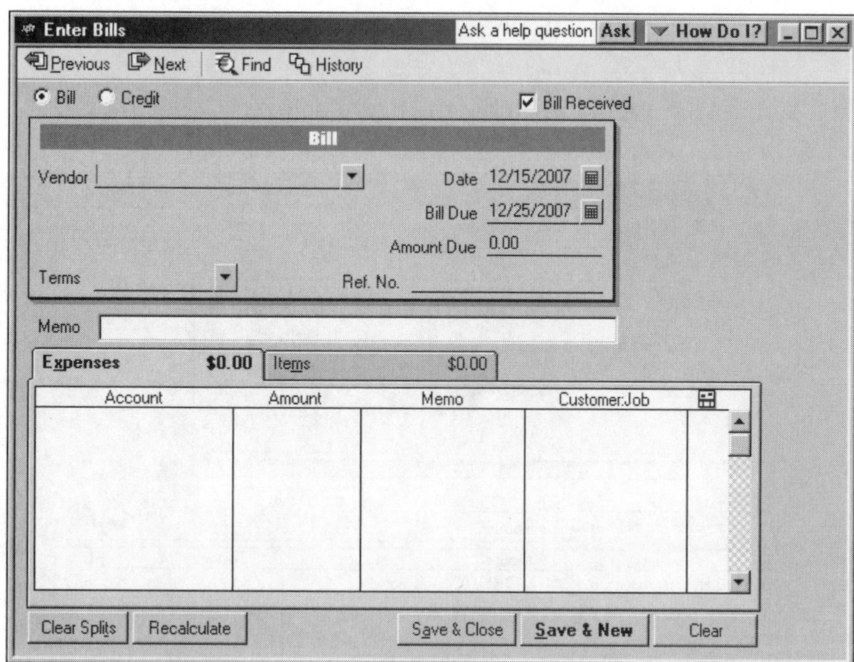

The top half of the window is where you enter the bill. The bottom half is the detail area where you can assign the bill amount to different expense accounts, customers, or jobs.

Notice that the Bill Received checkbox has a checkmark. The only time the Bill Received checkbox should be cleared is if you're using QuickBooks for inventory and you want to record items you've received that you haven't actually been billed for yet.

2 In the Vendor field, type ***Willis Advertising***, and then press Tab.

3 When QuickBooks displays a message telling you that Willis Advertising is not on the Vendor list, click Quick Add.

4 In the Amount Due field, type ***1500***.

5 Click in the Bill Due field.

Notice that QuickBooks supplies a date for you in the Bill Due field. The date displayed is ten days from the date in the Date field. You can change the date if you wish. If your Vendor list had payment terms entered for this vendor, QuickBooks would have used those terms to calculate the bill's due date.

6 Click in the Account column on the Expenses tab and type ***Printing***.

QuickFill completes the entry for you, and displays Printing and Reproduction as the account. QuickBooks lets you assign transactions to more than one account, so you can keep close track of where your company spends its money. Rock Castle Construction wants to assign the majority of this bill to a printing and reproduction expense account, and the rest to a freight delivery expense account.

7 Press Tab to accept Printing and Reproduction as the account.

8 Type ***1450*** to change the amount from 1,500 to 1,450.

9 Click in the Account column below Printing and Reproduction.

10 From the drop-down list, choose Freight & Delivery.

QuickBooks automatically assigns the remainder of the bill amount ($50.00) to Freight & Delivery.

Your screen should resemble the figure below.

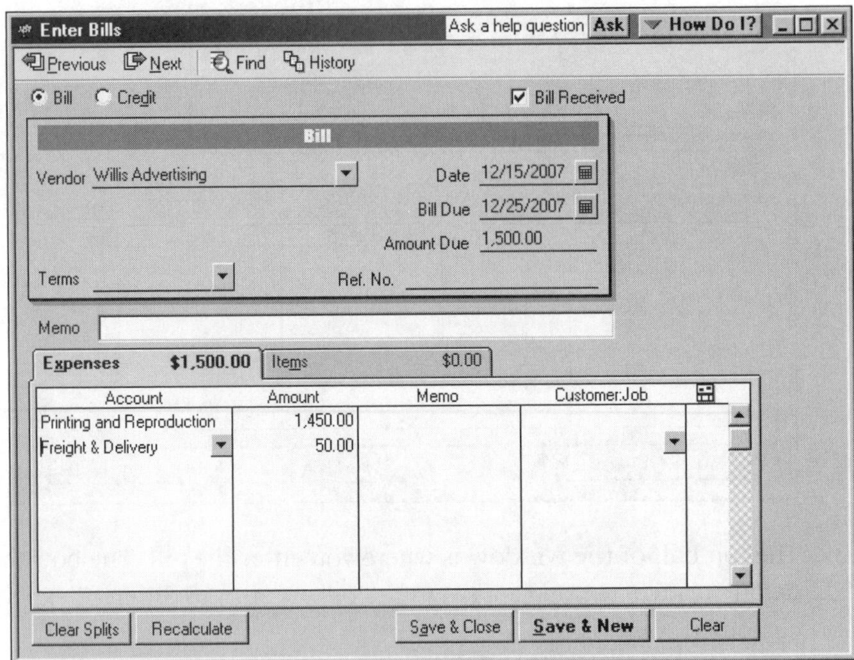

11 Click Save & Close to record the bill.

Tip: **You can enter bills and vendor credits directly in your accounts payable (A/P) register instead of using the Enter Bills window to create the transactions.** One benefit to using the register is speed: You can work more quickly in a register than you can if you fill out a separate bill for each transaction. And, since the register shows you all the transactions in the account to date (not just one transaction at a time), you have a better record of the entire account.

Paying bills

When you start QuickBooks or open a QuickBooks company file, a Reminders window appears that tells you whether you have transactions to complete, such as bills to pay or money to deposit.

Tip: **If you don't see the Reminders window when you start QuickBooks, you can turn it on by choosing Preferences from the Edit menu.** Click Reminders, click the My Preferences tab, and select "Show Reminders List when opening a Company file."

When QuickBooks tells you that you have bills due, you can display the Pay Bills window and select the bills you want to pay.

To pay a bill:

1 From the Vendors menu, choose Pay Bills.

QuickBooks displays the Pay Bills window.

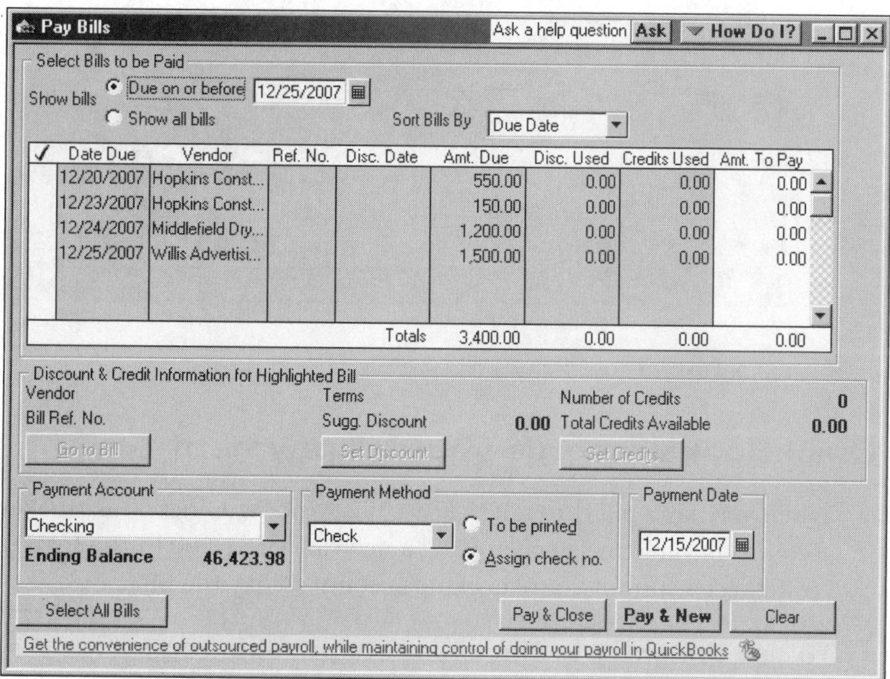

The Pay Bills window shows your unpaid bills as of any date you enter. You can pay by check, credit card, or with an online payment (if you are set up to make online payments).

For this exercise, you'll pay a bill using a QuickBooks check (rather than a handwritten one).

2 Select the "To be printed" option.

By selecting this option, you are telling QuickBooks that you will print this check later.

3 Select the Willis Advertising bill by clicking in the column to the left of the bill.

QuickBooks displays a checkmark next to the bill and changes the amount in the Ending Bank Balance to reflect a payment of $1,500.00. If you want to make a partial payment, you can enter the amount you want to pay in the Amt. To Pay column.

Your screen should resemble the figure below.

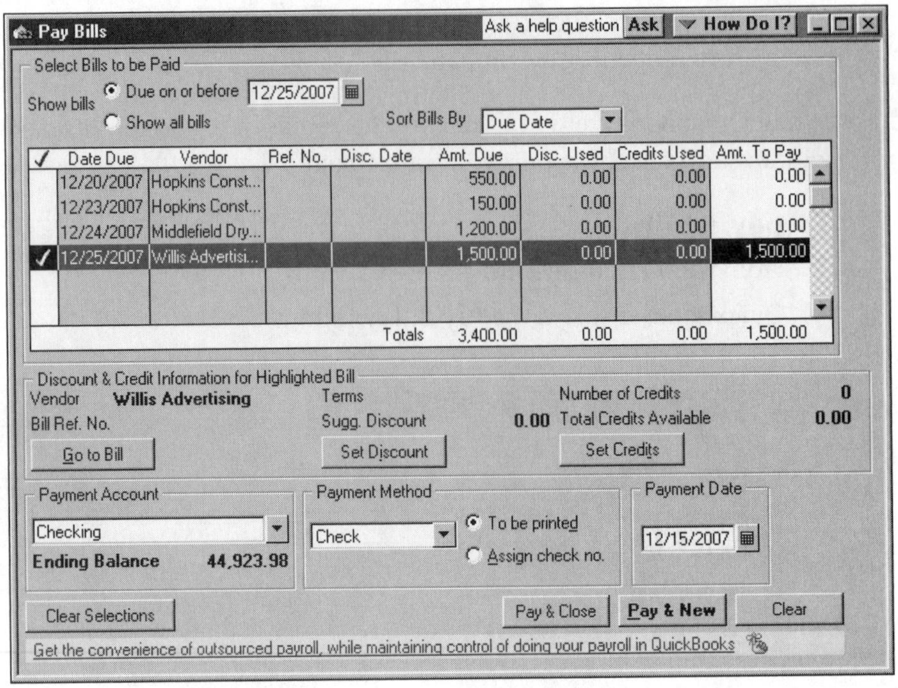

4 Click Pay & Close.

How QuickBooks records your bill payment

When you pay a bill through the Pay Bills window, QuickBooks makes an entry in the accounts payable register, showing a decrease of $1,500 in the total payables. It also creates a check from your checking account to pay the bill.

To see the entry in the accounts payable register:

1 From the Company menu, choose Chart of Accounts.

QuickBooks displays the chart of accounts.

2 In the chart of accounts, double-click the Accounts Payable account.

QuickBooks displays the accounts payable register.

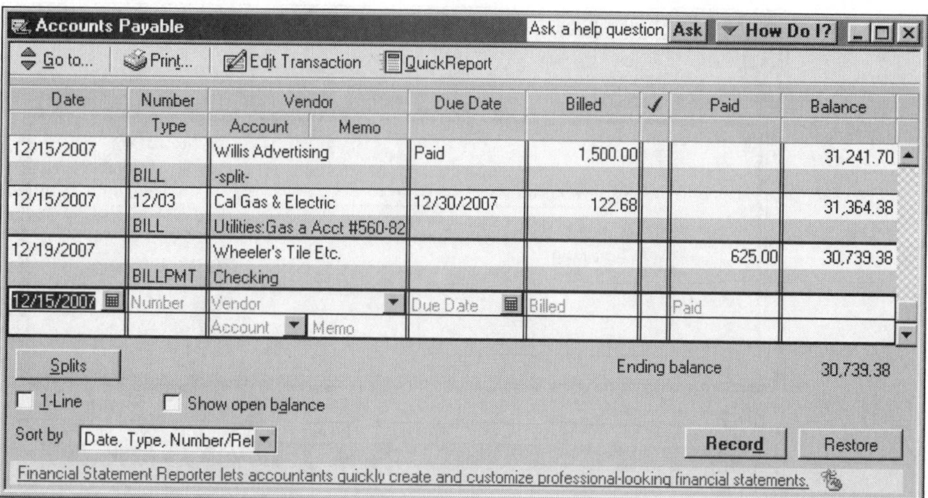

The register now shows the bill payment to Willis Advertising.

3 Close the accounts payable register.

At the same time QuickBooks recorded the entry in your accounts payable register, it made an entry in your Checking account.

To see the entry:

1 In the chart of accounts, double-click Checking.

QuickBooks displays the checking account register.

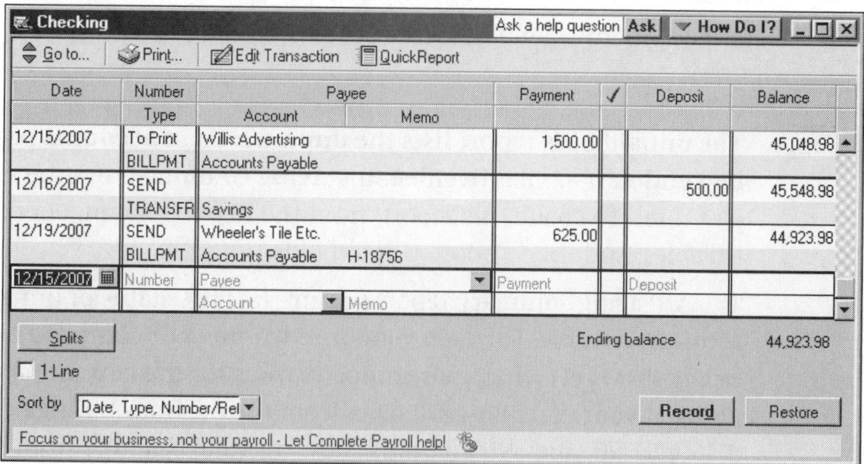

Notice that the third to the last entry in the register is the check for the payment to Willis Advertising.

2 Select the Willis Advertising transaction.

QuickBooks highlights the Willis transaction with a thick border to show that it is selected.

3 On the toolbar, click Edit Transaction.

QuickBooks displays the Bill Payments (Check) window.

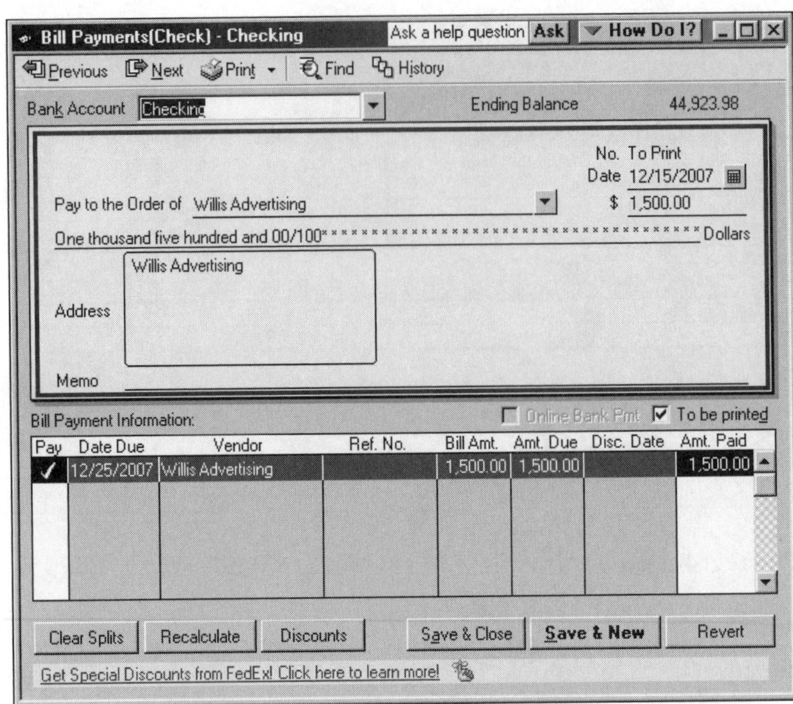

This check is called a "Bill Payment Check" and differs from the check form that you use to enter checks directly into the checking account. (That form shows expenses directly on the check voucher portion, while the bill payment form shows the bills paid by the check.)

4 Press Esc to close the Bill Payment Check window.

5 From the Window menu, choose Close All to close all the open QuickBooks windows.

Tip: **The unpaid bills report lists the unpaid bills in accounts payable, grouped by vendor.** If a bill is overdue, the Aging column shows the number of days past due. (To create this report, from the Reports menu, choose Vendors & Payables, and then choose Unpaid Bills.)

The A/P aging summary report summarizes the status of unpaid bills in accounts payable. For each vendor to whom your company owes money, the report shows (1) what your company owes for the current billing period, and (2) what your company still owes from the previous billing periods. The 1-30, 31-60, 61-90, and >90 columns show overdue balances from previous billing periods. For example, an amount in the 31-60 column is between 31 and 60 days overdue. (To create this report, choose Vendors & Payables from the Reports menu, and then choose A/P Aging Summary.)

Applying vendor discounts to bill payments

If you take advantage of discounts for early payment offered by some vendors, you can record the discounts directly in the Pay Bills window. You can set up QuickBooks to track the discount amounts.

In this section, you'll apply a discount for early payment to one of Rock Castle Construction's vendors.

To apply a discount for early payment:

1 From the Vendors menu, choose Pay Bills.

QuickBooks displays the Pay Bills window.

2 In the "Due on or before" field, type 1/16/2008 and press Tab.

QuickBooks displays all of Rock Castle Construction's bills due on or before 1/16/2008.

3 From the Sort Bills By drop-down list, choose Discount Date.

Your screen should look like this.

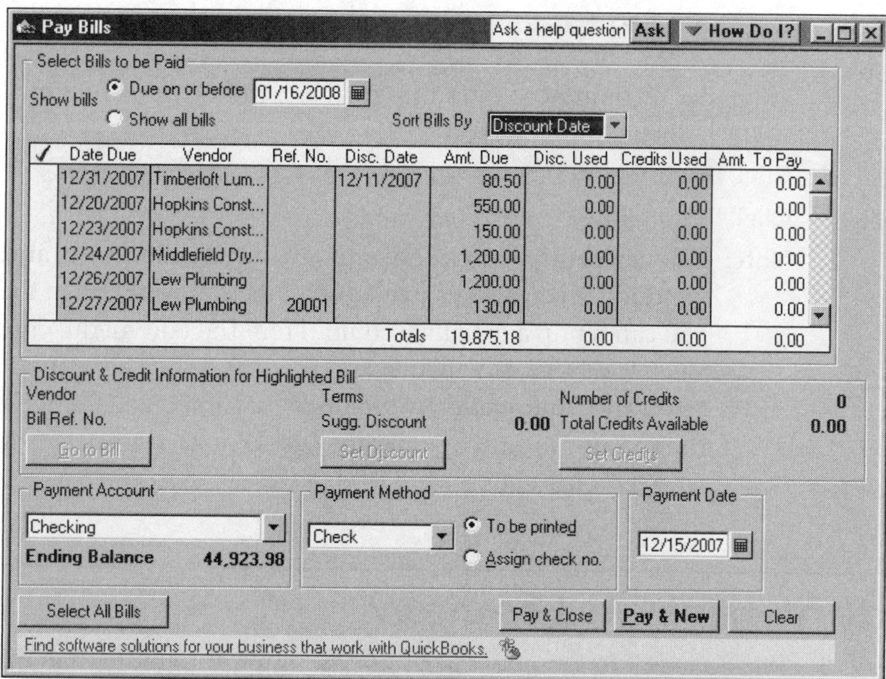

4 Click to put a checkmark next to the bill for Hamlin Metal with a due date of 1/10/2008.

QuickBooks displays the discount and credit information for Hamlin Metal.

5 Click Set Discount.

6 QuickBooks displays the Discount and Credits window prefilled with information about Rock Castle's terms with Hamlin Metal, and the amount of the discount based on those terms (in this case, two percent of $670.00, or $13.40).

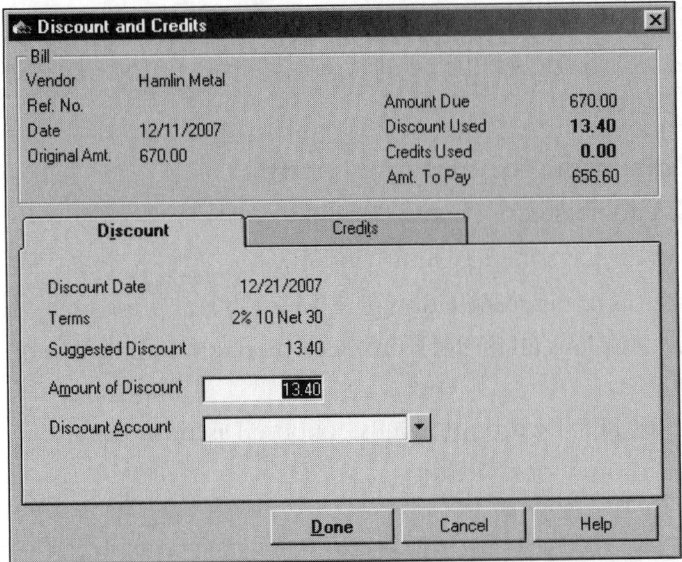

7 From the Discount Account drop-down list, choose Construction:Discounts given to track the discount amount.

8 Click Done.

9 Click Pay & Close.

Note: **You can set up QuickBooks to always use discounts and credits from vendors.** If you always track discounts from vendors in the same account, you can set up a default account. From the Edit menu, choose Preferences. Click Purchases & Vendors, and then click the Company Preferences tab. Select the "Automatically use discounts and credits" checkbox and choose the account in which you want QuickBooks to track the discounts you receive from vendors.

Student test and review

1 Write a check to a vendor, assigning the amount to more than one expense account.

2 Enter a bill in the Enter Bills window, and then view the bill transaction in the accounts payable register.

3 Pay the bill using the Pay Bills window.

LESSON 9 Analyzing financial data

Lesson objectives

- To discuss some of the tools QuickBooks gives you for analyzing financial data: QuickReports, preset reports, and graphs
- To create a QuickReport
- To add a column to a report
- To learn how to move a column in a report
- To learn about the types of preset reports QuickBooks offers
- To practice creating reports and viewing them onscreen
- To customize a report by changing how it looks and the data it covers (filtering)
- To learn how to process reports in batches
- To save reports as Portable Document Format (PDF) files
- To learn how to export a report to Microsoft Excel
- To practice filtering reports in Microsoft Excel
- To learn about the types of graphs QuickBooks offers
- To create and customize several graphs

Instructor preparation

- Review this lesson, including the examples, to make sure you're familiar with the material.
- Ensure that all students have a copy of qblesson.qbb on their computer's hard disk.

To start this lesson

Before you perform the following steps, make sure you have installed the exercise file (qblesson.qbb) on your hard disk. See "Installing the exercise file" in the Introduction to this guide if you haven't installed it.

The following steps restore the exercise file to its original state so that the data in the file matches what you see on the screen as you proceed through each lesson.

To restore the exercise file (qblesson.qbb):

1. From the File menu in QuickBooks, choose Restore.

   QuickBooks displays the Restore Company Backup window.
2. In the "Get Company Backup From" section of the window, click Browse and select your c:\QBtrain directory.
3. Select the qblesson.qbb file, and then click Open.

4 In the "Restore Company Backup To" section of the window, click Browse and select your c:\QBtrain directory.
5 In the File name field of the Restore To window, type ***lesson 9*** and then click Save.
6 Click Restore.

Reports and graphs help you understand your business

So far, you've been learning ways to track your data in QuickBooks. In this lesson, you'll work with two of the most valuable tools in QuickBooks: reports and graphs. Reports and graphs give you insight into your finances; they're two of the most important benefits of tracking your data in QuickBooks.

Often, people's perceptions of their business profitability don't match the facts. If you enter your data in QuickBooks, but don't take the time to analyze the data, your business decisions are based on incomplete knowledge. Reports let you summarize your financial data so you make decisions based on analysis of the numbers.

Reports give you the bottom line—you can see exactly how profitable your business is. If it's not doing as well as you'd hoped, you can create reports that show you which areas need improvement. QuickBooks has dozens of preset reports, but if you have specific reporting needs, you can customize any QuickBooks report to show exactly the data you want. And if you're interested in getting quick information, you can use a QuickReport that lets you summarize information from your lists, forms, or registers with one click of a button.

Some people find it easier to see a visual picture of their financial data. If you're interested in learning more about trends or patterns in your business data (for example, what proportion of your income comes from consulting services as compared to product sales), QuickBooks offers six types of QuickInsight graphs.

Creating QuickReports

One of the fastest ways to see a report on your QuickBooks data is to create a QuickReport. QuickReports are predesigned reports that give you information about the items you're currently viewing on screen. Whenever you have a list, a register, or a form displayed, you can click a button to have QuickBooks create a QuickReport.

When to use a QuickReport

Suppose you're viewing the Vendor list, and you want to see a history of all transactions for a certain vendor. Select the vendor's name, click the Report menu button, and then select QuickReport. You'll see a report listing information about each bill for that vendor.

Suppose that Rock Castle Construction wants to see what it owes to Patton Hardware.

To see what you owe a vendor:

1 From the Lists menu, choose Vendor List.

QuickBooks displays the Vendor list.

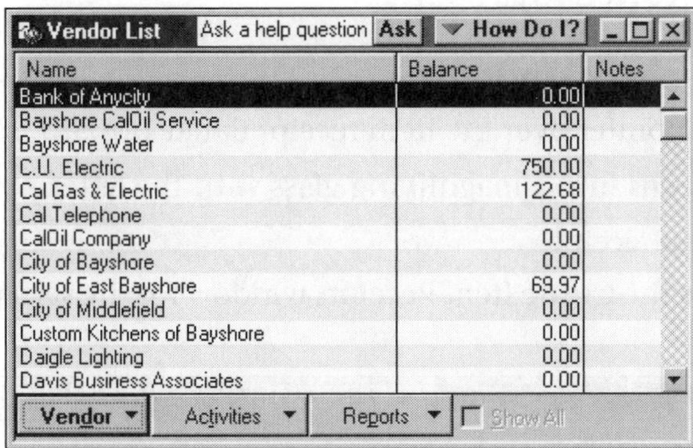

2 Select Patton Hardware Supplies.

3 Click the Reports menu button, and then select QuickReport:Patton Hardware Supplies.

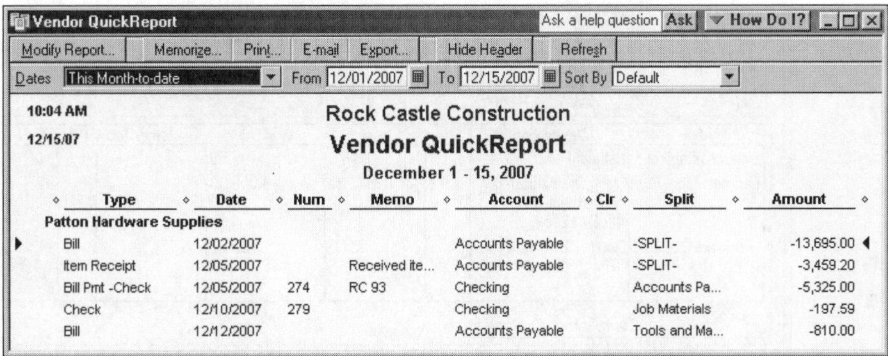

A vendor QuickReport shows all transactions for this month to date for the selected vendor, Patton Hardware Supplies. The transactions shown can include purchase orders, item receipts, bills, bill payments, and credits received from the vendor.

Note: If you want to see only unpaid bills and unapplied credits for the selected vendor, select Open Balance from the Reports menu button on the Vendor list.

Zooming in on a QuickReport

All QuickReports contain a summary of individual transactions. To help you better understand the information presented in reports, QuickBooks lets you trace report data to the individual transaction level using QuickZoom.

When you position the mouse pointer over a number in a report and you see the QuickZoom symbol (a magnifying glass with a Z in it), you can double-click the number to display the original transaction in QuickBooks.

Suppose you want more detail about the item receipt shown in the report. (You use an item receipt in QuickBooks when you want to record that you've received inventory items, but you haven't yet received a bill.)

To see more detail about an item:

1 Position the mouse pointer over the item receipt dated 12/05/07.

The arrow pointer turns into a magnifying glass with the letter Z (z for zoom).

2 Double-click the item receipt.

QuickBooks displays the Create Item Receipts window for the selected transaction.

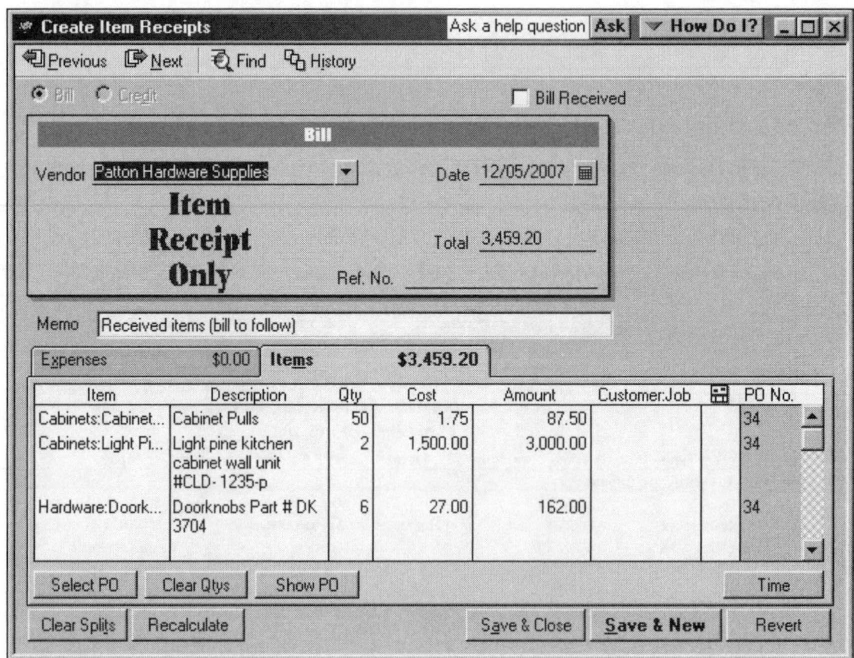

3 Click Save & Close to close the window.

QuickBooks returns you to the QuickReport.

Customizing QuickReports

Each QuickReport window has a buttonbar at the top of the report for customizing report content and layout.

In this exercise, you'll customize the QuickReport you just created to display transaction numbers in the report.

To add a column to a report:

1 In the QuickReport window, click Modify Report.

QuickBooks displays the Modify Report window.

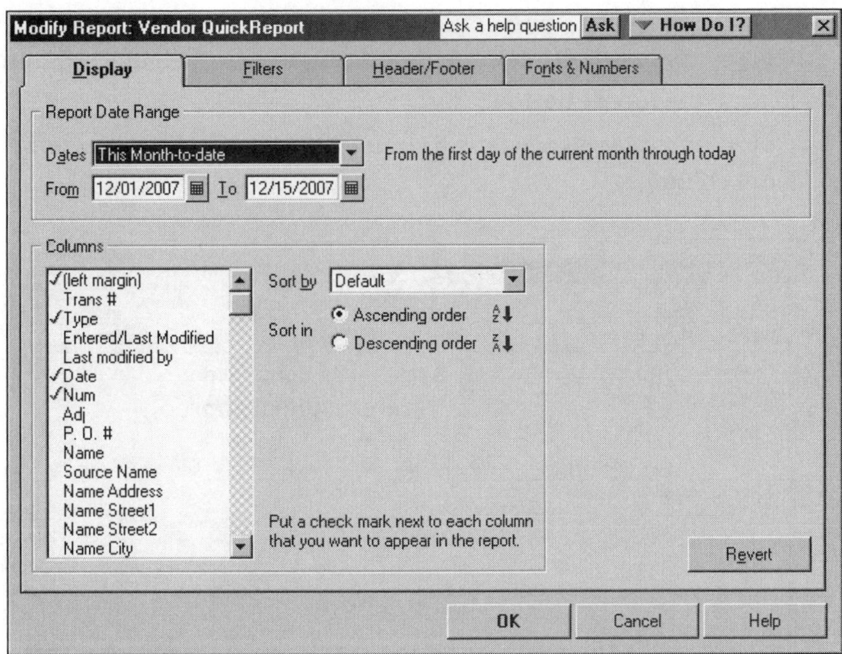

Use the Display tab of the Modify Report window to select the columns to include in the report and the date range of the report.

2 In the Columns list, select Trans #.

QuickBooks displays a checkmark next to Trans # to indicate that it's selected.

3 Click OK to accept the changes.

QuickBooks displays the customized vendor QuickReport.

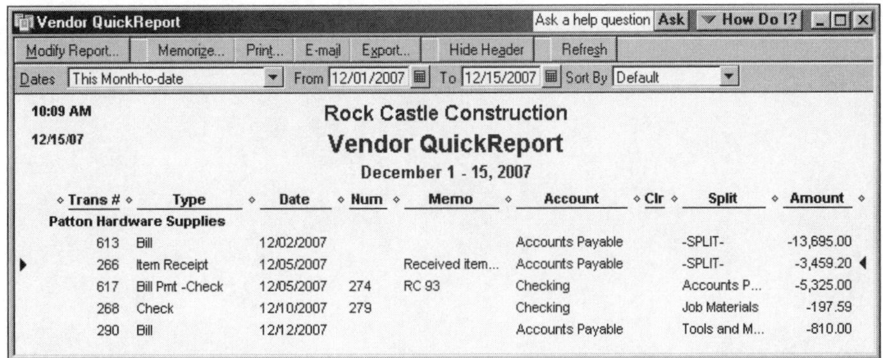

Notice that the item receipt from Patton Hardware Supplies is now listed as Transaction #266.

Next, you'll move the Trans # column to a new position in the report.

To move a report column:

1. Position your mouse pointer over the Trans # column that you added to the QuickReport.

   The mouse pointer changes shape to look like a hand.

2. Hold down the left mouse button and drag the Trans # column to the right until you see an arrow between the Date Column and the Num column.
3. Release the mouse button.

   QuickBooks places the Trans # column between the Date column and the Num column.

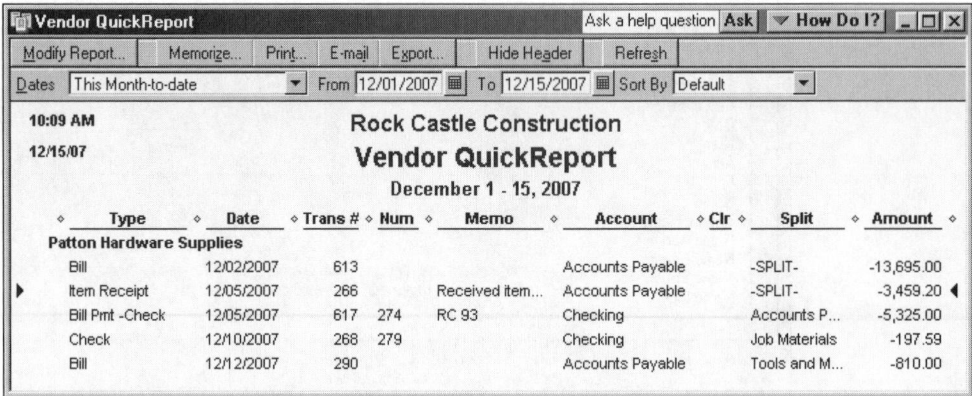

Next, you'll use the QuickReport buttonbar to customize the report header.

To change information in the report heading:

1. In the QuickReport window, click Modify Report, and then click the Header/Footer tab.

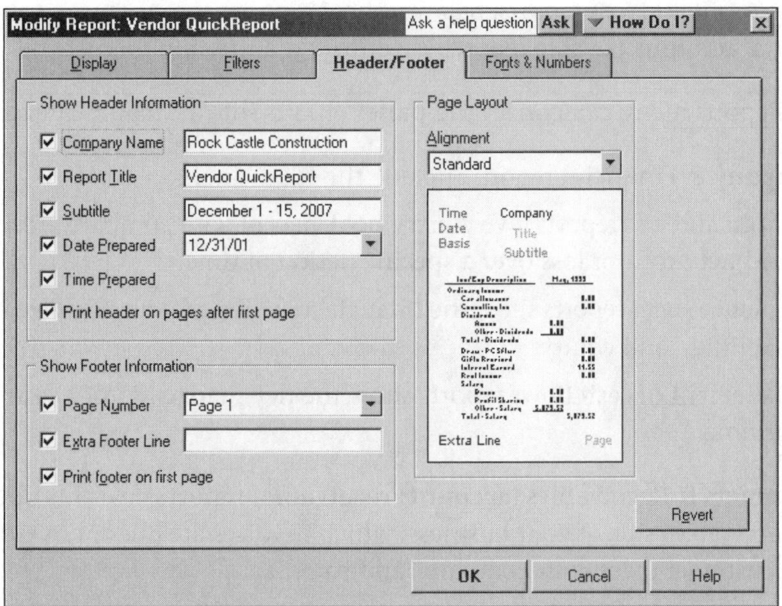

On the Header/Footer tab, you can change the company name, report title, subtitle, and date and time prepared. You can also specify whether to print the header on all pages or on just the first page. The Header/Footer tab is the same for all QuickBooks reports.

Use this window to change the report title from Vendor QuickReport to Vendor History Report.

2. In the Report Title field, select the text for "Vendor QuickReport," and type ***Vendor History Report*** to replace the title.
3. Click OK to close the Modify Report window.

   QuickBooks changes the title of the report and displays the new report.

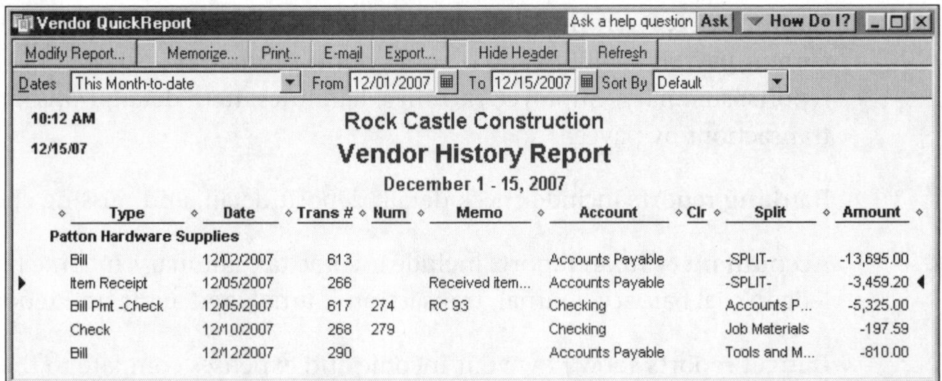

10:12 AM

12/15/07

Rock Castle Construction

Vendor History Report

December 1 - 15, 2007

Type	Date	Trans #	Num	Memo	Account	Clr	Split	Amount
Patton Hardware Supplies								
Bill	12/02/2007	613			Accounts Payable		-SPLIT-	-13,695.00
Item Receipt	12/05/2007	266		Received item...	Accounts Payable		-SPLIT-	-3,459.20
Bill Pmt -Check	12/05/2007	617	274	RC 93	Checking		Accounts P...	-5,325.00
Check	12/10/2007	268	279		Checking		Job Materials	-197.59
Bill	12/12/2007	290			Accounts Payable		Tools and M...	-810.00

4. Close the QuickReport window.
5. Close the Vendor list.

Creating and customizing preset reports

In addition to QuickReports, QuickBooks has dozens of preset report formats. You can create profit and loss reports, balance sheet reports, accounts receivable reports, sales reports, accounts payable reports, inventory reports, and many other types of reports.

The Reports menu categorizes the preset reports into 12 major categories:

Company & Financial reports include the following:

- Profit and loss reports give you a global view of your company's income, expenses, and net profit or loss over a specific period of time.
- Balance sheet reports show the financial position of your business by listing assets, liabilities, and equity.
- Statement of cash flows reports show the net change in your cash during a period of time.

Customers & Receivables (accounts receivable) reports give you information about the receivables side of your business: which invoices are due (or overdue), how much each customer owes your company, and so on.

Sales reports give you information about what you have sold and to whom.

Jobs, Time & Mileage reports (QuickBooks: Pro and Premier only) give information about the status and profitability of the jobs/projects you track in QuickBooks.

Vendors & Payables (accounts payable) reports give you information about the payables side of your business, including which bills are due, your sales tax liability, and your current balance with each vendor.

Purchases reports give you information about your purchases.

Inventory reports give you information about status (such as the quantities you have on hand or on order) and the value of your inventory.

Employees & Payroll reports summarize the information you need to pay your current payroll liabilities and fill out your tax forms. QuickBooks has these payroll reports: summary, employee earnings, liabilities, item detail, transaction detail, and transactions by payee.

Banking reports include check detail, deposit detail, and missing check reports.

Accountant & Taxes reports include income tax summary, income tax detail, general ledger, trial balance, journal, transaction journal, and audit trail reports.

Budget reports show how your income and expenses compare to the budgets you've set up.

List reports let you report on any information stored in a QuickBooks list.

Creating a balance sheet comparison report

The balance sheet comparison report compares the current year against the previous year in both dollar amount and percentage.

To create a balance sheet comparison report for Rock Castle Construction:

1 From the Reports menu, choose Company & Financial. Then choose Balance Sheet Prev Year Comparison.

The report on your screen should resemble the following figure.

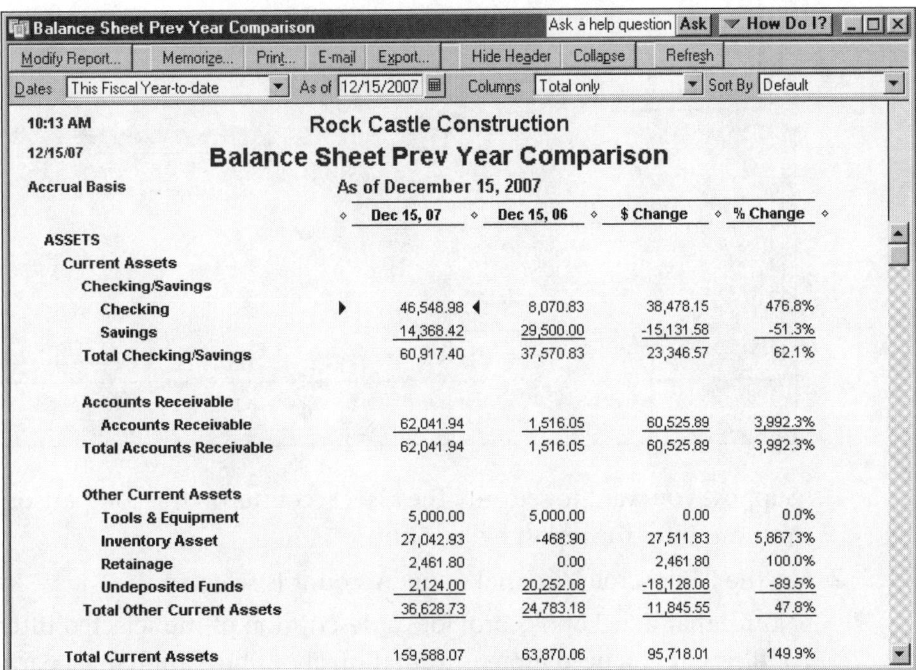

	Dec 15, 07	Dec 15, 06	$ Change	% Change
ASSETS				
Current Assets				
Checking/Savings				
Checking	46,548.98	8,070.83	38,478.15	476.8%
Savings	14,368.42	29,500.00	-15,131.58	-51.3%
Total Checking/Savings	60,917.40	37,570.83	23,346.57	62.1%
Accounts Receivable				
Accounts Receivable	62,041.94	1,516.05	60,525.89	3,992.3%
Total Accounts Receivable	62,041.94	1,516.05	60,525.89	3,992.3%
Other Current Assets				
Tools & Equipment	5,000.00	5,000.00	0.00	0.0%
Inventory Asset	27,042.93	-468.90	27,511.83	5,867.3%
Retainage	2,461.80	0.00	2,461.80	100.0%
Undeposited Funds	2,124.00	20,252.08	-18,128.08	-89.5%
Total Other Current Assets	36,628.73	24,783.18	11,845.55	47.8%
Total Current Assets	159,588.07	63,870.06	95,718.01	149.9%

2 Scroll the report window to see more of the report.

Notice that the buttonbar at the top of the report is the same buttonbar you saw in the QuickReport window.

3 Keep the report displayed on your screen. You'll use it in the next exercise.

Filtering reports

You can customize preset reports the same way you customize QuickReports. In this exercise you'll customize the balance sheet comparison report and *filter* it to include only the transactions you specify.

Report filters let you set custom criteria for the transactions you want included in a report. When you filter a report, QuickBooks includes only those transactions that match the rules you create.

To filter a preset report:

1 With the balance sheet comparison report displayed, click Modify Report on the report buttonbar, and then click the Filters tab.

QuickBooks displays the Filters tab of the Modify Report window.

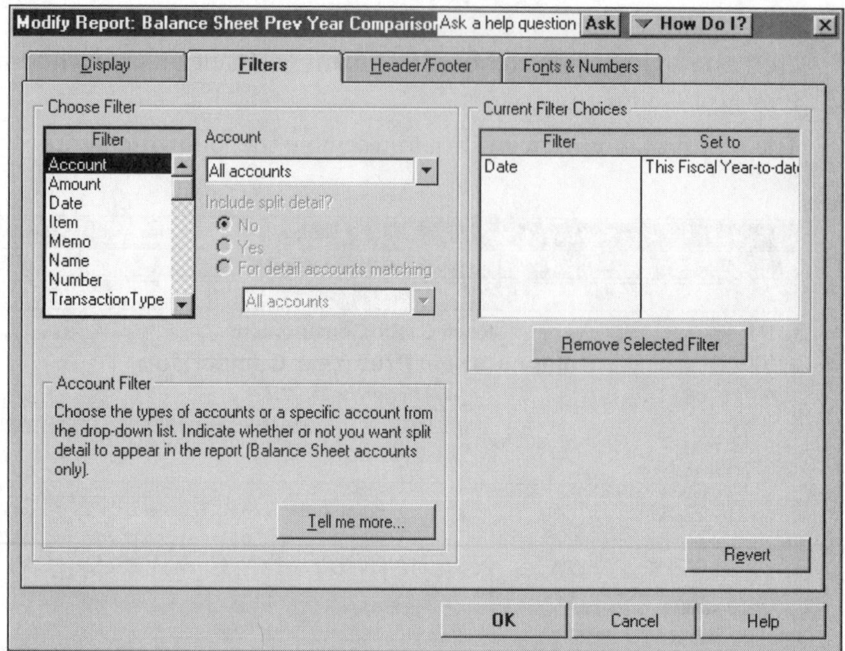

Suppose you want to see only the asset accounts on the comparison balance sheet. You can filter the report by account.

2 In the Filter scroll box, make sure Account is selected.

Notice that QuickBooks provides a description of the selected filter below the list of filters. If you need more information about how applying a particular filter will affect the report, click Tell me more.

3 In the Account field, choose All assets from the drop-down list.

4 Click OK.

QuickBooks displays the customized balance sheet comparison report.

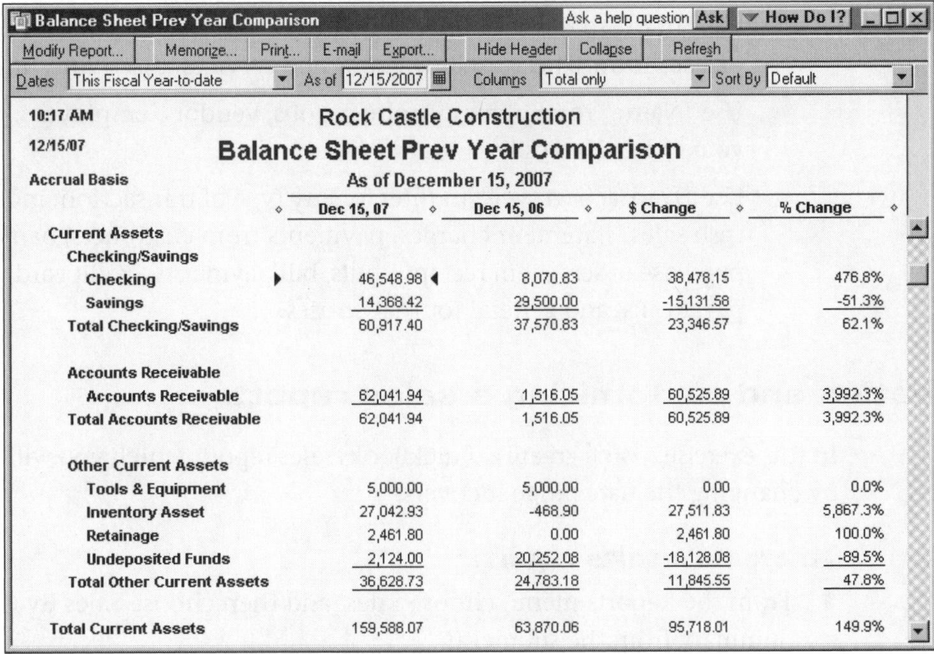

If you scroll to the bottom of the report, you'll see that QuickBooks removed the liability and other accounts from the report.

To keep a record of the information in the report as it exists today, you can save the report in Portable Document Format (PDF).

To save a report as a PDF file:

1 With the report open, choose Save as PDF from the File menu.
2 Navigate to the folder in which you want to store the file, and enter a filename.
3 Click Save.
4 Close the report window.
5 Click No when QuickBooks asks if you want to add this report to the Memorized Report list.

Tip: **Some filters represent more than one thing.** This may be a little confusing if you've never used report filters in QuickBooks before. Here are some tips on what to filter for:

Use "Item" to filter for any kind of line item that appears on a purchase order or sales form. These include goods and services, discounts, and sales tax.

Use "Name" to filter for customers, jobs, vendors, employees, or any name on your Other Names list.

Use "Transaction type" to filter for any type of transaction, including invoices, cash sales, statement charges, payments from customers, bank deposits, purchase orders, item receipts, bills, bill payments, credit card charges, checks, paychecks, and general journal entries.

Creating and customizing a sales report

In this exercise, you'll create a QuickBooks sales report, which you will then customize by changing the date range it covers.

To create a sales report:

1 From the Reports menu, choose Sales, and then choose Sales By Customer Summary from the submenu.

QuickBooks displays the sales by customer summary report.

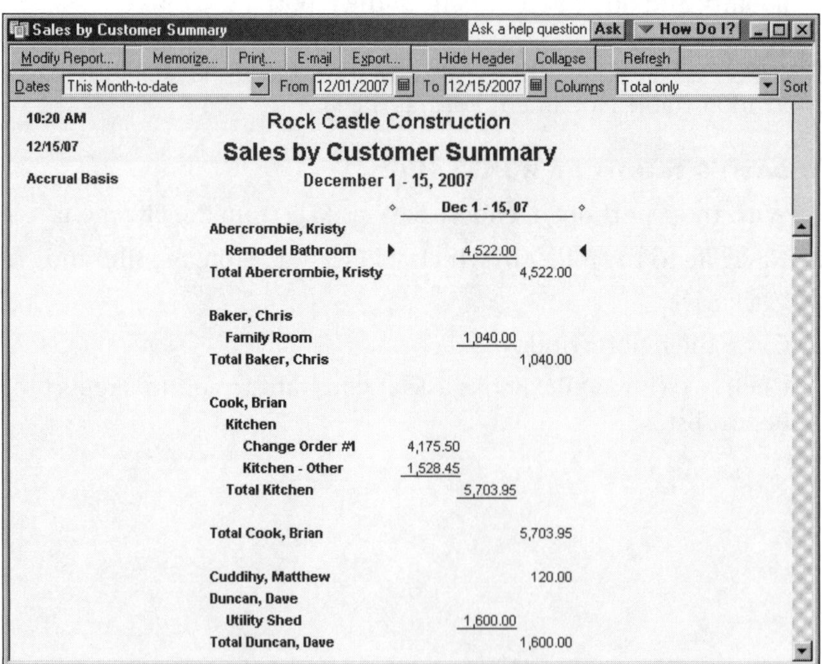

The Dates field in the report buttonbar shows that the report covers "This Month-to-date." Customize the report so you can see sales figures from January 2007.

To customize a report:

1 In the Dates field, select All from the drop-down list.

QuickBooks updates the report and displays the new data.

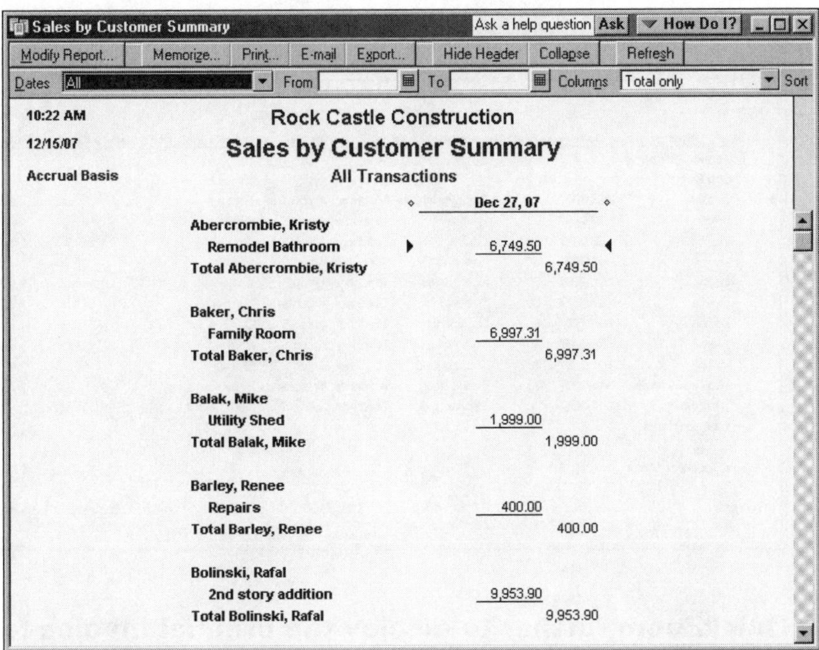

Using QuickZoom in a preset report

As with all QuickBooks reports, you can QuickZoom any item in the report to see more detail.

To QuickZoom on a report item:

1 Position the mouse pointer over the $11,105.00—the amount for Anton Teschner's sun room.

The arrow pointer turns into a magnifying glass with a Z in it.

2 Double-click $11,105.00.

QuickBooks displays a QuickZoom report showing sales by customer detail.

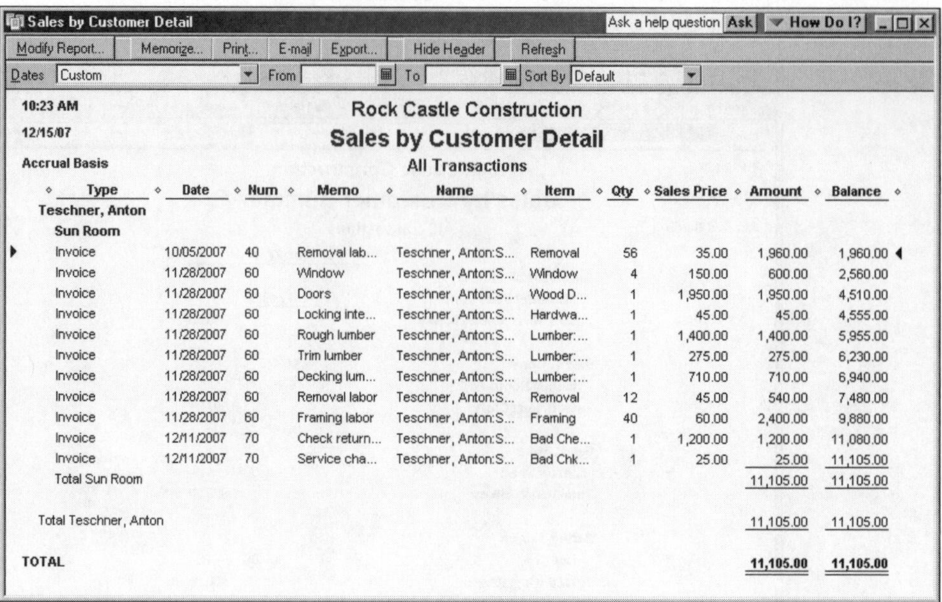

10:23 AM
12/15/07
Accrual Basis

Rock Castle Construction
Sales by Customer Detail
All Transactions

Type	Date	Num	Memo	Name	Item	Qty	Sales Price	Amount	Balance
Teschner, Anton									
Sun Room									
Invoice	10/05/2007	40	Removal lab...	Teschner, Anton:S...	Removal	56	35.00	1,960.00	1,960.00
Invoice	11/28/2007	60	Window	Teschner, Anton:S...	Window	4	150.00	600.00	2,560.00
Invoice	11/28/2007	60	Doors	Teschner, Anton:S...	Wood D...	1	1,950.00	1,950.00	4,510.00
Invoice	11/28/2007	60	Locking inte...	Teschner, Anton:S...	Hardwa...	1	45.00	45.00	4,555.00
Invoice	11/28/2007	60	Rough lumber	Teschner, Anton:S...	Lumber:...	1	1,400.00	1,400.00	5,955.00
Invoice	11/28/2007	60	Trim lumber	Teschner, Anton:S...	Lumber:...	1	275.00	275.00	6,230.00
Invoice	11/28/2007	60	Decking lum...	Teschner, Anton:S...	Lumber:...	1	710.00	710.00	6,940.00
Invoice	11/28/2007	60	Removal labor	Teschner, Anton:S...	Removal	12	45.00	540.00	7,480.00
Invoice	11/28/2007	60	Framing labor	Teschner, Anton:S...	Framing	40	60.00	2,400.00	9,880.00
Invoice	12/11/2007	70	Check return...	Teschner, Anton:S...	Bad Che...	1	1,200.00	1,200.00	11,080.00
Invoice	12/11/2007	70	Service cha...	Teschner, Anton:S...	Bad Chk...	1	25.00	25.00	11,105.00
Total Sun Room								11,105.00	11,105.00
Total Teschner, Anton								11,105.00	11,105.00
TOTAL								11,105.00	11,105.00

To QuickZoom further to display the original invoice for a transaction:

1 Position the mouse pointer over the first item on the report (invoice #40 dated 10/05/2007 for Removal labor).

2 Double-click anywhere in the first line.

QuickBooks displays Invoice #40 for Anton Teschner's sun room.

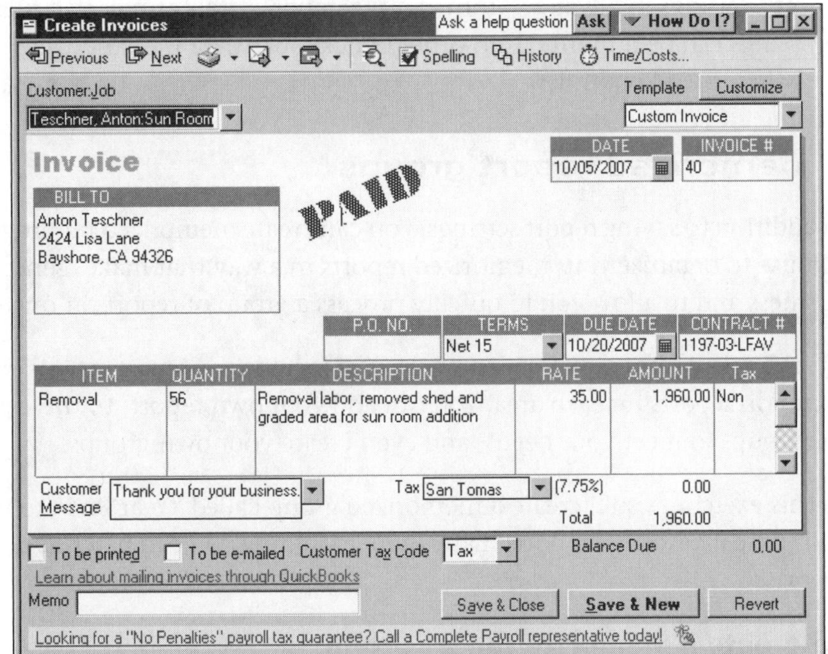

Notice that QuickBooks puts a paid stamp on invoices for which payment has been received in full.

3 From the Window menu, choose Close All.

4 Click No when QuickBooks asks if you want to memorize the report.

What you see when you QuickZoom in a report depends on the type of report displayed:

- If the report shows summary figures (like the sales by customer summary report we just displayed) and you QuickZoom an amount, QuickBooks displays a transaction report that includes the transactions which contribute to that amount.
- If the report shows transactions and you QuickZoom a transaction, QuickBooks displays the invoice, bill, or other form for the requested transaction.

Tip: **You can widen or narrow columns on any type of QuickBooks report.** To make a column wider, drag the small diamond at the right of the column header toward the right. To make a column narrower, drag the small diamond at the right of the column header toward the left.

Saving report settings

After you have customized a report to provide the information you need, you can have QuickBooks *memorize* the settings so you can quickly produce the same report in the future. (QuickBooks memorizes a report's settings, not the actual data.)

If you use one of the QuickBooks Premier products, you can export the settings for memorized reports as report templates. A report template lets you specify all of a report's settings in advance—for example, report date, format, and filters. Report templates can be imported into other QuickBooks data files and then accessed from the Memorized Report list.

Creating memorized report groups

In addition to saving report settings, you can create memorized report groups that you can use to organize your memorized reports in a way that makes sense for your business and to allow you to quickly process a group of reports at once.

QuickBooks comes preset with a number of memorized report groups each containing common reports for each area. You can add your own reports to these groups, modify the groups to meet your needs, and even create your own groups.

In this exercise, you'll create a memorized group called "Year End" to which you will add some memorized reports. Later, you learn how you can batch process memorized reports.

To create a memorize report group:

1 Choose Memorized Reports from the Reports menu, and then choose Memorized Report List.

QuickBooks opens the Memorized Report list.

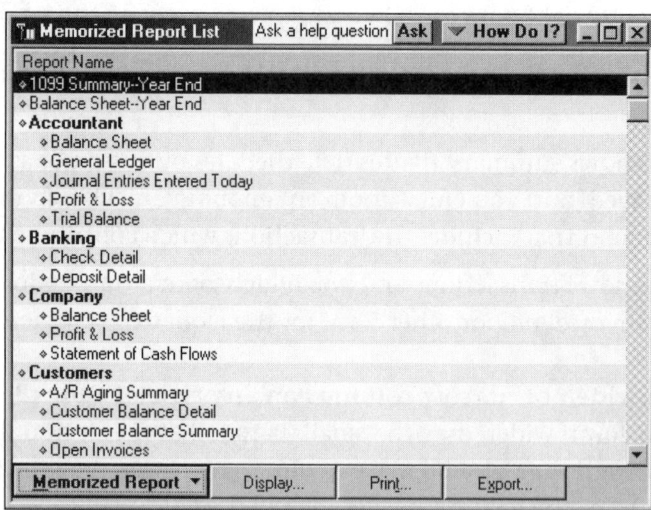

2 In the Memorized Report list, click the Memorized Report menu button, and choose New Group.

3 In the Name field of the New Memorized Report Group window, type ***Year End.***

Your window should look like this.

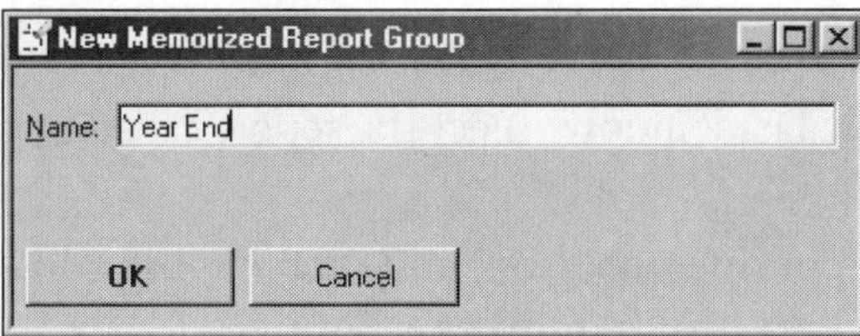

4 Click OK.

QuickBooks adds the new group to the Memorized Report list.

Memorizing preset reports

Now, you'll memorize a report and it to the memorized report group you just created.

To memorize a report:

1 From the Reports menu, choose Accountant & Taxes, and then choose Income Tax Summary.

2 On the report buttonbar, click Memorize.

QuickBooks displays the Memorize Report window.

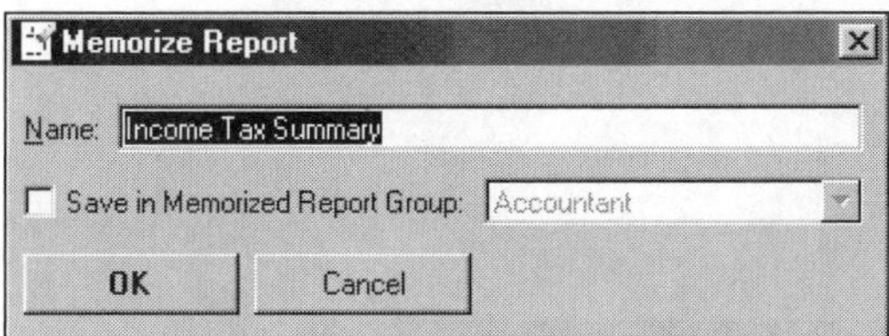

3 Leave the name of the report as is.

4 Click the "Save in Memorized Report Group" checkbox to select it, and then choose Year End from the drop-down list.

Your window should look like this.

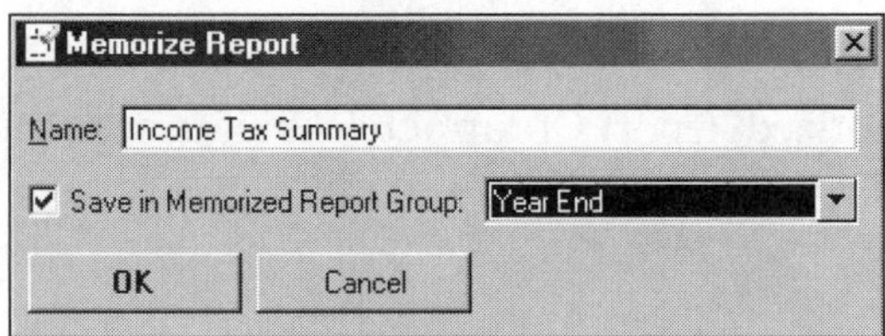

5 Click OK to memorize the report and add it to the Year End memorized report group.

6 Close the income tax summary report.

Adding reports to memorized report groups

Now, you'll add two previously memorized reports to the Year End group.

To add memorized reports to a memorized report group:

1 In the Memorized Report List window, select the report called "1099 Summary--Year End."

2 Click the Memorized Report menu button, and then choose Edit.

QuickBooks opens the Edit Memorized Report window.

3 Leave the report name as is.

4 Click the "Save in Memorized Report Group" checkbox to select it, and then choose Year End from the drop-down list.

5 Click OK.

QuickBooks moves the 1099 Summary report to the Year End memorized report group.

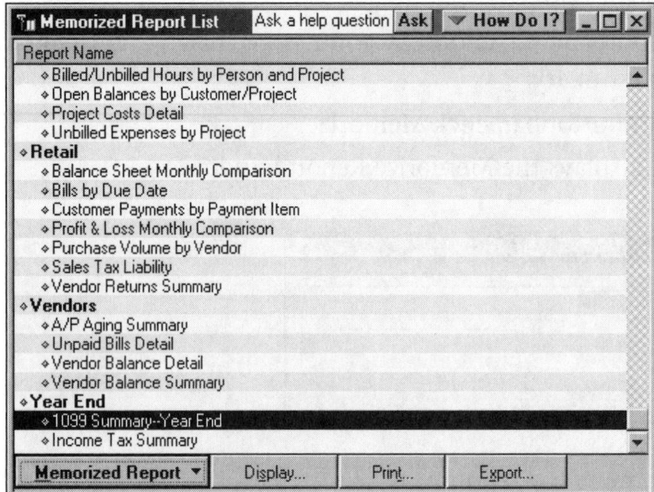

6 In the Memorized Report List window, select the report called "Balance Sheet--Year End."

7 Click the Memorized Report menu button, and then choose Edit.

8 Leave the report name as is.

9 Click the "Save in Memorized Report Group" checkbox to select it, and then choose Year End from the drop-down list.

10 Click OK.

Once a report is memorized, you can easily display it from the QuickBooks Memorized Report list.

To display a memorized report:

1 In the Memorized Report list, select "Balance Sheet--Year End."

2 Click Display.

QuickBooks displays the report.

3 Leave the report open.

Printing reports

Any time you have a report displayed in the report window, you can print it by clicking the Print button in the report buttonbar.

To print a report:

1 With the balance sheet summary report displayed, click Print.

QuickBooks displays the Print Reports window.

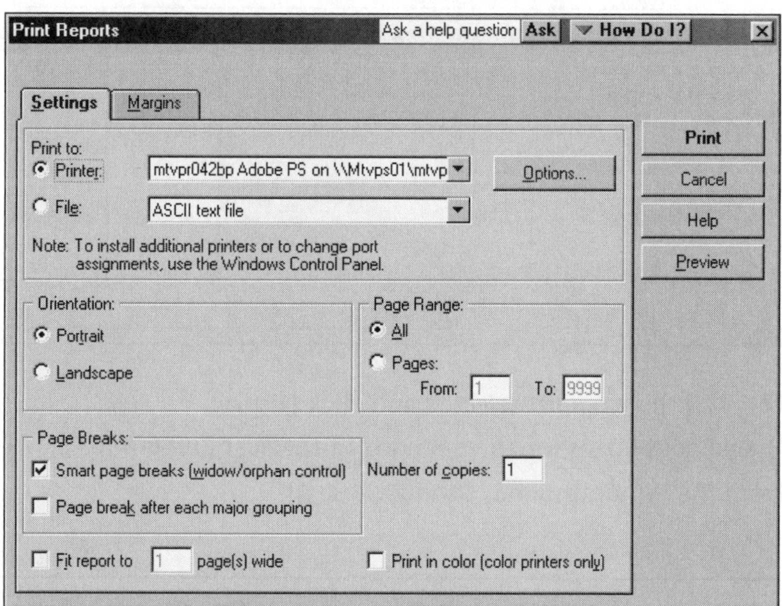

In the Print Reports window you can select the print orientation and tell QuickBooks where you would like the pages to break in multi-page reports.

2 Click Preview to see how the report will look when you print it.

QuickBooks displays a preview of your report onscreen.

3 Click Close to close the Print Preview window.

4 Close the Print Reports window, and then close the report.

Processing reports in groups

Organizing your memorized reports in groups makes it fast and easy to process several reports at once. Now, you'll process the reports you added to the Year End report group you created in the previous exercise.

To batch process reports:

1. In the Memorized Report list, select Year End.
2. Click Display.

   QuickBooks opens the Process Multiple Reports window. You can use this window to display or print the selected reports. You can also change the date range for reports in this window before you display or print them by clicking in the From or To columns.

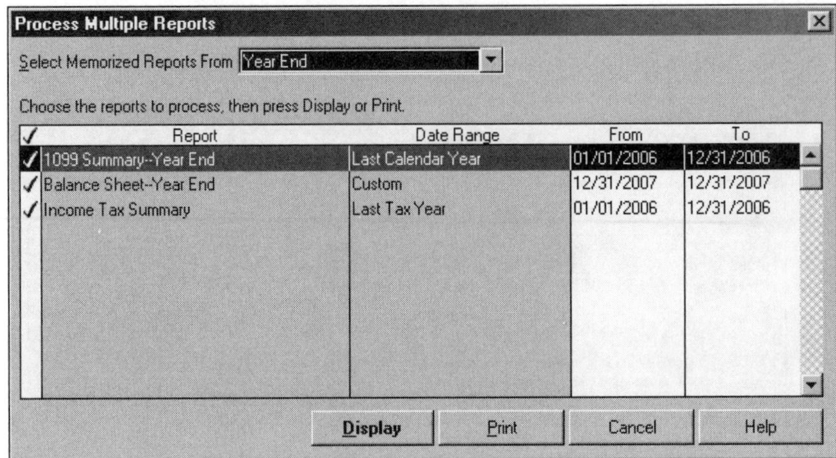

3. Leave all three reports selected and click Display.

   QuickBooks opens the three reports in the Year End group.
4. From the Window menu, choose Close All.

Exporting reports to Microsoft Excel

Occasionally, you may want to change a report's appearance or contents in ways that aren't available in QuickBooks, filter report data in ways that you can't in QuickBooks, or run "what-if" scenarios on your QuickBooks data.

You can send QuickBooks: Pro or QuickBooks: Premier reports to Microsoft Excel. Since the changes you make in Excel don't affect your QuickBooks data, you're free to customize reports as needed, and even change data to run what-if scenarios.

Note: **To proceed with this exercise, you need Pro or Premier and Microsoft Excel 97, 2000, 2002, or 2003.** If you don't have Excel, proceed to "Creating QuickInsight graphs" on page 202.

Sending a report to Microsoft Excel

When exporting a report to Microsoft Excel, you indicate whether or not you want to preserve the formatting from your QuickBooks report. You also have the option of turning on or off several Excel features from within QuickBooks.

By default, QuickBooks preserves the look of your report when exporting to Microsoft Excel, and turns on the following Excel features:

- **AutoFit** sets column widths in Excel wide enough to display your data without cutting off words or numbers.
- **Freeze panes** allows you to scroll through data while keeping the row and column headers in view.
- **Show Gridlines** turns on gridlines in Excel.

In this exercise, you learn how to select which QuickBooks report formatting options you want to preserve in Excel, and how to turn on and off certain Excel features from within QuickBooks.

To send a report to Microsoft Excel:

1 From the Reports menu, choose Company & Financial, and then choose Balance Sheet Standard.

2 On the Report buttonbar, click Modify Report.

QuickBooks displays the Modify report window.

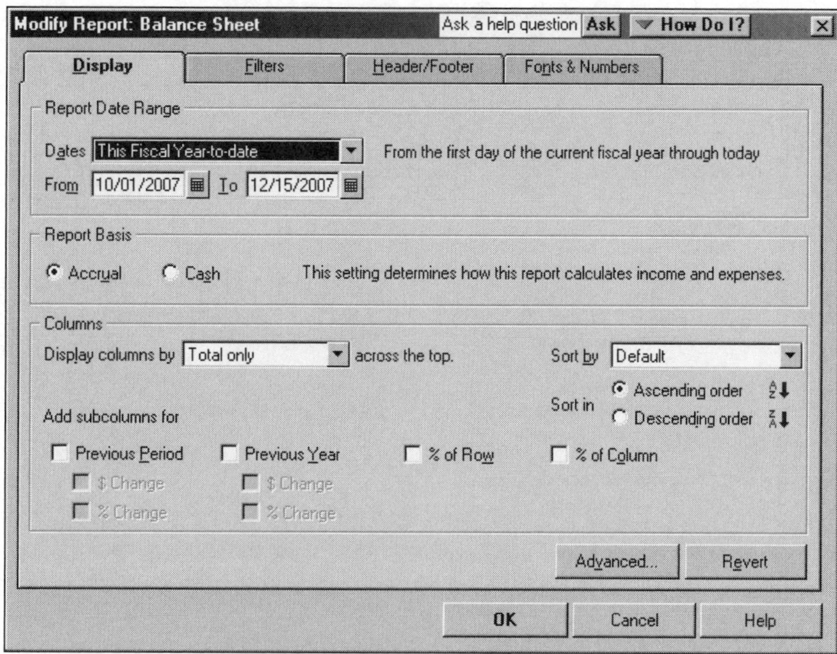

3 In the "Add subcolumns for" area, click the Previous Period checkbox, and then click the $ Change and % Change checkboxes.

Your screen should resemble the following.

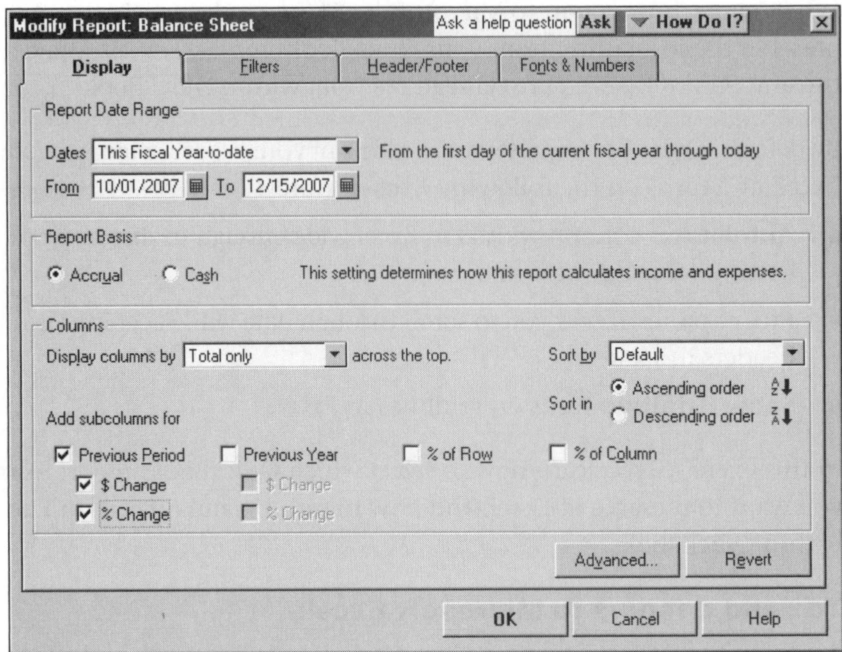

4 Click OK.

Your balance sheet should now look like this.

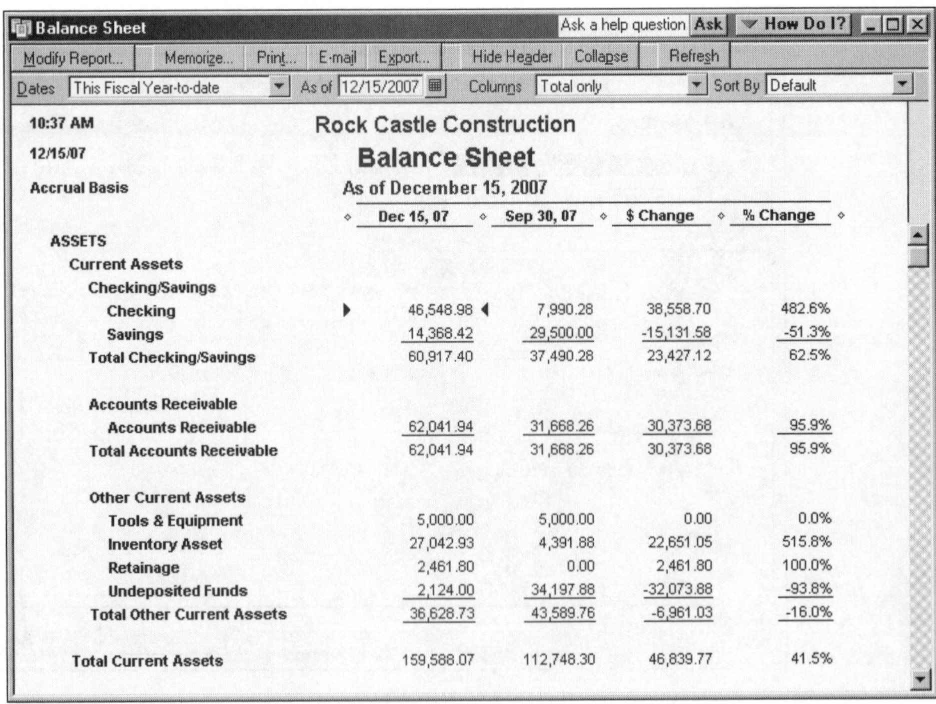

	Dec 15, 07	Sep 30, 07	$ Change	% Change
ASSETS				
Current Assets				
Checking/Savings				
Checking	46,548.98	7,990.28	38,558.70	482.6%
Savings	14,368.42	29,500.00	-15,131.58	-51.3%
Total Checking/Savings	60,917.40	37,490.28	23,427.12	62.5%
Accounts Receivable				
Accounts Receivable	62,041.94	31,668.26	30,373.68	95.9%
Total Accounts Receivable	62,041.94	31,668.26	30,373.68	95.9%
Other Current Assets				
Tools & Equipment	5,000.00	5,000.00	0.00	0.0%
Inventory Asset	27,042.93	4,391.88	22,651.05	515.8%
Retainage	2,461.80	0.00	2,461.80	100.0%
Undeposited Funds	2,124.00	34,197.88	-32,073.88	-93.8%
Total Other Current Assets	36,628.73	43,589.76	-6,961.03	-16.0%
Total Current Assets	159,588.07	112,748.30	46,839.77	41.5%

5 On the Report buttonbar, click Export.

QuickBooks displays the Export Report window.

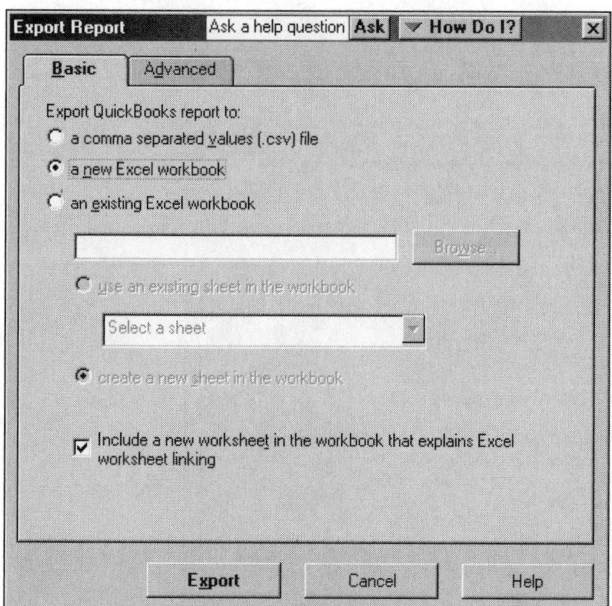

6 On the Basic tab, make sure that "a new Excel workbook" is selected.

If desired, you can also send the report to a new sheet in an existing Excel workbook, or to a comma separated value (.csv) file.

7 Click the Advanced tab.

8 Under Formatting options, click the Colors checkbox to clear it.

The title font will remain blue in QuickBooks, but display in black in Excel.

9 Under Excel features, select the Auto Filtering checkbox.

Your screen should now resemble the following.

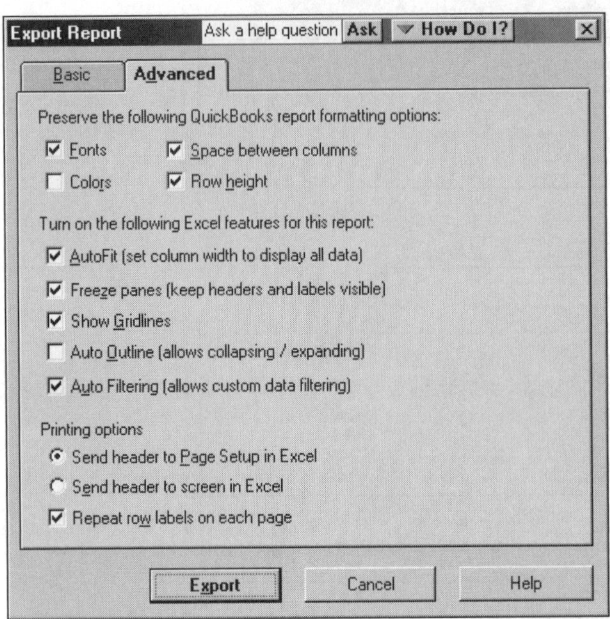

10 Click Export.

QuickBooks starts Excel (if it's not running already) and sends the report to a new spreadsheet.

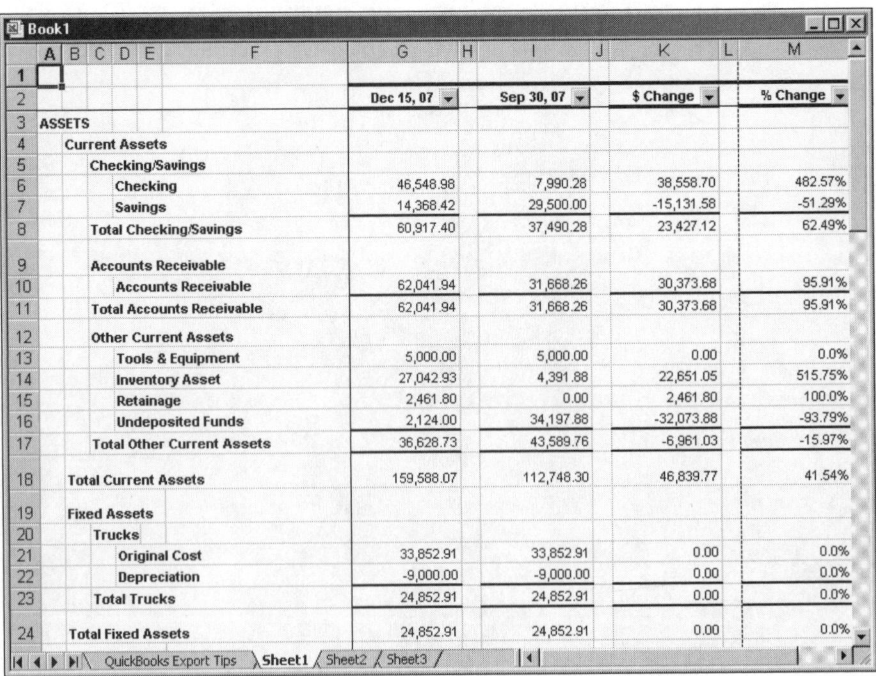

11 Leave the report open in Excel; you'll use it in the next exercise.

If you wanted to save the report, you would choose Save from the Excel File menu.

Filtering a report in Microsoft Excel

Within Microsoft Excel, you can filter on any column of data using a drop-down list at the top of the column. Using the drop-down list, you can apply a number of preset filters or create your own custom filter.

To find out if any of Rock Castle Construction's account balances have decreased since the previous period, you'll filter the balance sheet report you just created.

To filter a report in Microsoft Excel:

1. In the Excel window, click the down arrow in the $ Change column of the balance sheet report, and choose (Custom...) from the drop-down list.

   Excel displays the following window.

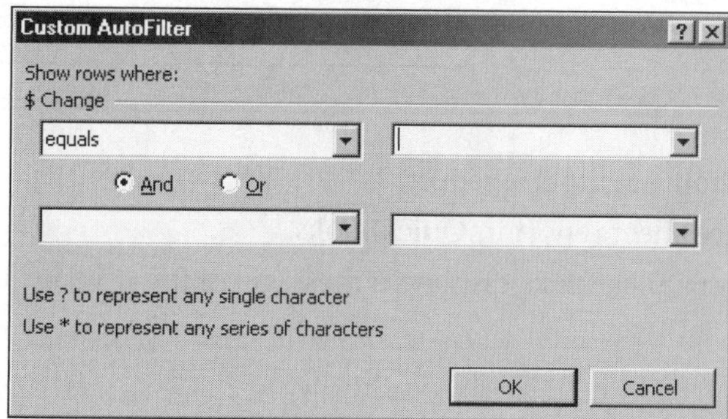

2. In the $ Change field, choose "is less than" from the drop-down list.
3. In the field to the right, type ***0***.

   Your screen should resemble the following.

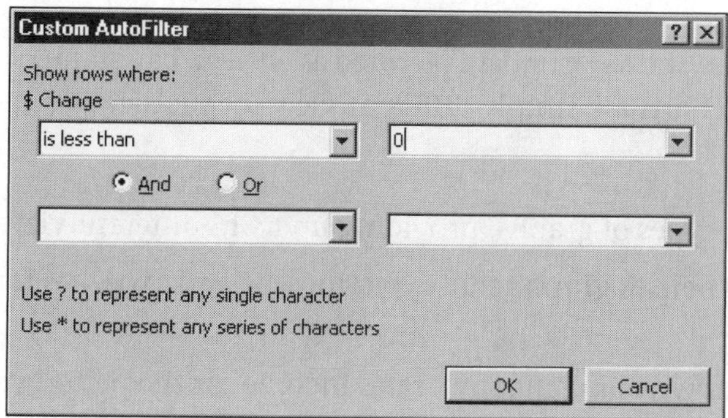

4 Click OK.

Excel filters the $ Change column for negative amounts and displays the results.

Book1

		Dec 15, 07	Sep 30, 07	$ Change	% Change
7	Savings	14,368.42	29,500.00	-15,131.58	-51.29%
16	Undeposited Funds	2,124.00	34,197.88	-32,073.88	-93.79%
17	Total Other Current Assets	36,628.73	43,589.76	-6,961.03	-15.97%
26	Pre-paid Insurance	1,041.85	3,364.51	-2,322.66	-69.03%
27	Total Other Assets	1,041.85	3,364.51	-2,322.66	-69.03%
43	Payroll Liabilities	3,302.06	3,781.99	-479.93	-12.69%
48	Bank of Anycity Loan	19,932.65	20,801.07	-868.42	-4.18%
50	Note Payable	3,440.83	20,500.00	-17,059.17	-83.22%
51	Truck Loan	5,662.38	7,149.32	-1,486.94	-20.8%
52	Total Long Term Liabilities	32,947.18	48,450.39	-15,503.21	-32.0%
55	Opening Bal Equity	-21,321.18	-11,937.68	-9,383.50	78.6%
58	Owner's Draw	-6,000.00	0.00	-6,000.00	-100.0%
59	Total Owner's Equity	19,000.00	25,000.00	-6,000.00	-24.0%
61	Net Income	38,013.44	76,530.28	-38,516.84	-50.33%

QuickBooks Export Tips / Sheet1 / Sheet2 / Sheet3

5 Close Excel without saving the report.

6 Close the balance sheet report in QuickBooks.

7 Choose No when QuickBooks displays a message asking if you want to memorize the report.

Creating QuickInsight graphs

A report gives you numbers that are essential if you want to stay on top of your business finances. But when you want a visual picture to plan current or future business decisions, a graph is another invaluable tool.

A QuickInsight graph shows your data pictured as either a bar graph or a pie chart. The bar graphs and pie charts are simply different views of the same company financial information.

QuickBooks has six types of graphs, providing up to 15 different views of your data:

- **Income and Expenses graphs** show your income and expenses for the period you specify.
- **Sales graphs** show your company's sales income for the period you specify.
- **Accounts Receivable graphs** show how much your customers owe.
- **Accounts Payable graphs** show how much you currently owe your vendors.
- **Net Worth graphs** show changes in your company's net worth.
- **Budget vs. Actual graphs** let you see the variance between your budgeted amounts and the actual amount you earned or spent.

To create a QuickInsight graph, select the type of graph you want from a report submenu.

Creating an Income and Expense graph

If you want your business to be profitable, you need to keep an eye on your expenses. The income and expense graph shows you exactly what you're spending and where.

You should be especially concerned with the proportion you're spending relative to the income you receive. As a simplistic example, if you're earning only $20,000 in income, you don't want to spend $30,000 in expenses.

To create an income and expense graph:

1 From the Reports menu, choose Company & Financial, and then choose Income & Expense Graph.

QuickBooks displays a graph depicting your income and expenses.

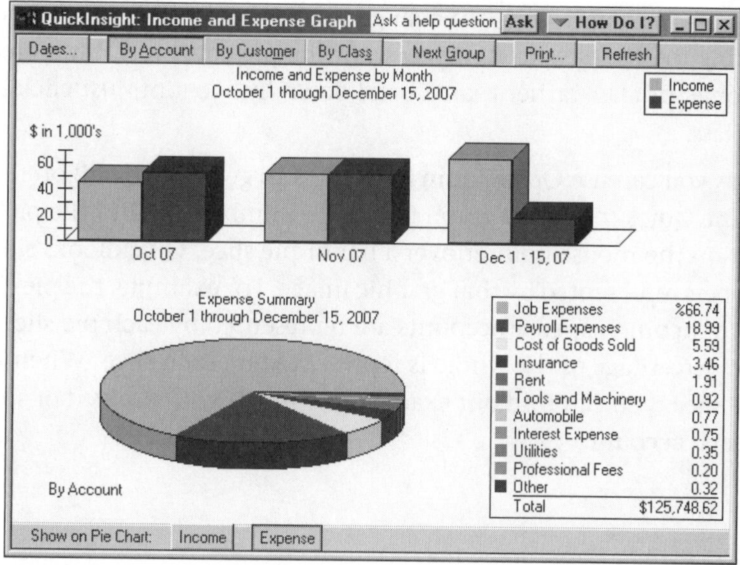

In the top portion of the graph window, QuickBooks displays a bar graph and legend showing total income and expenses. In the lower portion of the window, QuickBooks displays a pie chart and legend showing expense percentages by account.

2 QuickBooks can display only 10 accounts at a time. To display more accounts, click the Next Group button at the top of the graph window.

Features of QuickInsight graphs

These features are common to all QuickInsight graphs:

- Every graph window, except for the Net Worth and the Budget vs Actual graphs, shows a bar graph in the top part of the window and a pie chart in the bottom half.

  The bar graph usually shows totals. For example, the Income and Expense graph shows the total for income and the total for expenses in each month of the period.

  The pie chart shows a breakdown of the information shown in the bar graph; each pie slice in the Income and Expense graph represents a type of income or expense. The legend to the right of the pie chart shows you which income or expense account corresponds to the color shown in the pie chart; it also shows you what percentage of the pie each slice represents.
- Every graph window has a buttonbar with buttons you can click to customize the graph. For example, you can change the time period shown in the graph by clicking the Dates button. If you want the pie chart to show a breakdown by customer or class rather than a breakdown by account, just click By Customer or By Class.
- Just as you can use QuickZoom in a report to get more detail on the numbers, you can use QuickZoom in a graph to see the numbers behind the picture. When you position the mouse pointer over a bar or pie slice, QuickBooks shows you the numbers represented by that graphic image. For example, the pie chart legend tells which income/expense accounts are represented by each pie slice, and tells you what percentage of the whole is represented by each slice. When you zoom in on a pie slice, you can find out exactly how much you received or spent (in dollars) for each account.

Customizing graph data

To display income accounts instead of expense accounts:

1 Click Income at the bottom of the graph window.

2 Click By Customer.

QuickBooks changes the pie chart to display income by customers.

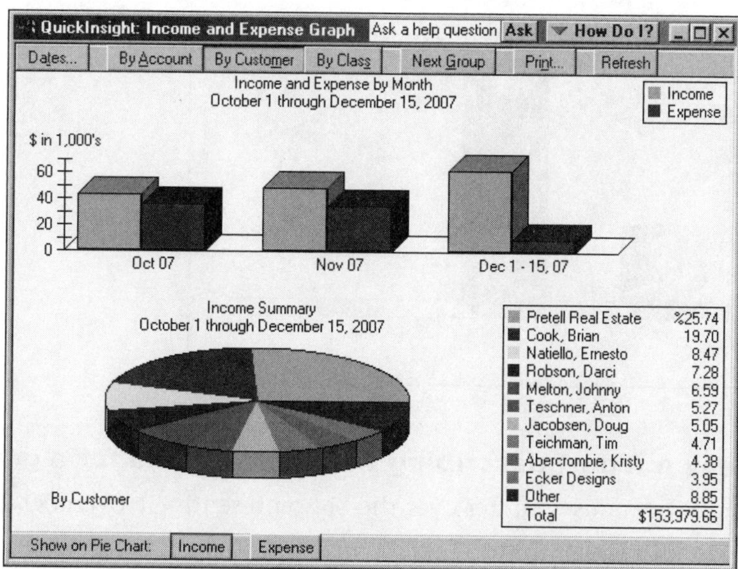

Using QuickZoom with graphs

To help you better understand the information shown in the graphs, QuickBooks lets you trace graphical data using QuickZoom graphs.

To display the sales for Anton Teschner:

1 Position the mouse pointer over the Teschner, Anton slice of the pie chart.

(Use the Key on the right side of the window.)

The pointer changes to a magnifying glass with the letter Z inside.

2 Double-click the Teschner, Anton slice.

Note: If a slice is too small to click, click on its legend representation instead.

QuickBooks displays a QuickZoom graph depicting sales for Anton Teschner by month.

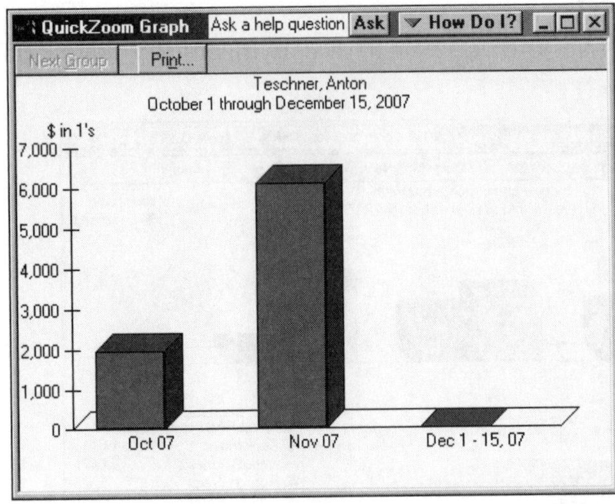

To display a report describing the transactions for a given month:

1 Position the mouse pointer over the bar representing November 2007.

The pointer turns into the QuickZoom symbol.

2 Double-click the bar.

QuickBooks displays the custom transaction detail report for the month of November 2007.

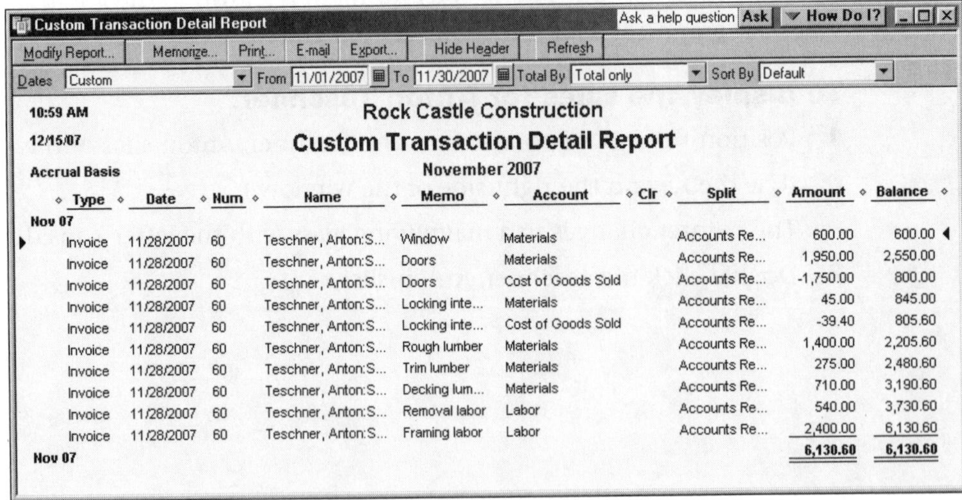

Custom Transaction Detail Report

Modify Report... Memorize... Print... E-mail Export... Hide Header Refresh

Dates Custom From 11/01/2007 To 11/30/2007 Total By Total only Sort By Default

10:59 AM

12/15/07

Accrual Basis

Rock Castle Construction

Custom Transaction Detail Report

November 2007

Type	Date	Num	Name	Memo	Account	Clr	Split	Amount	Balance
Nov 07									
Invoice	11/28/2007	60	Teschner, Anton:S...	Window	Materials		Accounts Re...	600.00	600.00
Invoice	11/28/2007	60	Teschner, Anton:S...	Doors	Materials		Accounts Re...	1,950.00	2,550.00
Invoice	11/28/2007	60	Teschner, Anton:S...	Doors	Cost of Goods Sold		Accounts Re...	-1,750.00	800.00
Invoice	11/28/2007	60	Teschner, Anton:S...	Locking inte...	Materials		Accounts Re...	45.00	845.00
Invoice	11/28/2007	60	Teschner, Anton:S...	Locking inte...	Cost of Goods Sold		Accounts Re...	-39.40	805.60
Invoice	11/28/2007	60	Teschner, Anton:S...	Rough lumber	Materials		Accounts Re...	1,400.00	2,205.60
Invoice	11/28/2007	60	Teschner, Anton:S...	Trim lumber	Materials		Accounts Re...	275.00	2,480.60
Invoice	11/28/2007	60	Teschner, Anton:S...	Decking lum...	Materials		Accounts Re...	710.00	3,190.60
Invoice	11/28/2007	60	Teschner, Anton:S...	Removal labor	Labor		Accounts Re...	540.00	3,730.60
Invoice	11/28/2007	60	Teschner, Anton:S...	Framing labor	Labor		Accounts Re...	2,400.00	6,130.60
Nov 07								**6,130.60**	**6,130.60**

You may need to scroll to the right to see the entire report.

To display the first transaction in the report:

1 Double-click any of the lines in the report for Invoice #60.

QuickBooks displays the invoice.

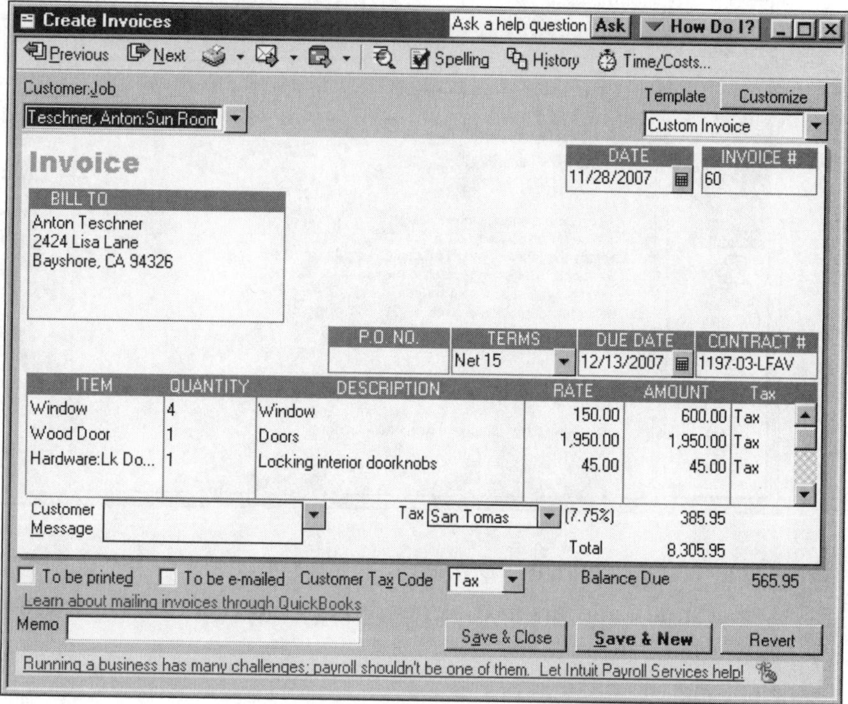

2 From the Window menu, choose Close All.

Customizing how graphs display

You can customize graphs to control what data they include and how the data is displayed. In this exercise, you'll change the display from three-dimensional (3D) to two-dimensional (2D) graphs.

To change from 3D to 2D:

1 From the Edit menu, choose Preferences.

QuickBooks displays the Preferences window.

2 In the left scroll box, click Reports & Graphs.

QuickBooks displays the Preferences window for Reports and Graphs.

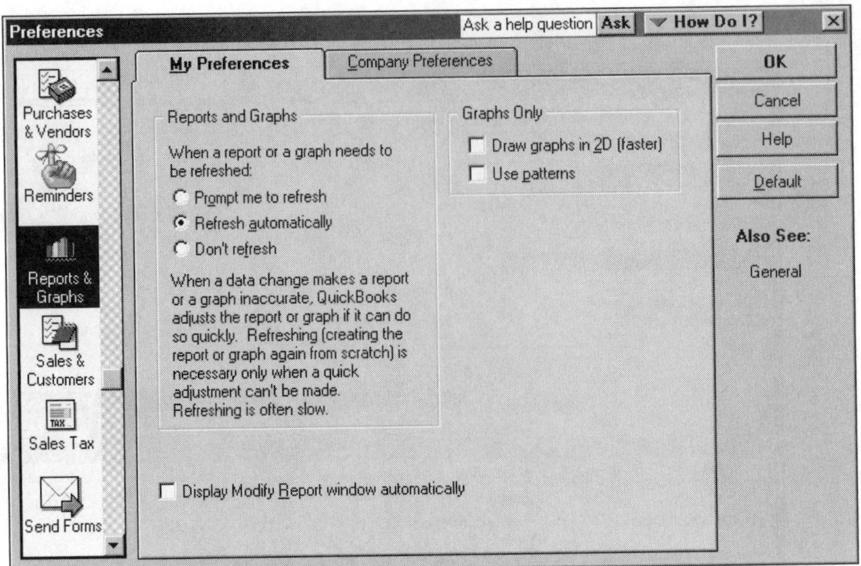

3 Click "Draw graphs in 2D (faster)."

A checkmark appears in the checkbox to indicate that Draw graphs in 2D (faster) is selected.

4 Click OK.

5 From the Reports menu, choose Sales. Then choose Sales Graph.

QuickBooks displays the sales graph in 2D.

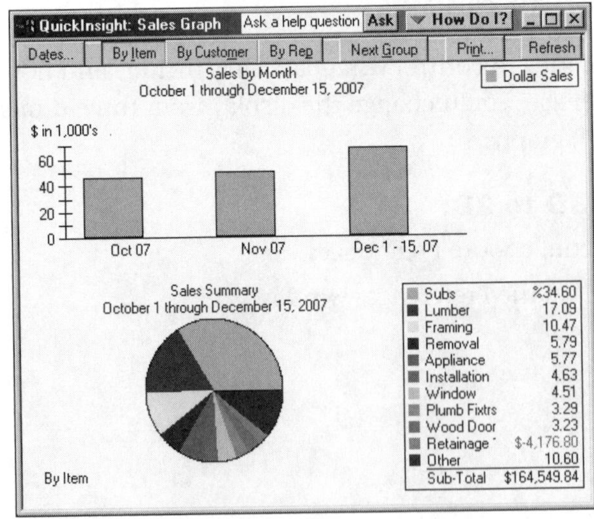

Displaying graphs in 2D often allows your computer to draw them on your screen faster than displaying them in 3D.

6 Close the graph.

Student test and review

1. Create a QuickReport on an item in one of Rock Castle Construction's lists.
2. Rock Castle Construction wants to create a report that shows how much they have spent on lumber for projects during November, 2007. Create an item summary purchase report, covering the date range from 11/01/2007 to 11/30/2007. Filter the report to show only Rock Castle Construction's purchases for Lumber.
3. Batch process the balance sheet, profit and loss statement, and statement of cash flows using the Process Multiple Reports window.

LESSON 10 Setting up inventory

Lesson objectives

- To get an overview of inventory in QuickBooks
- To practice filling out a purchase order for inventory items
- To track the receipt of the inventory items in QuickBooks
- To adjust inventory manually, to enter a stock loss or increase
- To create and build inventory assemblies (finished goods)

Handout materials

- Handout 5: Inventory workflow
- Handout 6: Group vs. inventory assembly items

Instructor preparation

- Review the lesson, including the examples, to make sure you're familiar with the material.
- Ensure that all students have copy of qblesson.qbb on their computer's hard disk.
- Have handouts 5 and 6 ready for distribution.

To start this lesson

Before you perform the following steps, make sure you have installed the exercise file (qblesson.qbb) on your hard disk. See "Installing the exercise file" in the Introduction to this guide if you haven't installed it.

The following steps restore the exercise file to its original state so that the data in the file matches what you see on the screen as you proceed through each lesson.

To restore the exercise file (qblesson.qbb):

1. From the File menu in QuickBooks, choose Restore.

   QuickBooks displays the Restore Company Backup window.
2. In the "Get Company Backup From" section of the window, click Browse and select your c:\QBtrain directory.
3. Select the qblesson.qbb file, and then click Open.
4. In the "Restore Company Backup To" section of the window, click Browse and select your c:\QBtrain directory.
5. In the File name field of the Restore To window, type ***lesson 10*** and then click Save.
6. Click Restore.

Turning on the inventory feature

The QuickBooks inventory feature is turned on in your exercise file, but you'll review how to turn on this feature so you become familiar with QuickBooks preferences. If you need to track inventory for your company, you can turn the feature on while completing the EasyStep Interview. If you want to turn on the inventory feature after you've completed the EasyStep Interview, follow this procedure.

To turn on the inventory feature:

1. From the Edit menu, choose Preferences.
2. Select Purchases & Vendors from the scroll box.
3. Click the Company Preferences tab.

   Note: Only the QuickBooks Administrator can change company preferences.
4. Click the "Inventory and purchase orders are active" checkbox to select it.

   A checkmark shows that the inventory feature is turned on.
5. Click OK.

Entering products into inventory

QuickBooks uses the average cost method to determine the value of inventory (rather than another method such as FIFO or LIFO). The average cost of an inventory item equals the total cost of the items currently in stock, divided by the number in stock.

Many small businesses that stock inventory don't know the number of units they have on hand or on order at any given time, and have no way of getting that information quickly. Using QuickBooks to manage your inventory, you'll be able to track the number of items in stock and the value of your inventory after every purchase and sale. As you order inventory items, receive the items, and later sell the items from inventory, QuickBooks tracks each inventory-related transaction. You will know the status of your inventory and will have a more accurate picture of your business's assets.

Refer to the diagram on Handout 5, "Inventory workflow" for the following discussion.

To track inventory, you must enter each product into the Item list as an inventory part. Once you enter a product, QuickBooks tracks it as you sell or reorder the product.

To enter a product into inventory:

1 From the Vendors menu, choose Item List.

QuickBooks displays the Item list.

2 Click the Item menu button, and then choose New.

QuickBooks displays the New Item window.

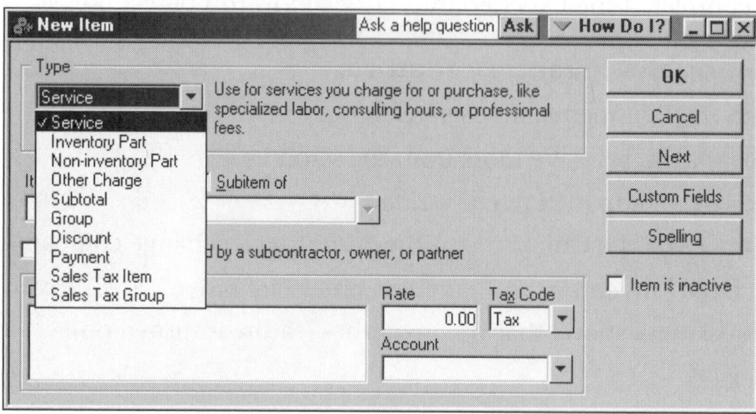

You'll enter one new item into your inventory.

3 In the Type field, choose Inventory Part from the drop-down list.

QuickBooks changes the New Item window to accept information for an inventory part.

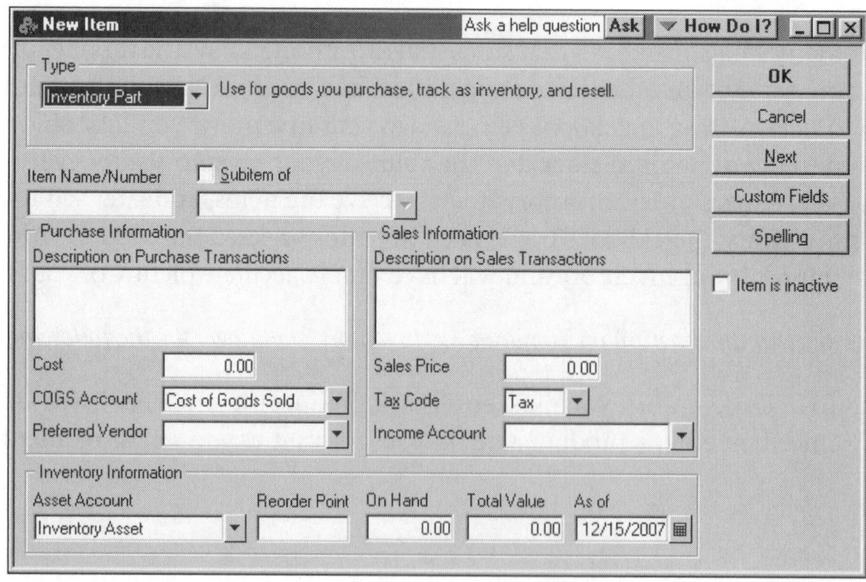

4 In the Item Name/Number field, type ***Cab 2015*** (2015 is the style number).

5 Select the "Subitem of" checkbox, and then choose Cabinets from the drop-down list.

6 In the "Description on Purchase Transactions" field, type ***Kitchen Cabinet #2015***, and then press Tab to move to the Cost field.

Notice that QuickBooks fills in the Description on Sales Transactions field with the same description you entered for the purchase side. You can leave the sales description the same or change it later.

7 In the Cost field, type ***169***.

8 In the Preferred Vendor field, choose Thomas Kitchen and Bath from the drop-down list.

Or, type the first few letters of your selection and QuickBooks fills in the rest.

9 In the Sales Price field, type ***225***.

10 Leave the Tax Code setting as is.

If you wanted to assign a different tax code, you could select a different code from the drop-down list when setting up the item.

11 In the Income Account field, choose Construction:Materials.

12 Press Tab to move to the Asset Account field.

Inventory Asset was filled in when you selected Inventory Part as the type of item. Leave this default setting.

13 In the Reorder Point field, type ***15***.

14 In the Qty-on-Hand field, type ***20***, and then press Tab to move to the Total Value field.

Notice that QuickBooks has calculated the value of your item by multiplying the number in the On Hand field by the number in the Cost field.

Your New Item window should resemble the following figure.

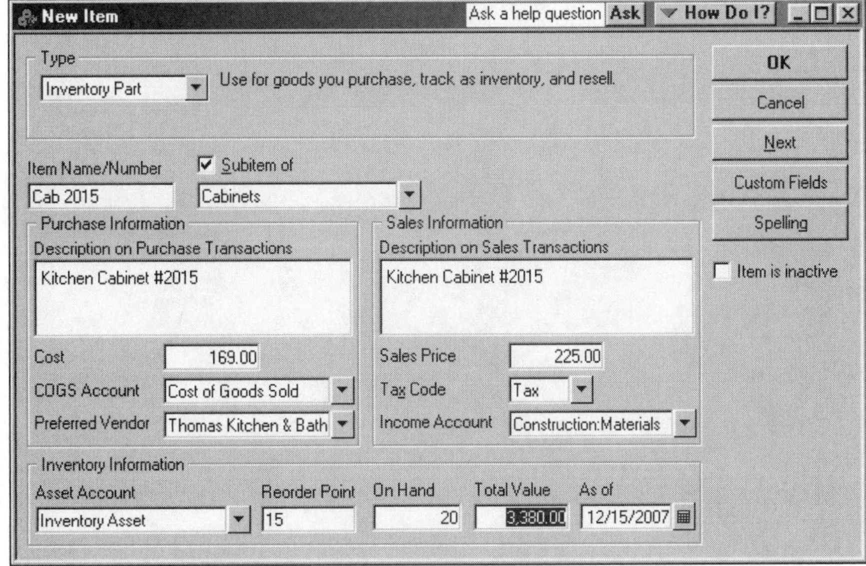

15 Click OK to close the New Item window.

QuickBooks adds the new item to the Item list.

16 Close the Item list.

Tip: **When you want to check on the status of your inventory stock, you can create a stock status by item report.** For every item in your inventory stock, the report gives you the reorder point, the current quantity on hand, the average cost to date, the quantity on order (and expected date of receipt), and the average sales per week.

Ordering products

Once you enter your current products and vendors into the Item and Vendor lists, you'll need to order products to keep your inventory stocked.

QuickBooks doesn't require you to use purchase orders, but you may want to recommend their use for students who track inventory. Using purchase orders lets you see items you have on order and when they're due to be received. You can also check items you receive against the PO.

If students don't order items in advance or don't want to use purchase orders, they can buy inventory directly by writing a check or entering a credit card transaction.

Creating purchase orders

In Lesson 6, you created a sales order for door frames. Now, create the purchase order to order the items from the vendor.

To order a product using a purchase order:

1 From the Vendors menu, choose Create Purchase Orders.

QuickBooks displays the Create Purchase Orders window.

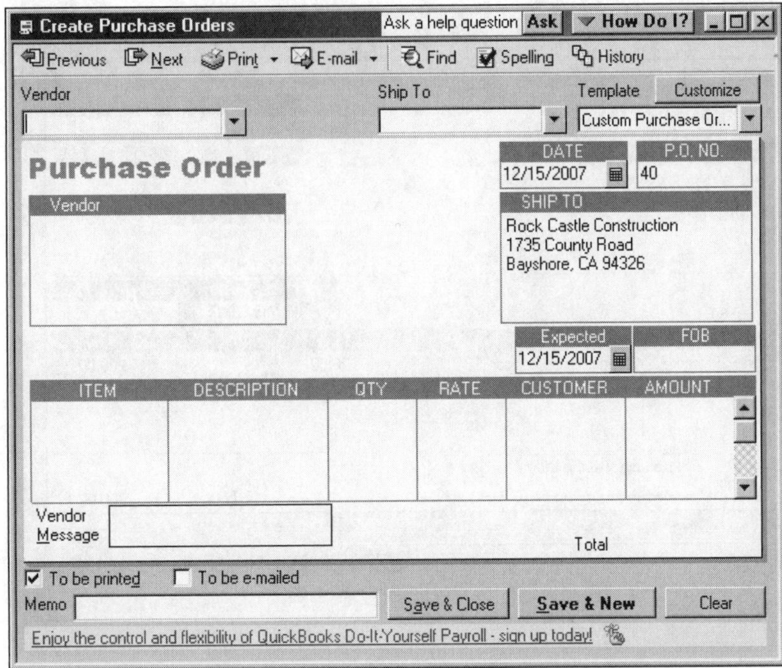

You use the Create Purchase Orders window to enter the products you wish to order, the quantities, and the vendor. As you fill in this information, QuickBooks automatically calculates purchase order number, item cost, and total cost.

Notice that QuickBooks has already entered today's date and a sequential purchase order number.

2 In the Vendor field, choose Perry Windows & Doors from the drop-down list.

Notice that QuickBooks displays all of the information about Perry Windows & Doors in the appropriate places on the purchase order form.

3 In the Item column, select Frames:Exterior Frame from the drop-down list.

4 In the QTY field, type ***10***.

5 In the Vendor Message field of the purchase order, type ***Please rush ship this order.*** Your Purchase Order should resemble the following figure.

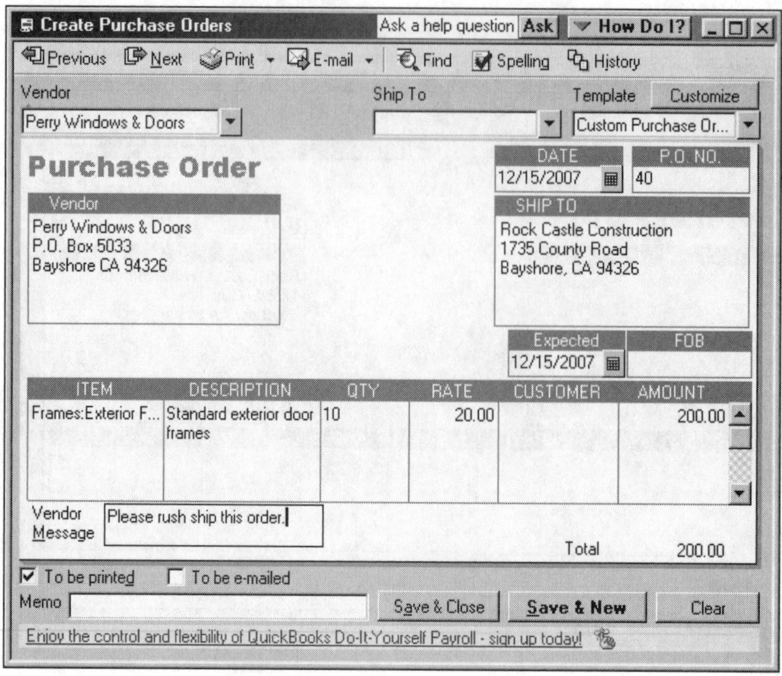

6 Click Save & Close to record the purchase order.

After you have created a purchase order, QuickBooks adds an account to the chart of accounts called Purchase Orders. This is a non-posting account and does not affect your balance sheet or income statement. The Purchase Orders account is used to produce a QuickReport showing current purchase orders so you always know what is on order.

Getting a report of purchase orders

To get a chronologically ordered report of all the purchase orders you have written:

1 From the Lists menu, choose Chart of Accounts.

2 In the chart of accounts, click Purchase Orders once to select it.

3 Click the Reports menu button and choose QuickReport:Purchase Orders. QuickBooks displays a report of all purchase orders.

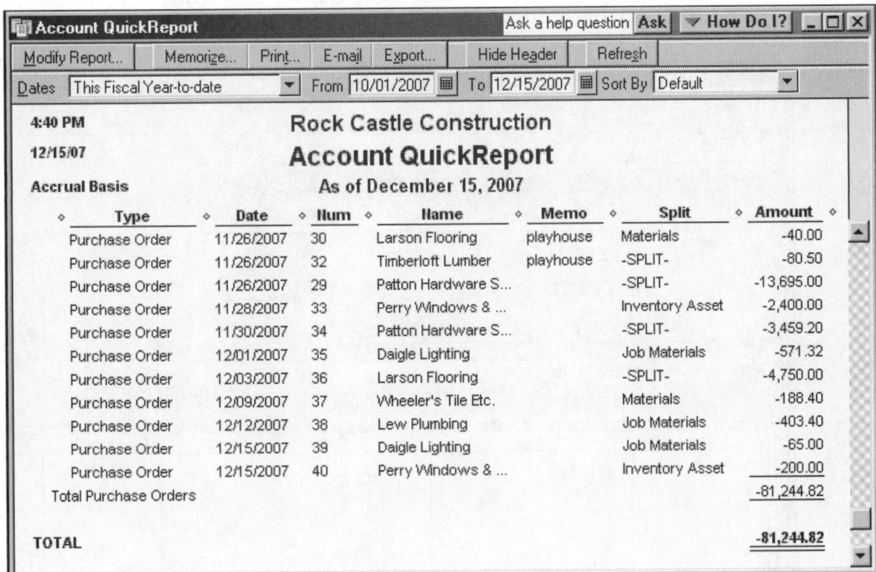

4:40 PM
12/15/07
Accrual Basis

Rock Castle Construction
Account QuickReport
As of December 15, 2007

Type	Date	Num	Name	Memo	Split	Amount
Purchase Order	11/26/2007	30	Larson Flooring	playhouse	Materials	-40.00
Purchase Order	11/26/2007	32	Timberloft Lumber	playhouse	-SPLIT-	-80.50
Purchase Order	11/26/2007	29	Patton Hardware S...		-SPLIT-	-13,695.00
Purchase Order	11/28/2007	33	Perry Windows & ...		Inventory Asset	-2,400.00
Purchase Order	11/30/2007	34	Patton Hardware S...		-SPLIT-	-3,459.20
Purchase Order	12/01/2007	35	Daigle Lighting		Job Materials	-571.32
Purchase Order	12/03/2007	36	Larson Flooring		-SPLIT-	-4,750.00
Purchase Order	12/09/2007	37	Wheeler's Tile Etc.		Materials	-188.40
Purchase Order	12/12/2007	38	Lew Plumbing		Job Materials	-403.40
Purchase Order	12/15/2007	39	Daigle Lighting		Job Materials	-65.00
Purchase Order	12/15/2007	40	Perry Windows & ...		Inventory Asset	-200.00
Total Purchase Orders						-81,244.82
TOTAL						-81,244.82

Notice the purchase order you have just created is at the bottom of the report.

4 Close the QuickReport.

5 Close the chart of accounts.

Receiving inventory

When you receive the items you have ordered with your purchase order, you have to enter the items into inventory. You can receive items with a bill or without a bill.

This exercise shows you how to enter into QuickBooks inventory items you've received when the bill for those items will follow later.

To receive inventory without a bill attached:

1 From the Vendors menu, choose Receive Items.

QuickBooks displays the Create Item Receipts window.

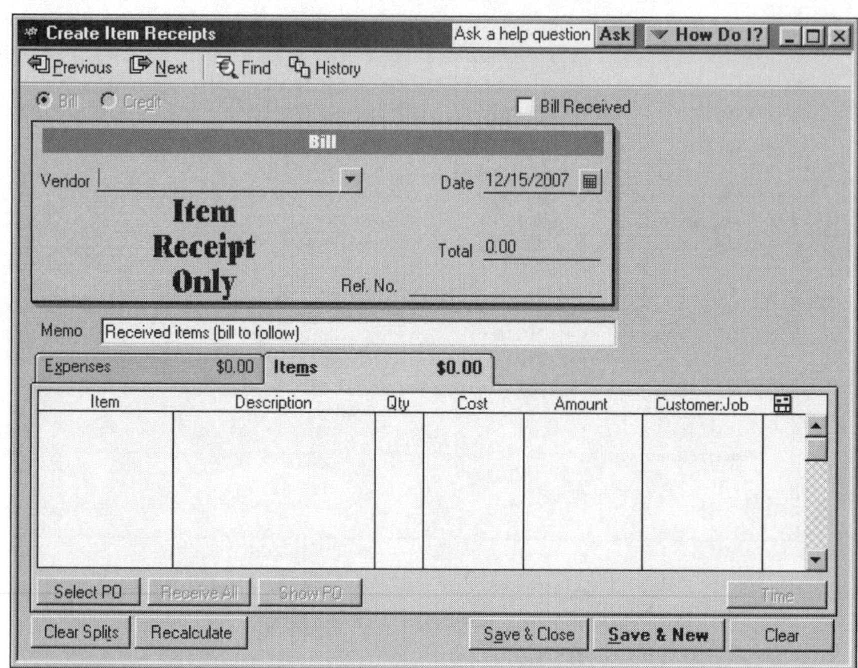

The Create Item Receipts window lets you enter information for inventory parts you've received.

2 In the Vendor field, choose Perry Windows & Doors from the drop-down list and press Tab.

QuickBooks tells you that there are open purchase orders for this vendor and asks if you wish to receive against one of these orders.

3 Click Yes.

QuickBooks displays the Open Purchase Orders for Perry Windows & Doors.

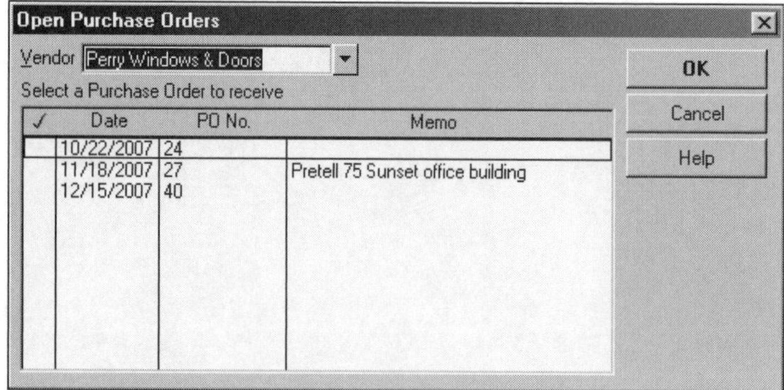

4 Click the third purchase order (#40, dated 12/15/2007) to select it.

QuickBooks places a checkmark in the left-most column for the item selected.

5 Click OK to move the information to the item receipt.

The Create Item Receipts window should resemble the following figure.

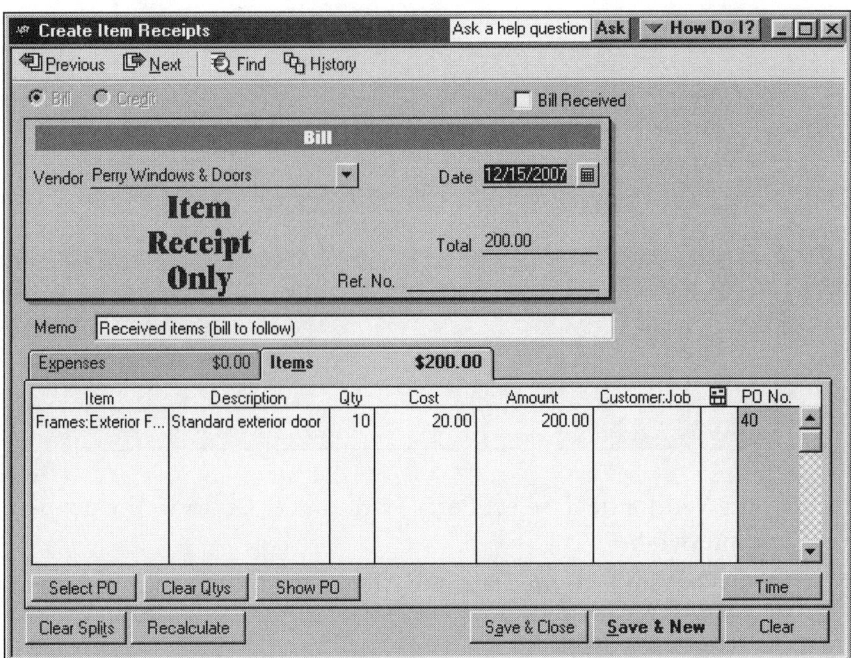

6 Click Save & Close to process the receipt.

QuickBooks processes the items and adds them to your inventory. If you display the Item list, you'll see that you now have 10 additional door frames on hand.

Entering a bill for inventory

If you've entered an item receipt for inventory, but the bill hasn't arrived yet, you can still record the bill amount in QuickBooks. Entering the bill as shown in this exercise records the amount in your accounts payable account so you can track how much you owe.

When the bill comes, you pay the bill just like you would pay any other bill in QuickBooks (from the Pay Bills window).

To enter the bill:

1 From the Vendors menu, choose Enter Bill for Received Items.

  QuickBooks displays the Select Item Receipt window, where you can select the vendor and the item for which you have a bill.

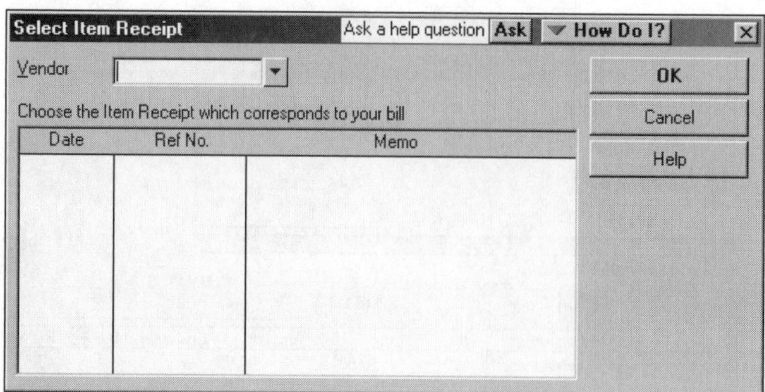

2 In the Vendor field, select Perry Windows & Doors in the drop-down list and press Tab.

  QuickBooks fills in the Date and Memo fields with information that corresponds to your bill.

3 Select "Received items (bill to follow)," dated 12/15/2007.

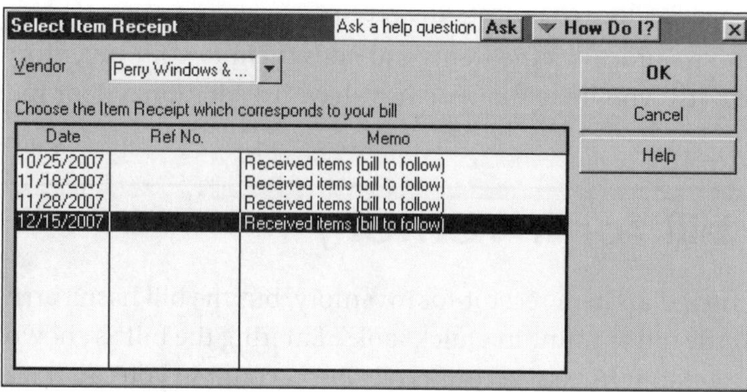

4 Click OK.

QuickBooks displays the Enter Bills window.

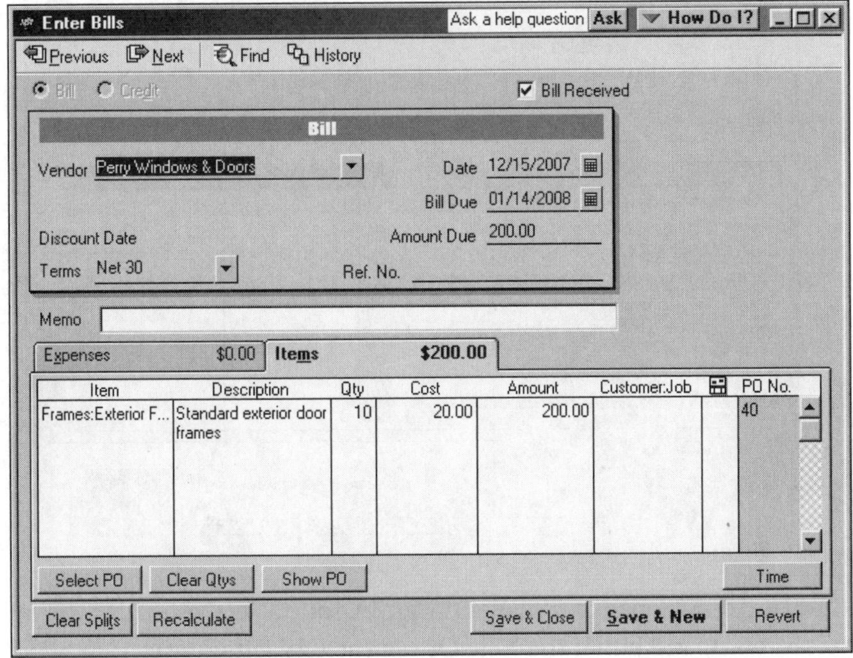

5 Click Save & Close.

QuickBooks changes the item receipt to a bill in the Accounts Payable account and lists the bill in the Pay Bills window. If you look at the Accounts Payable, you'll see that the balance increased by $200.00, based on the bill entered for Perry Windows & Doors.

Because you must have inventory on hand before you can enter a sale for inventory parts, we recommend that you enter you item receipts before entering sales.

Manually adjusting inventory

When you have spoilage or send out samples of your products, you can adjust your inventory manually.

To adjust the inventory manually:

1 From the Vendors menu, choose Inventory Activities, and then choose Adjust Quantity/Value on Hand.

QuickBooks displays the Adjust Quantity/Value on Hand window.

Adjust Quantity/Value on Hand

Previous Next

Adjustment Date 12/15/2007

Ref. No. 1 Customer:Job

Adjustment Account

Item	Description	Current Qty	New Qty	Qty Difference
Cabinets	Cabinets	0		
Cabinets:Cab ...	Kitchen Cabinet #2015	20		
Cabinets:Cabi...	Cabinet Pulls	110		
Cabinets:Light...	Light pine kitchen cabi...	9		
Frames		0		
Frames:Exterio...	Standard exterior door ...	12		
Frames:Interior...	Standard interior door f...	9		
Hardware		0		
Hardware:Bra...	Standard brass hinge	475		
Hardware:Doo...	Standard exterior door...	50		

Value Adjustment Memo

Total Value of Adjustment 0.00

Save & Close Save & New Cancel

The Adjust Quantity/Value on Hand window lets you enter the adjustment account, and either the New Qty or the Qty Difference.

Since two wood interior doors were damaged, you'll adjust the inventory account to remove two doors.

2 In the Adjustment Account field, type ***Inventory Adjustment*** and press Tab.

3 Click Set Up in the window telling you that Inventory Adjustment is not in the account list.

QuickBooks opens the New Account window.

4 In the Type field, choose Expense from the drop-down list, if it is not selected already.

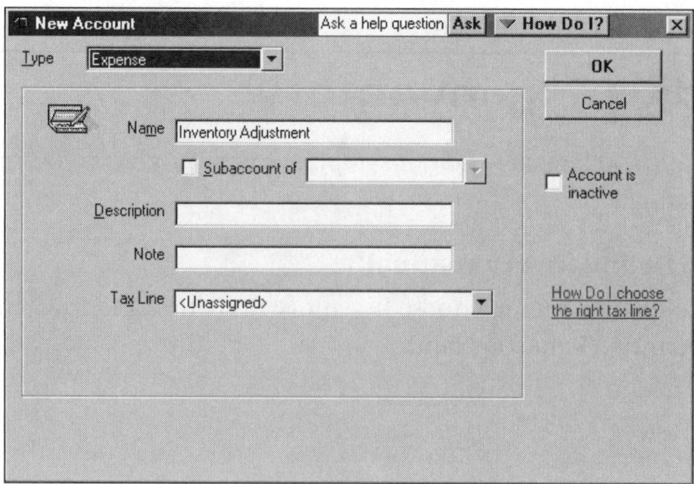

5 Click OK to close the New Account window.

6 In the Qty Difference column for Wood Door:Interior wood door, type *–2* (the number of damaged doors), and then press Tab.

QuickBooks calculates the value adjustment and decreases the inventory by two items.

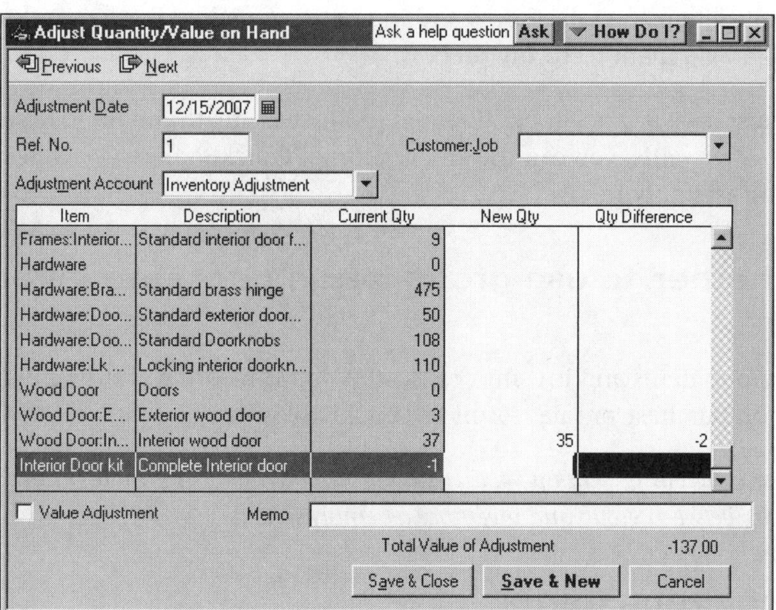

7 Click Save & Close.

Tip: **The inventory valuation reports in QuickBooks break down the value of your inventory and give you several statistical measures of its value.** The valuation summary report shows the quantity on hand, average cost, asset value, % of total asset value, retail value, and % of total retail value for each of your inventory items. The valuation detail report lists the opening balance, ending balance, and every transaction (purchase or sale) that has affected the inventory value of each inventory item during the period of time covered by the report.

Tracking finished goods

QuickBooks Premier products let you track the building and sale of finished goods using assembly items. When you define assembly items, you tell QuickBooks how many of each inventory item is needed to create the finished product.

Inventory assembly items allow you to create an item that contains assembled material units (finished goods) you buy or produce, track as inventory, and resell. You can keep track of how many items remain in stock after a sale, how many items you have on order, your cost of goods sold, and the value of your inventory. Note that inventory assembly items in QuickBooks are appropriate for indicating "light" assembled items on sales forms and in reports. QuickBooks does not track inventory throughout a manufacturing process.

You must have a QuickBooks: Premier product to create and build inventory assembly items. Afterwards, you can use any version of QuickBooks to view, sell, and report on existing assembly items.

Deciding whether to use group items or create inventory assemblies

Both group items and inventory assembly items record a group of items as a single entry on purchase or sales forms in QuickBooks.

Refer to Handout 6, "Group vs. inventory assembly items" for more information about choosing between group and inventory assembly items.

Using group items

Group items are useful for quickly entering a group of individual items that you've already set up as single items on your list and often sell together.

Group items let you track the items you sell in greater detail. For example, a construction firm that remodels houses could set up a group item that lists the significant components of a remodeling job: lumber, carpentry hours, markup, etc. Sales reports for the company would then show income broken down by each component instead of a single lump sum for all remodeling jobs.

If you need to track a lot of detail about your items but you also want to give your customers simple, uncluttered invoices, you can use group items to do both. You can set up a group item so that the printed version of an invoice reduces a group item to a single line item and one amount. Yet when you view the invoice on your screen, you see a separate line entry and amount for each item in the group.

Group items also give you a way to enter a great amount of line item detail quickly. On a sales or purchase form, all you have to do is enter the name of the group item—QuickBooks fills in all the details about the items in the group for you.

Using inventory assemblies

When you build an assembly, an assembled unit is automatically added to quantity on hand and its component parts (inventory items or other assembly items) are automatically deducted from quantity on hand. By using assembly items, you always know how many assembled and component items you actually have in stock.

You can specify a price for an assembly that's different than the sum of component items.

You can easily access the date items were assembled, quantity and cost of assembled items, and a detailed list of component items.

You can set a build point and QuickBooks will automatically remind you to build finished goods when stock is running low. At build time, QuickBooks will notify you if you don't have enough component items in stock to build the specified number of assembly items.

Note: **The ability to create inventory assemblies is available only in QuickBooks: Premier products.** To proceed through this exercise, you must be using QuickBooks: Premier.

Creating inventory assembly items

Creating assembly items in QuickBooks is a two-part process: first you define an assembly item, and then you build the assembly. Assembly item units are not added to inventory and assembly components (inventory parts or other assemblies) are not deducted from inventory until you build the assembly.

Inventory assembly items can include inventory part and other assembly items only. If you want to include a different type of item (a service item to charge for labor, for example), then you must include the assembly item and service item in a group item.

All items included in an inventory assembly item must be defined in the Item list. You can define them before you create the inventory assembly item, or as you create the assembly item. Note, however, that you cannot edit the items included in the assembly item once it's been used in transactions, or saved with a quantity on hand.

In addition to selling individual items, Rock Castle sells pre-assembled exterior door kits. In this exercise, you define the assembly item for the exterior door kits. All of the component items are already defined in the Item list.

To create an inventory assembly item:

1 From the Lists menu, choose Item List.

2 Click the Item menu button and select New.

QuickBooks displays the New Item window.

3 In the Type field, select Inventory Assembly.

4 In the Item Name/Number field, type ***Exterior Door Kit***.

5 In the Description field, type ***Complete exterior door kit.***

The New Item window should resemble the following graphic.

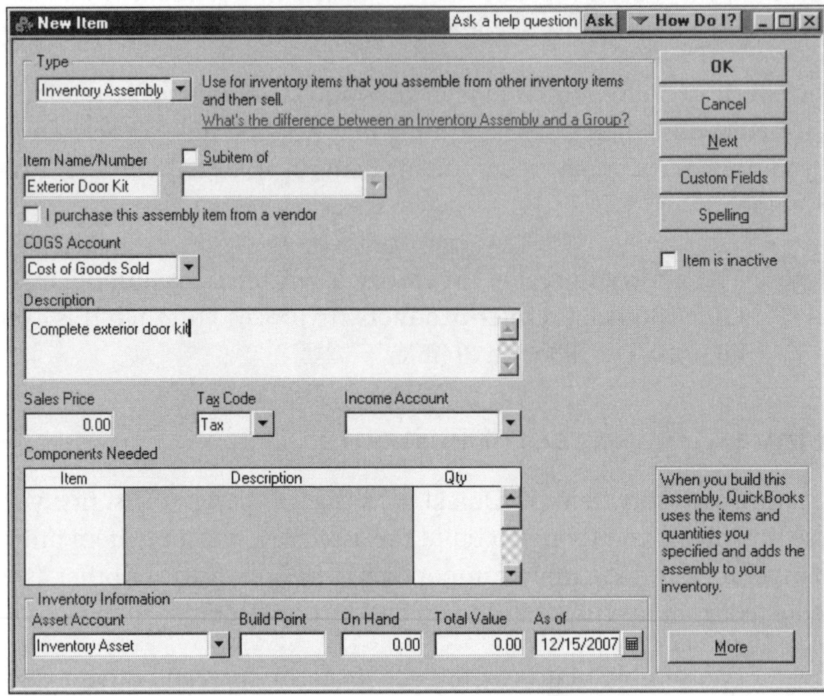

6 In the Sales Price field, type ***200***, and then press Tab twice.

QuickBooks allows you to set any price for assembled items; the price is independent of the sales price of the component items.

In this case, the assembly item uses the same sales tax code as the component parts, but you can use different sales tax codes for the assemblies, if necessary.

7 In the Income Account field, select Construction:Materials from the drop-down list.

8 In the Components Needed section, click in the Item column.

9 In the Item drop-down list, select Frames:Exterior Frame, and then press Tab.

10 In the Qty field, type ***1***, and then press Tab.

11 In the Item drop-down list, select Hardware:Doorknobs Locking Exterior, and then press Tab.

12 In the Qty field, type ***1***, and then press Tab.

13 In the Item drop-down list, select Hardware:Brass Hinges, and then press Tab.

14 In the Qty field, type ***3***, and then press Tab.

15 In the Item drop-down list, select Wood Door:Exterior, and then press Tab.

16 In the Qty field, type ***1***.

The New Item window should resemble the following graphic.

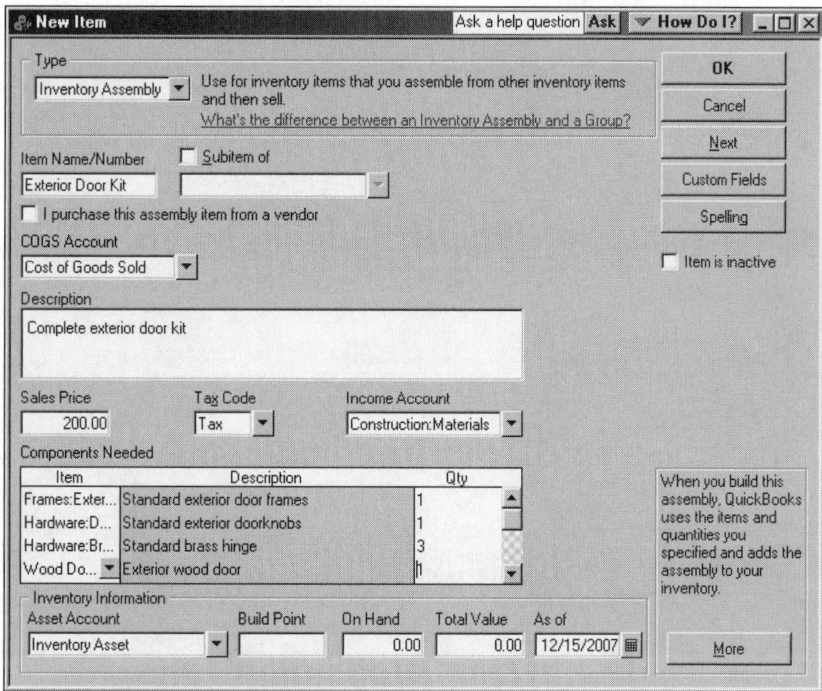

Assembly definition details, such as the list and quantity of components, can be edited until the assembly is used in a transaction. After an assembly has been used in a transaction, you can't edit the assembly's component list. However, you can still modify most other aspects of an assembly definition.

Because you cannot change components in an assembly, if a part changes, for example, you'll have to create a whole new assembly.

17 In the Build Point field, type ***5***.

18 Leave the On Hand and Total Value fields blank.

The New Item window should now resemble the following graphic.

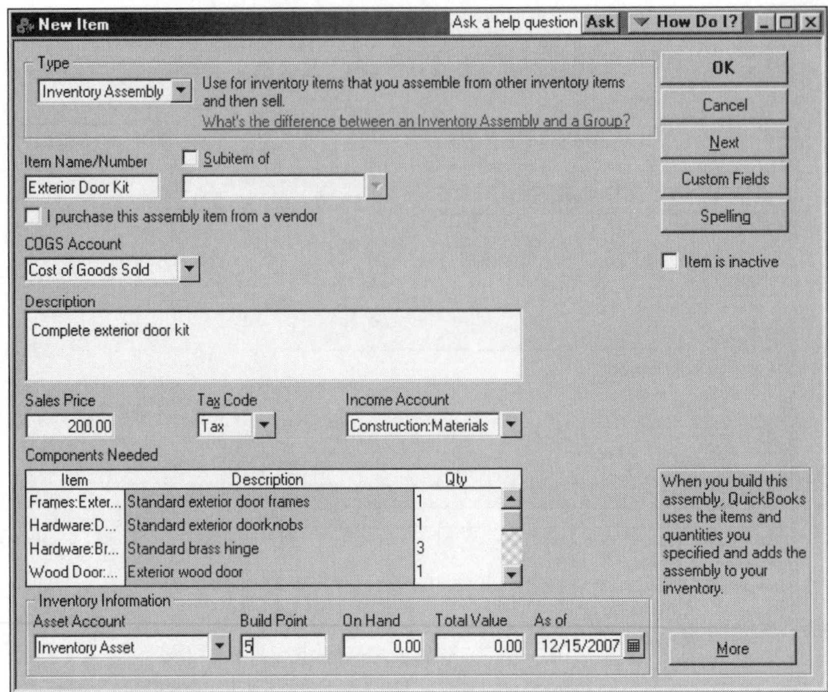

19 Click OK.

20 Close the Item list.

Building finished goods

Once you've defined assembly items that define the pieces you build, you are ready to enter the builds into QuickBooks. In this exercise, you build five exterior door kits for Rock Castle.

To build an inventory assembly:

1 From the Vendors menu, choose Inventory Activities, and then choose Build Assemblies from the submenu.

QuickBooks displays the Build Assemblies window.

2 In the Assembly Item field, select Exterior Door Kit from the drop-down list.

The Build Assemblies window should resemble the following graphic.

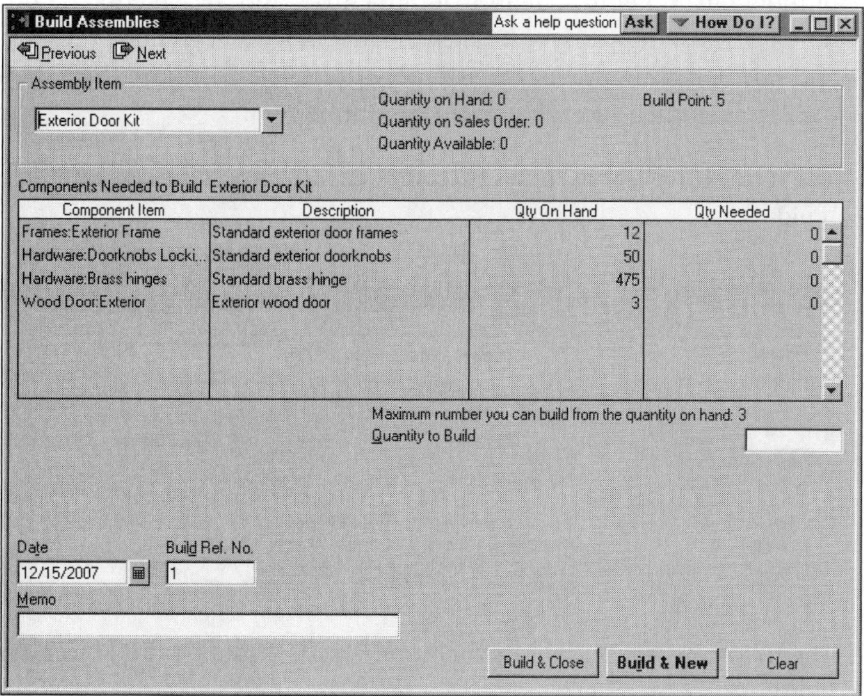

3 In the Quantity to Build field, type ***2***.

QuickBooks warns you when you do not have sufficient inventory items on hand to complete a build.

If you choose to build an assembly and do not have enough components in inventory to build the number of assemblies you have specified, you can postpone the build by marking it pending. If you don't mark the build as pending, you have to reduce the number of assemblies or you won't be able to save the build.

4 Click Build & Close.

Understanding the effect of builds on inventory

When you build an assembly item, QuickBooks decrements the appropriate number of individual inventory items from inventory and increments the number of inventory assembly items. It takes the inventory asset value of the component items and transfers the value to the assembly item. The parts and the values are combined into the quantity and value of the assembly item.

The following graphic shows the number of component and built items before the build.

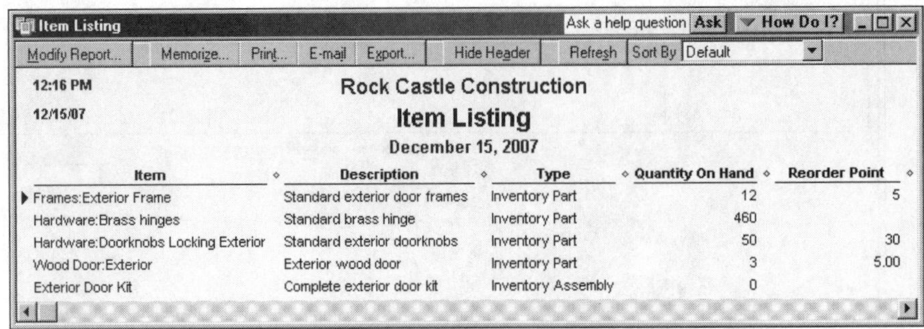

Item Listing — Rock Castle Construction — December 15, 2007 (12:16 PM, 12/15/07)

Item	Description	Type	Quantity On Hand	Reorder Point
Frames:Exterior Frame	Standard exterior door frames	Inventory Part	12	5
Hardware:Brass hinges	Standard brass hinge	Inventory Part	460	
Hardware:Doorknobs Locking Exterior	Standard exterior doorknobs	Inventory Part	50	30
Wood Door:Exterior	Exterior wood door	Inventory Part	3	5.00
Exterior Door Kit	Complete exterior door kit	Inventory Assembly	0	

The following graphic shows the number of component and built items after the build.

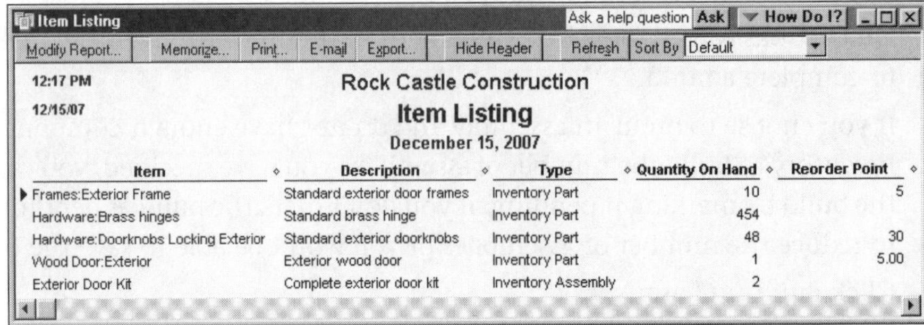

Item Listing — Rock Castle Construction — December 15, 2007 (12:17 PM, 12/15/07)

Item	Description	Type	Quantity On Hand	Reorder Point
Frames:Exterior Frame	Standard exterior door frames	Inventory Part	10	5
Hardware:Brass hinges	Standard brass hinge	Inventory Part	454	
Hardware:Doorknobs Locking Exterior	Standard exterior doorknobs	Inventory Part	48	30
Wood Door:Exterior	Exterior wood door	Inventory Part	1	5.00
Exterior Door Kit	Complete exterior door kit	Inventory Assembly	2	

Managing pending builds

A pending build is an inventory assembly build transaction that could not be finalized because there were not enough component parts in inventory to build the specified number of assemblies at build time. When a build is pending, "Pending" appears in the Build Assemblies window to remind you that these assemblies haven't been built.

If you modify or delete a previous build transaction, or change inventory quantities or the dates of purchase orders, invoices, or sales receipts, assembly builds that were finalized could change to pending. Finalized builds change to pending when the quantity of at least one component drops below the quantity needed to build the specified number of assemblies on the build transaction date. You can use the pending builds report to see a list of all builds that are currently pending.

In addition, you can choose to manually mark a build as pending even if you currently have enough components in stock to build the specified quantity. This allows you to set up build information but postpone building the assembly until later.

Disassembling inventory assemblies

There are several ways to disassemble inventory assemblies and return component items to inventory. You can do any of the following:

- Use the Adjust Quantity/Value on Hand window to adjust the quantity on hand for each assembly component and the assembly item.
- Reduce quantity to build in the Build Assemblies window and then click Build & Close. The quantity of assembly units in inventory are decreased and the quantity of component inventory parts are increased accordingly.
- Delete a build transaction completely. The quantity of assembly units in inventory are decreased and the quantity of component inventory parts are increased accordingly, but this method completely removes the build transaction from QuickBooks and should not be used if you want to maintain a record of the transaction.

Selling finished goods

When assembly items appear on any form (for example a sales receipt or in a report), their component items are hidden. Only the assembly name, description, and price appear.

If you attempt to sell more assembly units than you have available in inventory, QuickBooks warns you that quantities are insufficient to fulfill the order. If you decide to go ahead with this transaction, the quantity on hand for the specified assembly changes to a negative value. You can set a build point in the Build Assemblies window to remind you when assembly stock is getting low and you need to build more units. If you turn on reminders, a list of assemblies that need to be built appear in the Reminders window.

Student test and review

1. Enter a new inventory item using the following information.
   - Item Name/Number: Kitchen counter
   - Purchase Description: Kitchen counter
   - Cost: 280.00
   - COGS Account: Cost of Goods Sold
   - Preferred Vendor: Patton Hardware Supplies
   - Sales Description: Same as Purchase Description
   - Sales Price: 340.00
   - Income Account: Construction:materials
   - Asset Account: Inventory Asset
   - Reorder Point: 5
   - Qty on Hand: 6
2. Create a purchase order for 20 Standard doorknobs.
3. Receive the 20 Standard doorknobs into inventory and record the bill for the doorknobs.
4. Process the bill and pay for the 20 Standard doorknobs.

LESSON 11 Tracking and paying sales tax

Lesson objectives

- To get an overview of sales tax in QuickBooks (the steps involved in tracking, collecting, and paying it)
- To see how to set up QuickBooks to track sales tax
- To see how to apply sales tax to a sale
- To learn how to determine a business's sales tax liability
- To write a QuickBooks check to the appropriate tax agency for sales tax liability

Handout materials

- Handout 7: Sales tax

Instructor preparation

- Review the lesson, including the examples, to make sure you're familiar with the material.
- Ensure that all students have copy of qblesson.qbb on their computer's hard disk.
- Have Handout 7 ready for distribution.

To start this lesson

Before you perform the following steps, make sure you have installed the exercise file (qblesson.qbb) on your hard disk. See "Installing the exercise file" in the Introduction to this guide if you haven't installed it.

The following steps restore the exercise file to its original state so that the data in the file matches what you see on the screen as you proceed through each lesson.

To restore the exercise file (qblesson.qbb):

1. From the File menu in QuickBooks, choose Restore.

   QuickBooks displays the Restore Company Backup window.
2. In the "Get Company Backup From" section of the window, click Browse and select your c:\QBtrain directory.
3. Select the qblesson.qbb file, and then click Open.
4. In the "Restore Company Backup To" section of the window, click Browse and select your c:\QBtrain directory.
5. In the File name field of the Restore To window, type ***lesson 11*** and then click Save.
6. Click Restore.

Overview of sales tax in QuickBooks

If you have a business where you need to collect sales tax, you already know how complicated the process can be. These are some of the issues you may have to deal with:

- You may have to collect and pay more than one tax (for example, one rate for local taxes and one rate for state taxes).
- You may have some items that are taxable and some that aren't.
- You may tax some customers while others are non-taxable.

QuickBooks reduces some of the complication, because it lets you automatically apply sales tax on particular sales and keep track of how much you collect and from whom. Then, when you're ready to pay your taxes, QuickBooks can write a check for the correct amount.

Refer to Handout 7, "Sales tax in QuickBooks," for the following discussion.

To use QuickBooks to track and pay your sales tax:

1. **Set up your tax rates and agencies.**

   In the QuickBooks Item list, set up the separate tax rates you need to charge. In the Vendor list, set up the agencies to whom you submit the taxes you've collected.

   You can also set up sales tax codes, which can help you classify why a transaction (or part of one) is either taxable or non-taxable.

2. **Indicate who and what gets taxed.**

   Not all of the items you sell are taxable, and not all of your customers pay tax. In your Item and Customer:Job lists, you can indicate which items or customers are taxable.

3. **Apply tax to each sale.**

   When you fill out an invoice or sales receipt form, and choose a taxable item from your Item list, QuickBooks applies the appropriate sales tax.

4. **Find out what you owe.**

   As you record taxable sales, QuickBooks keeps track of the tax you've collected in your Sales Tax Payable account. When you're ready to pay your sales tax agency, you can open the Sales Tax Payable register to see how much you owe, or you can create a sales tax liability report.

5. **Pay your tax agencies.**

   When you go to the Pay Sales Tax window, QuickBooks shows the amount you owe and writes a check to the tax agency for that amount.

This lesson walks you through each of these steps.

Setting up your tax rates and agencies

The first step is to enter your sales tax rates, and then provide information about the tax agencies to which you pay the taxes.

Creating a tax item for each single tax you apply

Some businesses need to apply more than one sales tax to their sales; for example, they may collect a state sales tax as well as several county sales taxes. You need to create a separate sales tax item for each tax whose amount you must report (not necessarily for each tax you collect—some states want you to report state sales tax and county sales tax as separate items, while others let you report them as one item).

Even if you're paying more than one type of tax, you usually want your customers to see one overall tax amount, not separate taxes for the state and county. You'll learn how to do that in this lesson.

On the Item list, you already have sales tax for San Tomas and San Domingo County. Because Rock Castle Construction now does business in the city of Bayshore, you need to add sales tax items for that city.

To add a sales tax item:

1 From the Lists menu, choose Item List.

QuickBooks displays the Item list.

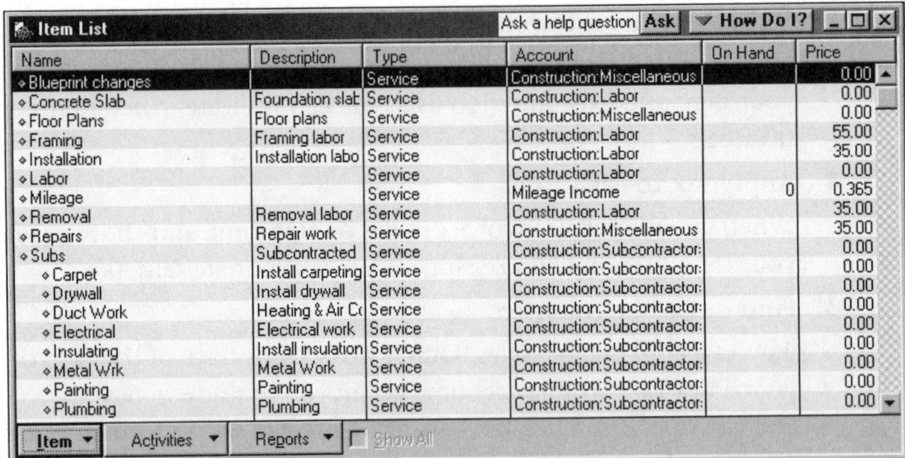

2 Click the Item menu button, and then choose New.

QuickBooks displays the New Item window.

3 In the Type field, choose Sales Tax Item from the drop-down list.

4 In the Tax Name field, type ***Bayshore***.

5 In the Description field, type ***Bayshore City***.

6 In the Tax Rate (%) field, type ***1***.

7 In the Tax Agency field, type ***Bayshore Tax Agency.***

Your New Item window should now resemble the following figure.

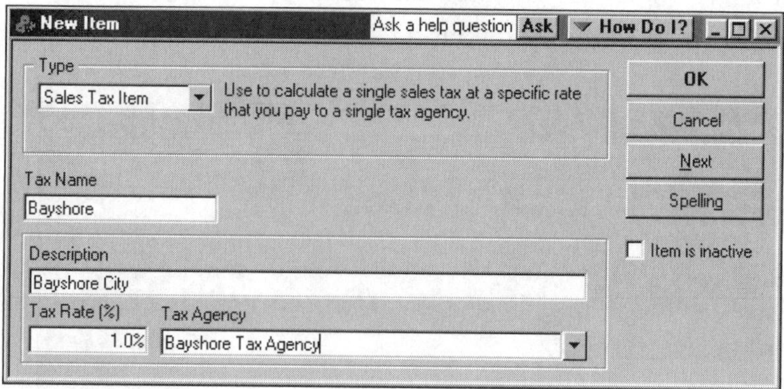

8 Click OK.

QuickBooks displays a message telling you that Bayshore Tax Agency is not on your Vendor list.

9 Click Quick Add.

QuickBooks adds Bayshore Tax Agency to the Vendor list.

10 Click OK.

Your Item list should resemble the following figure.

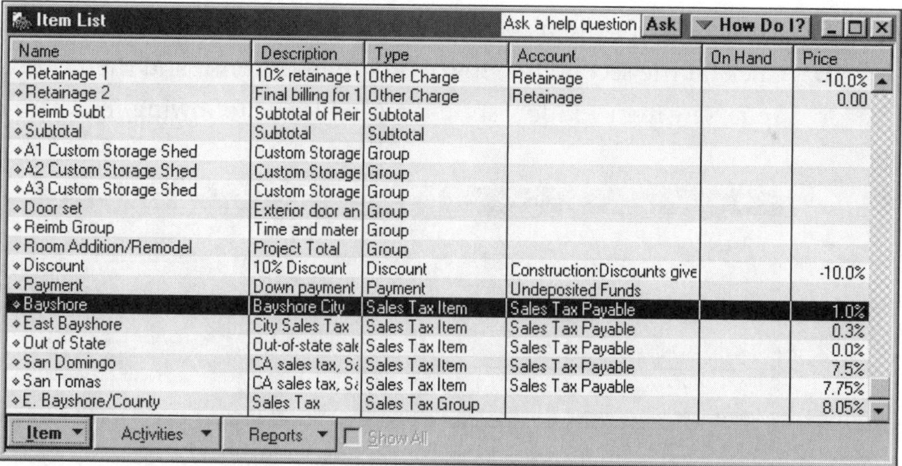

Grouping single taxes together

Even if you collect a combination of sales taxes (for example, city tax and county tax) that you report separately, you probably don't want to confuse customers by showing separate taxes on your invoices or sales forms. QuickBooks lets you group some or all of your tax items so that customers see a single tax amount on your invoices and sales receipts. Instead of a sales tax item, you'll be creating a sales tax group.

To create a sales tax group:

1 With the Item list displayed, click the Item menu button, and then choose New.

2 In the Type field, choose Sales Tax Group.

The New Item window on your screen should resemble the figure below.

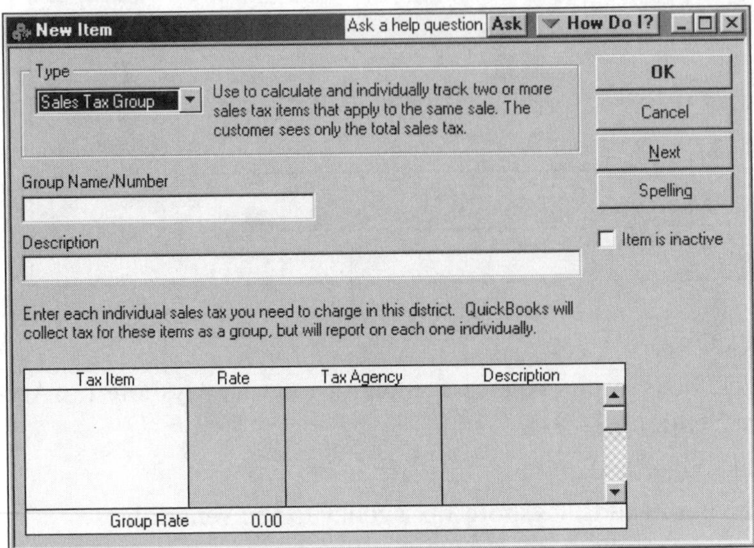

3 In the Group Name/Number field, type ***Bayshore Grp***.

4 In the Description field, type ***Sales Tax, Bayshore***.

5 Click in the Tax Item column, and then choose Bayshore from the drop-down list.

6 Click on the second line in the Tax Item column, and then choose San Tomas.

Your New Item window should resemble the following figure.

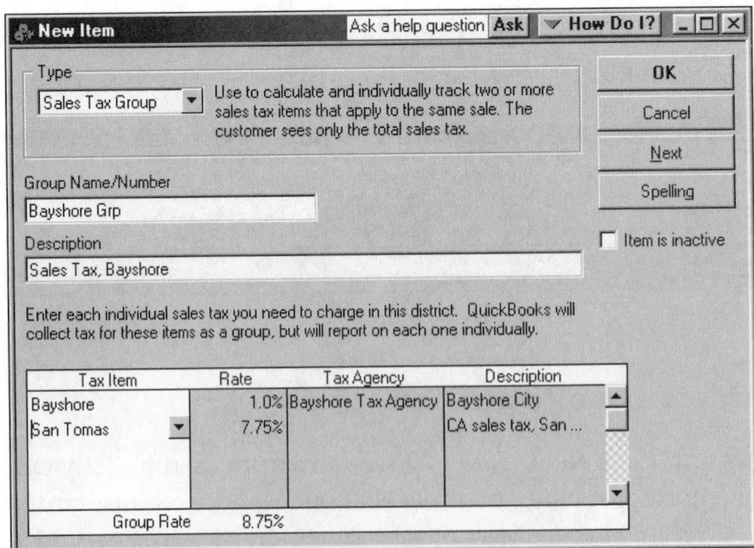

Notice that the total Group Rate is 8.75%.

7 Click OK.

QuickBooks adds the Bayshore Group to the Item list.

Identifying your most common tax

If you want QuickBooks to apply sales tax to your invoices and sales receipts, you have to tell it which sales tax item or group is the one you use most often. Once you do that, QuickBooks applies that sales tax when you fill out an invoice or a sales receipt. (You can choose a different sales tax from the sales form if you don't want the default tax.)

Assume Rock Castle Construction uses the San Tomas sales tax most often, and set that up as the default sales tax.

To set up a default sales tax:

1 From the Edit menu, choose Preferences.

QuickBooks displays the Preferences window.

2 In the Preferences window, click the Sales Tax icon in the left scroll box, and then click the Company Preferences tab.

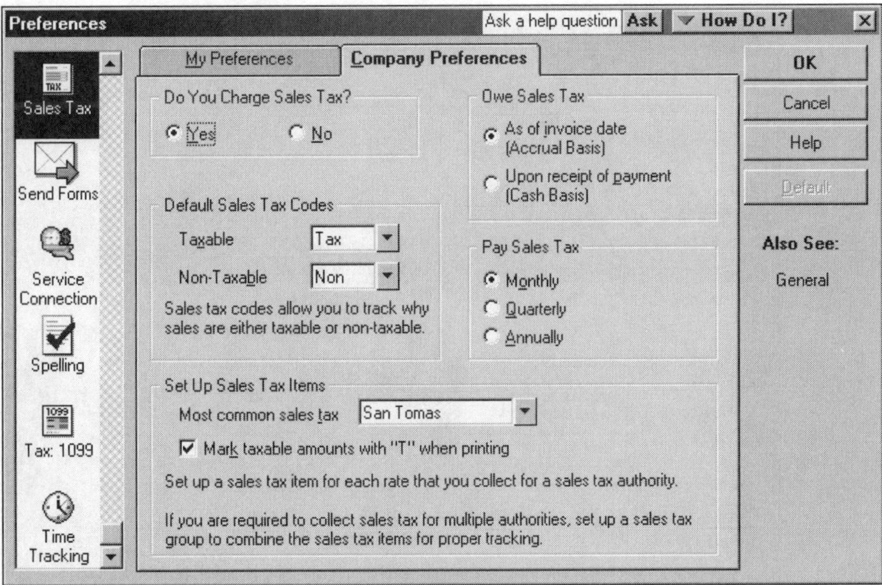

3 In the "Most common sales tax" field, make sure San Tomas is selected.

4 Click OK.

If you're using sales tax codes, you can use the Preferences window to tell QuickBooks which sales tax codes to use as the default taxable and non-taxable codes. You can use the codes that come preset with QuickBooks, or define your own. You can also manage sales tax codes using the Sales Tax Code list, which is available on the Lists menu when the sales tax feature is turned on in a company data file.

Indicating who and what gets taxed

The next step in setting up sales tax is to indicate who and what gets taxed. You have to tell QuickBooks whether or not a customer is taxable and assign a default tax item or tax group to that customer.

You must also distinguish between taxable and non-taxable items on the Item list. When you add an item to the Item list, there's a place in the window where you can indicate whether you charge tax for the item. QuickBooks remembers this information, and shows whether or not an item is taxable when you enter the item on a sales form.

In the next exercise, you'll take a look at an item on Rock Castle's Item list to see how to indicate that an item is taxable.

To indicate a taxable item:

1 In the Item list, select Doorknobs Std (under Hardware).

2 Click the Item menu button, and then choose Edit.

QuickBooks displays the Edit Item window.

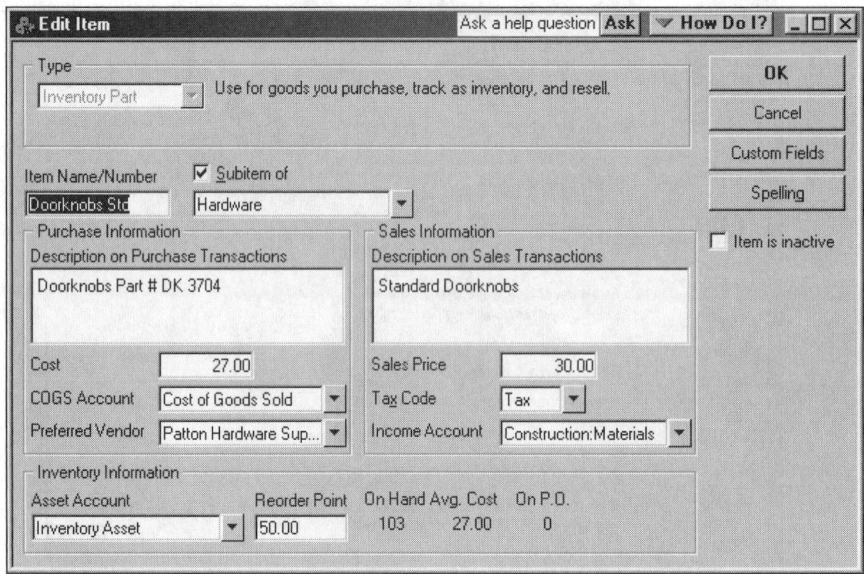

The code in the Tax Code field is a taxable code, which tells you that this item is taxable. When you choose the item to be included on a sales form, QuickBooks knows that the item is taxable and automatically applies the default sales tax (San Tomas sales tax with a rate of 7.75%).

To indicate that an item is non-taxable, select a non-taxable code from the drop-down list.

3 Click OK to close the Edit Item window.

4 Close the Item list.

In the same way that you can specify that an item in the Item list is taxable, you can indicate whether or not a particular customer is taxable or non-taxable in that customer's record.

To see an existing customer record:

1. From the Lists menu, choose Customer:Job List.

   QuickBooks displays the Customer:Job list.
2. Select Jimenez, Cristina.
3. Click the Customer:Job menu button, and then choose Edit.

   QuickBooks displays the Edit Customer window.

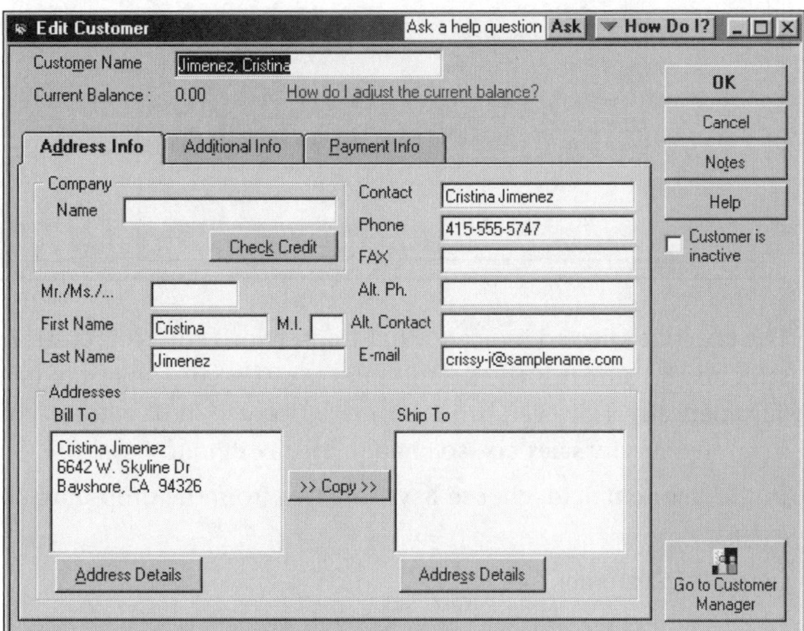

4 Click the Additional Info tab.

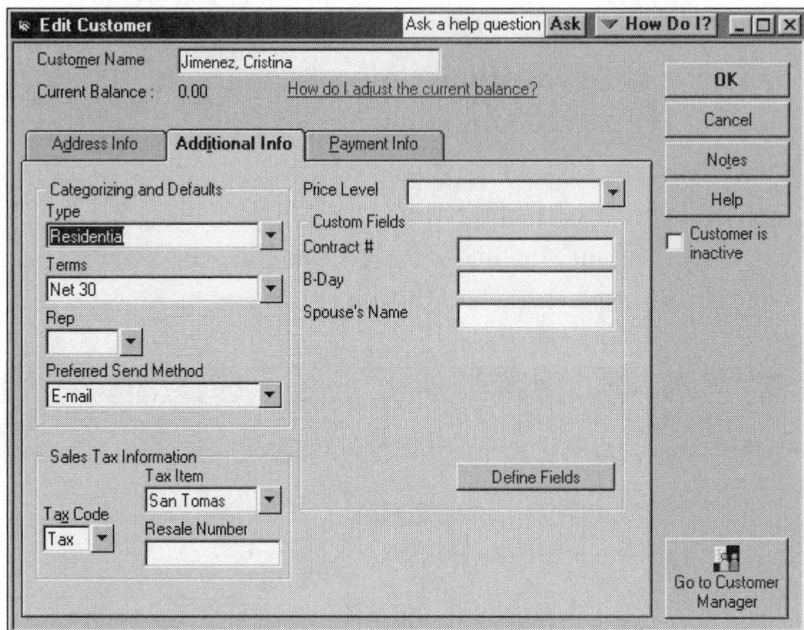

The tax code selected indicates that transactions with this customer are subject to sales tax. Because it is the default sales tax, the San Tomas tax item is assigned automatically. However, this customer is located in Bayshore, which has just instituted its city sales tax, so change the tax item to Bayshore Group.

5 In the Tax Item field, choose Bayshore Grp from the drop-down list.

6 Click OK.

7 Close the Customer:Job list.

Applying tax to each sale

If you've set up a default sales tax, assigned taxes to your customers, and marked taxable items you sell as taxable, QuickBooks automatically calculates and applies the tax when you make a sale.

To apply tax to a sale:

1 From the Customers menu, choose Create Invoices.

QuickBooks displays the Create Invoices window.

2 In the Customer:Job field, choose Jimenez, Cristina:Utility Shed from the drop-down list. (Select both the customer and the job.)

3 In Template field, select Custom Invoice from the drop-down list.

4 Click in the Item column and select Doorknobs Std from the drop-down list.

The Create Invoices window should resemble the figure below.

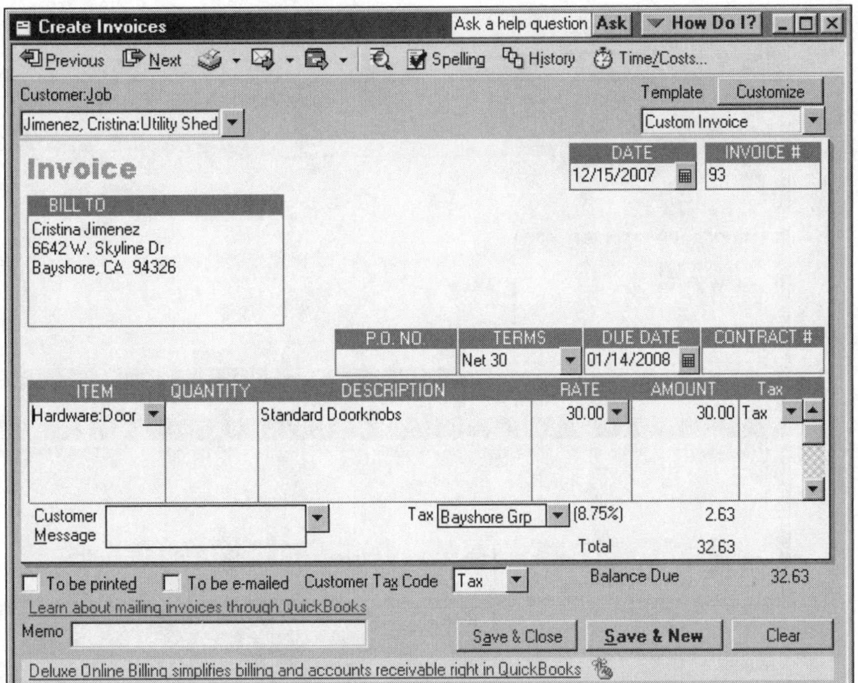

When you enter a taxable item, QuickBooks displays the tax code associated with that item in the Tax column (which appears to the right of the Amount column). If the customer is taxable, QuickBooks includes all items associated with a taxable tax code in its tax calculation.

Note: **You can select a different tax code from the list to turn taxable status on and off for unique situations.** You can also change the customer's taxable status by selecting a non-taxable code from the Customer Tax Code drop-down list.

Notice that QuickBooks applies to the Bayshore Group tax automatically because this is the sales tax you assigned to this customer.

5 In the Quantity column, type ***4***, and then press Tab.

The Create Invoices window should resemble the following figure.

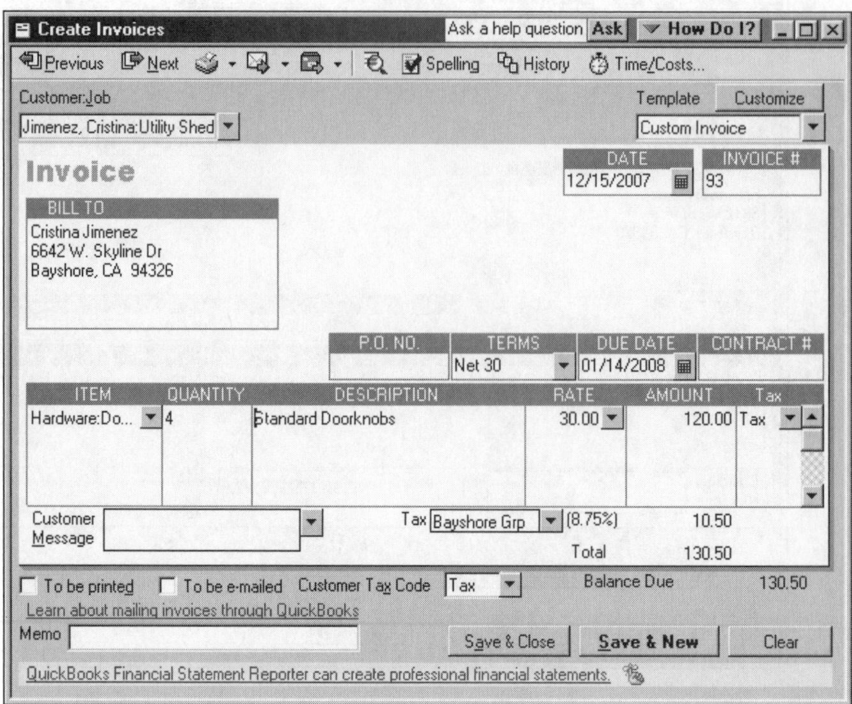

6 Click Save & Close.

Determining what you owe

If you're required to collect sales tax from customers, you also have to make periodic payments of the sales tax you've collected. QuickBooks gives you three ways to determine the amount of your sales tax liability: the sales tax liability report, the Sales Tax Payable register, and the Pay Sales Tax window.

Creating a sales tax liability report

The sales tax liability report provides complete information about the sales tax your company owes for a particular period of time.

To create the sales tax liability report:

1 From the Reports menu, choose Vendors & Payables, and then choose Sales Tax Liability.

Your report should resemble the following figure.

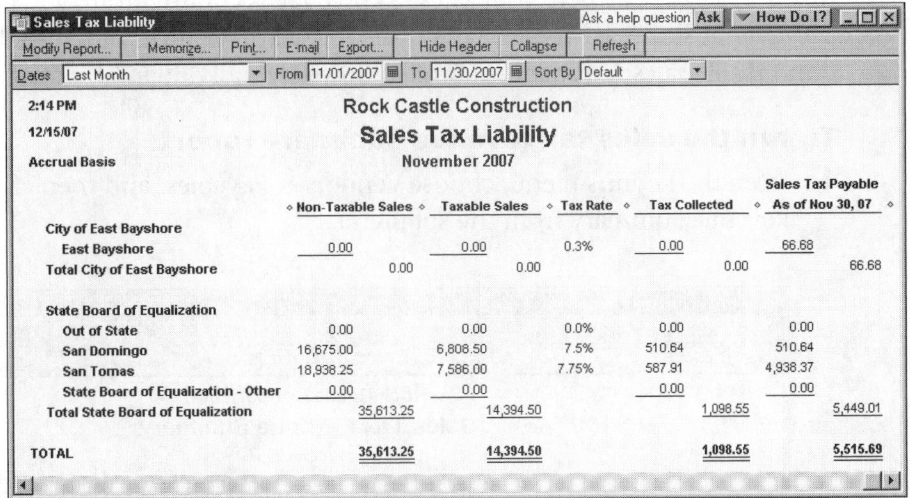

Sales Tax Liability

Dates: Last Month From 11/01/2007 To 11/30/2007 Sort By Default

2:14 PM
12/15/07
Accrual Basis

Rock Castle Construction
Sales Tax Liability
November 2007

	Non-Taxable Sales	Taxable Sales	Tax Rate	Tax Collected	Sales Tax Payable As of Nov 30, 07
City of East Bayshore					
East Bayshore	0.00	0.00	0.3%	0.00	66.68
Total City of East Bayshore	0.00	0.00		0.00	66.68
State Board of Equalization					
Out of State	0.00	0.00	0.0%	0.00	0.00
San Domingo	16,675.00	6,808.50	7.5%	510.64	510.64
San Tomas	18,938.25	7,586.00	7.75%	587.91	4,938.37
State Board of Equalization - Other	0.00	0.00		0.00	0.00
Total State Board of Equalization	35,613.25	14,394.50		1,098.55	5,449.01
TOTAL	35,613.25	14,394.50		1,098.55	5,515.69

2 In the Dates field, choose This Month-to-date from the drop-down list.

Your report should resemble the following figure.

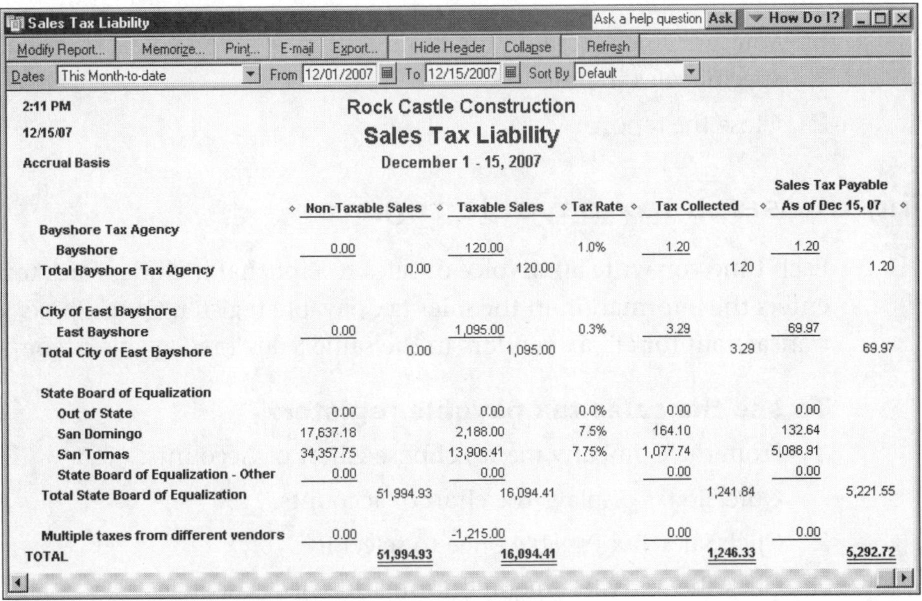

Sales Tax Liability

Dates: This Month-to-date From 12/01/2007 To 12/15/2007 Sort By Default

2:11 PM
12/15/07
Accrual Basis

Rock Castle Construction
Sales Tax Liability
December 1 - 15, 2007

	Non-Taxable Sales	Taxable Sales	Tax Rate	Tax Collected	Sales Tax Payable As of Dec 15, 07
Bayshore Tax Agency					
Bayshore	0.00	120.00	1.0%	1.20	1.20
Total Bayshore Tax Agency	0.00	120.00		1.20	1.20
City of East Bayshore					
East Bayshore	0.00	1,095.00	0.3%	3.29	69.97
Total City of East Bayshore	0.00	1,095.00		3.29	69.97
State Board of Equalization					
Out of State	0.00	0.00	0.0%	0.00	0.00
San Domingo	17,637.18	2,188.00	7.5%	164.10	132.64
San Tomas	34,357.75	13,906.41	7.75%	1,077.74	5,088.91
State Board of Equalization - Other	0.00	0.00		0.00	0.00
Total State Board of Equalization	51,994.93	16,094.41		1,241.84	5,221.55
Multiple taxes from different vendors	0.00	-1,215.00		0.00	0.00
TOTAL	51,994.93	16,094.41		1,246.33	5,292.72

The sales tax liability report shows the total taxable sales as of a date you choose, total non-taxable sales, and the amount of sales tax you owe each tax agency.

QuickBooks displays the sales tax liability report on an accrual basis (unless you changed the default setting in the Sales Tax Preferences window). The report shows exactly how much sales tax you collected.

3 Close the sales tax liability report.

4 If QuickBooks asks if you want to memorize the report, click No.

Determining the source of sales tax revenue

If you'd like to see where your sales tax revenue is coming from, you can run the sales tax revenue summary report, which shows you the sources of all taxable and non-taxable sales transactions, broken down by individual sales tax codes.

To run the sales tax revenue summary report:

1 From the Reports menu, choose Vendors & Payables, and then choose Sales Tax Revenue Summary from the submenu.

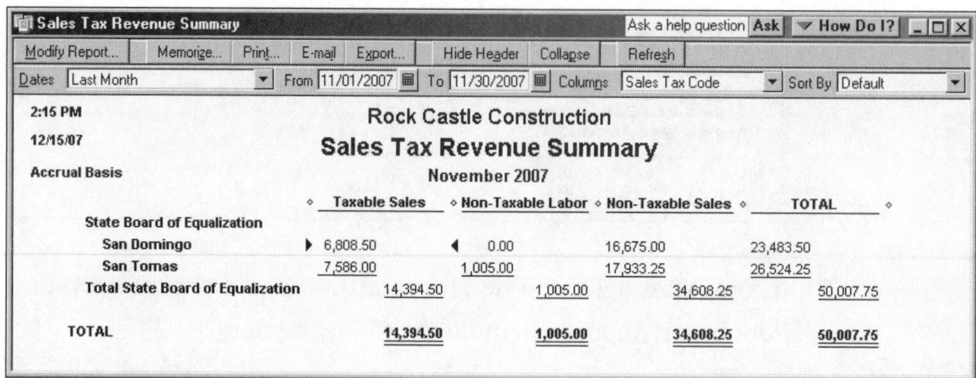

You can QuickZoom on the numbers in the report to get more information about specific sales transactions.

2 Close the report.

Using the sales tax payable register

Each time you write an invoice or sales receipt that includes sales tax, QuickBooks enters the information in the sales tax payable register. QuickBooks keeps track of transactions for all tax vendors in the same Sales Tax Payable account.

To see the sales tax payable register:

1 From the Company menu, choose Chart of Accounts.

QuickBooks displays the chart of accounts.

2 Click Sales Tax Payable once to select it.

3 Click the Activities menu button and select Use Register.

QuickBooks displays the Sales Tax Payable register.

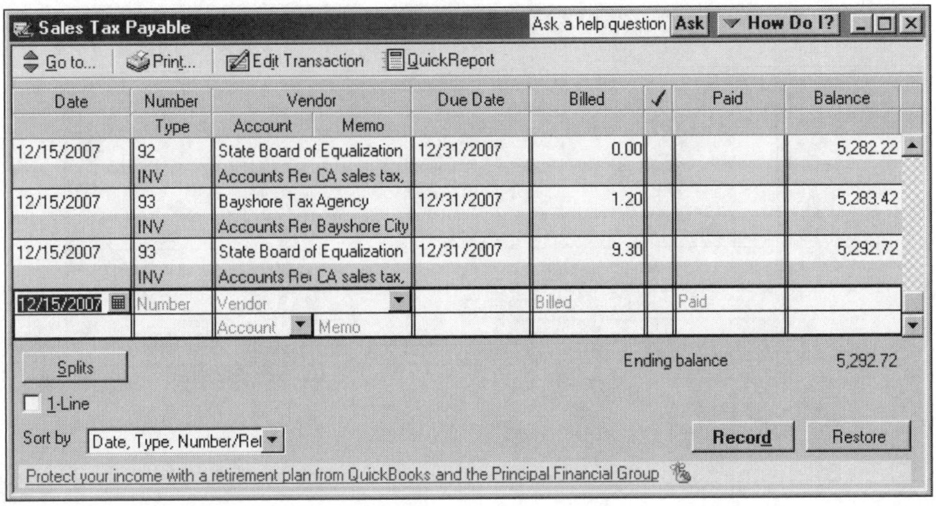

Each entry in the register is a single tax transaction. Taxes you record on invoices and sales receipts appear as increases, and payments you make to tax agencies appear as decreases. The ending balance of the register is your current tax liability.

Notice how some transactions have the same invoice number. When you record two tax rates on the same invoice or cash sale, the register shows a separate transaction for each tax agency. (This is because you have to make separate payments to individual tax agencies.)

4 Close the register.

5 Close the chart of accounts.

Paying your tax agencies

When it's time to pay sales tax, you use the Pay Sales Tax window to write a check to your tax agency or agencies. Suppose Rock Castle Construction is ready to make a sales tax payment.

To make a sales tax payment:

1 From the Vendors menu, choose Sales Tax, then choose Pay Sales Tax from the submenu.

QuickBooks displays the Pay Sales Tax window.

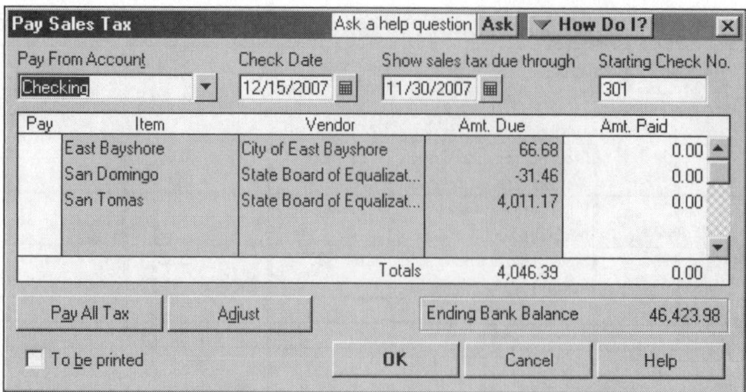

2 Select the "To be printed" checkbox.

3 In the "Show sales tax due through" field, type ***12/15/07***, and then press Tab.

QuickBooks displays tax agencies and the amounts you owe. To mark them for payment, click the Pay All Tax button.

The Pay Sales Tax window should resemble the figure below.

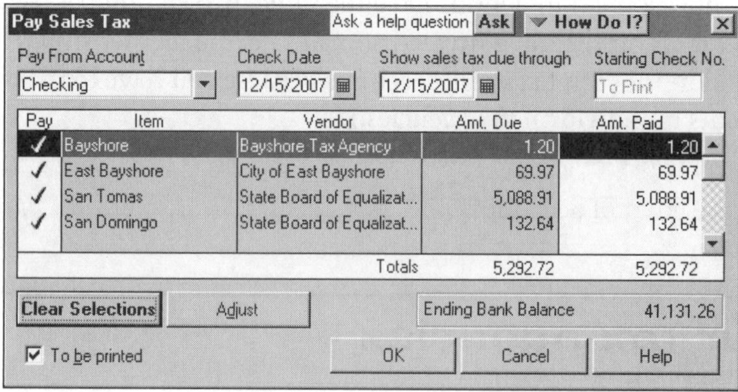

4 Click OK.

QuickBooks writes and records checks to the tax agencies you indicated. All you need to do is print the checks. QuickBooks updates your the tax report and sales tax payable register to show that you've paid the tax agencies.

Student test and review

1 Create an invoice for Pretell Real Estate's 155 Wilks Blvd. job, for 10 interior wood doors and 2 exterior wood doors.

2 After you record the invoice, open the sales tax payable register to see how QuickBooks has recorded the tax due from the invoice.

LESSON 12 Doing payroll with QuickBooks

Lesson objectives

- To gain an overview of payroll in QuickBooks
- To learn more about payroll setup
- To set up employee payroll information
- To practice writing and printing a payroll check
- To learn how QuickBooks tracks your tax liabilities
- To practice paying payroll taxes

Handout materials

- Handout 8: Employer payroll responsibilities
- Handout 9: Payroll item types
- Handout 10: List of payroll expenses and liabilities

Instructor preparation

- Review this lesson, including the examples, to make sure you're familiar with the material.
- Ensure that all students have a copy of qblesson.qbb on their computer's hard disk.
- Have Handouts 8 through 10 ready for distribution.

To start this lesson

Before you perform the following steps, make sure you have installed the exercise file (qblesson.qbb) on your hard disk. See "Installing the exercise file" in the Introduction to this guide if you haven't installed it.

The following steps restore the exercise file to its original state so that the data in the file matches what you see on the screen as you proceed through each lesson.

To restore the exercise file (qblesson.qbb):

1. From the File menu in QuickBooks, choose Restore.

   QuickBooks displays the Restore Company Backup window.
2. In the "Get Company Backup From" section of the window, click Browse and select your c:\QBtrain directory.
3. Select the qblesson.qbb file, and then click Open.
4. In the "Restore Company Backup To" section of the window, click Browse and select your c:\QBtrain directory.

5 In the File name field of the Restore To window, type ***lesson 12*** and then click Save.

6 Click Restore.

Overview of payroll tracking

Refer to Handout 8, "Overview of payroll tracking" for the following discussion.

This lesson is designed to demonstrate some of the QuickBooks payroll features. The way you process payroll for your company may differ from this lesson depending on which (if any) payroll service you subscribe to.

Because payroll information is already set up in the exercise file, you will not go through the payroll setup process in this lesson. For information about setting up payroll for your company in QuickBooks, see "Setting up payroll" in Chapter 17 of *QuickBooks Fundamentals*.

To calculate payroll, QuickBooks uses tax tables. The exercise file includes the tax table data needed to complete this lesson. To get the tax tables to use with your own QuickBooks company data file, you need to subscribe to one of the Intuit Payroll Services—either Do-It-Yourself Payroll or Assisted Payroll. Intuit also offers a full service payroll option. To learn about these options or subscribe to one of them, from the Employees menu, choose Payroll Services, and then choose Learn About Payroll Options from the submenu. Or see "About Intuit Payroll Services" in Chapter 17 of *QuickBooks Fundamentals* to get an overview of these services and to find contact information.

QuickBooks calculates each employee's gross pay, and then calculates taxes and deductions to arrive at the net pay. With QuickBooks, you can write the paycheck, record the transaction in your QuickBooks checking account, keep track of your tax liabilities, and pay them.

You, as the employer, must subtract taxes and other deductions before issuing an employee's paycheck. Some typical paycheck deductions are federal and state withholding (income) taxes, social security taxes (FICA), Medicare taxes, and state unemployment insurance. You may also deduct for benefits such as a 401(k) plan, or contributions to your company's medical/dental plan.

When you withhold social security, Medicare, and federal withholding taxes from employees' paychecks, you must submit regular deposits of the withheld tax money (semiweekly or monthly, depending on the size of your payroll), and file quarterly forms that list the total amounts you withheld from each employee's paycheck.

Calculating payroll with QuickBooks

To do its payroll calculations, QuickBooks needs four kinds of information:

- **Information about your company**

  Besides the company name and address, this includes information about your federal and state tax ID numbers. You enter this information in the EasyStep Interview when you set up your QuickBooks company data file. (You can view most company information by choosing Company Information from the Company menu.)

- **Information about your employees**

  The QuickBooks Employee list stores general information about each of your employees, and specific information related to payroll (such as the employee's salary or hourly rate, filing status, number of exemptions, and miscellaneous additions, deductions, and company contributions). You can store payroll information that most employees have in common in employee defaults. Whenever you have a new employee to add, simply enter information that's specific to that employee (name, address, and so on).

- **Information about your payroll items**

  QuickBooks maintains a list of items that affect the amount on a payroll check, including company expenses related to payroll. When you specify that you want to use payroll, QuickBooks creates a number of payroll items for you. You add others as you need them.

- **Tax tables for federal, state, and local withholdings**

  QuickBooks uses tax tables to calculate payroll. You get the current tax tables and keep them current when you subscribe to one of the Intuit Payroll Services mentioned on page 253. If you choose not to subscribe to one of these two payroll services, you need to calculate and enter your payroll tax deductions manually for each paycheck.

  Once you've set up your company, employee data, and payroll items, to run payroll you enter the number of hours worked during the pay period for each employee. QuickBooks calculates the gross wages for the employee, and then refers to its tax tables (if you've subscribed to one of the Intuit Payroll Services—Do-It-Yourself Payroll or Assisted Payroll) and the company and employee information you've entered to calculate all withholdings and deductions and to arrive at the net pay figure. QuickBooks also calculates your company payroll expenses (for example, your contributions to social security and Medicare).

Setting up for payroll

By default, the QuickBooks payroll feature is turned on.

To turn payroll off in a company data file:

1 From the Edit menu, choose Preferences, and click the Payroll & Employees icon.

2 Click the Company Preferences tab and select "No payroll."

Note: You can also turn off the payroll feature during the EasyStep Interview.

3 Click OK.

Understanding payroll items

Refer to Handout 9, "Items on the Payroll Item list," for this discussion.

QuickBooks maintains a list for everything that affects the amount on a payroll check and for every company expense related to payroll. This list is called the Payroll Item list. There are payroll items for compensation, taxes, other additions and deductions, and employer-paid expenses. QuickBooks uses payroll items to track individual amounts on a paycheck and accumulated year-to-date wage and tax amounts for each employee.

QuickBooks adds some items to the list for you, and you can add others as you need them. For common payroll items, such as compensation and benefits, QuickBooks provides extra assistance so you can set them up quickly and accurately.

You work directly with payroll items as you do payroll tasks. Behind the scenes, QuickBooks tracks your payroll liabilities in the Payroll Liabilities account (an Other Current Liability account) and your payroll expenses in the Payroll Expenses account.

To view the Payroll Item list:

1 From the Employees menu, choose Payroll Item List. (You must have payroll turned on to see this choice.)

QuickBooks displays the Payroll Item list.

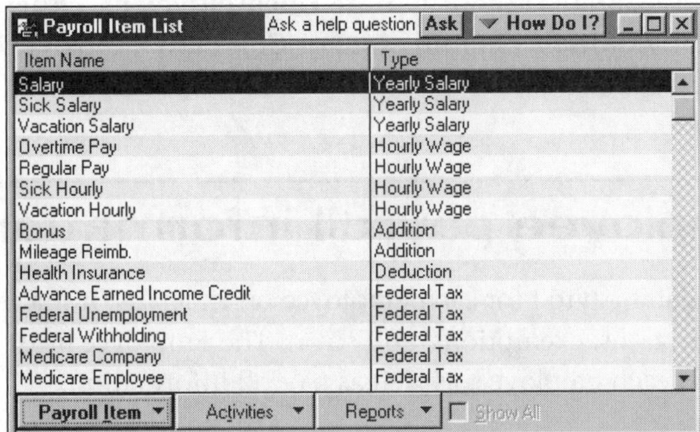

You've already used the QuickBooks Item list, so this list should look familiar. Just like the regular Item list, each payroll item has a Name and a Type.

The names of the payroll items are what you'll see on paychecks and in payroll reports.

2 Close the Payroll Item list.

You won't add a new payroll item in this lesson, but if you need to add an item after you've set up payroll in QuickBooks, you can use the following procedure.

To add a payroll item:

1. From the Employees menu, choose Payroll Item list.
2. Click the Payroll Item menu button, and then choose New.
3. QuickBooks displays the Add new payroll item window, which steps you through the payroll item setup process.

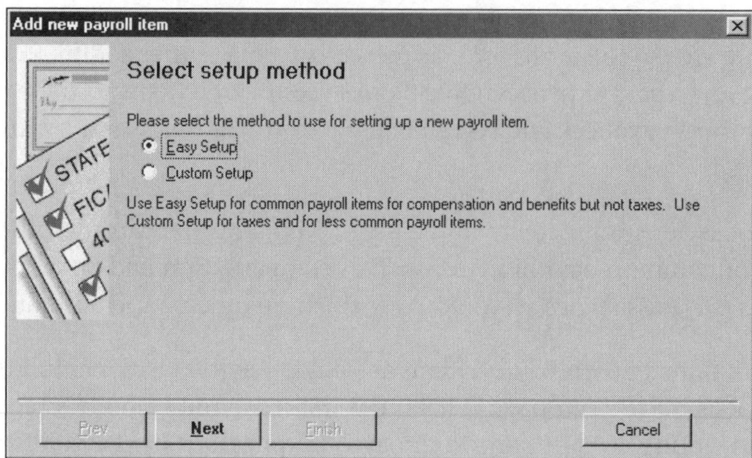

Select Easy Setup for common payroll items or compensation and benefits. Use Custom Setup for taxes and less common payroll items.

Tip: **Depending on your company's payroll, you may need additional payroll items of the following types: Yearly salary, Hourly Wage, State Withholding, State Disability, State Unemployment, Other Tax, Deduction, Addition, Commission, or Company Contribution.** Consult with your tax advisor.

Setting up employee payroll information

QuickBooks calculates payroll for each employee on the basis of that employee's pay rate, filing marital status, exemptions, and so on. The Employee list stores general information about each employee, as well as payroll information.

What information does QuickBooks store?

You're going to add a new employee to Rock Castle Construction payroll in a moment. First, look at the information QuickBooks stores in the Employee list.

To view information stored in the Employee list:

1 From the Employees menu, choose Employee List.

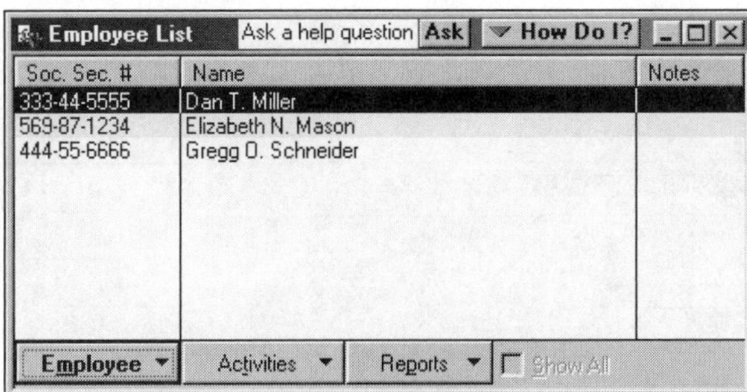

2 Select Dan T. Miller in the list, and then choose Edit from the Employee menu button.

QuickBooks displays the Edit Employee window for Dan T. Miller.

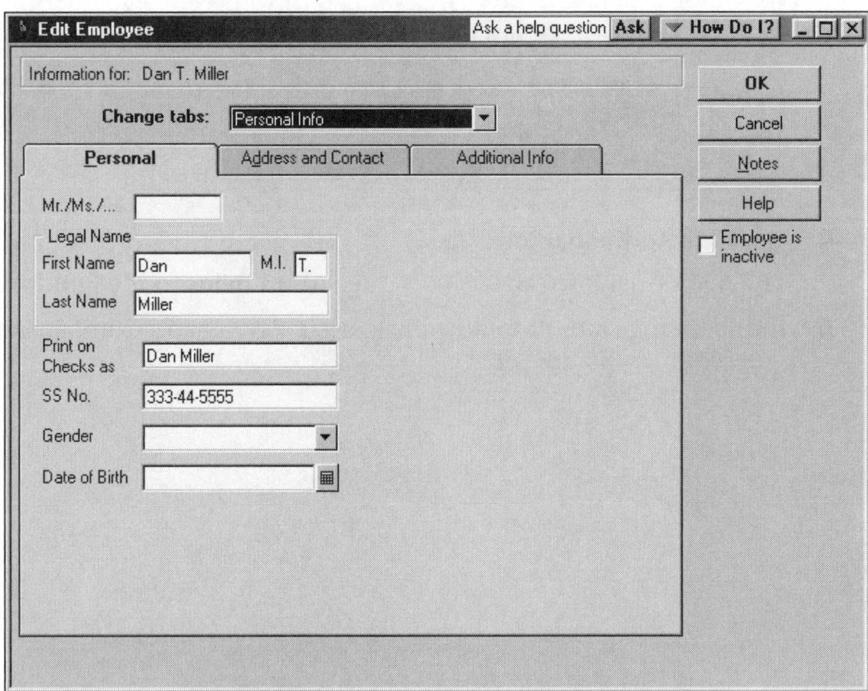

The Personal tab contains general information about Dan Miller, such as his name, social security number, and date of birth.

3 Click the Address and Contact tab.

This is where QuickBooks stores employees' addresses, telephone numbers, and other contact information.

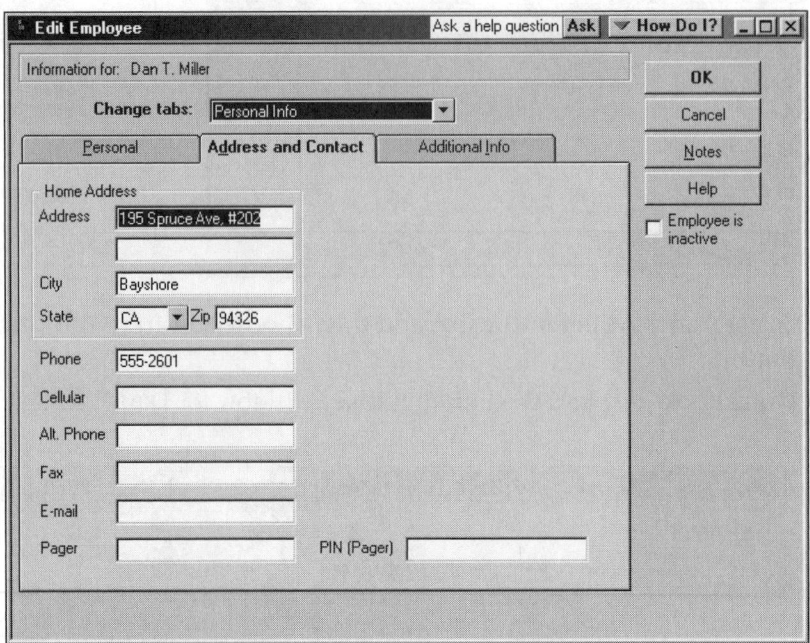

4 Click the Additional Info tab.

The Additional Info tab lets you add custom fields to the Employee list.

5 In the Change tabs drop-down list, select Payroll and Compensation Info.

QuickBooks displays the Payroll Info tab of the Edit Employee window. This is where QuickBooks stores payroll information.

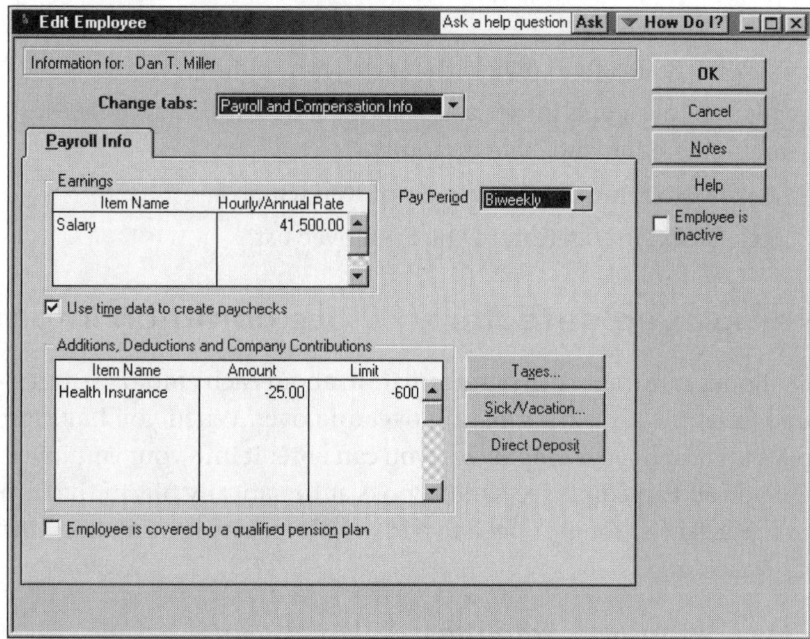

The Payroll Info tab contains an employee's specific salary or hourly rate, and any additions, deductions, or company contributions. You can see tax information for this employee (the type of information you get from a W-4) by clicking the Taxes button.

6 Click Taxes.

QuickBooks displays the Federal tab of the Taxes for Dan T. Miller window.

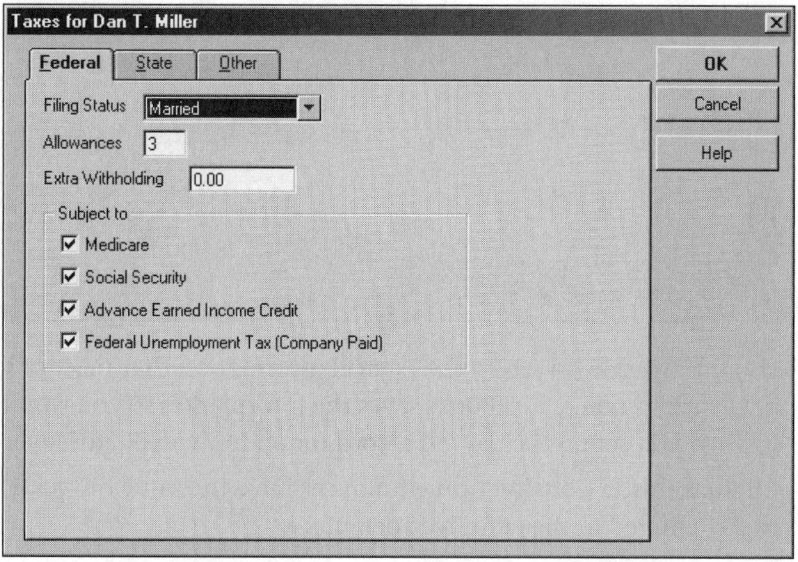

The checkboxes indicate the types of taxes the employee should have deducted from each paycheck. A checkmark in the Federal Unemployment checkbox indicates that this employee's pay is subject to the employer-paid federal unemployment tax.

7 Click the State tab to review the state withholdings.

This window stores information about state withholding taxes, state unemployment, and state disability.

8 Click OK to return to the Edit Employee window.

9 Click OK again to return to the Employee list.

Using the employee defaults to store common information

QuickBooks stores a wealth of information about each employee, but it doesn't require you to enter the same information over and over. When you have information that applies to most of your employees, you can enter it into your employee defaults. Then, when you add an employee, QuickBooks automatically fills in the information stored with the defaults. You just need to add or change any information that is different for a particular employee.

To view employee defaults:

1 With the Employee list displayed, choose Employee Defaults from the Employee menu button.

QuickBooks displays the Employee Defaults window.

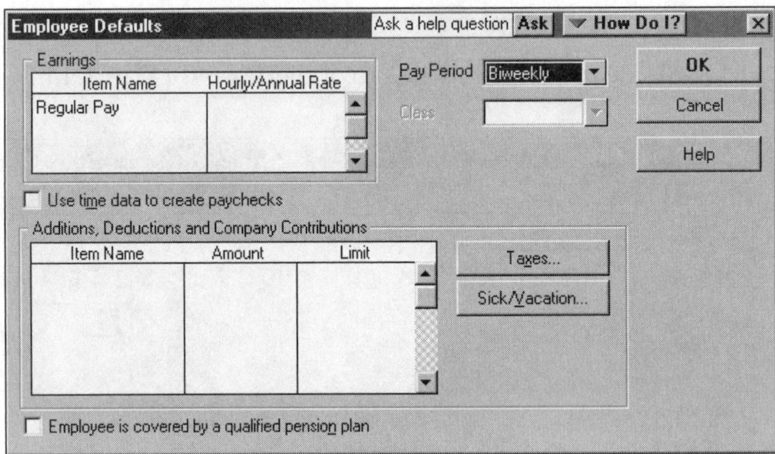

Use this window to set up the payroll information that most of your employees have in common. QuickBooks saves the information so you won't have to re-enter it when you set up the payroll record for an individual employee.

All Rock Castle Construction employees have the same biweekly pay period, so that is entered in the employee defaults.

In addition, all employees are subject to a deduction for health insurance, limited to a maximum of $1,200. This information isn't reflected in the defaults, so you can add it now.

2 Select the "Use time data to create paychecks" checkbox to include pay for time entered using the time tracking feature (available in QuickBooks Pro and Premier products only).

3 In the Additions, Deductions and Company Contributions area, click in the Item Name column, and then choose Health Insurance from the drop-down list.

4 In the Amount column, type ***50*** and press Tab.

Your screen should look like the following.

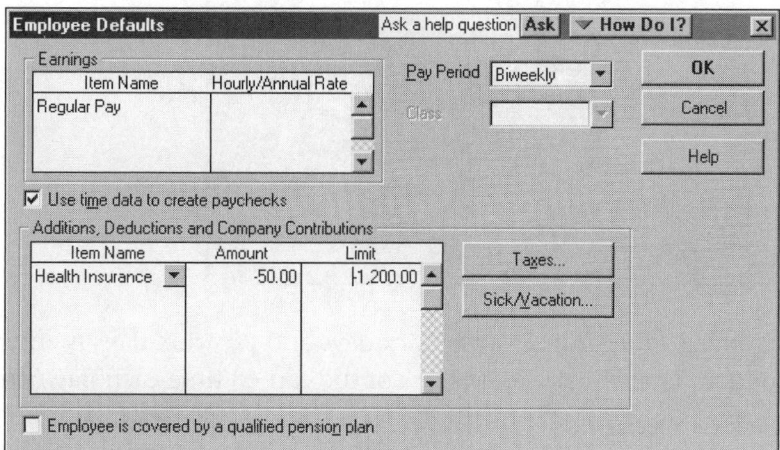

5 Click Taxes.

QuickBooks displays the Federal tab of the Taxes Defaults window.

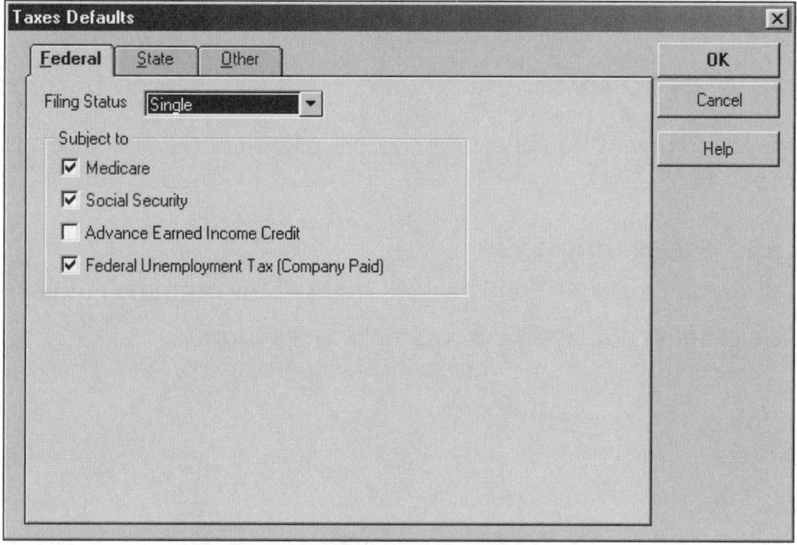

The withholding taxes that should be deducted from each employee paycheck are entered in this window.

6 Click Cancel to close the Taxes Defaults window.

7 Click Sick/Vacation.

QuickBooks displays the Sick & Vacation Defaults window.

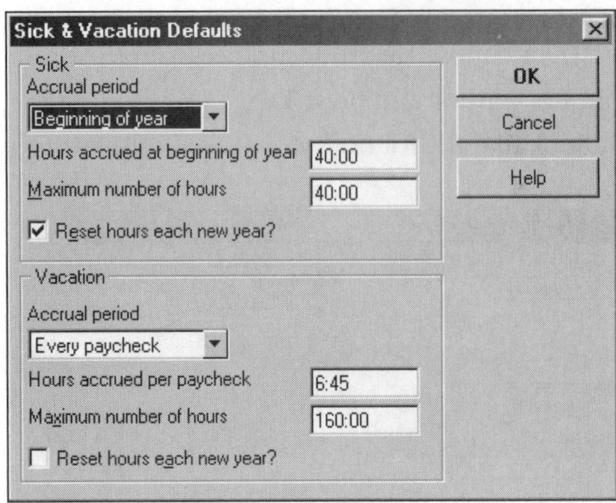

Information regarding earned sick days and vacation days is entered in this window. QuickBooks keeps track of the earned time each pay period.

8 Click Cancel to close the Sick & Vacation Defaults window.

9 Click OK to close the Employee Defaults window.

Tip: **The employee defaults affect employees you set up in the future.** If your employee list already contains names of employees but does not have payroll information for them, the defaults will not be applied to those employees.

Adding a new employee

Suppose you have a new employee on the payroll and want to add him to your records.

To add a new employee:

1 With the Employee list displayed, choose New from the Employee menu button.

QuickBooks displays the New Employee window.

2 On the Personal tab, enter the employee data as shown below.

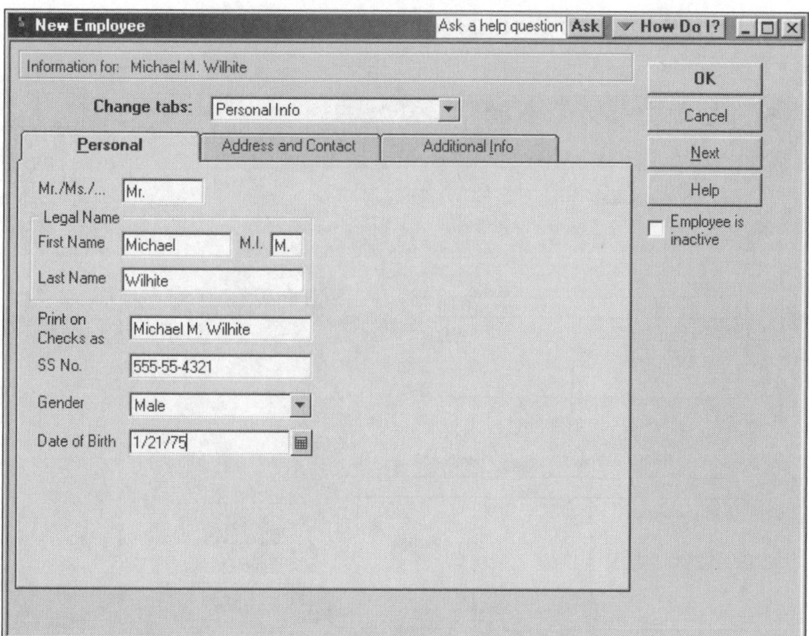

3 On the Address and Contact tab, enter the employee data as follows.

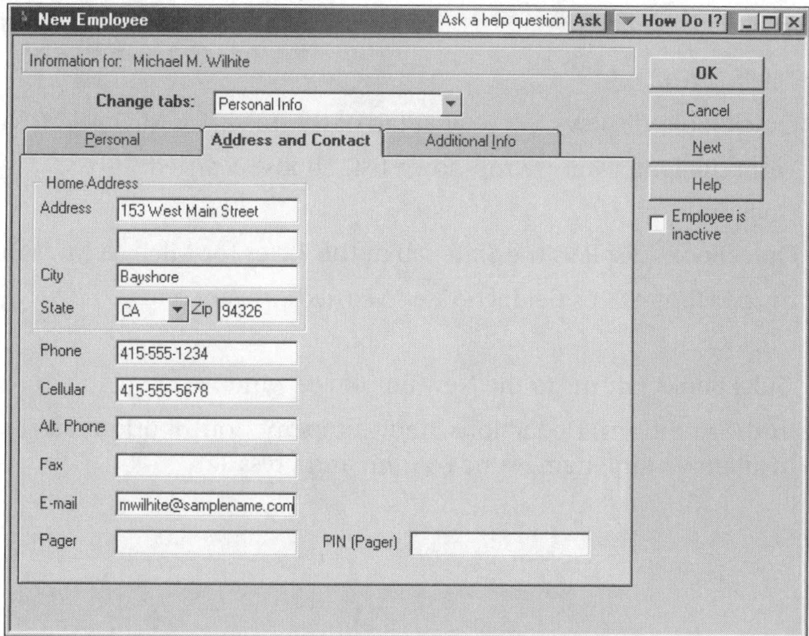

4 In the Change tabs drop-down list, select Employment Info.

5 In the Hire Date field, enter 11/28/2007.

6 In the Change tabs drop-down list, select Payroll and Compensation Info.

7 In the Earnings section of the window, click the Item Name column and press Tab. (Notice that the Regular Pay item is displayed already.)

8 In the Hour/Annual Rate column for the Regular Pay payroll item, type ***15***. Then press Tab.

The Payroll Info tab should look like the following.

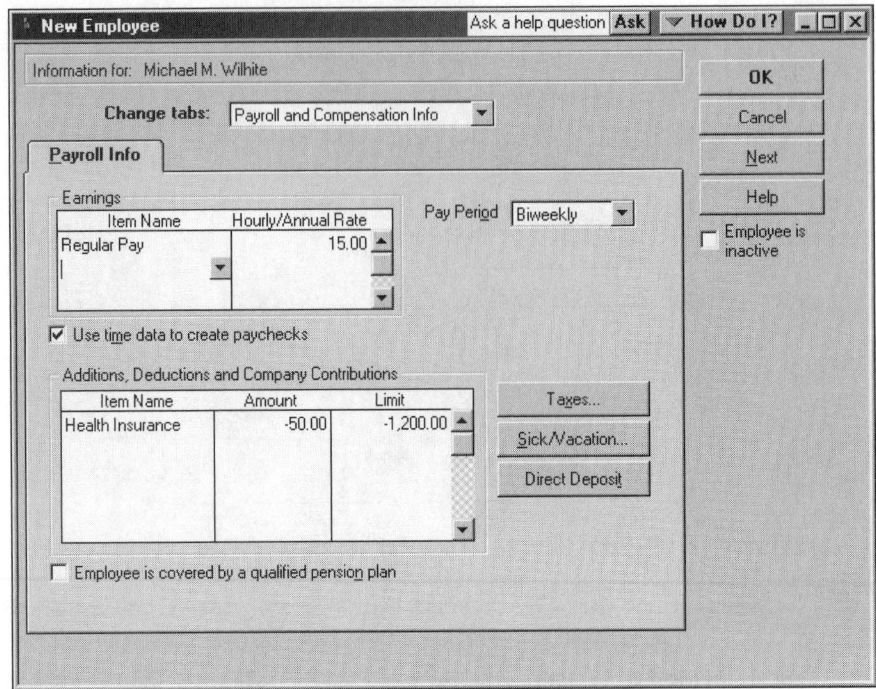

9 Click Taxes.

QuickBooks displays the Federal tab of the Taxes for Michael M. Wilhite window.

10 From the Filing Status drop-down list, choose Married.

11 Click State.

QuickBooks displays the State tab of the Taxes for Michael M. Wilhite window.

12 In the Filing Status field, choose "Married (two incomes)."

13 Click OK.

QuickBooks returns to the New Employee window.

14 In the Additions, Deductions, and Company Contributions area, select Health Insurance in the Item Name column and press Tab.

15 In the Amount column, type ***15*** and press Tab.

QuickBooks enters –15.00 in the Amount column. The New Employee window should now look like this.

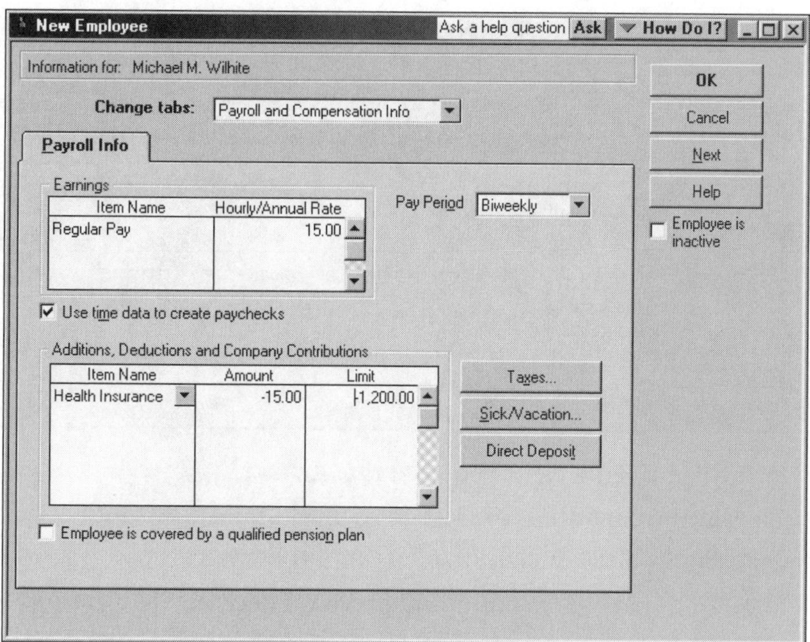

16 Click OK.

17 When QuickBooks asks whether you want to set up additional payroll information, click Leave As Is.

QuickBooks returns to the Employee list, where the new employee's name is now displayed.

18 Close the Employee list.

Writing a paycheck

QuickBooks lets you print payroll checks in a batch or one at a time. You may want to process the paychecks of salaried employees in a batch, and do payroll for the hourly employees one at a time.

To run a paycheck:

1 From the Employees menu, choose Pay Employees.

QuickBooks displays the Select Employees To Pay window.

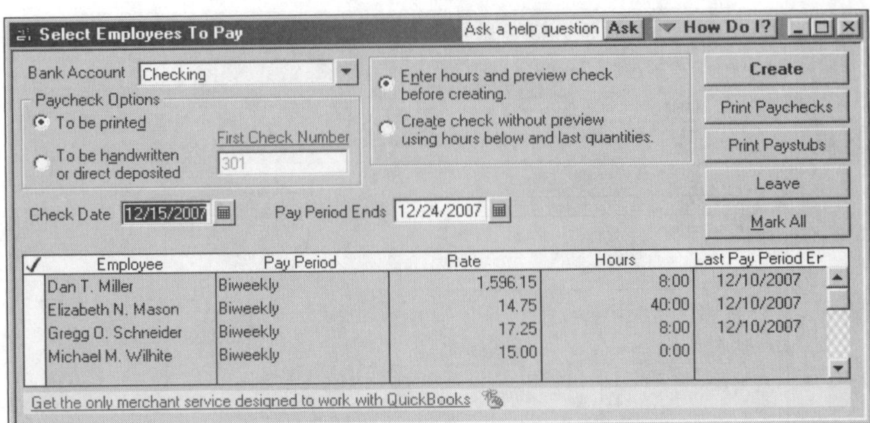

2 In the Period Ends field, type ***12/15/2007***.

3 Click in the column to the left of Michael M. Wilhite's name.

QuickBooks places a checkmark next to the name.

4 Make sure that "Enter hours and preview check before creating" is selected.

5 Click Create.

6 If QuickBooks indicates that there is no time data for this employee, click OK.

QuickBooks displays the Preview Paycheck window. Now you can enter the time Michael worked.

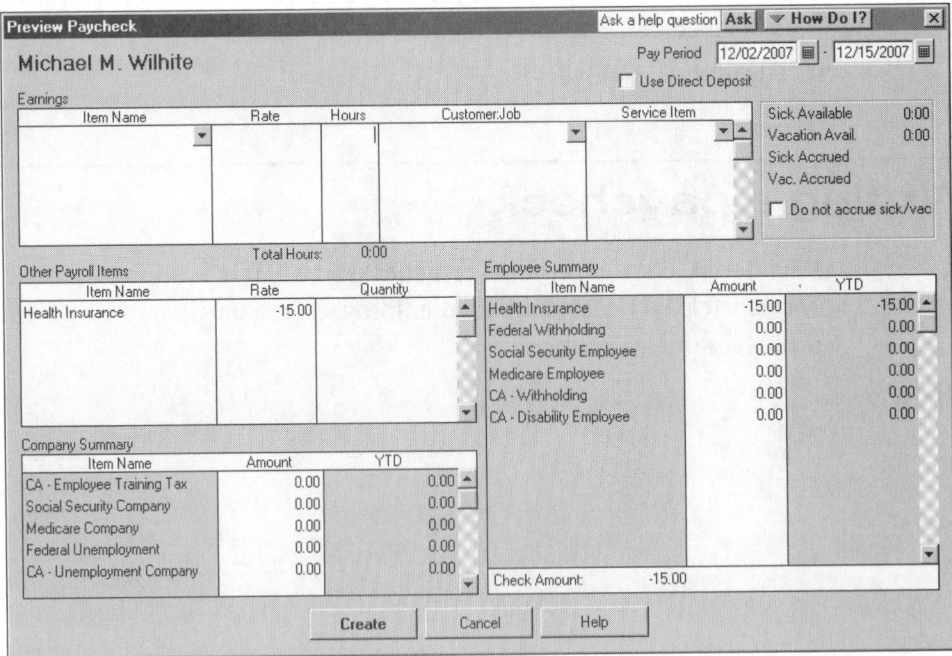

7 In the Earnings section, click in the Item Name column, and then select Regular Pay from the drop-down list.

8 Tab to the Rate column and type ***15***.

9 In the Hours column, type ***80*** and press Tab.

QuickBooks fills in the Employee Summary area of the Preview Paycheck window, showing the gross regular pay and all of the deductions from Michael's paycheck. The net amount of the check appears at the bottom.

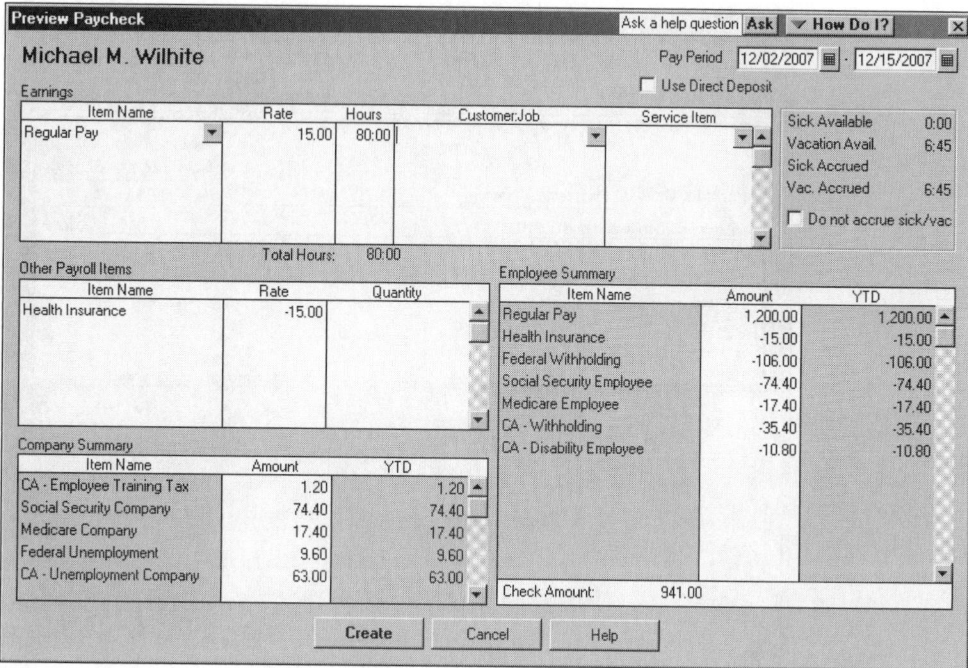

Because payroll tax rates change regularly, your numbers may vary from this illustration.

The Company Summary area of the window shows company-paid taxes and contributions that don't affect the amount of the paycheck (company-paid benefits).

10 Click Create.

QuickBooks writes a payroll check for the correct net amount, showing the deductions in the voucher area.

QuickBooks displays the Select Employees To Pay window.

11 You don't want to pay another employee now, so click Leave.

Viewing the paycheck

QuickBooks records payroll checks in your QuickBooks checking account register. You can see the check by going to the register.

To view the paycheck from the register:

1 From the Lists menu, choose Chart of Accounts.

2 Double-click "Checking."

QuickBooks displays the Checking account register.

3 Select the paycheck transaction for Michael M. Wilhite, and click Edit Transaction.

QuickBooks displays the Paycheck – Checking window for Michael. Notice that the Paycheck Summary shows a summary of the check's deductions. If you want to see the deductions that make up this total, you can click the Paycheck Detail button.

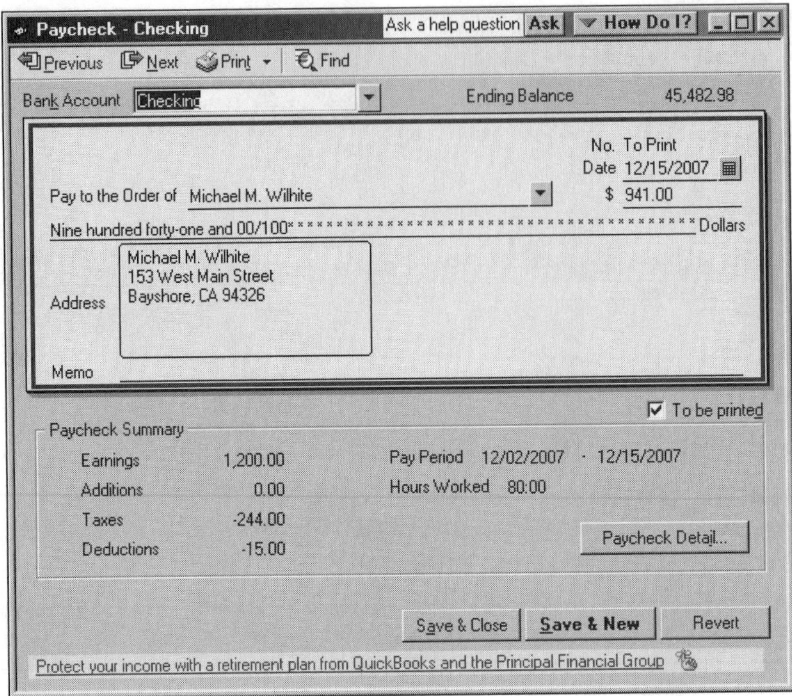

4 Click Save & Close to close the Paycheck – Checking window.

5 Close the checking account register, but leave the chart of accounts open.

Printing paycheck stubs

You can print paychecks as you would any QuickBooks check. If you use voucher checks, QuickBooks prints the payroll item detail in the voucher area. If you don't use voucher checks, you can print a paystub to give to your employees.

To print a paycheck:

1 From the File menu, choose Print Forms, and then choose Paychecks. QuickBooks displays the Select Paychecks to Print window.

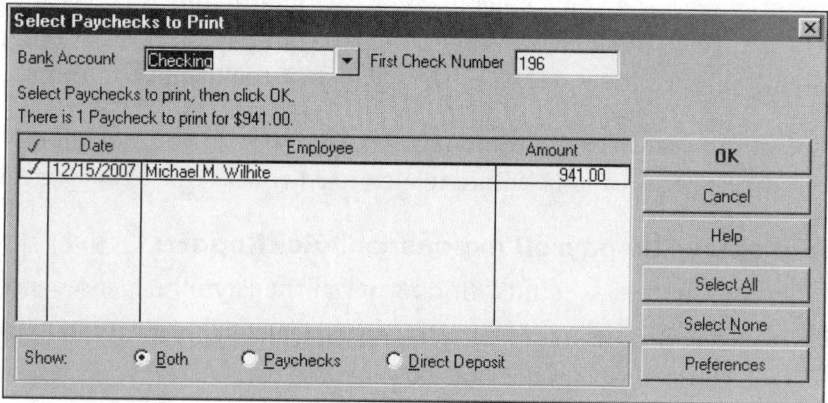

2 In the First Check Number field, type ***301***.

3 Make sure there's a checkmark next to Michael Wilhite's name, and then click OK.

4 Click Print.

Tracking your tax liabilities

Refer to Handout 10, "Tracking payroll expenses and payroll liabilities."

As an employer, you need to track both payroll expenses and payroll liabilities. These are the company payroll expenses you need to track:

- Employees' gross pay
- Employer payroll taxes, such as contributions to social security (FICA), Medicare, federal and state unemployment insurance, and state disability insurance

QuickBooks uses an expense account called Payroll Expenses to track these actual costs to your company. (The funds you deduct from employee paychecks aren't considered an actual cost because they're monies you're holding for the government; they don't come directly from your company assets.) Whenever you run your payroll, QuickBooks keeps track of your company's expenses for each employee. You can then see totals for these expenses on the payroll summary by employee report and on the profit and loss statement.

QuickBooks uses the Payroll Liabilities account (an Other Current Liability account) to track what you owe to the government. When you do your payroll, QuickBooks calculates how much you owe for each tax, deduction, or company contribution payroll item and records that information as a transaction in the liability account. This produces a record of how much tax you owe at any time, so you can plan to have the cash available for payment. When you pay your payroll taxes or other payroll liabilities, QuickBooks decreases the balance of the liability account.

Look at the payroll expense and liability accounts, so you can see how QuickBooks recorded expenses and liabilities related to Michael Wilhite's paycheck.

To display the payroll expenses QuickReport:

1 In the Chart of Accounts window, select the Payroll Expenses account.

2 From the Reports menu button, choose QuickReport: Payroll Expenses.

QuickBooks displays the QuickReport. You can scroll through the report to see the expense items paid by the company for Michael Wilhite's paycheck.

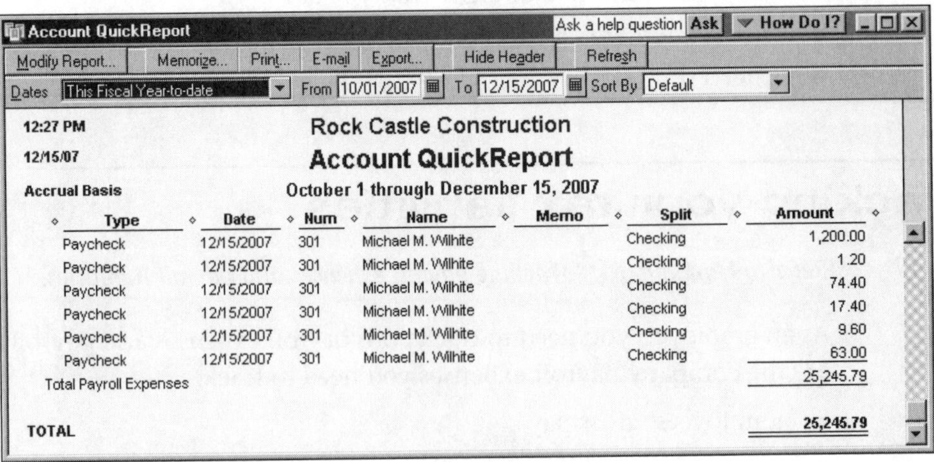

12:27 PM
12/15/07
Accrual Basis

Rock Castle Construction
Account QuickReport
October 1 through December 15, 2007

Type	Date	Num	Name	Memo	Split	Amount
Paycheck	12/15/2007	301	Michael M. Wilhite		Checking	1,200.00
Paycheck	12/15/2007	301	Michael M. Wilhite		Checking	1.20
Paycheck	12/15/2007	301	Michael M. Wilhite		Checking	74.40
Paycheck	12/15/2007	301	Michael M. Wilhite		Checking	17.40
Paycheck	12/15/2007	301	Michael M. Wilhite		Checking	9.60
Paycheck	12/15/2007	301	Michael M. Wilhite		Checking	63.00
Total Payroll Expenses						25,245.79
TOTAL						25,245.79

3 Close the QuickReport.

4 In the chart of accounts, double-click the Payroll Liabilities account.

QuickBooks displays the register for the account. The register shows a separate transaction for each item from Michael's paycheck. The running balance shows an increase for every liability.

Payroll Liabilities — Ask a help question | Ask | How Do I?

Go to... | Print... | Edit Transaction | QuickReport

Date	Ref / Type	Payee / Account	Memo	Increase	✓	Decrease	Balance
12/15/2007	301 / PAY CHK	Michael M. Wilhite / Checking [split]		15.00			3,193.06
12/15/2007	301 / PAY CHK	Michael M. Wilhite / Checking [split]		1.20			3,194.26
12/15/2007	301 / PAY CHK	Michael M. Wilhite / Checking [split]		106.00			3,300.26
12/15/2007	301 / PAY CHK	Michael M. Wilhite / Checking [split]		74.40			3,374.66
12/15/2007	301 / PAY CHK	Michael M. Wilhite / Checking [split]		74.40			3,449.06
12/15/2007	301 / PAY CHK	Michael M. Wilhite / Checking [split]		17.40			3,466.46
12/15/2007	301 / PAY CHK	Michael M. Wilhite / Checking [split]		17.40			3,483.86
12/15/2007	301 / PAY CHK	Michael M. Wilhite / Checking [split]		9.60			3,493.46
12/15/2007	301 / PAY CHK	Michael M. Wilhite / Checking [split]		35.40			3,528.86
12/15/2007	301 / PAY CHK	Michael M. Wilhite / Checking [split]		10.80			3,539.66
12/15/2007	301 / PAY CHK	Michael M. Wilhite / Checking [split]		63.00			3,602.66

Splits — Ending balance 3,726.66

1-Line

Sort by Date, Type, Number/Ref — Record — Restore

Focus on your business, not your payroll - Let Complete Payroll help!

5 Close the register.

6 Close the chart of accounts.

Tip: The employee earnings summary report summarizes the wages, taxes, and adjustments, the gross pay (total and adjusted), and the taxes withheld for each employee and the entire company.

The payroll summary report shows information similar to the employee earnings summary report, but in a much different layout. The report has a column for each employee and a row for each payroll item. To create either of these reports, choose Employees & Payroll from the Reports menu.

Paying payroll taxes

As long as you have a valid subscription to one of the Intuit Payroll Services, QuickBooks uses current tax tables to keep track of your tax liabilities as they accrue, so you know how much you owe at any time.

Figuring out what you owe

If you're about to pay taxes or other liabilities, the payroll liabilities report shows you how much to pay. Suppose you are ready to make a tax payment, and you want to see how much you owe.

To create a payroll liabilities report:

1. From the Reports menu, choose Employees & Payroll, and then choose Payroll Liability Balances.
2. Click Modify Report, select "Display columns by **Year** across the top," and then click OK.

   QuickBooks displays a report that shows what you owe for each payroll item.

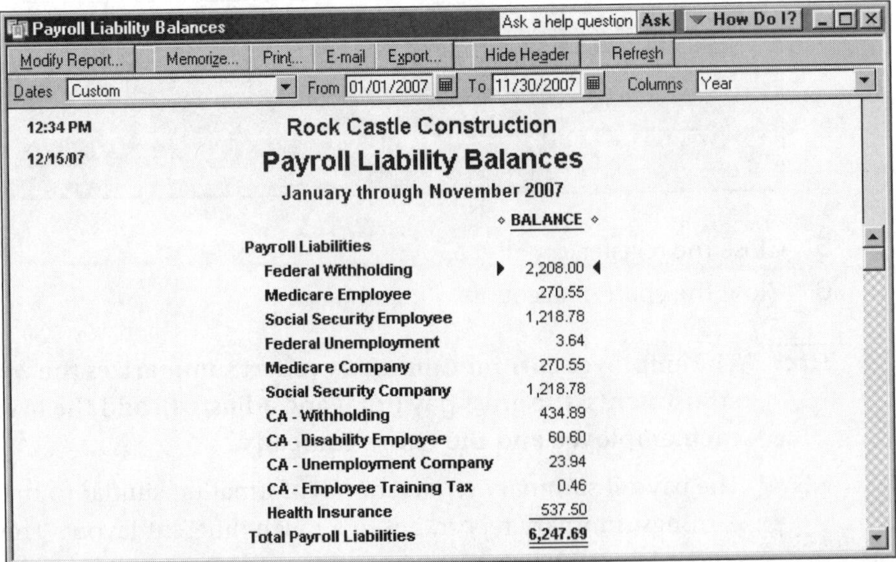

Payroll Liability Balances

Ask a help question | Ask | How Do I?

Modify Report... | Memorize... | Print... | E-mail | Export... | Hide Header | Refresh

Dates: Custom | From 01/01/2007 | To 11/30/2007 | Columns: Year

12:34 PM
12/15/07

Rock Castle Construction
Payroll Liability Balances
January through November 2007

	BALANCE
Payroll Liabilities	
Federal Withholding	2,208.00
Medicare Employee	270.55
Social Security Employee	1,218.78
Federal Unemployment	3.64
Medicare Company	270.55
Social Security Company	1,218.78
CA - Withholding	434.89
CA - Disability Employee	60.60
CA - Unemployment Company	23.94
CA - Employee Training Tax	0.46
Health Insurance	537.50
Total Payroll Liabilities	**6,247.69**

3. Close the report.
4. Click No at the message asking if you'd like to memorize the report.

Writing a check for payroll taxes

When it's time to deposit payroll taxes with your deposit institution, use the Liability Check window to fill out a QuickBooks check.

Note: Don't just open the Write Checks window and write a check from there. QuickBooks can't properly adjust your Payroll Liabilities account unless you use the Pay Liabilities feature.

To pay payroll liabilities:

1. From the Employees menu, choose Process Payroll Liabilities, and then choose Pay Payroll Liabilities from the submenu.

   QuickBooks displays the Select Date Range For Liabilities window.

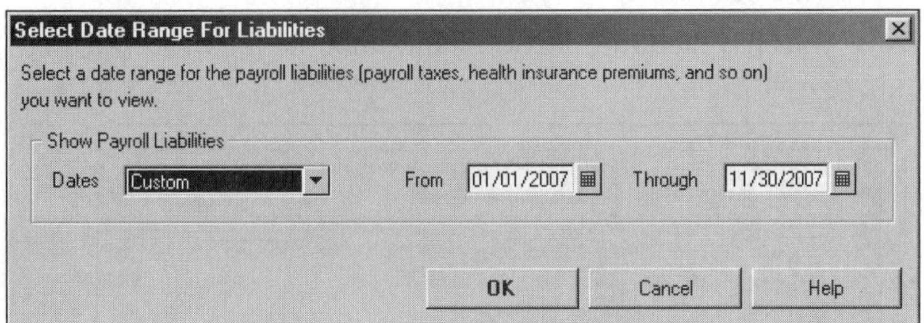

2. In the "From" field type ***11/30/2007***, and then type ***12/15/2007*** in the "Through" field.
3. Click OK.

   QuickBooks displays the Pay Liabilities window.

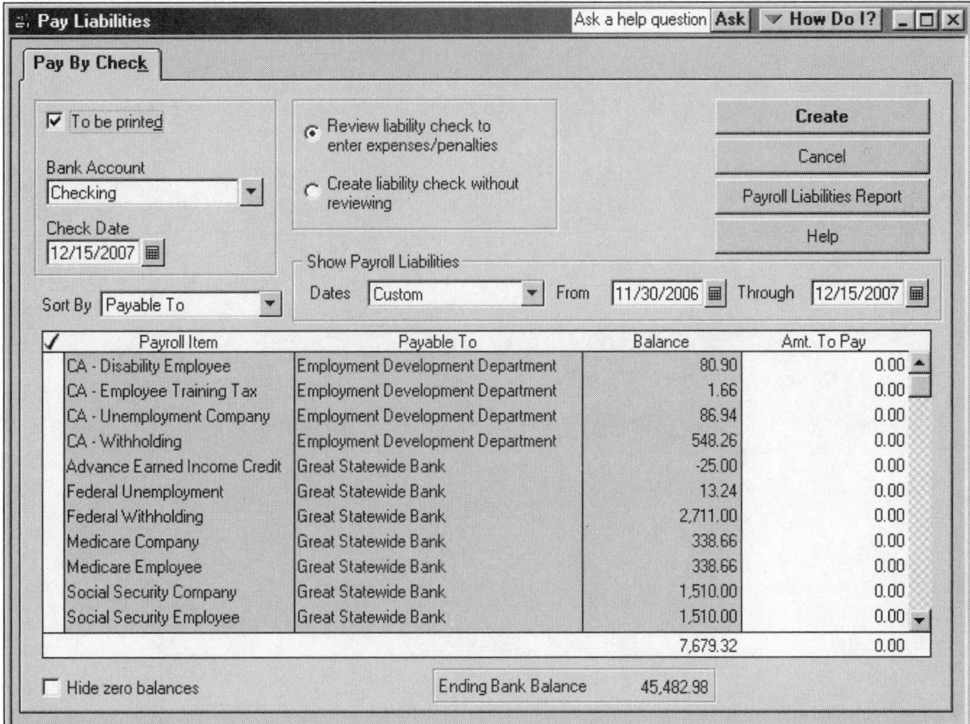

4 Click in the column to the left of the Federal Withholding payroll item.

QuickBooks places a checkmark in the column to show that the item will be paid. It also places a checkmark next to the Advanced Earned Income Credit item.

5 Click in the column to the left of the Medicare Company payroll item.

QuickBooks places checkmarks in the column for both Medicare Company and Medicare Employee.

6 Click in the column to the left of the Social Security Company payroll item.

QuickBooks places checkmarks in the column for both Social Security Company and Social Security Employee.

Now your Pay Liabilities window should look like the following.

✓	Payroll Item	Payable To	Balance	Amt. To Pay
	CA - Disability Employee	Employment Development Department	20.30	0.00
	CA - Employee Training Tax	Employment Development Department	1.20	0.00
	CA - Unemployment Company	Employment Development Department	63.00	0.00
	CA - Withholding	Employment Development Department	113.37	0.00
✓	Advance Earned Income Credit	Great Statewide Bank	-25.00	-25.00
	Federal Unemployment	Great Statewide Bank	9.60	0.00
✓	Federal Withholding	Great Statewide Bank	503.00	503.00
✓	Medicare Company	Great Statewide Bank	68.11	68.11
✓	Medicare Employee	Great Statewide Bank	68.11	68.11
✓	Social Security Company	Great Statewide Bank	291.22	291.22
✓	Social Security Employee	Great Statewide Bank	291.22	291.22
			1,431.63	1,196.66

7 Make sure "Review liability check to enter expenses/penalties" is selected and then click Create.

QuickBooks displays the Liability Check window, with your check displayed.

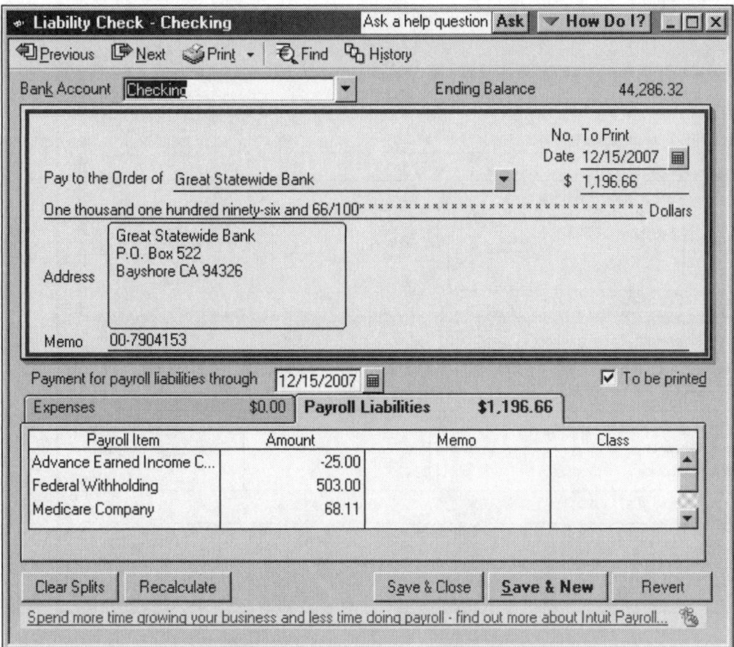

You should use a separate check for each type of deposit coupon (for example, 941 or 940).

8 In the Memo field, type ***EIN 96-4820567, Form 941***.

The Liability Check window should now look like the following.

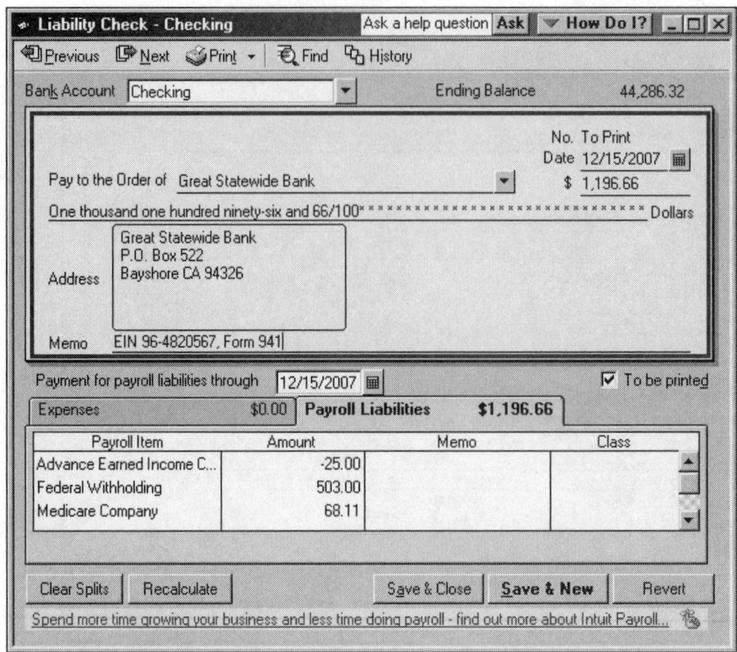

9 Click Save & Close to record the check.

10 Click Yes if QuickBooks asks if you wish to save changes made to this transaction.

Whenever you make a payment and record your check this way, QuickBooks decreases the balance of the Payroll Liabilities account.

Student test and review

1 Add a salaried employee to the employee list. Enter the employee's personal information, federal and state tax information, and at least one additional paycheck deduction.

2 Process a paycheck for the new employee. Then, view the check in QuickBooks. Open at least one payroll liability account register to see how the paycheck changes the account's balance.

3 Select one of the payroll expense accounts from the chart of accounts. Create a QuickReport for that expense account.

LESSON 13 Estimating and progress invoicing

Lesson objectives

- To learn how to create job estimates
- To find an estimate in a data file
- To learn to duplicate an existing estimate
- To create an invoice from an estimate
- To display project reports for estimates
- To update a job's status
- To make an estimate inactive

Instructor preparation

- Confirm that you are using QuickBooks: Pro or QuickBooks: Premier to complete this lesson.
- Review the lesson, including the examples, to make sure you're familiar with the material.
- Ensure that all students have copy of qblesson.qbb on their computer's hard disk.

To start this lesson

Before you perform the following steps, make sure you have installed the exercise file (qblesson.qbb) on your hard disk. See "Installing the exercise file" in the Introduction to this guide if you haven't installed it.

The following steps restore the exercise file to its original state so that the data in the file matches what you see on the screen as you proceed through each lesson.

Note: **To proceed through this lesson, you must be using QuickBooks: Pro or QuickBooks: Premier. Estimates are not available in QuickBooks: Basic.**

To restore the exercise file (qblesson.qbb):

1. From the File menu in QuickBooks, choose Restore.

   QuickBooks displays the Restore Company Backup window.
2. In the "Get Company Backup From" section of the window, click Browse and select your c:\QBtrain directory.
3. Select the qblesson.qbb file, and then click Open.
4. In the "Restore Company Backup To" section of the window, click Browse and select your c:\QBtrain directory.
5. In the File name field of the Restore To window, type ***lesson 13*** and then click Save.
6. Click Restore.

Creating jobs and estimates

An estimate is a description of work or products you propose to sell to a current or prospective customer. You can create multiple estimates for each name (customer or customer:job combination). If the customer accepts an estimate, you can turn the estimate into an invoice, modifying it as necessary. When you have actual costs and revenues, you can compare them to your estimated costs and revenues to see if you were over or under the estimate.

Estimates are "non-posting" transactions—they do not affect any financial reports or income and expense balances. QuickBooks allows you to create invoices from estimates either by transferring the entire estimate to an invoice or by allowing you to choose a percentage or selected items to invoice from the estimate. The ability to bill for only a percentage of the estimate or selected items on an estimate is called *progress invoicing*.

When you create a new QuickBooks company using the EasyStep Interview, QuickBooks asks you if you use estimates and/or progress invoicing. If you respond yes, QuickBooks turns on these features for you. If you respond no, you need to turn on these features in order to use them. Rock Castle Construction already has estimates and progress invoicing turned on, but you'll review how to do this so you become familiar with QuickBooks preferences.

Turning on estimates and progress invoicing

To turn on estimates and progress invoicing:

1. From the Edit menu, choose Preferences.
2. Click Jobs & Estimates in the left scroll box.
3. Click the Company Preferences tab to display the job and estimate preferences.

QuickBooks displays the Jobs & Estimates section of the Preferences window.

4 Click Yes for "Do You Create Estimates?"

5 Click Yes for "Do You Do Progress Invoicing?"

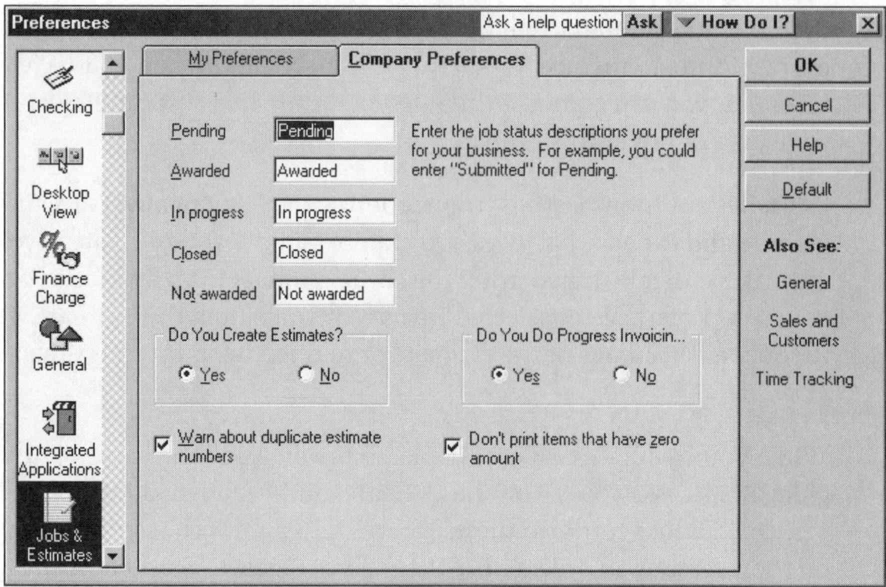

6 Click OK to record your selections and close the Preferences window.

Tip: **If your industry uses a term other than "estimate" (for example, "bid" or "proposal"), you can change the title that appears on the QuickBooks estimate form using the Cusomize Forms window and the Layout Designer.** (To customize a form, choose Templates from the Lists menu.)

Creating a new job

Now that you've turned on the estimates feature, you can add a new job for a bathroom remodel project for your customer, Ernesto Natiello. Then you'll create an estimate for the job.

To create a new job:

1 From the Customers menu, choose Customer:Job List.

2 In the Customer:Job list, select Natiello, Ernesto.

3 Click the Customer:Job menu button, and then choose Add Job.

QuickBooks displays the New Job window.

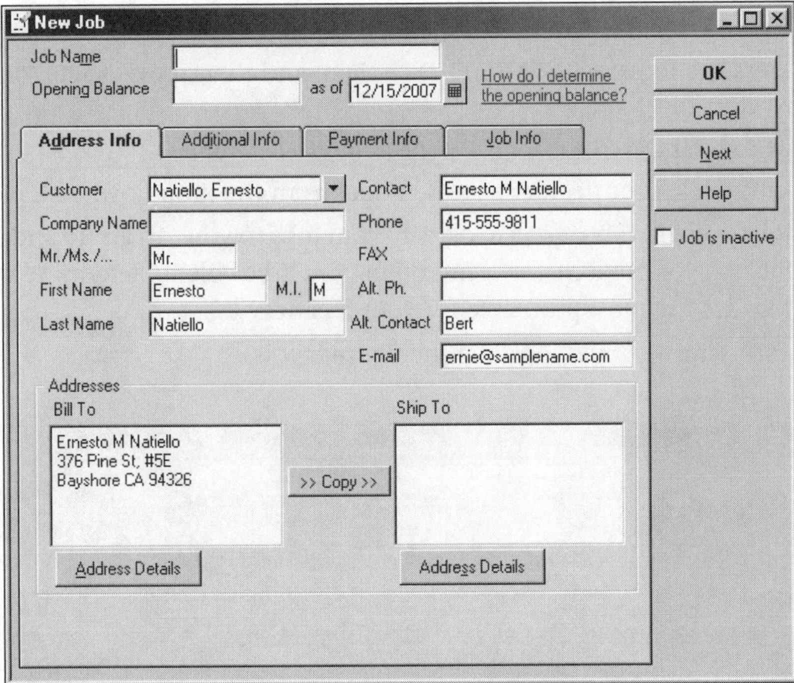

4 In the Job Name field, type ***Bathroom remodel***.

5 Click the Job Info tab.

QuickBooks displays the Job Info portion of the New Job window.

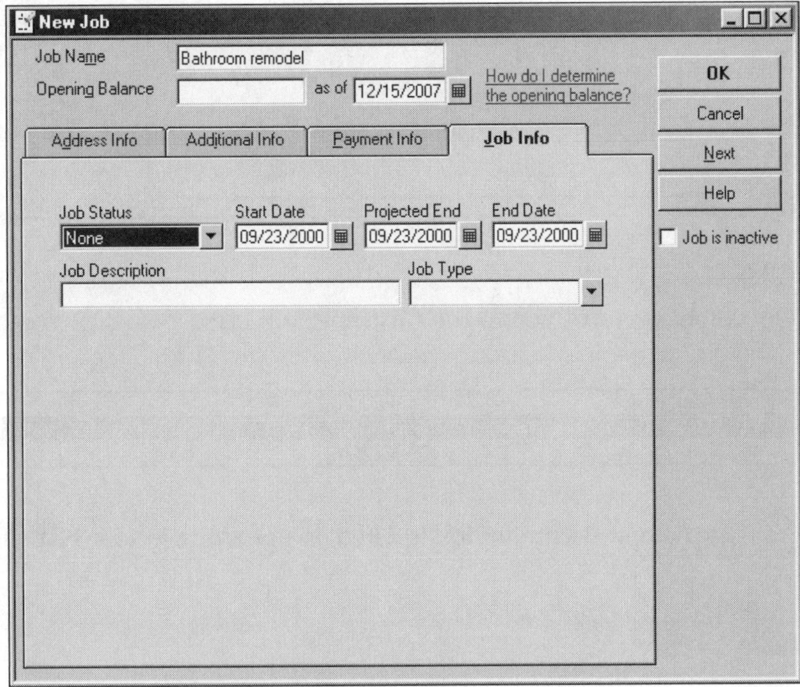

The New Job window is unique to QuickBooks: Pro and QuickBooks: Premier.

6. In the Job Status field, select Pending from the drop-down list.
7. In the Start Date field, type ***1/4/08***, and then press Tab.
8. In the Projected End field, type ***2/28/08***.
9. Press Tab to move to the End Date field, and then press Delete (on the keyboard) to clear this field.
10. In the Job Description field, type ***Remodel bathroom***.
11. In the Job Type field, choose Remodel from the drop-down list.

    Job types give you a way to classify your jobs so you can group and subtotal similar jobs on your reports. By using them, you'll be able to determine which kinds of jobs are the most profitable for your business.

    Your screen should look like the figure below.

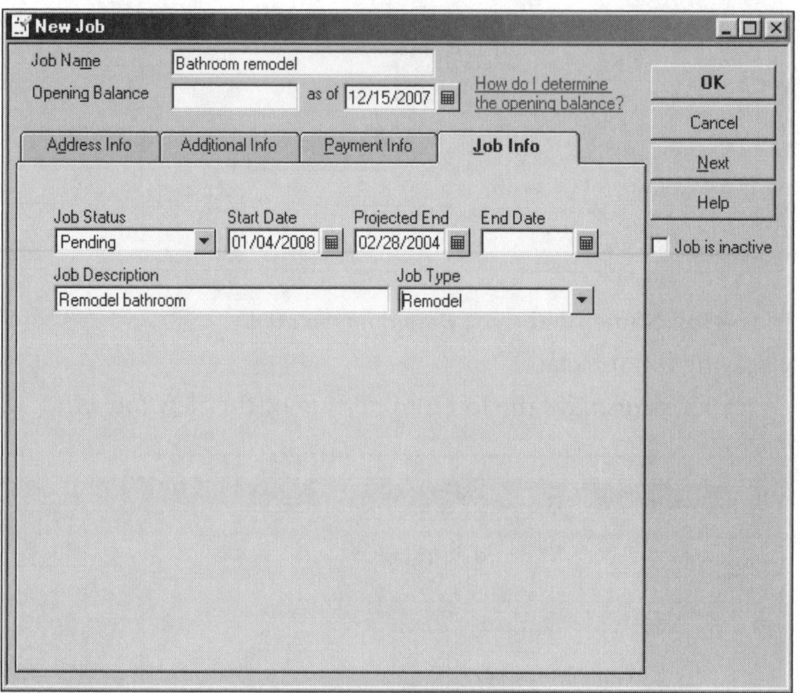

12. Click OK.

    QuickBooks returns you to the Customer:Job List.

◆Natiello, Ernesto	-622.26			14,595.25
◆Bathroom Remodel	0.00		Pending	
◆Kitchen	-622.26		Closed	14,595.25

Notice that the new Bathroom job is listed as a pending job for Natiello, Ernesto.

Writing an estimate

Now that you've created a new job for the bathroom remodel, you can create an estimate for it.

To create an estimate:

1 In the Customer:Job list, select Natiello, Ernesto:Bathroom remodel.

2 Click the Activities menu button, and then choose Create Estimates.

QuickBooks displays the Create Estimates window for this customer and job. You learned in Lesson 6 how to fill out an invoice form, so this form should look familiar.

3 Press Tab to accept Natiello, Ernesto:Bathoom remodel in the Customer:Job field.

Notice that QuickBooks enters the customer's name and address in the appropriate area of the form.

4 Select "Custom Estimate" in the Template field.

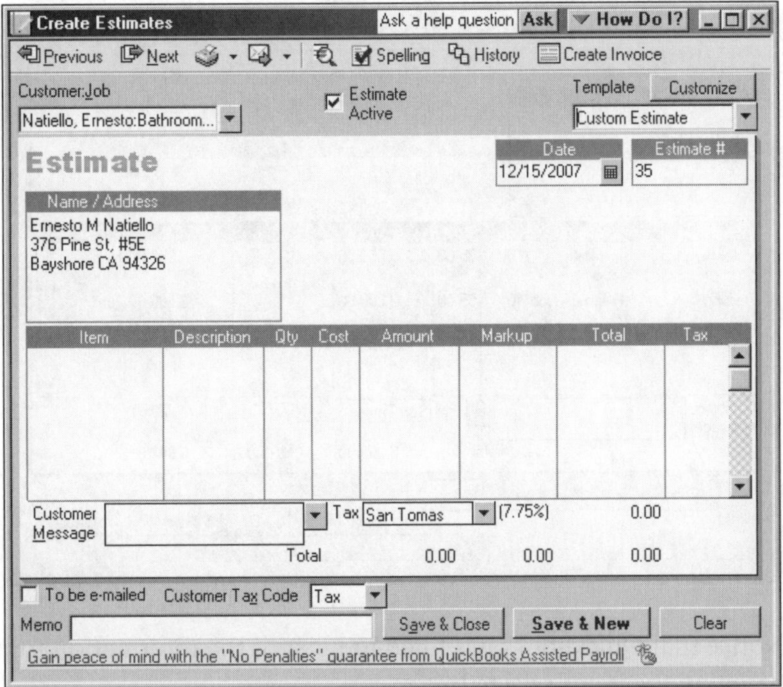

5 Click in the Item column in the middle of the form.

A Down Arrow appears, indicating that a drop-down list of choices is available.

The Item list, which contains all the services and goods your business provides, is the same list that is available to you on invoice forms and throughout QuickBooks.

6 Type ***Installation***.

Before you can finish typing, QuickBooks has filled it in for you, and QuickBooks fills in the default description for this item when you exit the field.

7 Press Tab twice to move to the QTY column.

8 Type ***10*** in the QTY column, and then press Tab.

The total amount is calculated by QuickBooks when you move out of this field.

9 Click the line under "Installation" in the Item column.

10 Type ***Framing***.

11 Press Tab twice to move to the QTY column, and then type ***40***.

12 In the line under Framing in the Item column, type ***Rough***.

QuickBooks completes the field with the item Lumber:Rough.

13 Press Tab three times to move to the Cost column, and then type ***2500***.

14 Press Tab to move to the Markup column.

15 Type ***15%***, and then press Tab twice.

Your estimate should look like the following figure.

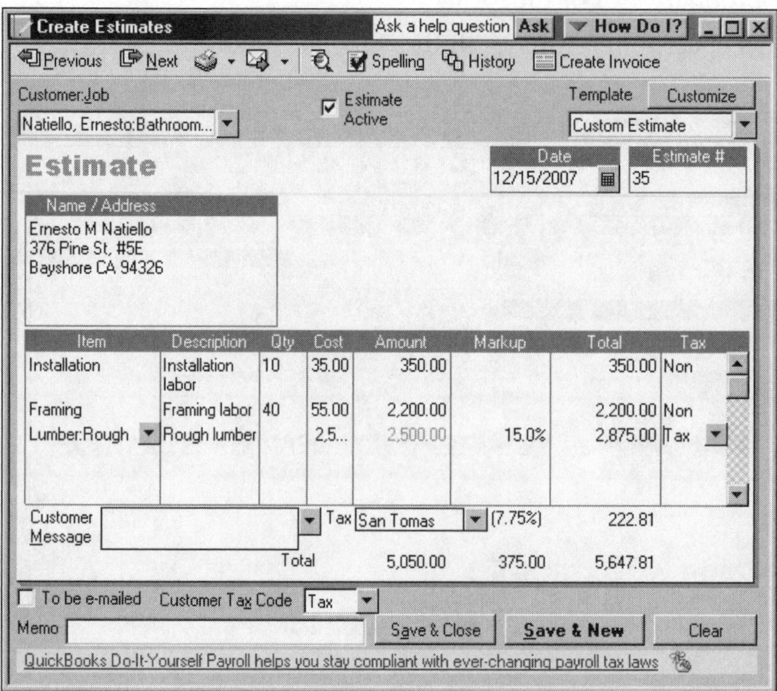

Notice that QuickBooks has filled in most of the information for the estimate based on the items selected.

16 Click Save & Close to save the estimate.

QuickBooks returns you to the Customer:Job list. Notice the Estimate Total column for the Pending Bathroom remodel job for Ernesto Natiello now has a balance of 5,647.81.

◆Natiello, Ernesto	-622.26			20,243.06
◆Bathroom Remodel	0.00		Pending	5,647.81
◆Kitchen	-622.26		Closed	14,595.25

17 Close the Customer:Job list.

Creating multiple estimates

Just as you've completed the estimate for this customer, he calls and asks you to prepare a second estimate for the same job. He'd like you to price a couple of different options.

Finding estimates

Because you just created the estimate, you can open the Create Estimates window and press Prev and that will take you to the correct estimate. However, when you don't know where an estimate is, there are a couple of methods you can use to locate the estimate you want quickly. You'll use one of them here.

1 From the Customers menu, choose Create Estimates.

2 From the Edit menu, choose Find Estimates.

QuickBooks displays the Find Estimates window.

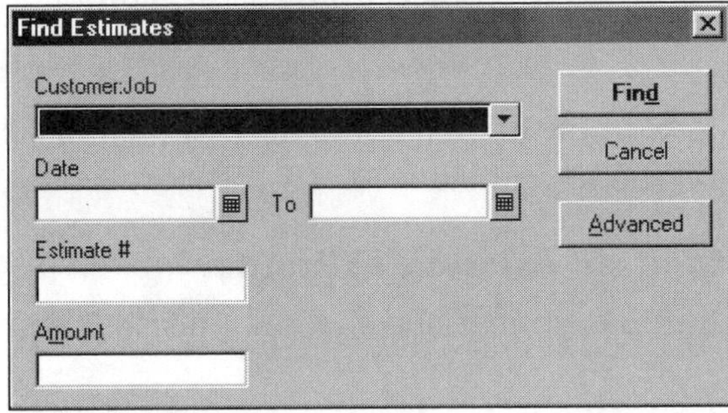

3 In the Customer:Job drop-down list, select Natiello, Ernesto:Bathroom remodel.

4 Click Find.

QuickBooks displays the estimate that you've already created for this job (Estimate # 35).

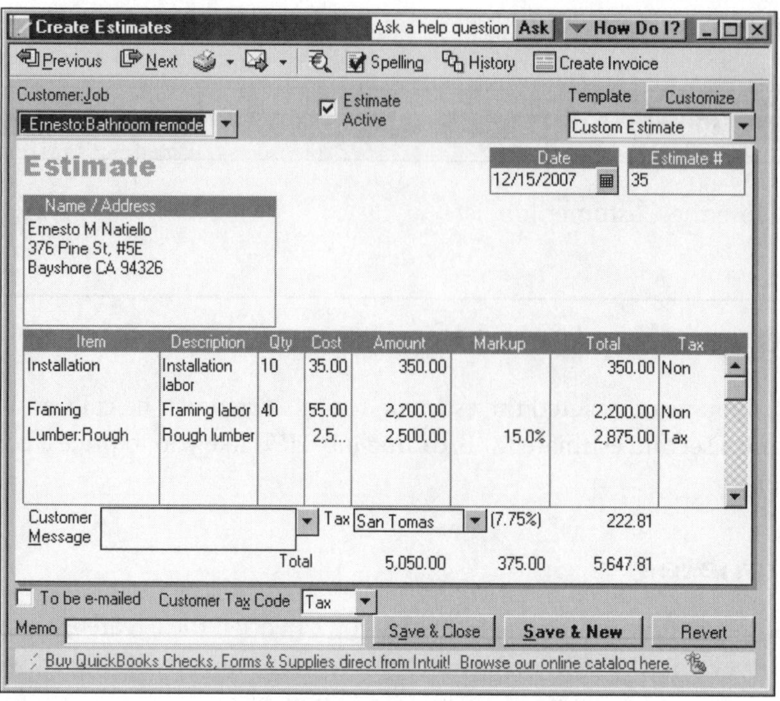

5 Keep the estimate open; you'll use it in the next exercise.

Duplicating estimates

Your customer wants you to prepare a second estimate for the bathroom remodel job because he is considering buying the cabinets from you in addition to having you do the installation work.

First, you'll create a duplicate of the original estimate, and then make the modifications necessary for the second bid.

To create a duplicate of an existing estimate:

1 Right-click in the body of the estimate and choose Duplicate Estimate from the list that displays.

QuickBooks duplicates the estimate and displays the new version on your screen. Notice that QuickBooks assigns the next available estimate number to the new form.

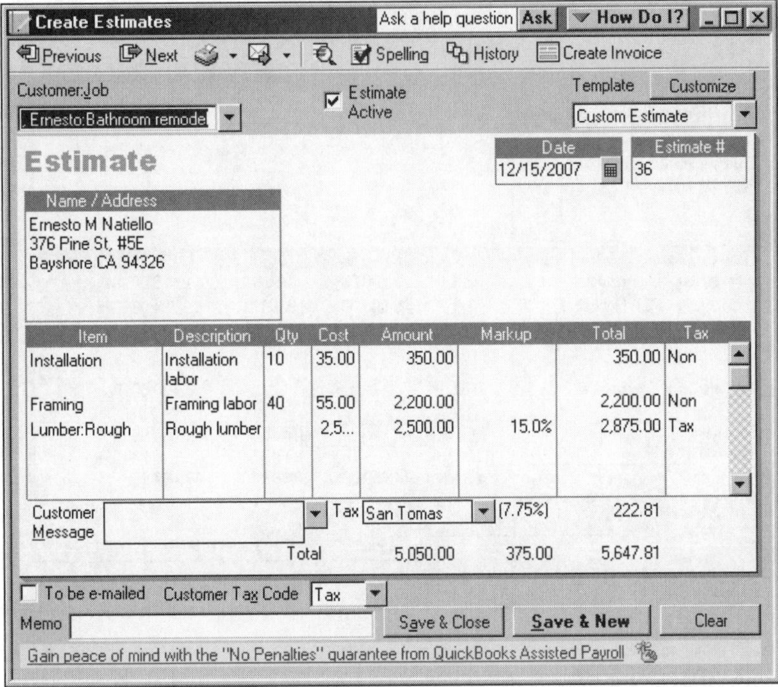

2 Highlight the number in the QTY column on the line for Installation.

3 Type ***18***.

4 Click in the Item column in the line below Lumber:Rough, and select Cabinets:Light Pine from the drop-down list.

5 Press Tab twice and type ***6*** in the QTY column.

6 Click in the Item column in the line below Cabinets:Light Pine and select Cabinets:Cabinet Pulls from the drop-down list.

7 Press Tab twice and type ***12*** in the QTY column.

8 Press Tab and type ***10*** in the Cost field.

9 Press Tab.

Your estimate should look like the following figure.

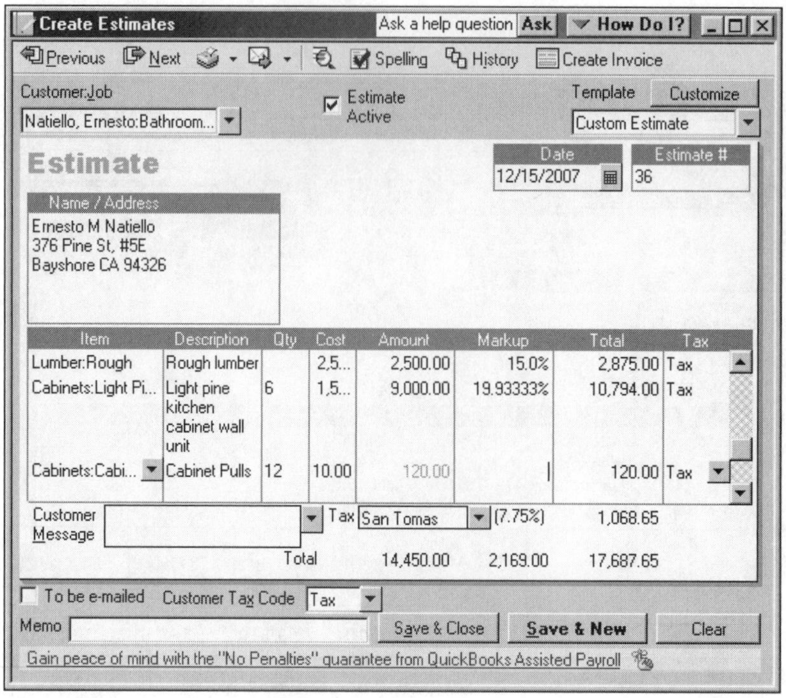

10 Click Save & Close.

Creating an invoice from an estimate

Once you have created an estimate and the customer has approved it, you can use the estimate to invoice the customer. In this exercise, you'll be using the QuickBooks progress invoicing feature.

Progress invoicing (also known as progress billing), lets you invoice for jobs that you work on and complete in phases. When using progress invoicing, you start by creating an estimate for the job (you don't have to give this estimate to the customer). Then, as you complete each phase, you can easily transfer items from the original estimate to an invoice. You can specify which items to include on each invoice and change estimated amounts or percentages. When you use estimates to create progress invoices, you can run reports to help you track your estimated versus actual costs.

To create an invoice from an estimate:

1. From the Lists menu, choose Customer:Job list.
2. In the Customer:Job list, select Natiello, Ernesto:Bathroom remodel.
3. Click the Activities menu button, and then choose Create Invoices.

   QuickBooks displays the Create Invoices window.
4. Press Tab to leave the Customer:Job field.

QuickBooks displays a list of estimates created for this job.

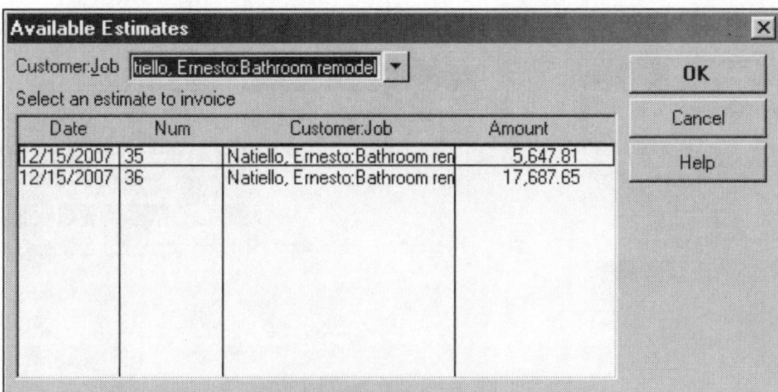

5 The customer accepted the first estimate you created, so select the line containing Estimate #35, and click OK.

QuickBooks displays the Create Progress Invoice Based On Estimate window.

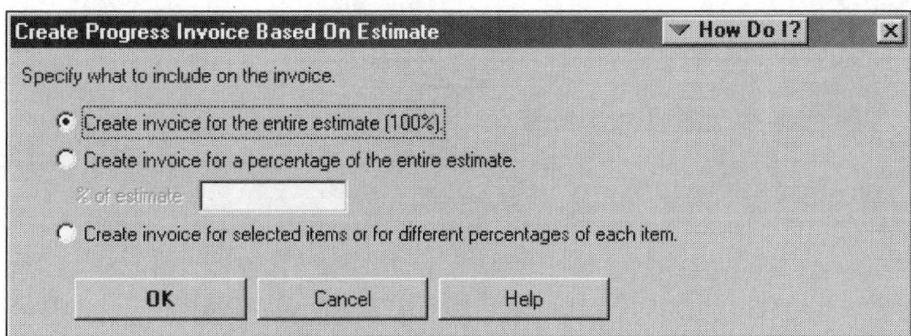

Rock Castle Construction typically bills for one-third of the job before starting work, one-third when the project is one-third complete, and the final one-third when the job is completed.

6 Select "Create invoice for a percentage of the entire estimate."

7 Type ***33.333*** in the "% of estimate" field.

If you need to invoice for only selected items on an estimate or for varying percentages or amounts for different items, select the option "Create invoice for selected items or for different percentages of each item." QuickBooks then displays a table of all items on the estimate and allows you to select which items you want to include and the amounts for each item.

8 Click OK.

9 In the Template drop-down list, select Progress Invoice.

QuickBooks completes the invoice for one-third of each item on the estimate. Your invoice should resemble the following figure.

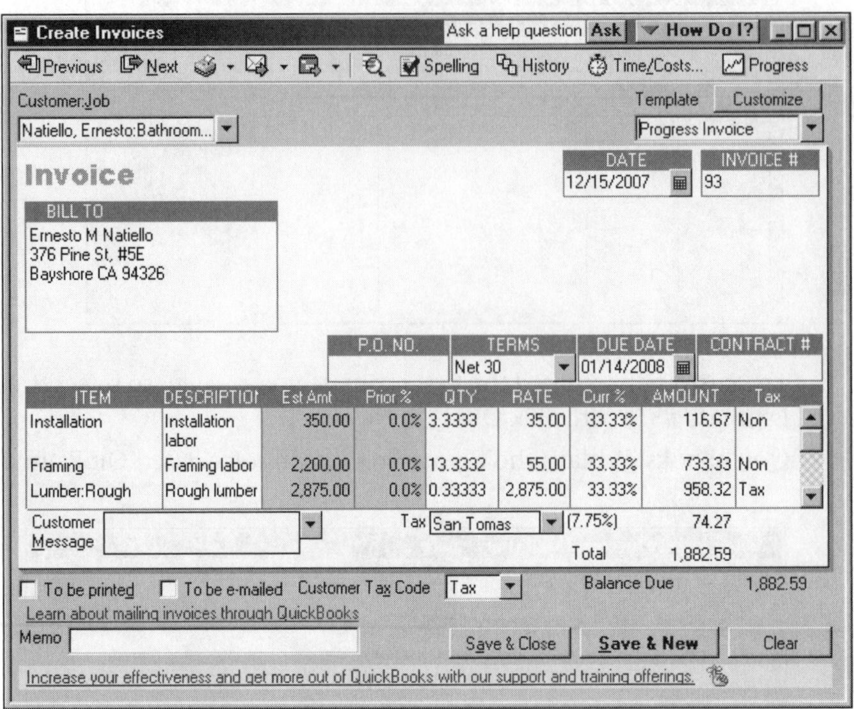

Notice that QuickBooks changed the invoice template to Progress Invoice and added fields for Estimate Amount, Prior %, and Current %. QuickBooks also tracks that one-third of the Natiello bathroom remodel job has been invoiced and that two-thirds has not yet been invoiced.

Note: **If you don't want your customers to see this level of detail on the invoice you send them, you can customize the invoice to remove some of these columns from the printed form.** See Lesson 15, "Customizing forms and writing QuickBooks Letters" for more information.

10 Click Save & Close to record the invoice.

11 Close the Customer:Job list.

Tip: **If you don't want your customers to see this level of detail on the invoice you send them, you can customize the invoice to remove some of these columns from the printed form.** See Lesson 15, "Customizing forms and writing QuickBooks Letters" for more information.

Displaying reports for estimates

QuickBooks provides five reports on estimates, as described in the following table. You can create these reports from the Jobs, Time & Mileage submenu of the Reports menu.

Report	Description
Job Estimates vs. Actuals Summary	Compares estimated cost to actual cost and estimated revenue to actual revenue for all customers and jobs.
Job Estimates vs. Actuals Detail (for one job)	For a particular customer or job, compares estimated costs to actual costs and estimated revenues to actual revenues.
Job Progress Invoices vs. Estimates	Compares each estimate with progress invoices based on the estimate.
Item Estimates vs. Actuals	For each item, compares estimated cost to actual cost and estimated revenue to actual revenue.
Estimates by Job	Lists all estimates by job.

Displaying the job progress invoices vs. estimates report

Because you've just completed a progress invoice, you can see how QuickBooks records this on the job progress invoices vs. estimates report. This report shows job status, estimate total, total invoiced from the estimate on progress invoices, and the percentage of the estimate already invoiced on progress invoices.

To display the job progress invoices vs. estimates report:

1 From the Reports menu, choose Jobs, Time & Mileage.

QuickBooks displays a submenu of project reports that deal with customer jobs and estimates.

2 Choose Job Progress Invoices vs. Estimates.

QuickBooks displays the job progress invoices vs. estimates report.

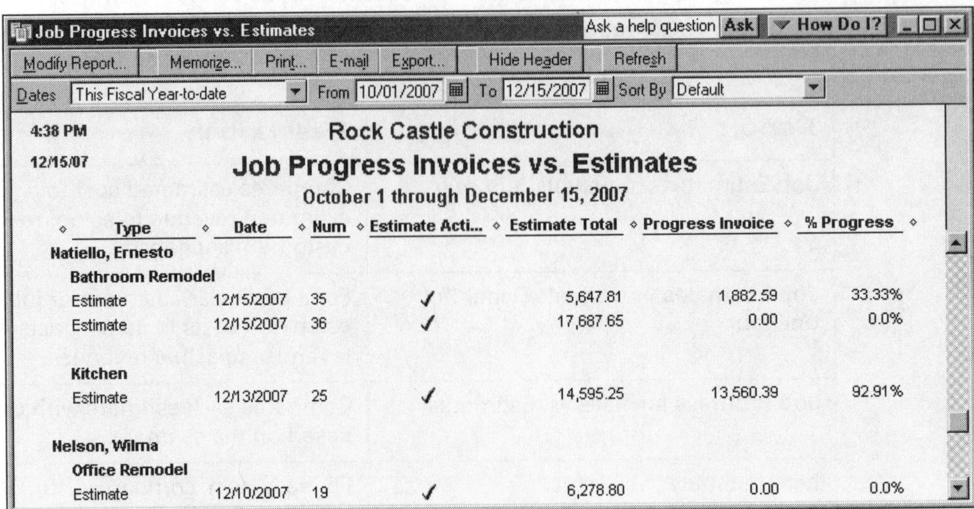
4:38 PM Rock Castle Construction
12/15/07
Job Progress Invoices vs. Estimates
October 1 through December 15, 2007

Type	Date	Num	Estimate Acti...	Estimate Total	Progress Invoice	% Progress
Natiello, Ernesto						
Bathroom Remodel						
Estimate	12/15/2007	35	✓	5,647.81	1,882.59	33.33%
Estimate	12/15/2007	36	✓	17,687.65	0.00	0.0%
Kitchen						
Estimate	12/13/2007	25	✓	14,595.25	13,560.39	92.91%
Nelson, Wilma						
Office Remodel						
Estimate	12/10/2007	19	✓	6,278.80	0.00	0.0%

Notice that the progress invoice you completed for Ernesto Natiello is listed in the Prog. Invoice column. The % Progress column shows how much of the total estimate you've invoiced for so far.

3 Close the report window.

Updating job status

Every time you change the status of a job, you should update its job status in the Customer:Job list. For example, the estimate for the bathroom remodel is no longer pending: Ernesto Natiello awarded you the job and you have started work.

To update the status of a job:

1 From the Customers menu, choose Customer:Job List.

QuickBooks displays the Customer:Job list.

2 In the list, select Natiello, Ernesto:Bathroom remodel.

3 Click the Customer:Job menu button, and then choose Edit.

QuickBooks displays the Edit Job window.

4 Click the Job Info tab.

QuickBooks displays the Job Info portion of the Edit Job window.

5 In the Job Status field, select "In progress."

Your screen should look like this.

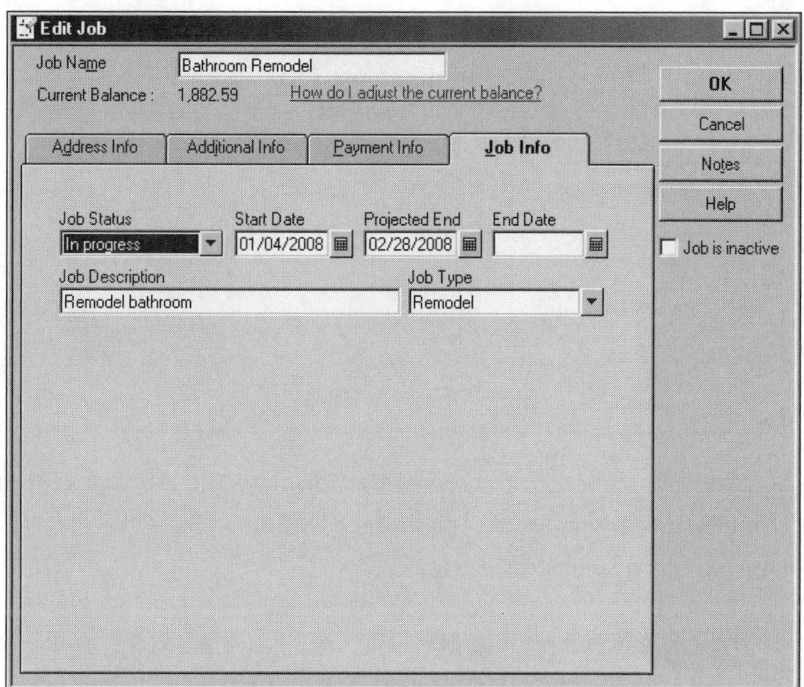

6 Click OK.

QuickBooks returns you to the Customer:Job list. The Customer:Job list now shows this project as being in progress.

7 Close the Customer:Job list.

Making estimates inactive

Now that the customer has accepted one of the estimates for the bathroom remodel job and you have started work, you might want to make the unaccepted estimate inactive. When you make an estimate inactive QuickBooks keeps a record of it, but does not use the numbers in reports.

To mark an estimate inactive:

1 From the Reports menu, choose Jobs, Time & Mileage.

2 Choose Estimates by Job from the submenu.

QuickBooks displays the estimates by job report.

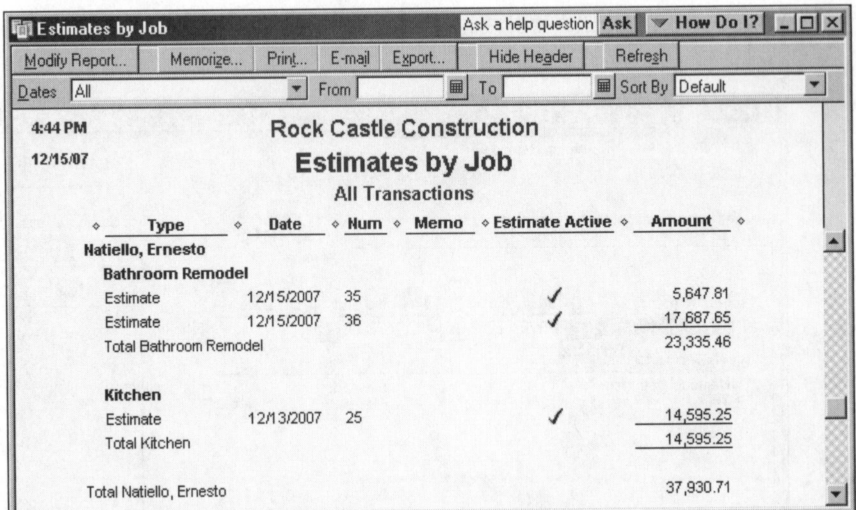

Type	Date	Num	Memo	Estimate Active	Amount
Natiello, Ernesto					
Bathroom Remodel					
Estimate	12/15/2007	35		✓	5,647.81
Estimate	12/15/2007	36		✓	17,687.65
Total Bathroom Remodel					23,335.46
Kitchen					
Estimate	12/13/2007	25		✓	14,595.25
Total Kitchen					14,595.25
Total Natiello, Ernesto					37,930.71

3 Scroll to the section of the report that displays the estimates for Ernesto Natiello.

4 Double-click anywhere on the line for Estimate #36.

QuickBooks displays the estimate.

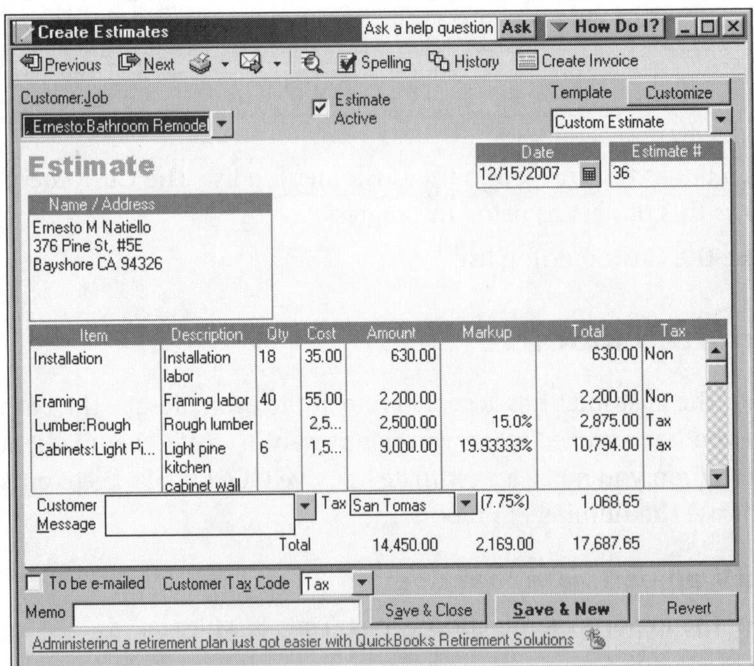

Item	Description	Qty	Cost	Amount	Markup	Total	Tax
Installation	Installation labor	18	35.00	630.00		630.00	Non
Framing	Framing labor	40	55.00	2,200.00		2,200.00	Non
Lumber:Rough	Rough lumber		2,5...	2,500.00	15.0%	2,875.00	Tax
Cabinets:Light Pi...	Light pine kitchen cabinet wall	6	1,5...	9,000.00	19.93333%	10,794.00	Tax

5 Click to clear the checkmark in the Estimate Active checkbox.

6 Click Save & Close.

7 Answer Yes to the message asking if you want to save the changes you made to the transaction.

8 Close the report.

Student test and review

1 Create an estimate for the 75 Sunset Rd. job for Pretell Real Estate. The estimate is for 6 hours of installation labor, 18.5 hours of plumbing work, and 4 hours of drywall work.

2 Create a progress invoice for 50% of the estimate just created for the 75 Sunset Rd. job for Pretell Real Estate.

LESSON 14 Tracking time

Lesson objectives

- To learn how to track time worked on a project
- To learn how to invoice a customer for time worked on a project
- To learn how to track and invoice a customer for mileage
- To create project reports for time tracking and learn about other project reports
- To learn how to set up items used to track time worked by owners or partners
- To learn how to pay nonemployees for time worked

Instructor preparation

- Confirm that you are using QuickBooks: Pro or QuickBooks: Premier to complete this lesson.
- Review the lesson, including the examples, to make sure you're familiar with the material.
- Ensure that all students have copy of qblesson.qbb on their computer's hard disk.

To start this lesson

Before you perform the following steps, make sure you have installed the exercise file (qblesson.qbb) on your hard disk. See "Installing the exercise file" in the Introduction to this guide if you haven't installed it.

The following steps restore the exercise file to its original state so that the data in the file matches what you see on the screen as you proceed through each lesson.

Note: **To proceed through this lesson, you must be using QuickBooks: Pro or QuickBooks: Premier.** Time tracking is not available in QuickBooks: Basic.

To restore the exercise file (qblesson.qbb):

1. From the File menu in QuickBooks, choose Restore.

   QuickBooks displays the Restore Company Backup window.
2. In the "Get Company Backup From" section of the window, click Browse and select your c:\QBtrain directory.
3. Select the qblesson.qbb file, and then click Open.
4. In the "Restore Company Backup To" section of the window, click Browse and select your c:\QBtrain directory.
5. In the File name field of the Restore To window, type ***lesson 14*** and then click Save.
6. Click Restore.

Tracking time and mileage

QuickBooks provides time tracking for any job. Time tracking lets you keep track of the time a person spends on each job (including sick and vacation time and time spent for general overhead). The person whose time you track can be an employee, an owner or partner, or a subcontractor.

You can use time data to do the following:

- Invoice the customer for the time spent doing a job.
- Provide hours worked on an employee's paycheck, or a check to a nonemployee (vendor, owner, or partner).
- Track the cost of employees' gross pay by job.
- Report on the number of hours worked—by person, by job, or by item.

Turning on time tracking

The following procedure shows how to turn on the time tracking feature, (it is turned on already in the exercise file).

To turn on time tracking:

1 From the Edit menu, choose Preferences.

2 Click Time Tracking in the left scroll box. Then click the Company Preferences tab. QuickBooks displays the Time Tracking Preferences window.

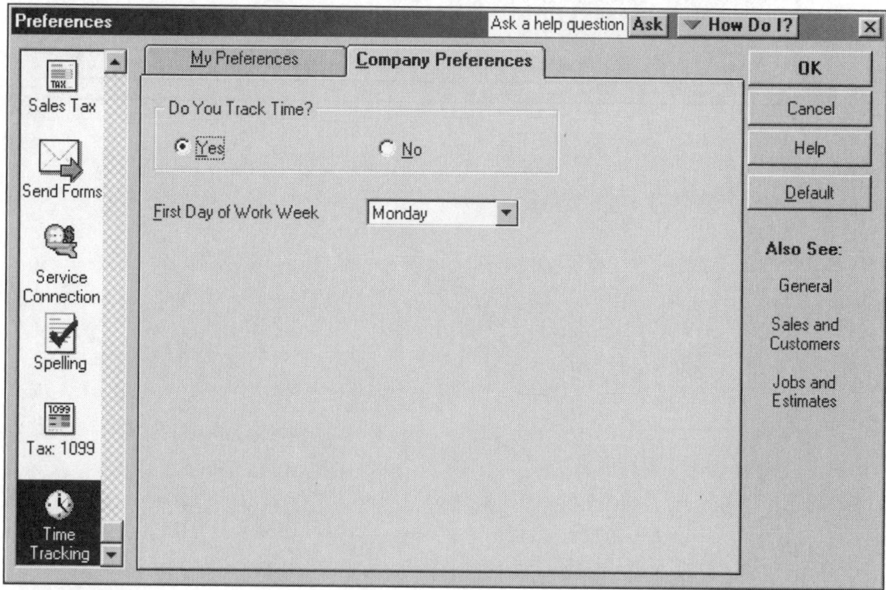

3 Make sure Yes is selected as the answer to the question "Do You Track Time?"

4 Click OK to save the preference setting.

Entering time data

There are three ways to get time data into a company file:

- Enter time directly onto a weekly timesheet or single activity form in QuickBooks.
- Use the Stopwatch to time an activity while you are performing it.
- Use the QuickBooks Timer program to track time and then import the time directly into QuickBooks. (The Timer is available in QuickBooks: Pro and Premier only.)

When you track time with QuickBooks, you have a choice of two forms to enter time: Weekly Timesheet or Time/Enter Single Activity window. If you want to enter time for multiple jobs or multiple days, then the Weekly Timesheet is the best choice.

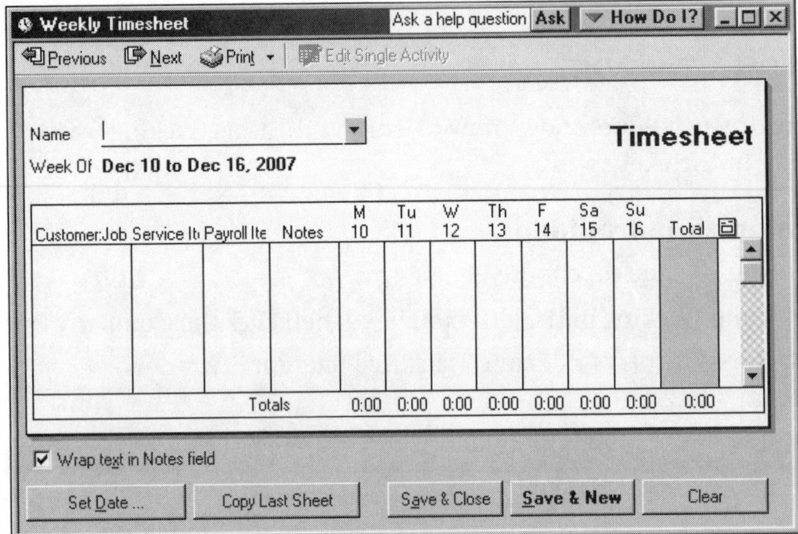

If you tend to enter a lot of detailed notes about your activities, or you prefer to enter time data as you complete an activity, use the Time/Enter Single Activity window instead.

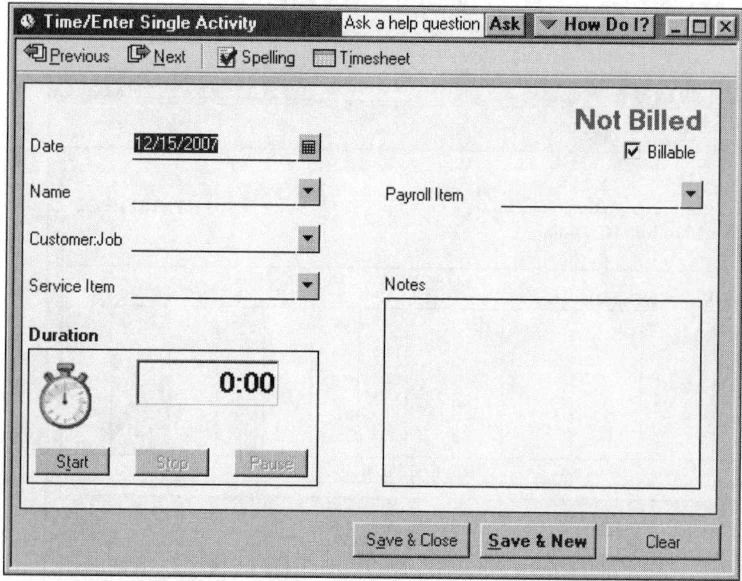

Information you enter in the Time/Enter Single Activity window displays in the Weekly Timesheet, and vice versa. They're different views of the same information.

The Timer program is useful when you have employees or subcontractors who need to track their time but don't need or want to run QuickBooks. When time is imported into QuickBooks from the Timer application, you view the imported time data on the same timesheets you would use if you did the data entry directly into QuickBooks.

If you have employees who don't have access to a computer or who don't have access to QuickBooks, you can print blank copies of the weekly timesheet for your employees to fill out by hand.

To print a blank timesheet:

1 From the Employees menu, choose Time Tracking and then choose Use Weekly Timesheet.
2 From the Print drop-down menu, choose Print Blank timesheet.
3 In the Print Timesheets window, click Print.

Recording employee time on a weekly timesheet

In this exercise, you'll complete a weekly timesheet for Gregg Schneider. In a later exercise, you'll learn how to invoice a customer for the time Gregg spent working on a job for that customer.

To enter information on a weekly timesheet:

1 From the Employees menu, choose Time Tracking, and then choose Use Weekly Timesheet from the submenu.

QuickBooks displays the Weekly Timesheet window.

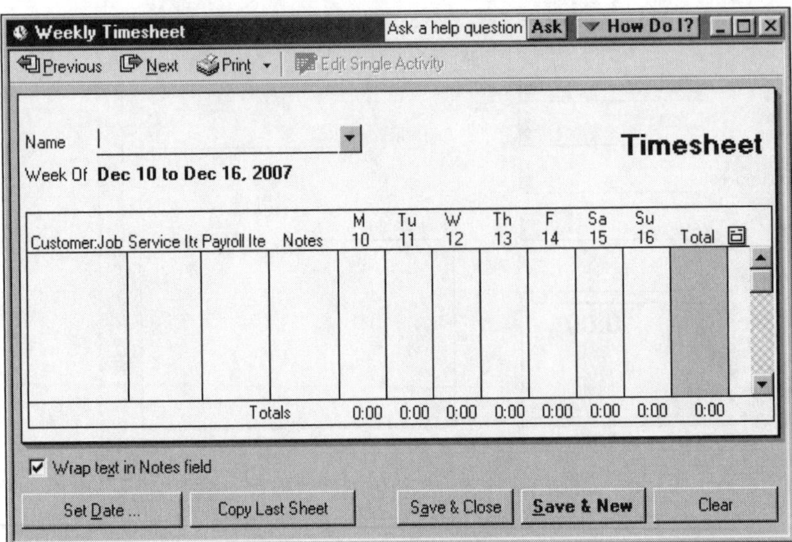

2 In the Name field, select Gregg O. Schneider from the drop-down list.

QuickBooks will track the time you enter for this employee and display it when you are ready to pay employees. Notice that there are already hours listed for Gregg for this week.

3 On the line below the existing entries, click in the Customer:Job column, and then choose Melton, Johnny:Dental office from the drop-down list.

QuickBooks will associate the time that you enter in this window with the office repairs being completed for Johnny Melton.

4 In the Service Item column, type ***Installation***.

After you type a few characters, QuickBooks fills in the rest of the item for you. The Item list, which contains all the services and goods your business provides, is the same list that is available to you on invoice forms and throughout QuickBooks.

Notice that QuickBooks fills in the information in the Payroll Item column for you.

Gregg Schneider is paid by the hour. QuickBooks has his hourly rate stored in the Employee list, on the Payroll Info tab.

Note: **If you try to select a payroll item that is not associated with this employee, QuickBooks displays a warning message.** For example, if you try to select Salary as the payroll item for Gregg Schneider, QuickBooks tells you that you do not have that type of payroll item set up for the employee. (It still lets you make the selection, but it warns you that the Salary is set up with a $0.00 rate.)

5 Click in the W 12 column for the row in which you entered Johnny Melton's job. W stands for Wednesday and 12 for the date, Wednesday, the 12th of December, 2007. Note that you can change the first day of your workweek in the QuickBooks time tracking preferences. (From the Edit menu, choose Preferences, and then click Time Tracking.)

6 Type ***8*** to enter the number of hours worked on Wednesday.

7 In the Th field, type ***8***.

8 In the F field, type ***8***, and then press Tab.

As you enter hours for each day, the Total column displays the total hours for the week.

Your screen should resemble the figure below.

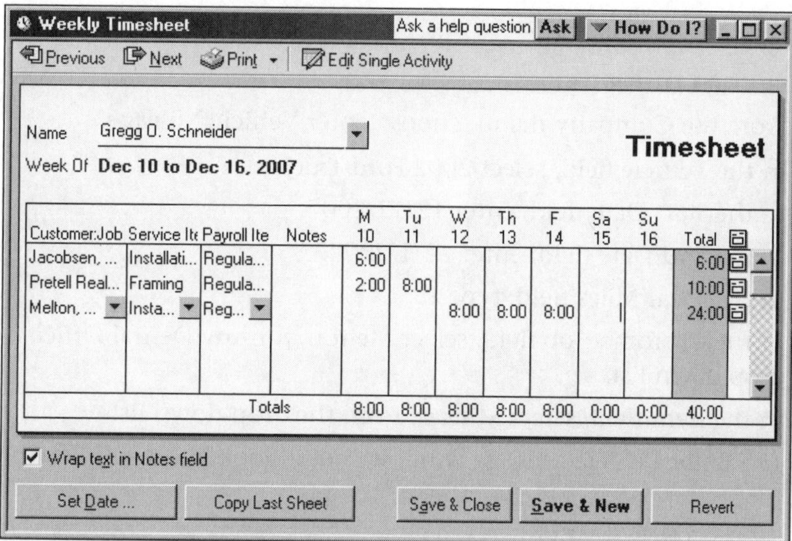

The invoice icon to the right of the Total column tells QuickBooks if the time will be transferred onto an invoice. In its current setting, you're telling QuickBooks that you *do* want to invoice the customer for time worked.

If you do not plan on invoicing the customer for time worked, you can click the invoice icon and QuickBooks displays a red "X" over it.

9 Click Save & Close to record the Weekly Timesheet.

QuickBooks records the time for Gregg Schneider and for Johnny Melton's dental office job.

This time can now be transferred onto an invoice for Johnny Melton's dental office job and to create a paycheck for Gregg Schneider.

Entering mileage

By tracking your vehicle mileage, you can enter, sort, and print lists of your vehicles and the mileage you've driven for work-related tasks. You can use this information for your tax deductions and for billing your customers.

You cannot use this feature to reimburse employees or vendors for mileage. Nor can you track specific vehicle expenses, such as gas, tolls, etc. with this feature. However, you can track these types of expenses by entering bills for them as the expenses are incurred by employees.

Important: Intuit recommends that you consult with your tax advisor, accountant, or the IRS to determine if you can deduct the costs of operating and maintaining your vehicle and which method you should use.

To record mileage:

1 From the Company menu, choose Enter Vehicle Mileage.

2 In the Vehicle field, select 2002 Ford Truck.

3 In the Start Date field, enter 12/12/2007.

4 In the End Date field, enter 12/12/2007.

5 In the Total Miles field, type ***25***.

6 In the Customer:Job field, select Melton, Johnny:Dental Office from the drop-down list.

7 In the Item field, select Mileage from the drop-down list.
The Enter Vehicle Mileage window should look like the following.

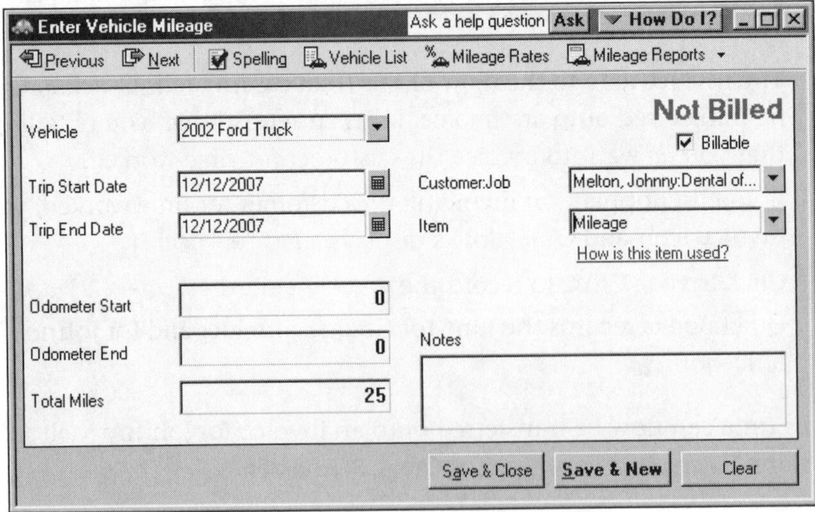

8 Click Save and New.

9 Repeat the steps above to enter 25 miles for the same vehicle and customer:job for December 13 and an additional miles for December 14.

10 Click Save & Close.

Tip: **Instead of entering time on a weekly timesheet, QuickBooks: Pro and QuickBooks: Premier products also let you enter single activities at the time they occur.** A single activity entry shows the time spent by one person doing a single activity for a single job on a single date. If you prefer to jot down the details of one day's work as the day progresses, this method might work best for you. For example, an attorney could use a single activity entry to record the time he or she just spent on a phone conversation with a client.

You can move back and forth between the two time entry forms. If you are viewing a single activity entry, you can display that person's weekly timesheet with a click of the mouse. On a weekly timesheet, you can select any hourly entry and view it as a single activity entry. The two forms are simply different views of the same data.

Invoicing a customer for time and mileage

Now you can invoice Johnny Melton for the time Rock Castle Construction's employee, Gregg Schneider, spent on the dental office job.

1. From the Customers menu, choose Create Invoices.
2. Select Melton, Johnny:Dental office as the customer:job.
3. Click Cancel in the Available Estimates window.
4. In the Date field, type ***12/17/2007***.

5 Click Time/Costs, and then click the Time tab.

QuickBooks displays the Choose Billable Time and Costs window.

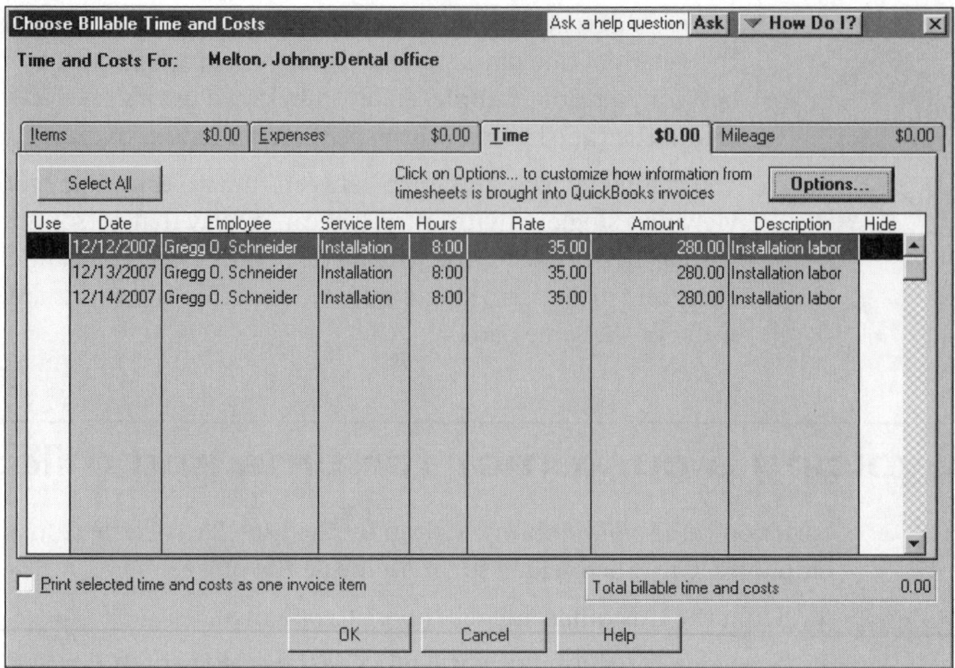

QuickBooks displays the time information entered on the timesheet for Gregg Schneider for the Johnny Melton dental office job.

Note: **By default, QuickBooks combines time for activities that have the same service item, and lists them as one line item on the invoice.** If you prefer to have each individual line from the timesheet displayed as a line item on the invoice, click the Options button and select "Enter a separate line on the invoice for each activity." In the Options for Transferring Billable Time window, you can also select to transfer notes about time activities (in addition to descriptions) onto invoices.

6 Click in the Use column to select each of the lines that represents time worked by Gregg Schneider.

QuickBooks places a checkmark in the Use column to the left of each entry to indicate it is selected.

7 Click OK.

The top part of the invoice should resemble the figure below.

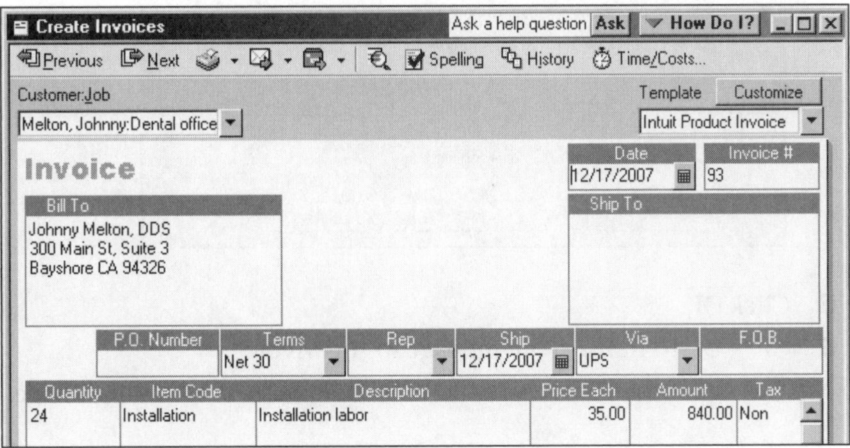

8 Keep the invoice open. You'll use it in the next exercise.

To invoice a customer for mileage:

1 In the Create Invoices window, click Time/Costs, and then click the Mileage tab.

QuickBooks displays the mileage you entered earlier for this job.

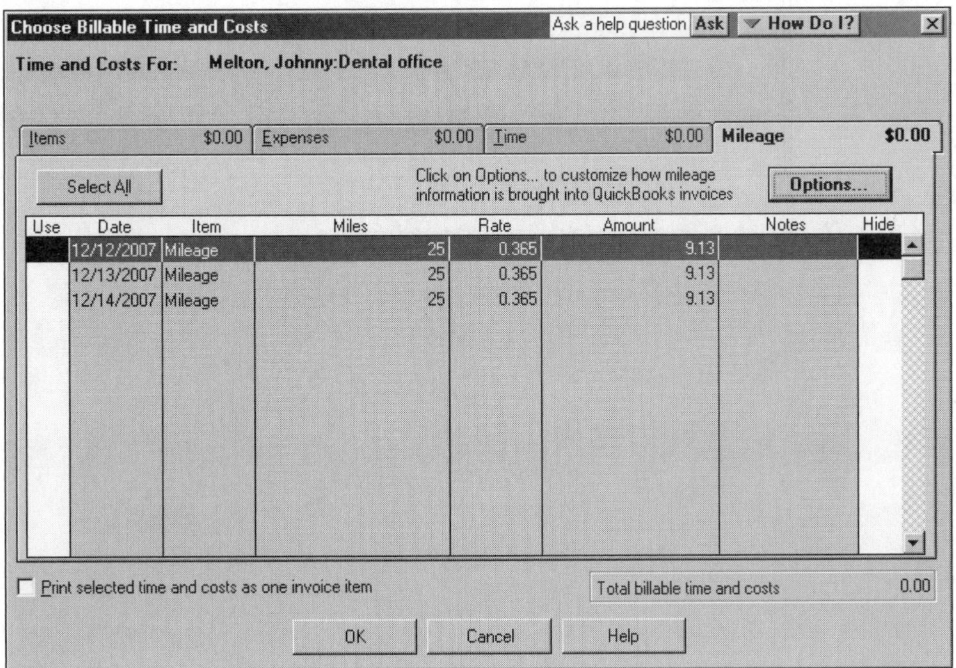

2 Click in the Use column to select each of the lines that represents the mileage for this job.

3 You want to combine mileage on a single line, so click Options.

4 Select the "Combine activities with the same service items" option.

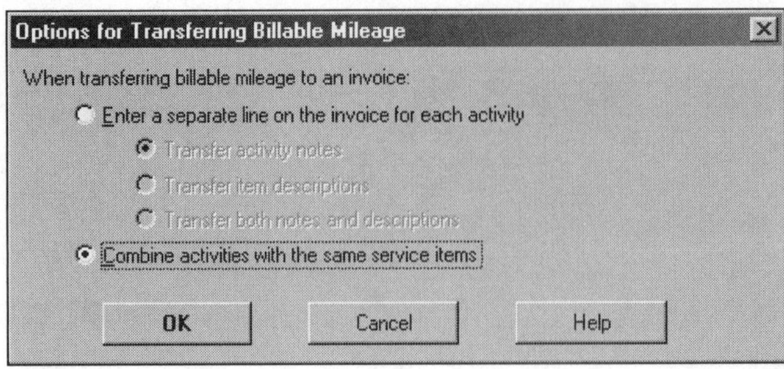

5 Click OK.

6 Click OK to transfer the mileage to the invoice.

The top of the invoice should now look like the following image.

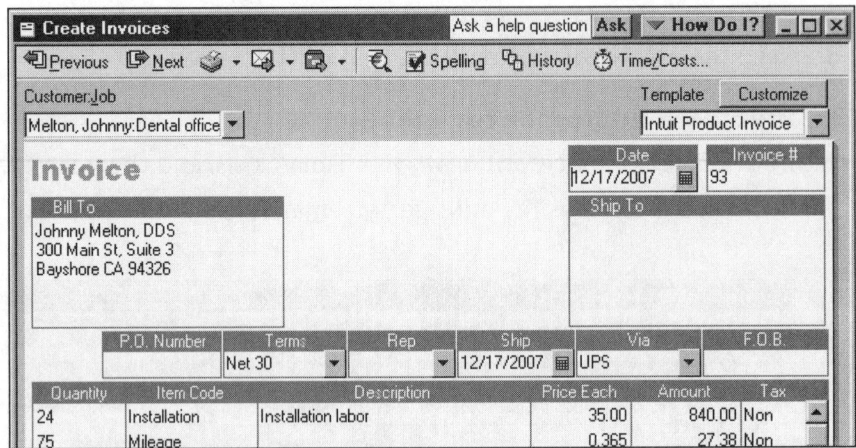

7 Click Save & Close to record the invoice.

Displaying project reports for time tracking

QuickBooks provides four reports on time, as described in the following table. You can create these reports by choosing Jobs & Time from the Reports menu.

Project report	Description
Time by Job Summary	Shows hours worked subtotaled first by customer or job and then by service item.
Time by Job Detail	Lists each time activity (that is, work done by one person for a particular customer or job on a specific date), and shows whether the work is billed, unbilled, or not billable. The report groups and subtotals the activities first by customer and job and then by service item.
Time by Name	Shows hours worked (or tracked as sick or vacation time), subtotaled first by the name of the person who performed the work and then by the customer or job the person performed the work for.
Time by Item	Shows the hours worked, subtotaled first by service item and then by customer or job.

Displaying the time by job report

The time by job summary report summarizes the total hours for each job, and the time by job detail report breaks down those summary figures into hours for each service item and hours for each customer:job.

To create a time by job report:

1. From the Reports menu, choose Jobs, Time & Mileage.
2. From the submenu, choose Time by Job Summary.

   QuickBooks displays the time by job summary report.

3 Scroll the report until you see the time worked for the Melton, Johnny:Dental office job.

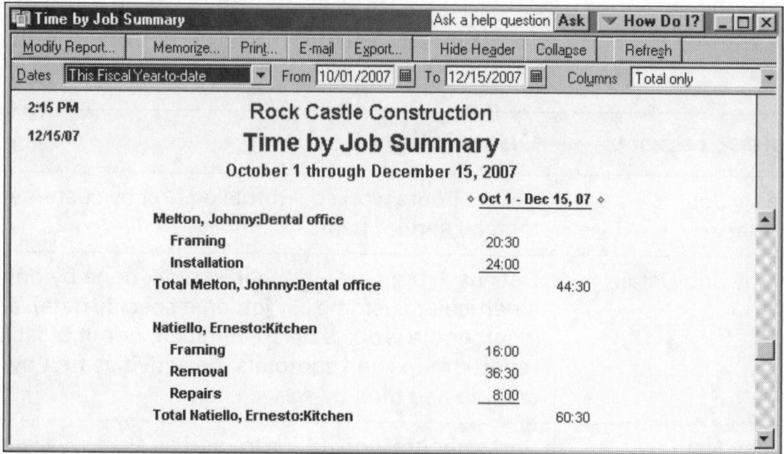

Notice that the report shows the 24 hours for Installation work performed by Gregg Schneider.

Viewing time data in more detail

Like all QuickBooks reports, you can QuickZoom any of the numbers in a report to see more detail. Suppose you want to see who worked the eight hours on installation for Johnny Melton. You can point to that number in the report and double-click to get more information.

To view more time detail in the report:

1 Position your mouse pointer over the 24 hours for Installation on the Melton, Johnny:Dental office job, and then double-click.

When you position your mouse pointer over the number, the pointer changes into a magnifying glass with a Z in it. After you double-click, QuickBooks displays a time by job detail report for the time data you selected. (This functionality is called QuickZoom.)

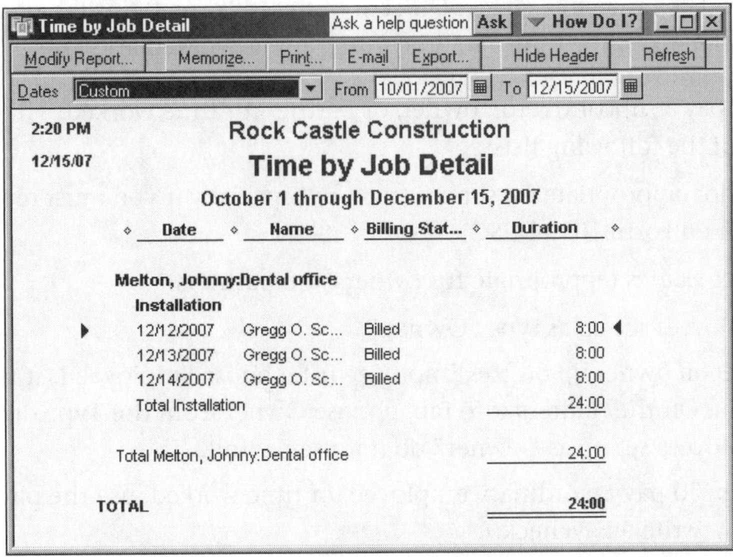

You can see that Gregg Schneider did the work and the time has already been billed to the customer.

2 Close the time by job detail and the time by job summary reports.

When QuickBooks asks if you want to memorize the report, click No.

3 Close the time by job summary report.

Displaying other project reports

In addition to the estimate and time reports, QuickBooks provides several project reports to track job profitability, as described in the following table.

Project report	Description
Job Profitability Summary	Compares the actual cost to the actual revenue for all customers and jobs. The report subtotals the data first by customer and then by job.
Job Profitability Detail (for one customer:job)	For a particular customer or job, compares actual costs to actual revenues and shows the difference between the two amounts. The report subtotals the data first by item type and then by item.
Item Profitability	For each item, compares the actual cost to actual revenue and shows the difference between the two amounts. The report subtotals the data first by item type and then by item.

Paying nonemployees for time worked

When the company file has time data for a person who is not on your payroll, you can write checks based on the time worked. QuickBooks can transfer time data for a specified date range to a check. QuickBooks prefills the Items tab of a check with information from the time data, including hours worked and rate.

You can pay a subcontractor, owner, or partner for time worked. The person must be on one of the following lists:

- Vendor (appropriate for subcontractors, especially if you must report payments to them on Form 1099-MISC)
- Other Names (appropriate for owners and partners)
- Employees set up as type "Owner."

  To set an owner up on the Employee list, choose Employee List from the Lists menu. On the Address Info tab, choose Owner from the Type drop-down list. Employees set up as "Owner" do not use payroll.

  Note: To pay an ordinary employee for time worked, use the payroll feature to write a paycheck.

Creating service items for subcontractors, owners, or partners

When you use service items for subcontractors, QuickBooks records expenses and income for the work in separate accounts. You can use such items on both purchase forms and sales forms.

In this section, you learn how to do the following:

- Set up a service item to use to track work performed by an owner or partner
- Enter time worked for an owner or partner
- Prepare a check to pay an owner or partner for time worked

To set up a service item for owners or partners:

1. From the Lists menu, choose Item List.
2. Click the Item menu button, and choose New.
3. In the Type field of the New Item window, choose Service from the drop-down list.
4. In the Item Name/Number field, type ***Planning***.

5 Select the "This service is performed by a subcontractor, owner, or partner" checkbox.

QuickBooks changes the window to display fields for sales and purchase information.

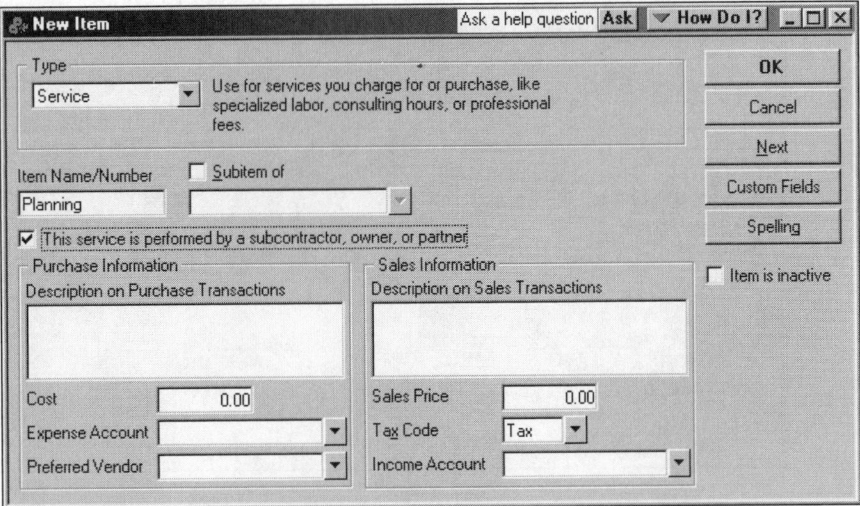

6 In the Description on Purchase Transactions field, type ***Job Planning*** and press Tab.

QuickBooks copies the text into the Description on Sales Transactions field.

7 In the Cost field, type ***50*** and press Tab.

8 From the drop-down list in the Expense Account field, choose the equity subaccount called *Owner's Draw.*

If you pay owners (or partners) for time worked, you need a service item that records the cost of the work as a draw against equity, rather than an expense.

9 In the Sales Price field, type ***90.***

10 In the Tax Code drop-down list, select Non.

11 In the Income Account field, type ***Planning*** and press Tab.

12 When QuickBooks tells you that Planning is not on the Account list, click Set Up.

13 In the New Account window, make sure Income is selected in the Type drop-down list and click OK.

Your screen should now look like this.

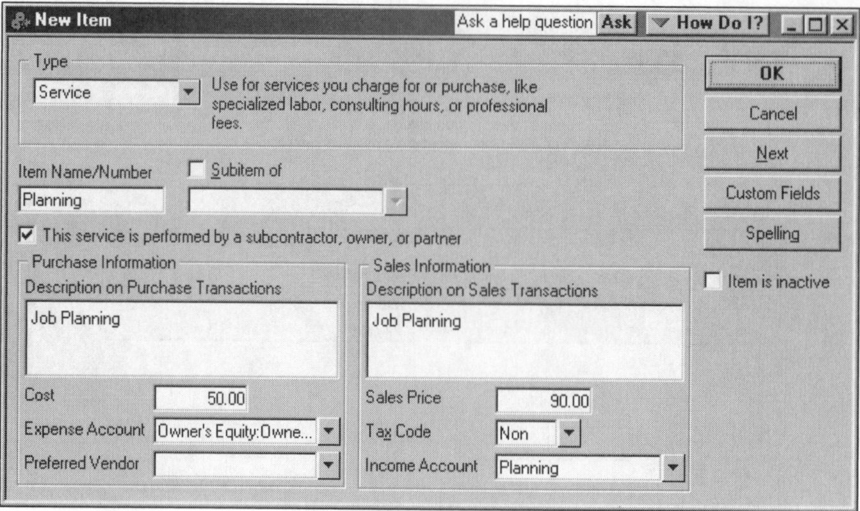

14 Click OK to close the New Item window.

15 Press Esc to close the Item list.

In the next section, you learn how to use the Planning item you've just created to track time performed by the owner of Rock Castle Construction.

Recording nonemployee time worked

You record data for time worked by nonemployees the same way you enter it for employees.

To enter time for nonemployee time worked:

1 From the Employees menu, choose Time Tracking. Then choose Time/Enter Single Activity.

QuickBooks displays the Time/Enter Single Activity window.

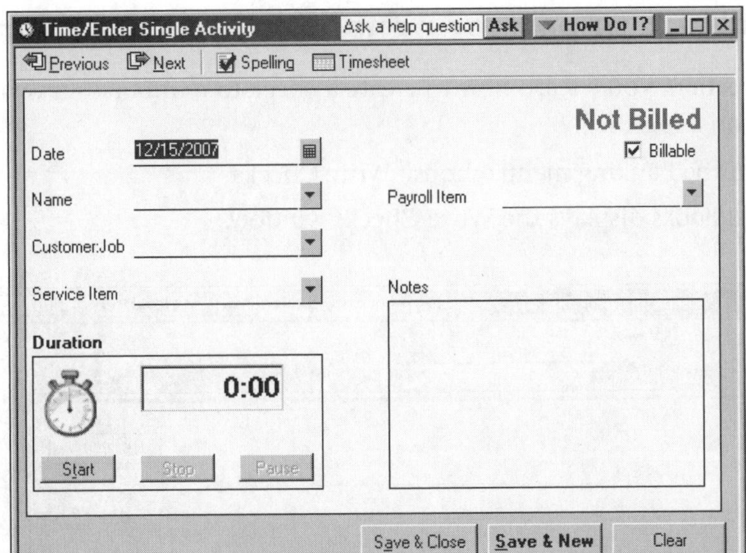

2 In the Name field, choose Tom Ferguson from the drop-down list.

Note: When you selected the owner's name, QuickBooks removed the Payroll Item field from the window. (When class tracking is on, this field is replaced with the class field.) Owners and partners should be set up on the Other Names list, or on the Employee List with the Type set to "Owner" because they are not paid with payroll checks.

3 In the Customer:Job field, choose Abercrombie, Kristy:Family Room.

4 In the Service Item field, select Planning from the drop-down list and press Tab.

5 Type ***8*** in the Duration field and press Tab.

Your screen should resemble the following.

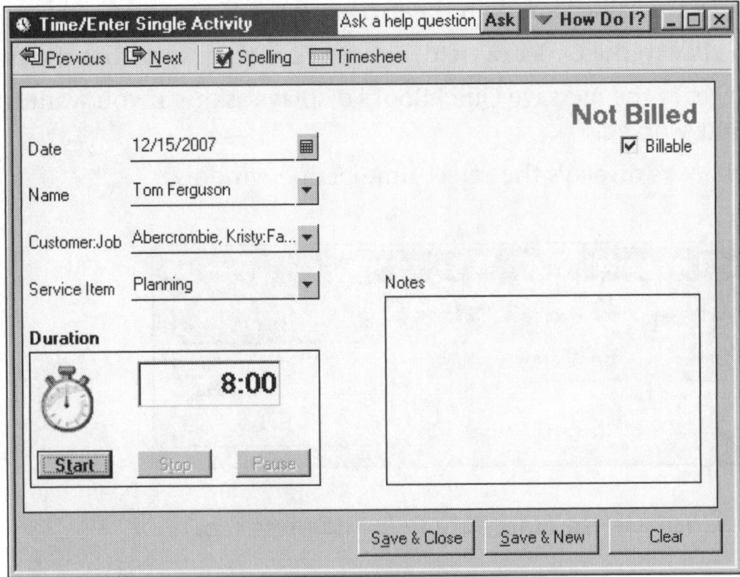

6 Click Save & Close.

Preparing a check to pay for nonemployee time worked

In this section, you'll learn how to create a check to reimburse an owner for time worked on a specific job.

1 From the Banking menu, choose Write Checks.

QuickBooks displays the Write Checks window.

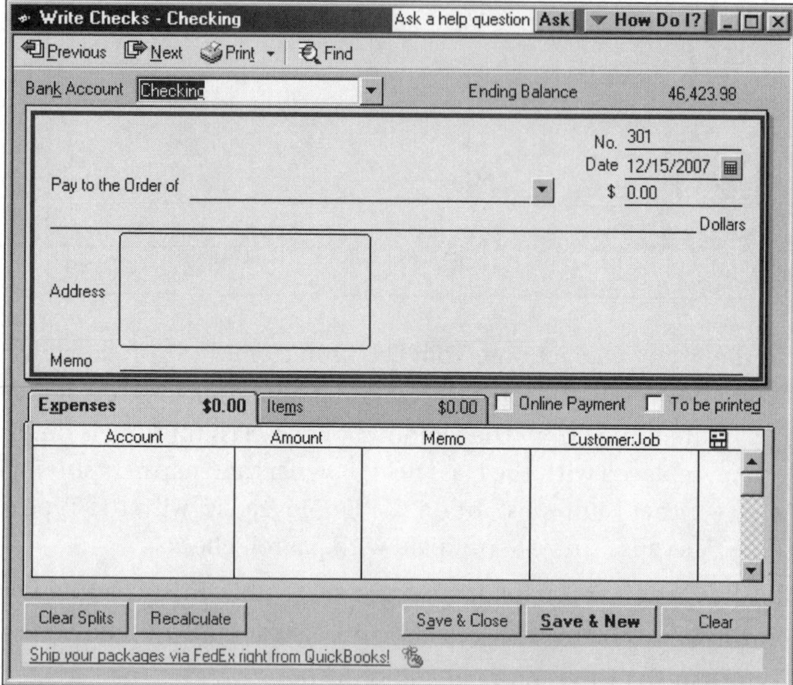

2 Make sure that Checking is selected in the Bank Account field.

3 Click to put a checkmark in the "To be printed" checkbox.

4 In the Pay to the Order of field, choose Tom Ferguson from the drop-down list.

5 Click Yes at the message QuickBooks displays asking if you want this check to pay for time worked.

QuickBooks displays the Select time period window.

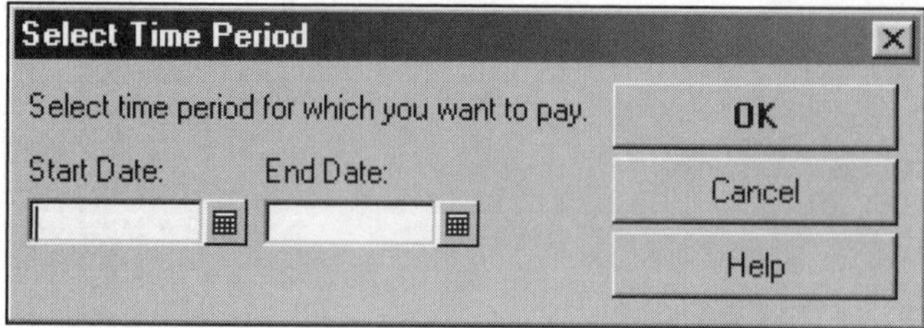

6 Type ***12/15/07*** in the Start Date field and press Tab.

7 Type ***12/19/07*** in the End Date field and click OK.

QuickBooks prefills the Items tab of the check with information from the time data, including hours worked and rate.

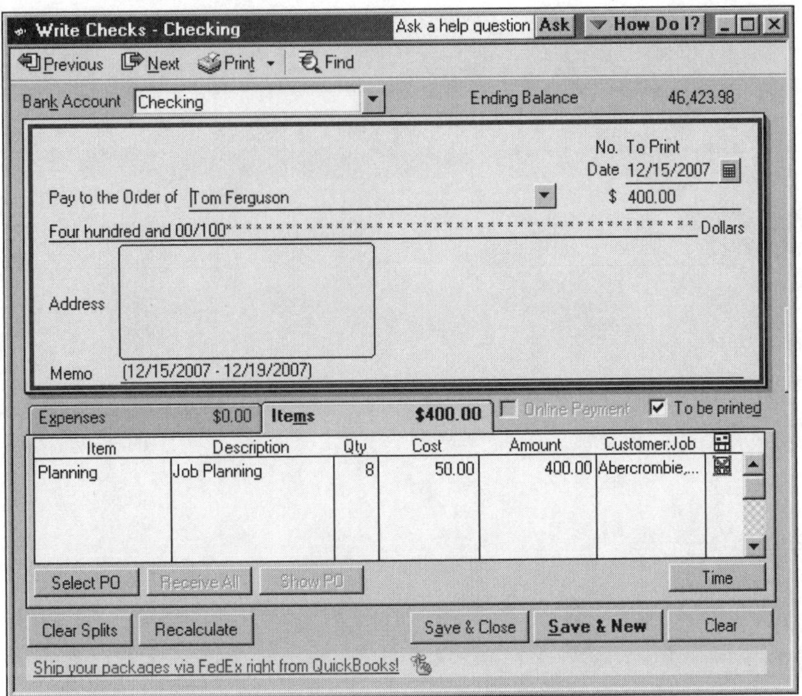

8 Click Save & Close in the Write Checks window.

Notice that time activity is marked unbillable so that it is not billed twice—as a time activity and an item.

Student test and review

1. Create a single activity timesheet for Gregg Schneider, for eight hours worked on the Anton Teschner Sun Room job.
2. Transfer the time you just entered for Gregg Schneider onto an invoice for the Teschner Sun Room job.

   On the invoice, click the Time/Costs button and then click the Time tab to display the hours recorded for this job. Select the time by clicking in the Use column and then clicking OK.
3. Display a time by name job report to see how many hours Gregg Schneider has worked for each job.

• • • • • • • • • •

LESSON 15 Customizing forms and writing QuickBooks Letters

Lesson objectives

- To learn how to modify a preset invoice form
- To design a custom invoice form
- To see how to print invoices
- To learn how to prepare a collection letter for overdue customers
- To learn how to edit a prewritten letter in QuickBooks

Instructor preparation

- Review the lesson, including the examples, to make sure you're familiar with the material.
- Ensure that all students have copy of qblesson.qbb on their computer's hard disk.

To start this lesson

Before you perform the following steps, make sure you have installed the exercise file (qblesson.qbb) on your hard disk. See "Installing the exercise file" in the Introduction to this guide if you haven't installed it.

The following steps restore the exercise file to its original state so that the data in the file matches what you see on the screen as you proceed through each lesson.

To restore the exercise file (qblesson.qbb):

1. From the File menu in QuickBooks, choose Restore.

   QuickBooks displays the Restore Company Backup window.
2. In the "Get Company Backup From" section of the window, click Browse and select your c:\QBtrain directory.
3. Select the qblesson.qbb file, and then click Open.
4. In the "Restore Company Backup To" section of the window, click Browse and select your c:\QBtrain directory.
5. In the File name field of the Restore To window, type ***lesson 15*** and then click Save.
6. Click Restore.

About QuickBooks forms

Each form you use in QuickBooks has its own layout—that is, its own arrangement of fields and columns for entering information. If the layout of a particular form doesn't meet your needs, you can create your own custom layout and use your version instead of the QuickBooks version.

In Lesson 6, you learned about the three preset formats for invoices: professional, service, and product. If these formats don't precisely meet your needs, you can create your own invoice templates. You can also create templates for other sales and purchase forms.

For each form, you can decide which fields and columns to include, what they are called, and where to place them. Once you have created your forms, you can save the new layouts as *templates*—to use whenever you wish, and to modify whenever you want. The forms you can customize in QuickBooks are the invoice, sales receipt, credit memo, statement, purchase order, estimate (QuickBooks Pro and Premier only), and sales order (QuickBooks Premier editions only).

Note: **You can create custom forms in all QuickBooks products, but some of the customization and layout options described in this lesson are available only in QuickBooks Pro and Premier products.** For example, adding colored backgrounds, using rounded borders on fields, and using fields on forms multiple times are available only in QuickBooks Pro and Premier products.

Customizing invoices

QuickBooks lets you customize an invoice form to suit the needs of your business, but there may be times when you want to design a completely different invoice form. QuickBooks lets you do that, too. You can use the Layout Designer to create a new form design for your business. In the Layout Designer, you can move, resize, or change the width of columns, turn on or off borders around fields, and control font type and size for each field.

In the following exercises, you'll use both the customize forms and Layout Designer features in QuickBooks to create a custom invoice.

Note that these features affect only the printed forms; you cannot customize the onscreen version of QuickBooks forms.

Creating new templates

To create a new invoice template:

1 From the Lists menu, choose Templates.

QuickBooks displays the Templates list.

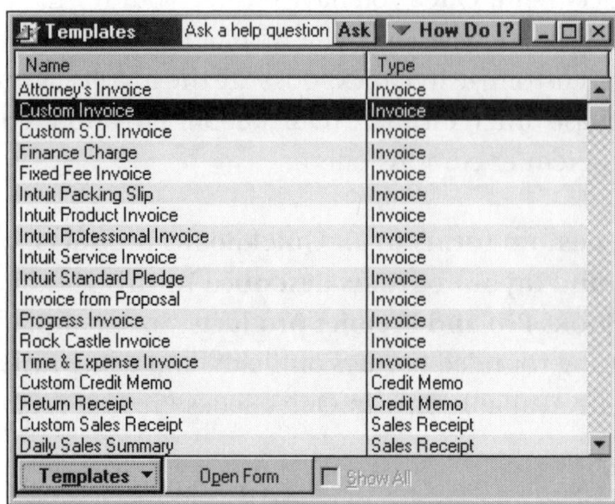

2 Click the Templates menu button, and then choose New.

QuickBooks displays the Select Template Type window.

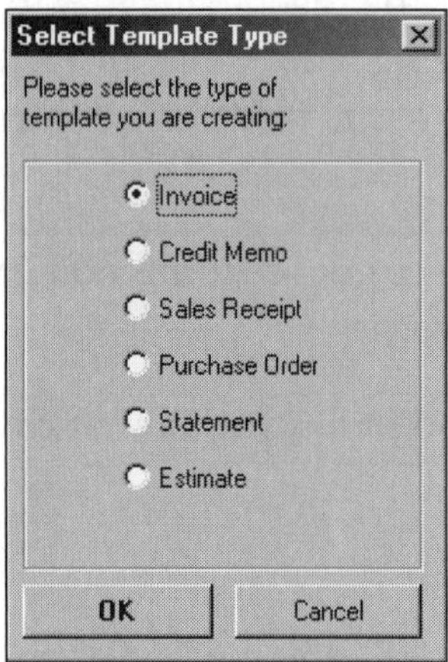

3 Click OK to select the invoice form.

QuickBooks displays the Customize Invoice window, which uses multiple tabs to display several sets of formatting options. Each area of the form is represented by a tab. To display the available formatting options, click the tab for the area of the form you want to change.

4 In the Template Name field, type ***My Invoice***.

This is the name you'll use for the new template. Your window should look like this.

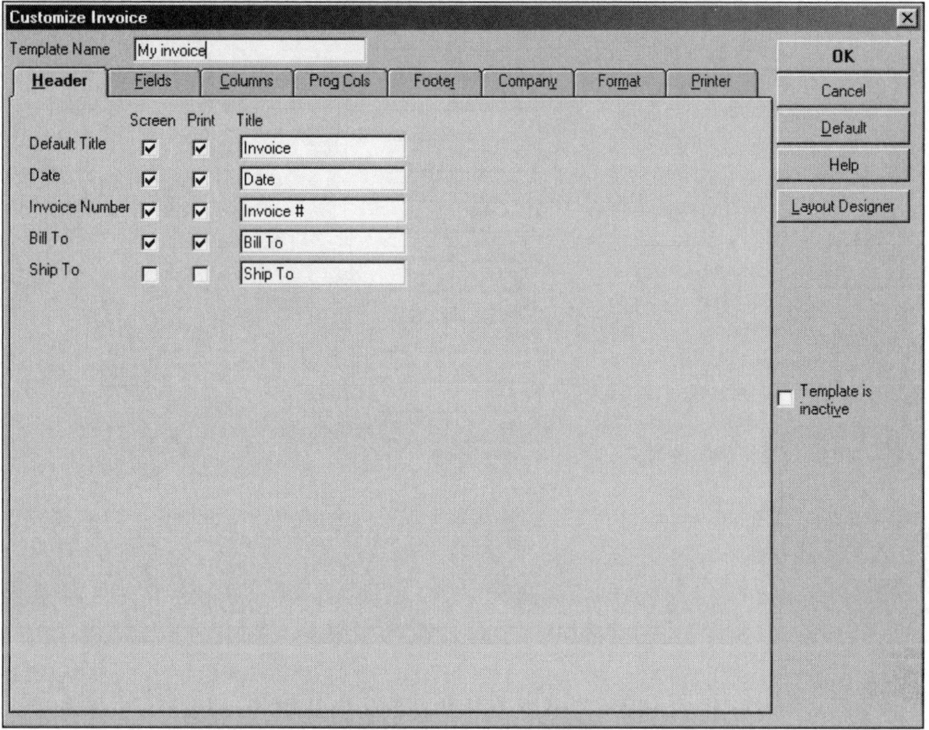

Notice that the Header tab is currently selected. The Header tab displays the formatting options you have for the top part of the invoice form. For each field, you can specify the title you want and whether you want the field displayed onscreen, on paper, both, or neither. You can enter a new title by highlighting the current title text and typing your new one.

If you want to track information about a particular invoice, but don't want your customer to see this information, select the Screen checkbox and clear the Print checkbox.

5 Click the Fields tab.

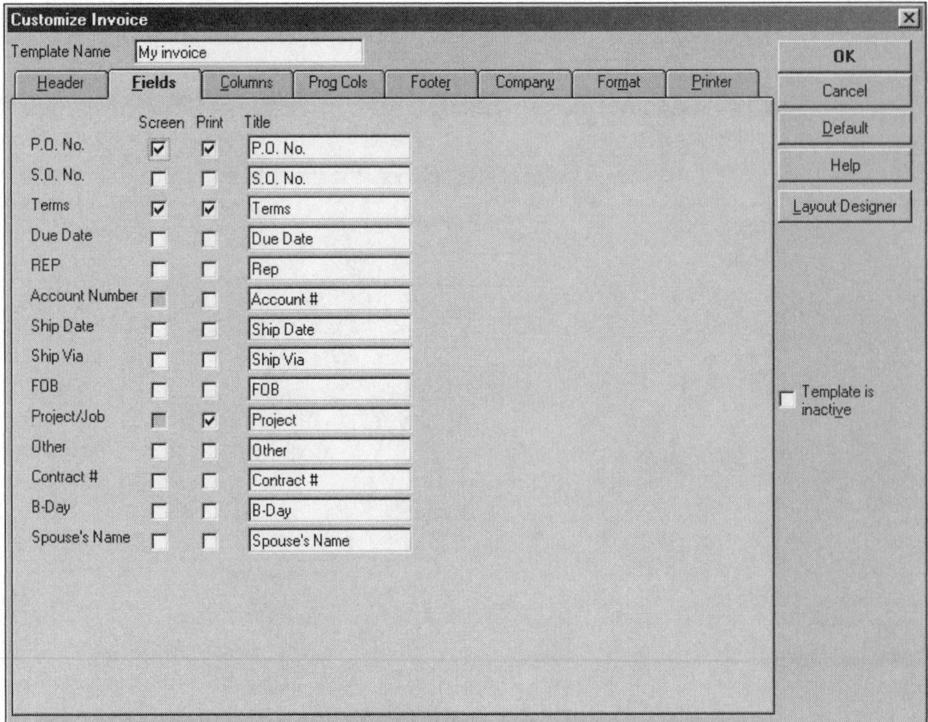

The Fields tab is where you select which fields you want to appear on screen and on paper. You can specify your own title (label) for each field.

Suppose you want to remind customers of payment due dates at the time you send the invoice. You can customize the invoice form to display the Due Date field.

6 To have the Due Date field display both on screen and on the printed form, click the Screen and Print columns for Due Date to select both checkboxes.

Checkmarks appear in both checkboxes.

7 Clear the Screen and Print checkboxes for the P.O. field to remove the field from the form.

Changing field order on forms

The lower half of the standard QuickBooks invoice form is where you enter details about the items or services purchased by the customer. You can change the order of these fields as they appear on your invoices.

The Order column shows you how fields display from left to right on the invoice form. Currently, Item is the first column and Amount is the last column. Suppose you want the Qty field to appear after the Item field, and before the Description field.

To change the order of fields on a form:

1 Click the Columns tab.

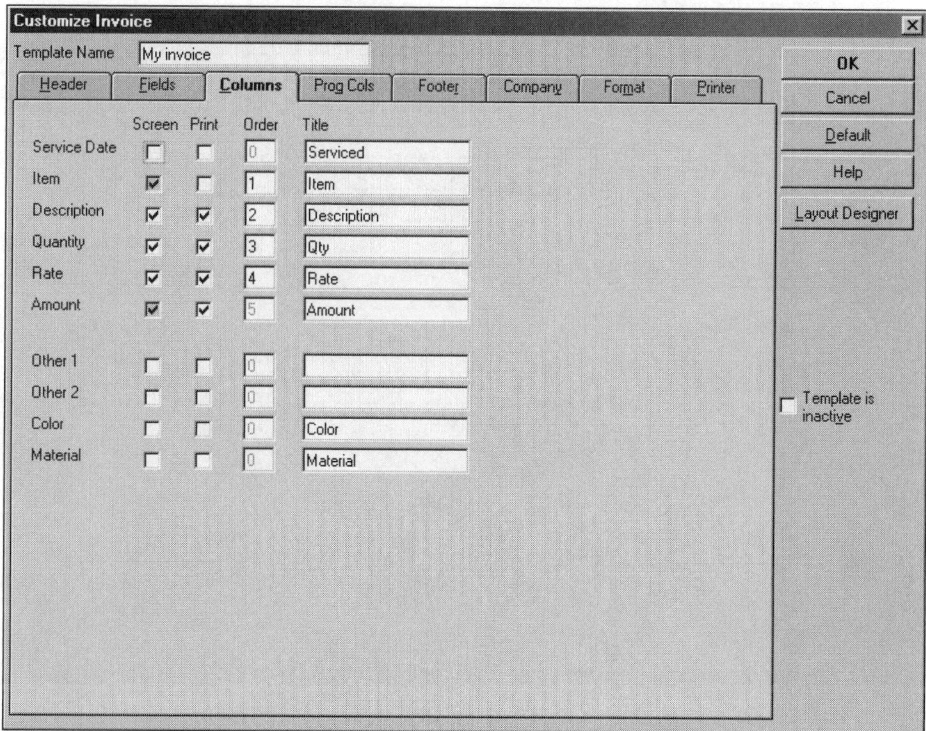

2 Double-click the Order column in the Quantity row to select the number.

3 Type *2*.

4 Double-click the Order column in the Description row to select it.

5 Type *3*.

Your screen should look like the following figure.

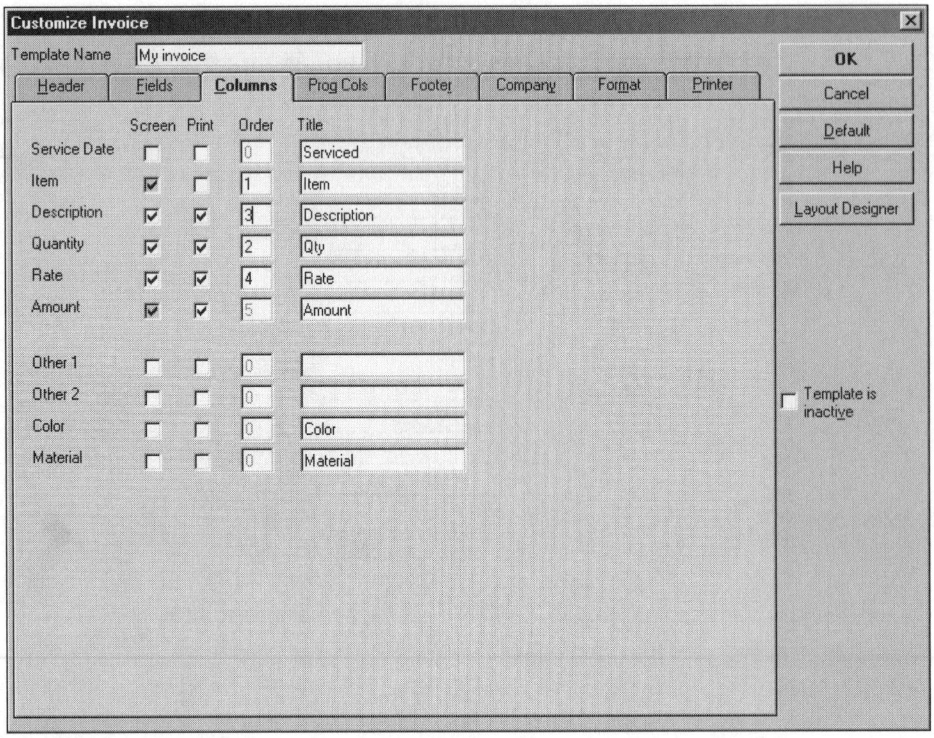

If you use progress invoices or sales orders, use the Prog Cols tab to customize the columns on those forms.

6 Click the Footer tab.

The Footer tab contains information that you usually find at the bottom of the form. It also provides a place for you to enter free-form text, such as a disclaimer, on your form. In the next exercise, you'll learn how to move fields on forms.

7 Click the Company tab.

Use the Company tab to specify which pieces of company information to include on your sales and purchase forms.

8 Select the Print Phone Number checkbox.

Your window should look like the following graphic.

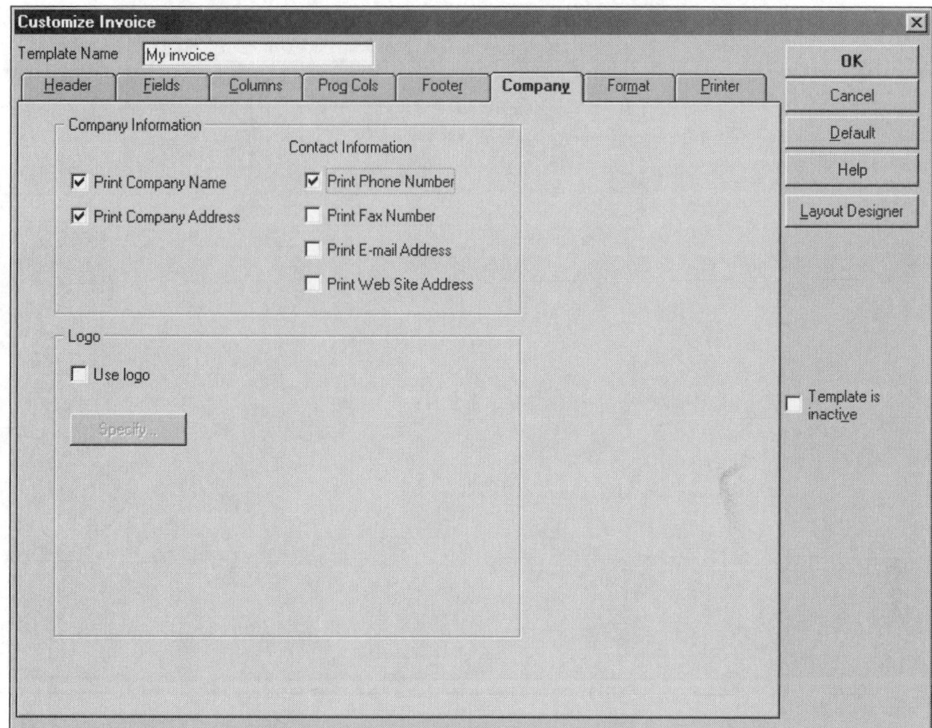

If you wanted to add your company logo to the form, you would select the Use Logo checkbox and tell QuickBooks which file to use. QuickBooks supports BMP, JPEG, TIFF, and GIF graphic formats.

9 Click the Format tab.

Use the Format tab to change the fonts for various textual elements on the form. If your forms print on multiple pages, use the checkbox on this tab to indicate whether or not you want to print page numbers.

If you don't want QuickBooks to print the status stamp (paid, pending, etc.) on forms, clear the Print Status Stamp checkbox on this tab.

10 Click the Printer tab.

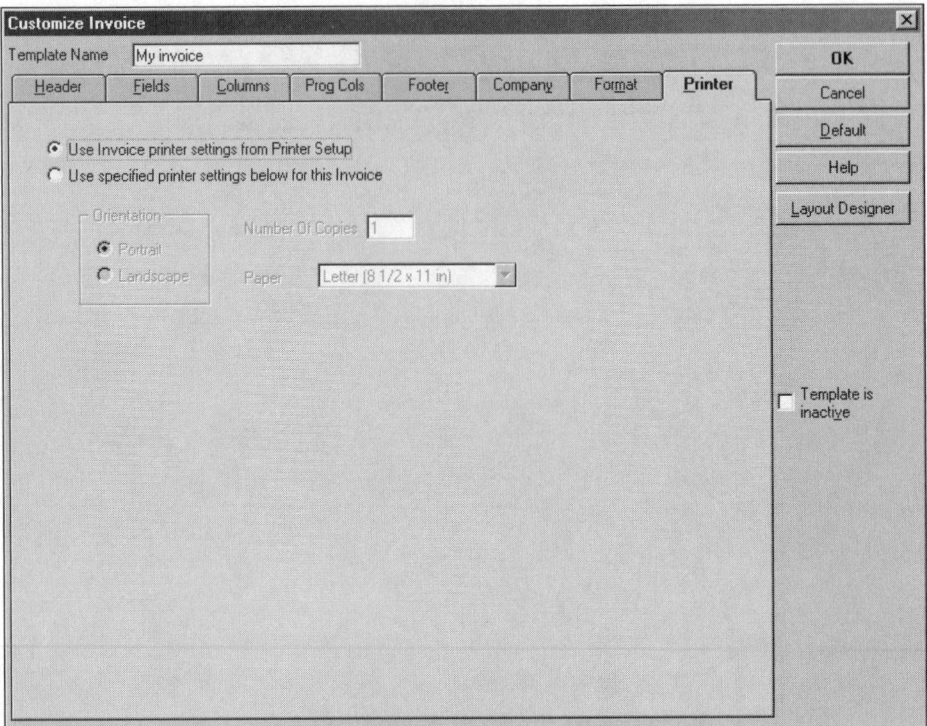

Use the Printer tab to associate print settings with individual form templates. For example, if you print most forms in Portrait mode, but have one form that you print in Landscape, you can associate the Landscape print setting with that form's template. When you send the form to the printer, QuickBooks knows to print it in Landscape.

11 Click OK to record the changes.

12 Close the Templates window.

Displaying your customized form

Now display the customized form to see the changes you made in the previous exercise.

To display the custom form:

1 From the Customers menu, choose Create Invoices.

QuickBooks displays the Create Invoices window with the Intuit Product Invoice template displayed.

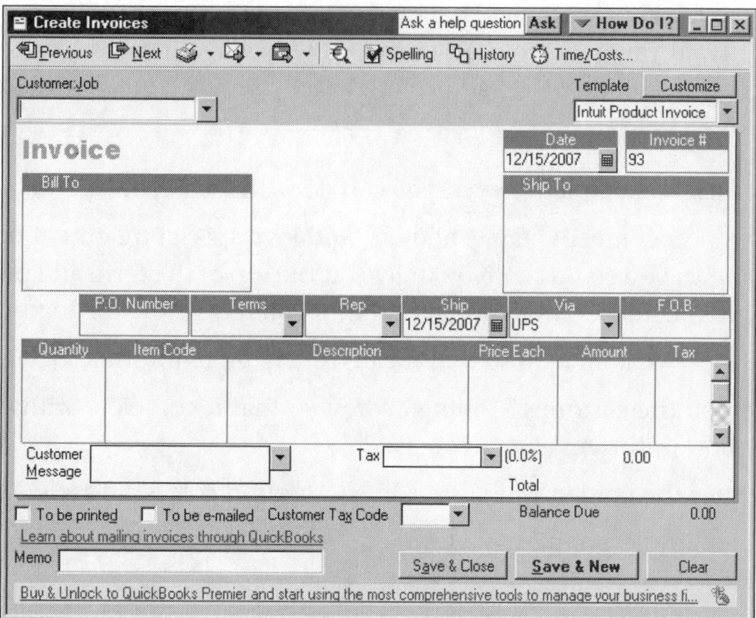

2 In the Template field, choose My Invoice from the drop-down list.

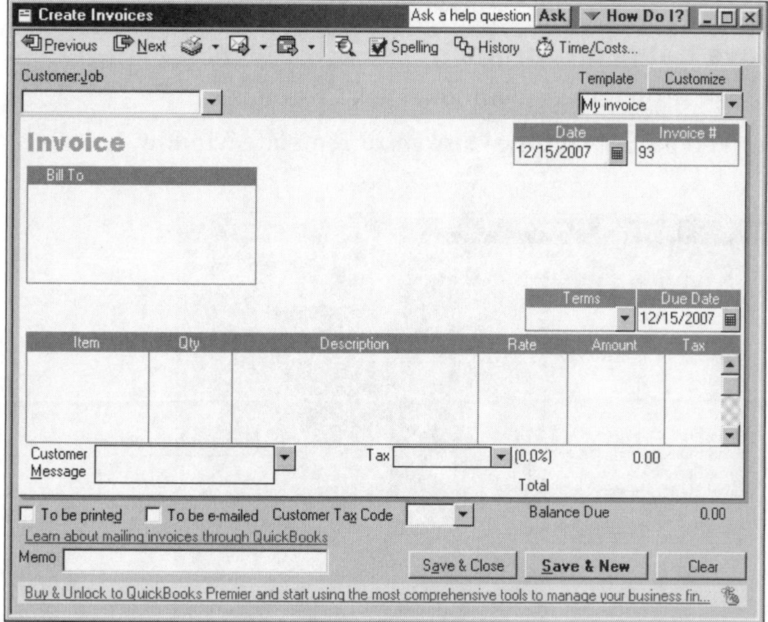

Notice how this form reflects the changes you made in the Customize Invoice window. The Due Date field now displays onscreen and the Qty column appears in its new order before the Description field.

The phone number field that you added to the form only shows on the printed form, so you do not see it onscreen.

3 Leave the Create Invoices window open, you'll use it in the next exercise.

Designing custom layouts for forms

With the QuickBooks Layout Designer, you can change the design or layout of a form. In the Layout Designer, you can move, resize, change the width of columns, turn on or off borders around fields, add colored backgrounds, and control the font type and size for each field.

Here are a few examples of what you can do with a custom layout:

- Give your company name, address, and logo special treatment on the form. For example, you could center your logo at the top of the form and put your company name and address in a special font immediately below the logo.
- Enlarge a custom field so that it can display more information.
- Position the customer's billing address so that it coincides with the address window in the envelopes you use.
- Change the borders on fields, add background colors, and add extra text fields.
- Add multiple graphics to a form.

Changing the position of fields on forms

Next, you'll use the Layout Designer to move the Phone # and Bill To fields, and to decrease the width of the Quantity column.

To move fields on forms:

1 In the Create Invoices window, click Customize.

QuickBooks displays the Customize Template window.

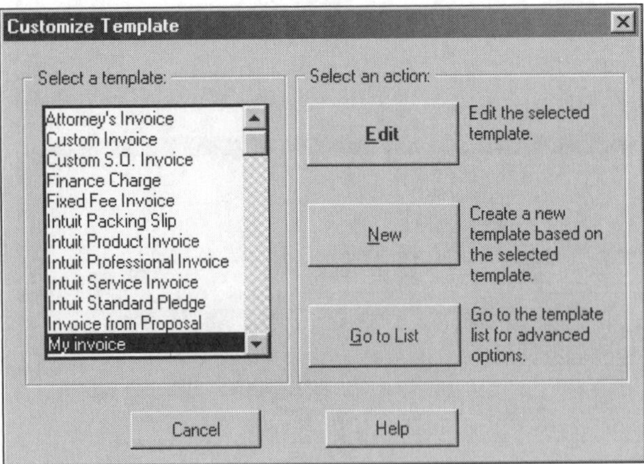

2 Make sure that My Invoice is selected and click Edit.

QuickBooks displays the Customize Invoice window that you used to customize the form.

Now, you'll use the Layout Designer to change the design of the form.

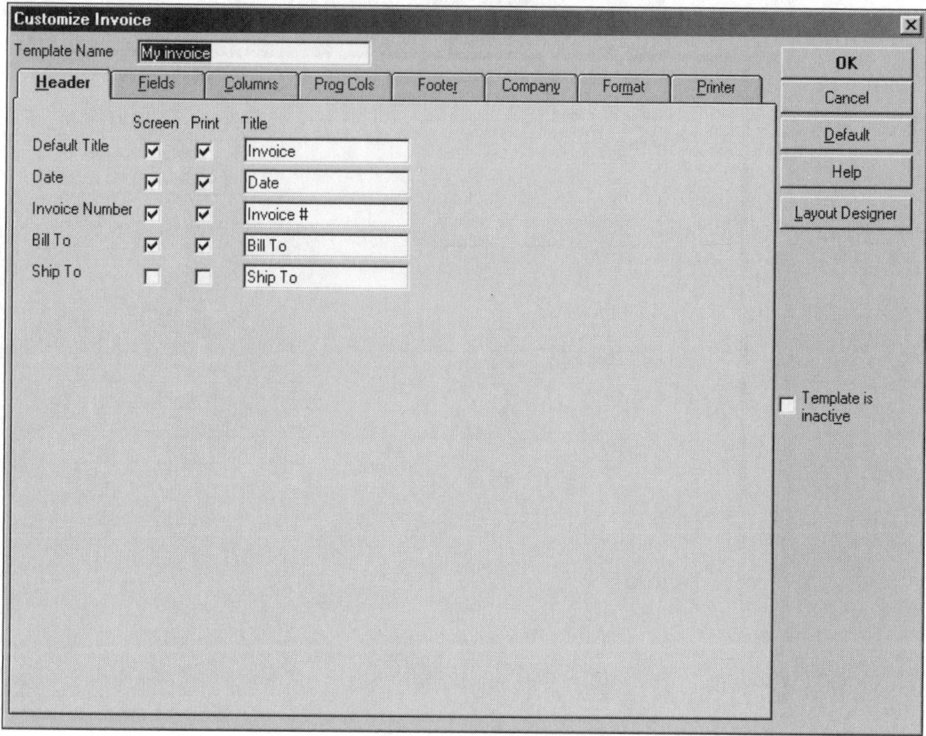

3 Click Layout Designer.

QuickBooks displays the Layout Designer window.

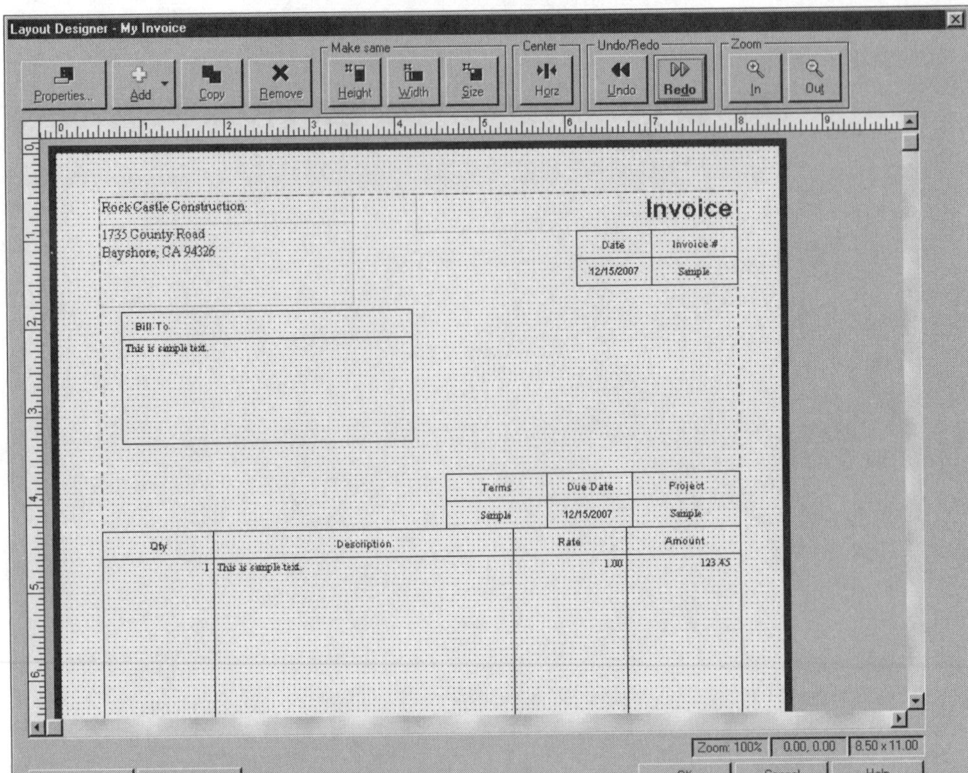

By clicking the Zoom buttons, you can zoom out to see an overall view of the form or zoom in for a closer look at a small section of the form.

4 Click the Bill To field.

5 Press and hold the Shift key.

Holding down the Shift key when clicking on an object allows you to select multiple fields at the same time. Having multiple fields selected lets you move the fields together.

6 Click the field directly below the Bill To field (the field containing the words "This is sample text").

Notice the four-directional arrow that appears when you move the cursor over the selected fields. The selected fields on your screen should look like this.

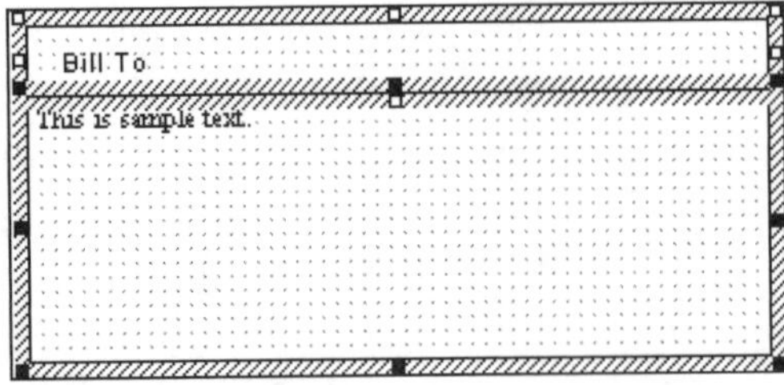

7 Release the Shift key.

8 With the cursor over the selected fields, press and hold the left mouse button.

9 Drag the selected fields down about one inch.

10 Release the mouse button.

Your screen should now look like this.

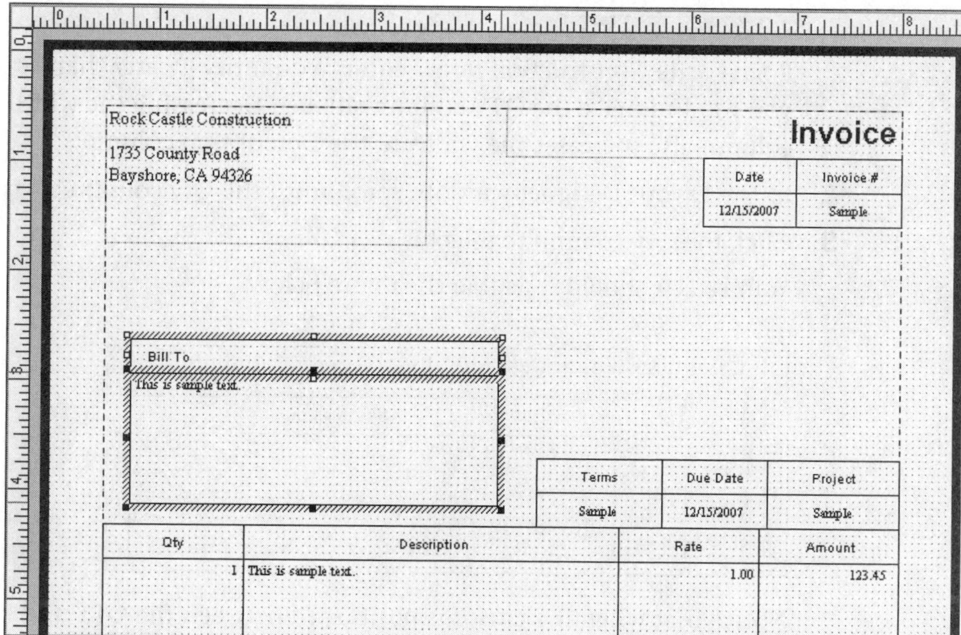

11 Select the field containing Rock Castle's address.

12 Move the mouse over one of the dark squares on the bottom of the field and then hold the mouse button while you drag the bottom of the field up to a point just below the address.

13 Scroll to the bottom of the screen and select the Phone # field.

14 Click Remove.

15 Select the field containing the numbers 555-555-5555.

16 Holding down the mouse button, drag the field so that it sits just below Rock Castle's address.

Changing field widths

In the next exercise, you'll change the font size for Rock Castle's phone number to make it match the address, but first you want to make the field wider so that the phone number isn't cut off.

To change the width of a field:

1 Select the field containing the telephone number and drag the right border further to the right while holding down the mouse button.

The fields should resemble the figure below.

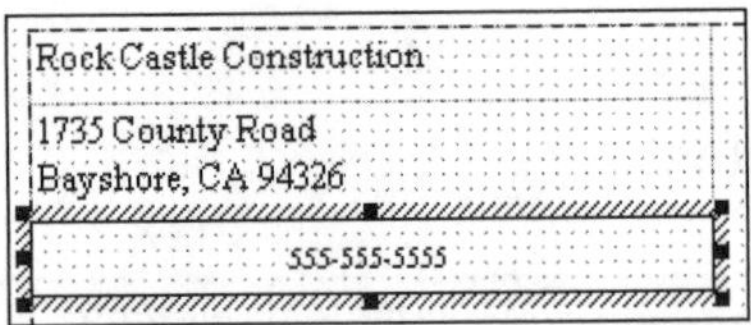

Rock Castle Construction rarely enters a quantity greater than two characters, so you want to make the QTY column smaller. Decreasing the width of the QTY column also increases the width of the Description column.

2 In the Layout Designer window, scroll until the Qty column is visible.

3 Click the Qty column to select it.

Your screen should resemble the figure below.

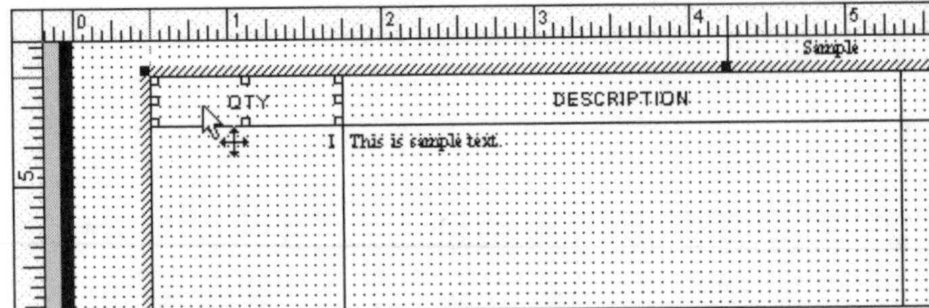

Notice that when the cursor is positioned between the QTY and DESCRIPTION columns, it turns into a two-directional arrow.

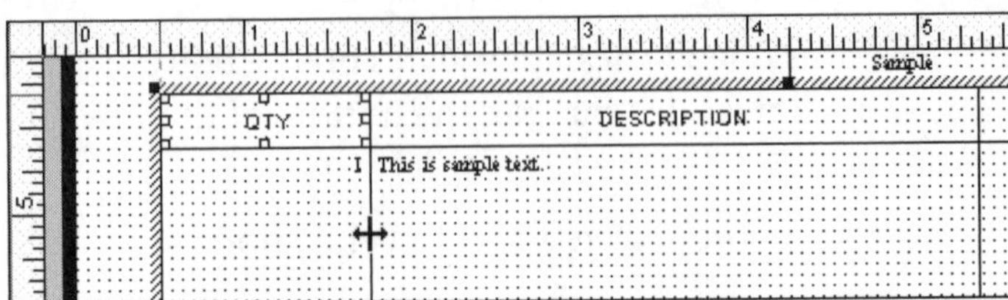

4 Click and hold the left mouse button on the line separating the Qty and Description columns.

5 While holding down the mouse button, drag the column line to the left (to the one-inch mark on the ruler).

6 Release the mouse button.

The forms area on your screen should resemble the figure below.

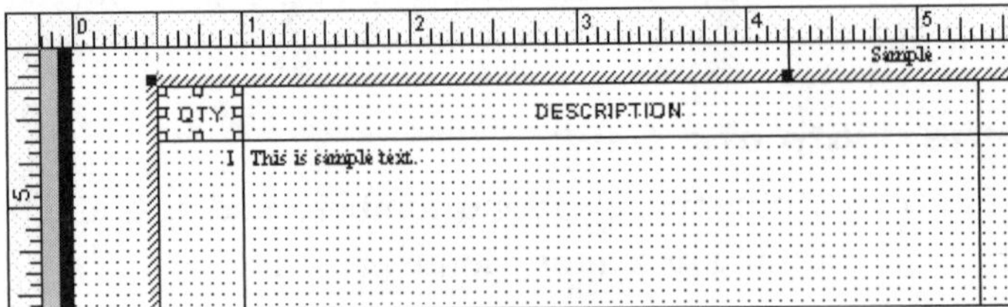

Changing fonts, borders, and colors

Using the Properties window in the Layout Designer, you can change font size and style, text justification. You can also add, remove, or change the borders around fields.

1 With the phone number field selected, click Properties.

   QuickBooks displays the Properties window.

2 On the Text tab, select Left for horizontal justification.

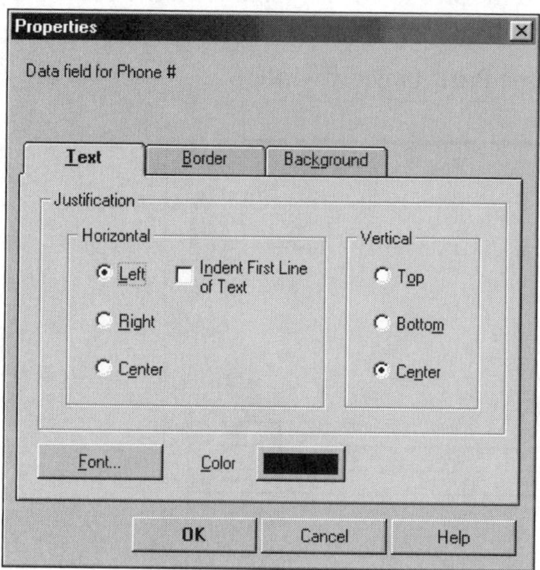

3 Click the Font button.

4 In the Size drop-down list, select 12, and then click OK.

5 Click the Border tab.

6 Click to remove the Top, Bottom, Right, and Left checkboxes.

7 Click OK to save your changes in the Properties window.

8 Click OK to save the changes in the Layout Designer.

9 Click OK to close the Customize Invoice window.

This exercise covers only a portion of the changes you can make with the customization and layout tools. For example, if you wanted to add a background color to the field, you could do so using the Background tab. You could use the Add button to add empty fields into which you can enter your own text—or to add data fields that you forgot to select in the Customize window. If you want a field to appear on a form more than once, select the field and click Copy.

We encourage you to experiment with the tools available to create your own custom forms. For examples of what you can achieve, visit the forms library at http://templategallery.quickbooks.com/forms/.

If you are using QuickBooks: Pro or QuickBooks: Premier, you can download templates from the forms library to use in your own business.

Previewing new forms

Notice that the invoice form displayed by QuickBooks doesn't show the changes you just made in the Layout Designer. This is because changes made in the Layout Designer only affect the printed invoice and not the invoice QuickBooks displays onscreen for data entry.

To preview the invoice:

1. To see how the printed invoice form will look, click the Print drop-down list on the Create Invoices window toolbar, and then choose Preview.

   QuickBooks displays the Print Preview window.

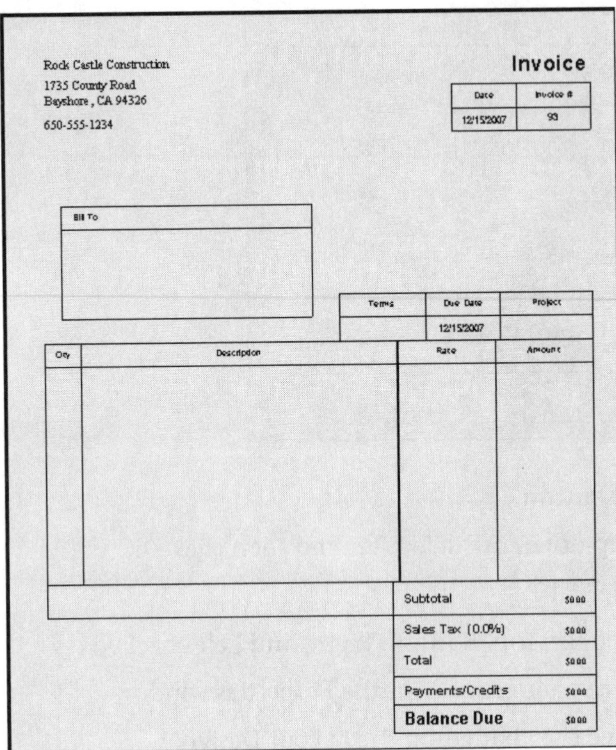

Rock Castle Construction
1735 County Road
Bayshore, CA 94326
650-555-1234

Invoice

Date	Invoice #
12/15/2007	93

Bill To

Terms	Due Date	Project
	12/15/2007	

Qty	Description	Rate	Amount

Subtotal	$0.00
Sales Tax (0.0%)	$0.00
Total	$0.00
Payments/Credits	$0.00
Balance Due	$0.00

   The invoice displayed in the Print Preview window shows exactly how the printed invoice will look. Notice that the changes you made in the Layout Designer are reflected in this preview.

2. When you are finished looking at the preview, click Close.
3. Press Esc to close the Create Invoices window without saving.

Using QuickBooks Letters

From time to time, you may need to send a letter to a customer or vendor (or someone on your employee list or other names list), or to another list of people. With QuickBooks Pro and Premier, you can easily add the pertinent QuickBooks data (such as name, address, and balance information) to a letter without having to re-type it.

QuickBooks provides a number of business letters focusing on collections, news, and announcements. You can edit these letters as needed to suit your business and style of communication.

Note: **To proceed with this lesson, you must be using QuickBooks: Pro or Premier and Microsoft Word 97, 2000, 2002, or 2003.** The QuickBooks Letters feature is not available in QuickBooks: Basic.

Preparing collection letters

In this exercise, you'll learn how to prepare a collection letter to send to customers with overdue payments.

To prepare a collection letter:

1 From the Company menu, choose Write Letters.

2 If QuickBooks prompts you to find letters, click Copy. QuickBooks will copy the QuickBooks letters from your installation directory to your QBtrain folder.

QuickBooks opens the Write Letters wizard.

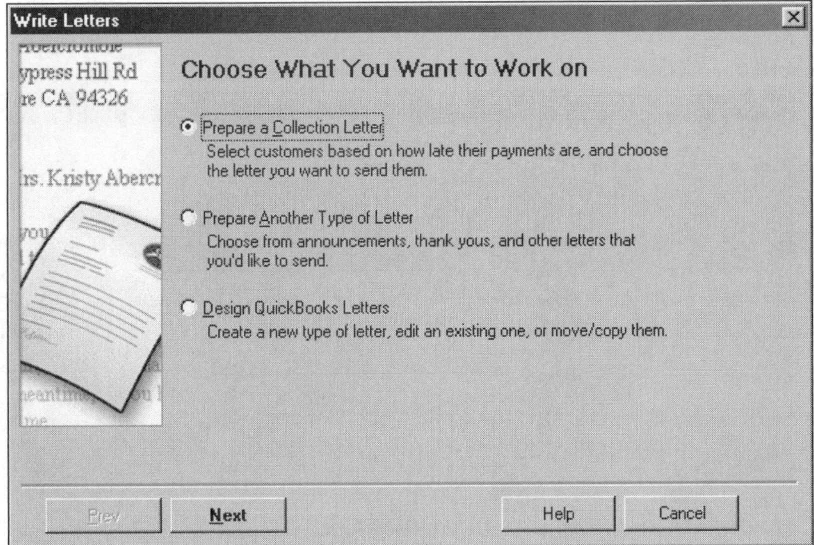

3 Make sure that "Prepare a Collection Letter" is selected and click Next.

4 When QuickBooks prompts you to choose who you want to write to, make the following selections:

- For number 1, choose Active.
- For number 2, choose Customer.
- For number 3, choose 31 days or more.

Your screen should look like this.

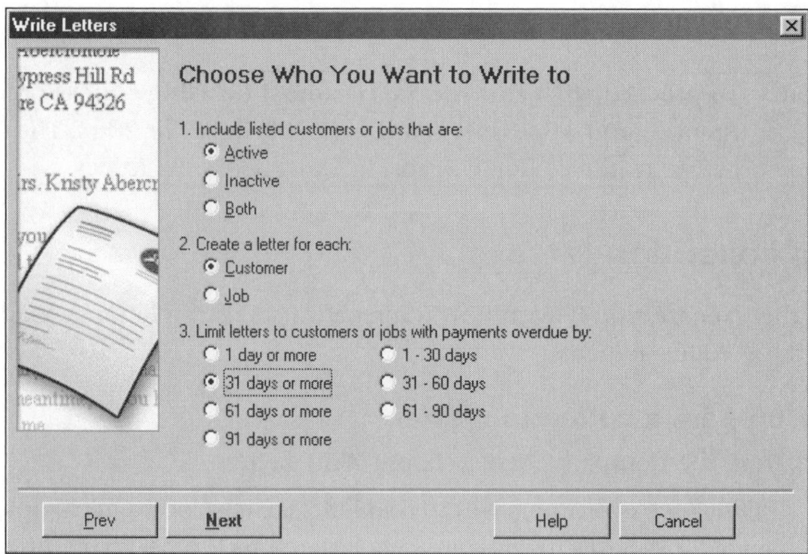

5 Click Next.

QuickBooks displays a list of all active customers with payments 31 days or more past due.

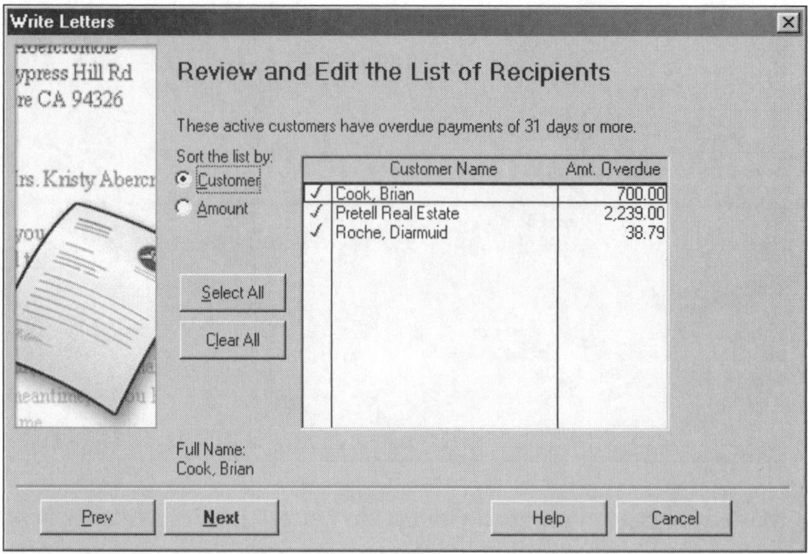

6 Leave all of the names selected and click Next.

7 When QuickBooks prompts you to choose the letter you want to use, click "Friendly collection" and click Next.

8 In the Name field of the next screen, type ***Tom Ferguson***. In the Title field, type ***President***.

Your screen should look like the following.

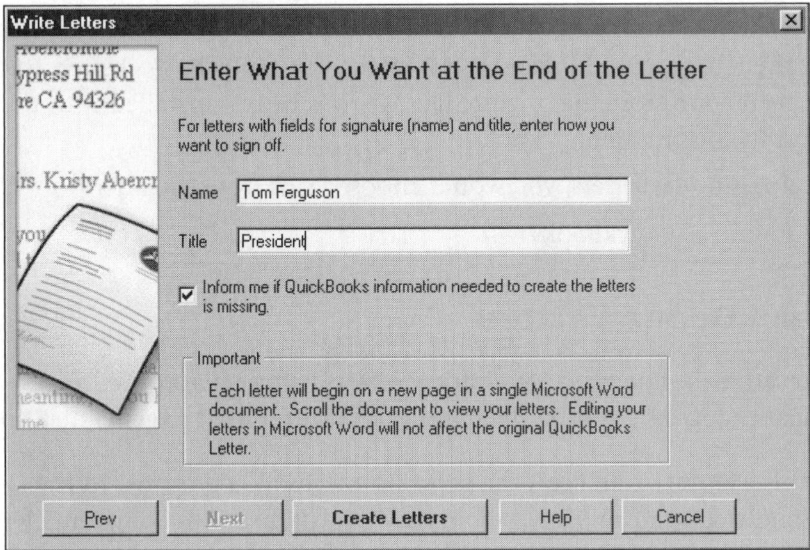

9 Click Create Letters.

10 If QuickBooks displays a message about missing information, click OK.

QuickBooks starts Microsoft Word (if it's not running already) and displays collection letters for the three customers that you selected.

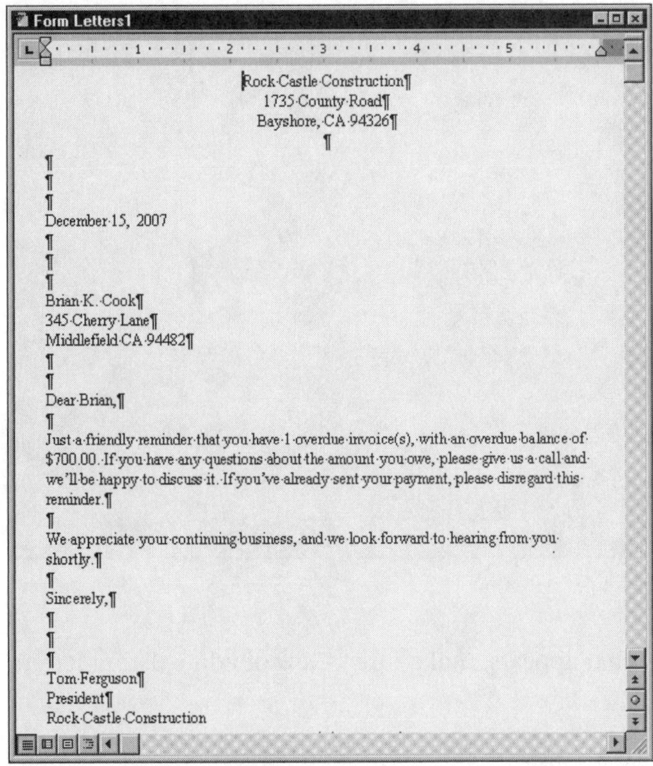

Form Letters1

Rock Castle Construction
1735 County Road
Bayshore, CA 94326

December 15, 2007

Brian K. Cook
345 Cherry Lane
Middlefield CA 94482

Dear Brian,

Just a friendly reminder that you have 1 overdue invoice(s), with an overdue balance of $700.00. If you have any questions about the amount you owe, please give us a call and we'll be happy to discuss it. If you've already sent your payment, please disregard this reminder.

We appreciate your continuing business, and we look forward to hearing from you shortly.

Sincerely,

Tom Ferguson
President
Rock Castle Construction

You can scroll through the Microsoft Word document to see all of the letters. Notice that QuickBooks entered Tom Ferguson's name and title at the end of each letter.

11 Close the Microsoft Word file without saving the letters.

When you do save letters you've created using QuickBooks Letters, don't save them to the QuickBooks Letters folder. The QuickBooks Letters folder should only be used to store the original QuickBooks Letters installed with the QuickBooks software program.

To print the letters, you would choose Print from the Microsoft Word File menu.

12 Return to QuickBooks.

Editing QuickBooks Letters

You can make changes to individual letters using Microsoft Word, or you can make global changes by editing the QuickBooks Letter used to generate a specific letter.

In this exercise, you'll edit the collection letter you prepared in the last exercise (Friendly collection). However, instead of working with completed letters with customer information already filled in, you'll work with the underlying QuickBooks Letter used to create the letters.

To edit a QuickBooks Letter:

1 From the Company menu, choose Write Letters.

2 Click Design QuickBooks Letters.

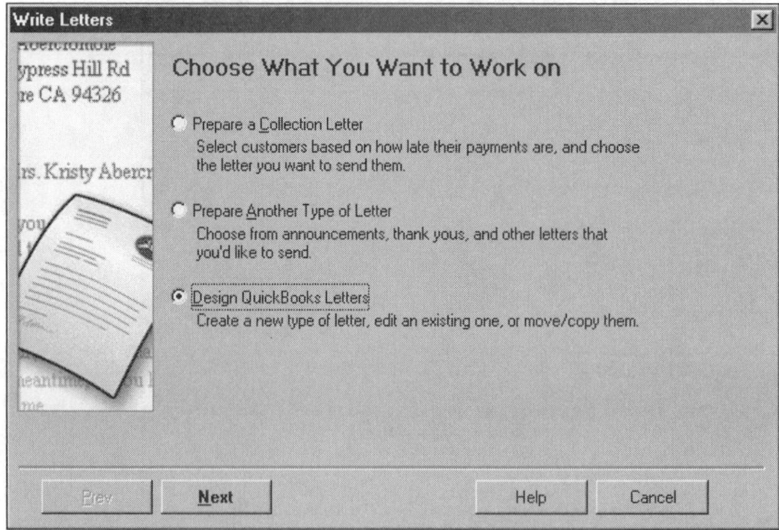

3 Click Next.

4 In the screen that appears, make sure "View or edit existing letters" is selected and click Next.

5 When QuickBooks prompts you to choose the QuickBooks Letter you want to view or edit, click Overdue customers (collection letters), and then select "Friendly collection" from the list of available letters.

Your screen should look like this.

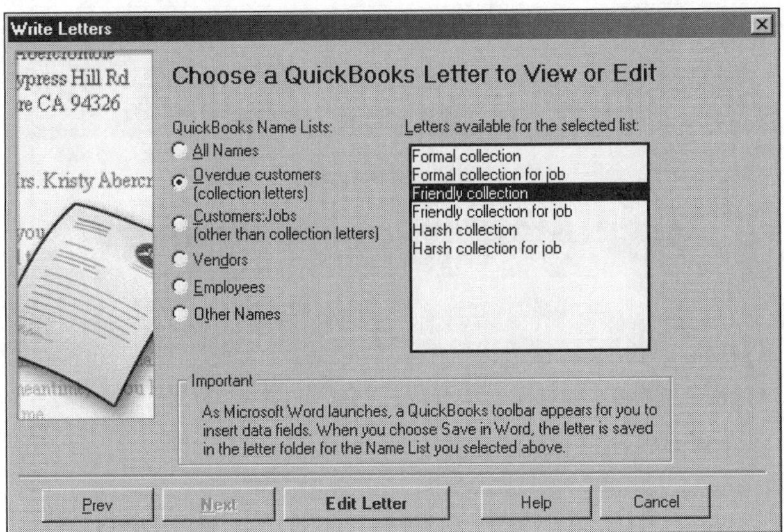

6 Click Edit Letter.

QuickBooks opens Microsoft Word (if it's not running already) and displays the QuickBooks Letter (Friendly collection) and a toolbar (QuickBooks Collection Letter Fields) that you'll use to add information from QuickBooks to the letter in Word.

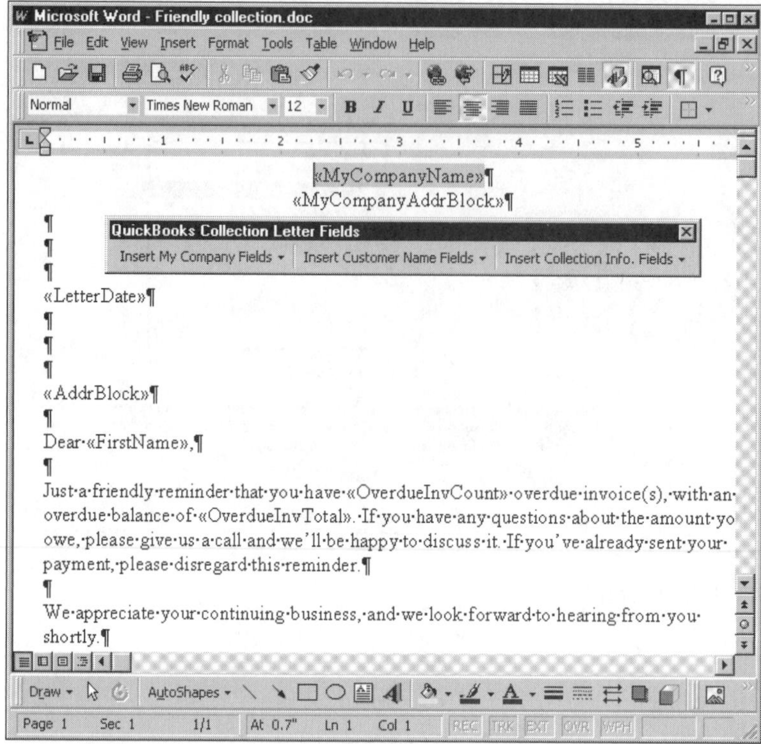

Note that you can move the toolbar by clicking it with your mouse pointer and dragging it to a new location.

Now, you'll enter more text and use the toolbar to insert data from QuickBooks into the "Friendly collection" letter.

7 Click your mouse pointer after the period at the end of the first sentence and the press the Space bar once. (You'll insert a sentence into the paragraph.)

8 Type ***Our records show that your balance is past due.***

9 Click your mouse pointer after the word *is* in the sentence you just typed, and press the Space bar again.

10 From the Insert Collection Info. Fields drop-down list on the QuickBooks Collection Letter Fields toolbar, select Range(days) of Overdue Invoices.

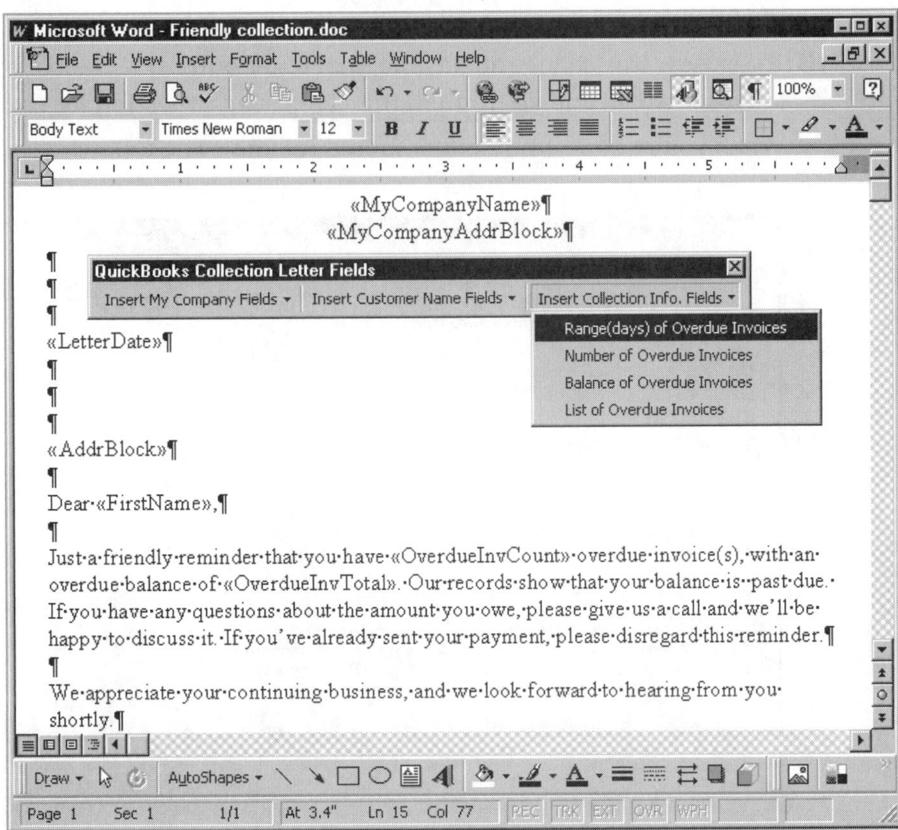

QuickBooks adds the <<OverdueRange>> field to the sentence you just typed.

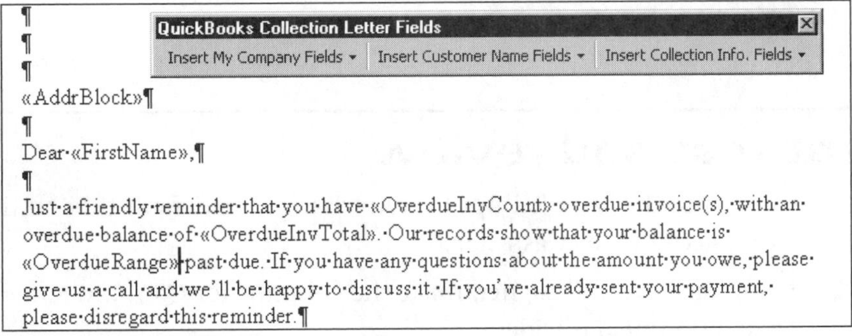

When you create letters using this modified QuickBooks letter, QuickBooks will replace the <<OverdueRange>> field with the number of days each customer you create a letter for is past due.

11 From the Word File menu, choose Save As.

12 Navigate to the Collection Letters folder in your Qbtrain directory and click Save.

If you save the file to your QuickBooks directory (instead of the Qbtrain folder you created to use with this guide) without changing the filename, you will overwrite the original QuickBooks Letter.

13 To see how this change affects the final letter output, close the letter file in Microsoft Word and go through the "Preparing collection letters"exercise again.

When you're done, your letters should resemble the following.

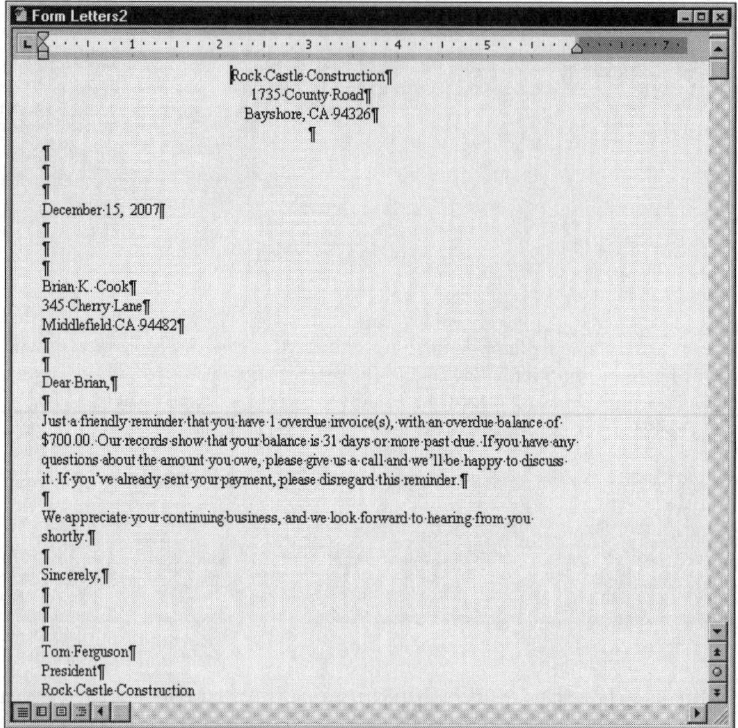
Form Letters2

Rock Castle Construction
1735 County Road
Bayshore, CA 94326

December 15, 2007

Brian K. Cook
345 Cherry Lane
Middlefield CA 94482

Dear Brian,

Just a friendly reminder that you have 1 overdue invoice(s), with an overdue balance of $700.00. Our records show that your balance is 31 days or more past due. If you have any questions about the amount you owe, please give us a call and we'll be happy to discuss it. If you've already sent your payment, please disregard this reminder.

We appreciate your continuing business, and we look forward to hearing from you shortly.

Sincerely,

Tom Ferguson
President
Rock Castle Construction

14 Close Microsoft Word.

Student test and review

1 Customize the Sales Receipt form to change the default title on the header from "Sales Receipt" to "Cash Sale."

2 Using the Layout Designer, make the columns for QTY and Rate narrower so the Description field is wider.

3 Customize the P.O. form to include the Terms field.

APPENDIX A What's new in QuickBooks 2004

New features in QuickBooks 2004

QuickBooks Financial Software offers features that give you fast access to information about your finances, improve your productivity, and provide new services that can simplify your day-to-day business transactions.

The products listed below start with our most basic offering and progress to our most comprehensive product. Our comprehensive products contain all of the features and functionality found in the more basic editions.

QuickBooks Financial Software: Basic Edition

- **Checklist for new businesses.** QuickBooks now contains a checklist for new businesses. The checklist provides information about local, state, and federal requirements; necessary forms, permits, and licenses; finding funding; taxes and insurance, and more.
- **Undo reconciliations.** If the last reconciliation was in error, you can undo it without having to identify and manually clear each affected transaction.
- **Find reconcile discrepancies.** An improved Reconcile Discrepancy report shows changes and deletions made to previously reconciled transactions, making it easier to find discrepancies. Also, the previous reconciliation summary and detail reports are viewable as PDF files. To further facilitate reconciliation, you can now select the columns you want to display in the Reconcile window, showing only the information you want to see.
- **Copy and paste an entire address.** You can now copy an entire address at one time; you no longer have to cut, copy, and paste address information one line at a time. In addition, each line of an address list exported to Excel now occupies a different column.

QuickBooks Financial Software: Pro Edition

QuickBooks: Pro contains these additional features as well as all of the QuickBooks: Basic features:

- **E-mail and save reports and forms.** Save reports and forms to Portable Document Format (PDF), making files accessible to anyone. In addition to invoices, statements, and estimates, you can now e-mail purchase orders, sales receipts, credit memos, sales orders (Premier and Enterprise only), and reports directly from QuickBooks. (Registration and Internet access required. Service subject to change. Fees may apply.)

- **Print packing slips from the invoice form.** You can now print packing slips directly from the invoice form without having to toggle between the invoice template and a separate customized invoice template. To create packing slips from invoices, simply select Print Packing Slips from drop-down Print menu in the Create Invoices window. QuickBooks creates a packing slip based on the contents of the invoice.
- **Suppress printing of mailing labels to inactive customers.** Now printing mailing labels is easier and more efficient. You can print shipping labels directly from the Create Invoices window, and you have the option to not to print mailing labels for inactive customers—or one for each job a customer has.
- **Import data from Microsoft Excel.** QuickBooks now allows you to import information without having to put data into IIF format. Simply map each column in an Excel spreadsheet to a corresponding QuickBooks "field," such as inventory item, phone number, or price. You can preview data before you import it and save import settings for future use. (Requires Microsoft Excel '97, 2000, 2002, or 2003.)
- **Update report data in existing Excel spreadsheets.** You can now specify an existing spreadsheet and have QuickBooks export report data to that spreadsheet, replacing any existing data with data from the current report. Existing cell references and formulas from other worksheets referencing that data are maintained.
- **Include total customer balances on printed invoices.** You can add a customer's total balance to printed invoices by adding these fields to the invoice form using the Layout Designer or Customize Forms window. Because the customer balance totals are active fields, when you reprint the invoice later the balance reflects any subsequent changes.
- **Add more price levels.** You can now define up to 100 price levels by percent.
- **Bring both item descriptions and notes to invoices.** QuickBooks now allows you to bring both item descriptions *and* notes from timesheets to invoices so you don't have to choose one and then retype the other on the invoice.
- **Manage loan information in QuickBooks.** Now you can track and manage loan information from within QuickBooks. The Loan Manager lets you enter new or existing loans, enter loan payments, and create "what-if" scenarios to compare different loans. QuickBooks also calculates loan amortization and the breakdown of principal and interest. (From the Banking menu, choose Loan Manager.)
- **Track and report on vehicle mileage.** The Enter Vehicle Mileage window lets you track vehicle mileage including date, amount, and type of expense for tax purposes. Once mileage is recorded, you can use the information to create reports and invoice customers for billable mileage. (From the Company menu, choose Enter Vehicle Mileage.)

- **Track asset information.** The Fixed Asset Item list lets you track important details such as asset names, serial numbers, warranty information, and acquisition and disposal dates. Clients can use items from the Fixed Asset Item list on sales and purchase transactions. This allows you to track all transactions related to fixed assets, including repairs, improvements, damage—anything that affects value and depreciation amounts. You can use the Fixed Asset Item list with or without the Fixed Asset Manager tool available in Accountant Edition.
- **Estimate cash flow**. The Cash Flow Projector uses QuickBooks data to project and model cash flow for the next six weeks. The tool also lets you run "what-if" scenarios to see how changing receipts and disbursements could affect a business's weekly cash balance. (From the Company menu, choose Planning & Budgeting and then choose Cash Flow Projector.)

QuickBooks Financial Software: Premier Edition

QuickBooks: Premier contains these additional features as well as all of the new QuickBooks Basic and QuickBooks Pro features:

- **Create sales orders from estimates.** QuickBooks Premier products allow you to quickly create sales orders from estimates without having to re-enter information. This saves time and helps minimize data entry errors.
- **Create purchase orders from estimates.** In addition to invoices, you can now also create purchase orders from estimates without having to re-enter information. In the Create Estimates window, simply select the form you want to create (invoice or purchase order) from the drop-down list.
- **Set "per item" price levels.** In addition to setting fixed percentage price levels, you can now set prices for individual items in a price level.
- **Generate purchase orders from sales orders.** QuickBooks Premier now allows you to easily create purchase orders from estimates (and purchase orders from sales orders) without having to re-enter data. Simply select the form you want to create from the drop-down menu in the Create Estimates or Create Sales Orders windows. You can choose whether to transfer all of the items or only selected items.
- **See quantities invoiced against sales orders.** The Sales Order by Item report now displays the quantity invoiced against the sales orders listed.

Industry-specific QuickBooks products

In addition to its core QuickBooks product line (Basic, Pro, and Premier), Intuit now makes a number of industry-specific versions of QuickBooks Premier. This section lists each of the products currently available and highlights some of the key functionality.

In addition to the functionality described in this section, many of the industry-specific products also contain the following:

- Help topics written by industry experts
- Sample data files that can be used to learn better ways to use the features included with the product or to experiment with new features without affecting real company data
- Navigators and menus to provide easy access to frequently used features for a particular industry

QuickBooks Financial Software: Premier Accountant Edition

QuickBooks: Premier Accountant Edition contains these additional features as well as all of the new QuickBooks: Basic, Pro, and Premier features.

- **Manage fixed assets.** Use the Fixed Asset Manager to manage fixed assets from acquisition to disposition. With the Fixed Asset Manager, you can compute depreciation for up to six asset bases (including tax and book), create depreciation journal entries (including disposals), print up to 20 reports (including asset schedules by G/L account, location, and category), calculate gains and losses on asset sales, and import data from the new fixed asset list maintained by your clients. (From the Accountant menu, choose Manage Fixed Assets.)
- **Calculate, allocate, and track loans in one place with the Loan Manager.** With loan amortization, you can compute "what if" scenarios to help clients make better financial decisions about loans and lines of credit. You can also print amortization schedules and calculate loan payments, allocate the loan payment between principal and interest, and track the allocation over the life of the loan.
- **Use features from all nine QuickBooks editions.** Accountant Edition is the only edition you need to work with clients who use QuickBooks Financial Software products. In addition to Basic, Pro, and Premier, QuickBooks: Premier Accountant Edition 2004 supports six industry-specific editions. Accountant Edition includes the reports and features of each industry-specific edition.
- **Track Adjusting Journal Entries and run Adjusted Trial Balance reports.** Use the Adjusting Entry checkbox in the Make General Journal Entries window to record and mark adjusting entries you make to clients' original balances. See all adjusting entries you made during a specified time period in the Adjusting Journal Entries report. You can view clients' original balances, your adjustments, and the final adjusted balances in the Adjusted Trial Balance report.

- **Find deletions and changes to previously cleared transactions.** Use the improved Reconcile Discrepancy report to quickly identify transactions that have been changed since the last bank reconciliation.
- **Keep closed periods closed.** You can protect closed periods by selecting the closing date (end of period, end of fiscal year) in your clients' files and setting a closing date password to prevent changes. Use the Closing Date Exception report to quickly find all changes made prior to the closing date.
- **Export G/L balances to Lacerte® or ProSeries® software.** Using Premier, you can easily export G/L balances to Lacerte or ProSeries tax software.

QuickBooks Financial Software: Premier Contractor Edition

- **Assign all expenses to customer:jobs.** To get more accurate job costing, Contractor Edition allows you to assign expenses to customer:jobs. To assign job costs, simply select the appropriate job in the Customer:Job field in the Enter Bills, Timesheet, or Write Checks windows.
- **Compare estimated costs to actual costs.** Many contractors create estimates outside of QuickBooks and then enter invoices in QuickBooks. To compare costs, at least a summary of each estimate must be entered into QuickBooks. Contractor Edition saves time by allowing users to enter estimates directly into QuickBooks and create invoices (or progress invoices) from the estimates by clicking the Create Invoices button in the Create Estimates window. Entering estimates directly into QuickBooks allows you to get estimated cost and revenue amounts to compare to actual costs and revenues on job costing reports.
- **Track change orders automatically.** You can create change orders simply by editing existing estimates. Contractor Edition tracks the changes, lets you enter comments, and then prints the change order.
- **Run reports designed for contractors.** In addition to job costing and job profitability reports, Contractor Edition provides a set of new reports designed specifically for contractors, such as Job Status, Job Costs by Vendor, and Expenses Not Assigned to Jobs. (From the Reports menu, choose Contractor.)

QuickBooks Financial Software: Premier Manufacturing & Wholesale Edition

- **Choose from predefined charts of accounts.** The Manufacturing & Wholesale Edition contains pre-defined charts of accounts for wholesalers, manufacturers, and distributors. The sample data files included with this edition contain examples of how to use classes, customer types, and other features in these types of businesses.
- **Run reports designed for manufacturing and wholesale businesses.** As with other QuickBooks products, you can customize standard reports or choose from more than 10 reports that have already been customized for manufacturers and wholesalers, including Profitability by Product, Inventory Reorder Report by Vendor, Open Sales Order by Customer, and Open Purchase Orders by Item.

- **Manage inventory with more accuracy.** Manufacturing & Wholesale Edition lets you track both individual inventory items (components, raw materials) and assemblies (combined inventory items, finished goods or products). QuickBooks makes it easy to assign a unique sales price to any assembly, and to set reminders to build new assemblies. QuickBooks removes component items from inventory when you "build" assembly items.
- **Create purchase orders directly from estimates and sales orders.** Save time by instantly copying information from an estimate or sales order onto a purchase order. You can edit the purchase order as necessary and even e-mail the purchase order directly to the vendor. (To e-mail, registration and Internet access required. Service subject to change. Fees may apply.)

QuickBooks Financial Software: Premier Nonprofit Edition

- **Use the customized chart of accounts.** The Nonprofit Edition includes the Unified Chart of Accounts (UCOA) developed by nonprofit accounting professionals. Using this customized chart of accounts allows you to create IRS Form 990 and other nonprofit reports more easily.
- **Create financial and program reports for owner and boards of directors.** The Nonprofit Edition provides a set of reports designed specifically for nonprofits. Customized nonprofit reports include Budget by Programs, Donors/Grants, Biggest Donor, and Statement of Financial Position.
- **Track donations, pledges, or grants.** With the Nonprofit Edition, you can enter donations and pledges as they come in and instantly dispatch thank you notes with contact data you've already entered in QuickBooks.
- **Use customized forms and letters.** QuickBooks provides professionally designed nonprofit forms and letters. You can use the forms and letters as is, or customize them further, adding special fields and logos.
- **File IRS 990 Form easily**. Use the Statement of Functional Expenses (990) Report to view all of the totals in the exact format that the IRS requires. Using the nonprofit chart of accounts to categorize each transaction ensures that data is "clean" and able to be used for reports required by the government, board members, and donors.

QuickBooks Financial Software: Premier Professional Services Edition

- **Choose from several pre-defined company files.** Choose from six predefined company files, each based on a different type of professional services business. When you select a predefined company file, QuickBooks automatically sets up the accounting records for the file including a professional services-specific chart of accounts, an item list for services, and prebuilt reports. You can use the EasyStep Interview for further customization.

- **Track time and transfer time information to invoices.** Use the weekly timesheet or Enter Single Activities window to record the time that each employee, partner, or subcontractor spend on each client or project and then transfer the time data (including notes and descriptions) to invoices. When you are creating invoices, QuickBooks now alerts you when there is outstanding billable time or expenses for the client for which you are creating the invoice.
- **Run industry-specific reports.** Professional Services Edition provides 11 reports designed specifically for professional services firms (from the Reports menu, choose Professional Services). This edition includes reports that identify unbilled expenses or expenses not assigned to projects to help you avoid underbilling. Also, you'll find reports that help you see what client, project, or activity each employee is working on, track billable and non-billable hours, and analyze resource utilization. These reports also provide backup detail for invoices.
- **Take advantage of more flexible invoicing options.** Professional Services Edition includes professional-looking templates for proposals and invoices that display information and use terminology appropriate for this industry. The enhanced price level functionality provides the flexibility needed to set different billing rates by client, which saves time and increases accuracy when creating invoices.

QuickBooks Financial Software: Premier Retail Edition

- **Choose from several pre-defined company files.** Retail Edition includes five pre-defined company files from which you can choose. Each file is designed for a different type of retail business. When you select a pre-defined file, QuickBooks automatically sets up a retail-specific chart of accounts, customized icon bar, preferences, customized forms, and report templates.
- **Record daily summaries quickly.** To allow you to track daily sales summaries easily, Retail Edition lets you enter the daily sales totals from the cash register or point of sale system in the Daily Sales Summary Form. This form lets you track taxable and non-taxable daily sales totals, breakdown sales by type of payment (cash, check, MasterCard, Visa, American Express), and confirm that end-of-day sales totals match the payments received. Tracking sales using this method also lets you use reports to track sales by type of payment and save time on routine reconciliation tasks.
- **Run industry-specific reports.** Retail Edition includes reports designed to help you analyze sales and profitability, track vendor purchases, and manage accounts payable. Retail Edition provides reports that you can use to compare profitability this month to last month, identify trends in customer sales over the past year, track sales tax liability, understand vendor return history, and prioritize bills by due date.
- **Use letters and forms customized for retail businesses.** Retail Edition includes letter templates customized for retailers on topics such as customer follow-up after a return and reminders for overdue maintenance or service appointments.

APPENDIX B Instructor demonstration of QuickBooks

Restoring the demo data file

The following demonstration is meant to be presented by the instructor with the class observing. It gives students an introduction to the major QuickBooks features, and lets them see how QuickBooks automates day-to-day bookkeeping.

Before you start the demonstration, restore the file "qblesson.qbb" in the QBtrain folder you set up using the instructions in the introduction to this guide.

To restore the data file:

1. From the File menu in QuickBooks, choose Restore.
   QuickBooks opens the Restore Company Backup window.
2. In the Get Company Backup section, click Browse, and then select the QBtrain directory you set up following the instructions in the introduction of this guide.
3. Click Open.
4. Select the qblesson.qbb file, and click Open.
5. In the Restore Company Backup To section, click Browse and select your QBtrain directory.
6. Click Open.
7. In the File name field, type ***demo.qbw*** and click Save.
8. When you see the message about the sample file's default date, click OK.
9. If you are not starting the demonstration now, exit QuickBooks.

Explain to students that later they'll be learning how to create their own QuickBooks company. For most of the course, however, they'll be using a sample file for a fictitious construction company called Rock Castle Construction.

Entering sales

One of a business's primary concerns is revenue, so let's begin with that. Suppose your business has made a sale and you need to invoice the customer. To do that in QuickBooks, you fill out an invoice that looks just like a paper form.

Creating an invoice

You can choose any QuickBooks task from the QuickBooks menu bar located on the top of the screen. The menu bar is organized by business areas (for example, customers, vendors, employees).

To create an invoice:

1 From the Customers menu, choose Create Invoices.

The Create Invoices window looks just like a paper invoice form. The upper part of the form is where you enter customer information; the bottom part of the form is where you enter the items or services you've sold.

You can move from field to field by pressing Tab, or you can use the mouse to point to the field you want, and then click the mouse button.

2 Click the drop-down list next to the Customer:Job field.

If you see this arrow next to a field, it means there's a QuickBooks list where you can choose an entry.

3 Choose Kitchen under Jacobsen, Doug from the Customer list.

Notice how QuickBooks automatically fills in other information about the customer.

Point out the address and payment terms.

4 Press Tab three times to move to the Date Field.

QuickBooks automatically displays today's date here (the sample data file is set up with December 15, 2007 as today's date). If you want to change it, all you have to do is press the Plus key (+) or Minus key (-). Now change the date to December 17.

5 Press the Plus key (+) twice to display 12/17/2007.

When you're finished, this is how the top half of the invoice should look.

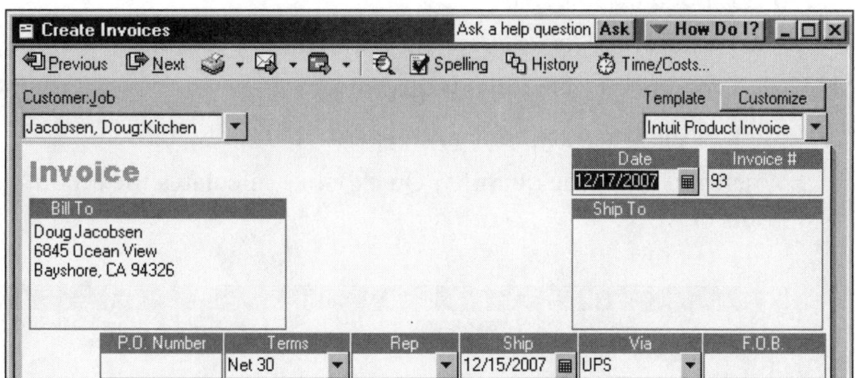

Now you're ready to fill out the bottom half of the invoice form.

Filling in the details

The bottom part of the invoice is where you list the items the customer has purchased. You list each service or product you're selling on its own line of the invoice, along with the amount the customer owes for each item. The lines on this part of the invoice are called line items, because each individual item is on its own line.

All the information about your line items is in the QuickBooks Item list. The Item list stores information about each service you render and each product you sell. It also stores information about other types of line items you'll want to put on invoices, like discounts, sales taxes, and subtotals. You'll be learning more about the Item list later in the course.

To fill in details:

1 Click in the Item Code column. Then click the arrow next to the field to display the drop-down list.

When you click in the Item Code column, QuickBooks displays a drop-down list where you can choose the items you want to invoice the customer for.

Suppose you've done nine hours of installation for Doug's kitchen remodelling project.

2 Choose Installation from the drop-down list.

This item is already entered in Rock Castle Construction's Item list, so QuickBooks can automatically fill in the item description and a rate ($35.00). It also knows that this is not a taxable item.

Point out the 0.00 for sales tax below the Amount column.

Now you just need to enter a quantity.

3 Click in the Quantity field, and type ***9***. Then press Tab.

When you enter the quantity, QuickBooks calculates the amount for the nine hours of work.

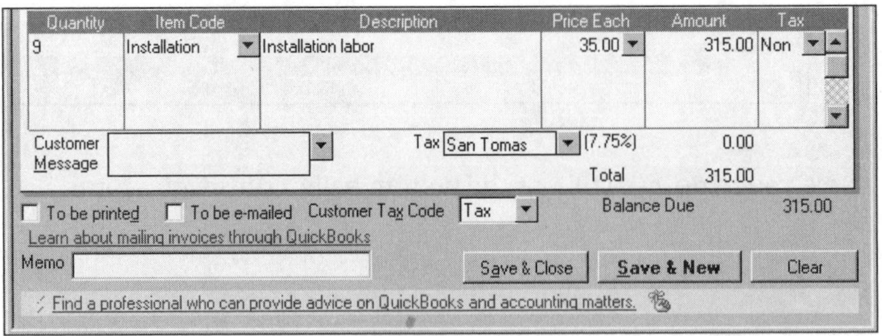

4 Click Save & Close to record the invoice.

Viewing the customer's register

The money owed to your business, by customers or from other sources, is your accounts receivable. When you fill out and save an invoice form, QuickBooks automatically makes an entry for you in your customer's accounts receivable register.

To display the register:

1 From the Customers menu, choose Customer:Job list.

2 Click Jacobsen, Doug once to select it.

3 Click the Activities menu button, and then choose Use Register.

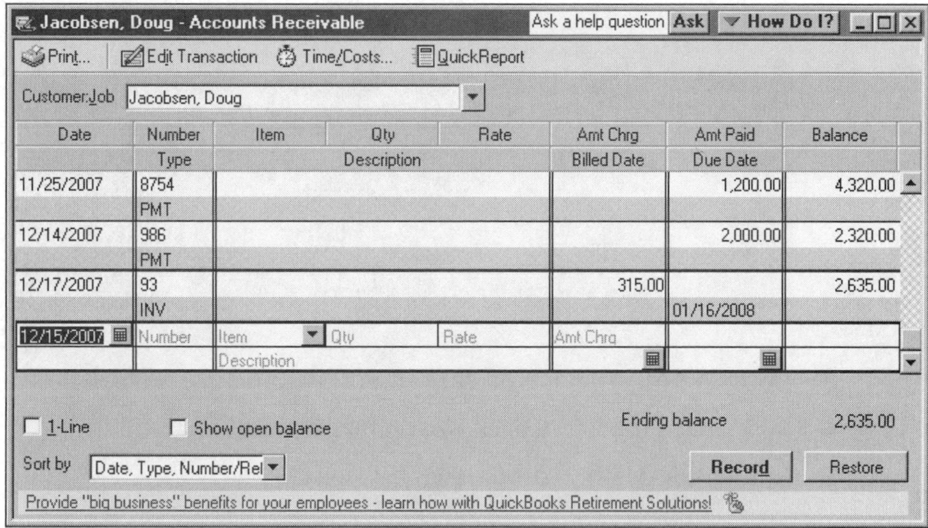

The customer accounts receivable register looks similar to a paper check register. The register shows every transaction for this customer that affects your company's receivables. The invoice you just recorded is in the register in order of its date. The second column shows the invoice number and the type of transaction it is (invoice). When you wrote the invoice, QuickBooks automatically updated the register and account balance.

4 Close the register and then close the Customer:Job List.

Receiving a customer payment

When you receive a payment from a customer for outstanding invoices, you want to record receipt of the payment and indicate which invoices are being paid. Suppose you've received a check in the mail from Pretell Real Estate, a customer that has several outstanding invoices for different jobs. This check is for the job at 155 Wilks Blvd.

To receive a payment:

1 From the Customers menu, choose Receive Payments.

2 From the drop-down list in the Customer:Job field, choose the 155 Wilks Blvd. job under Pretell Real Estate.

QuickBooks lists all the outstanding invoices for the job you entered.

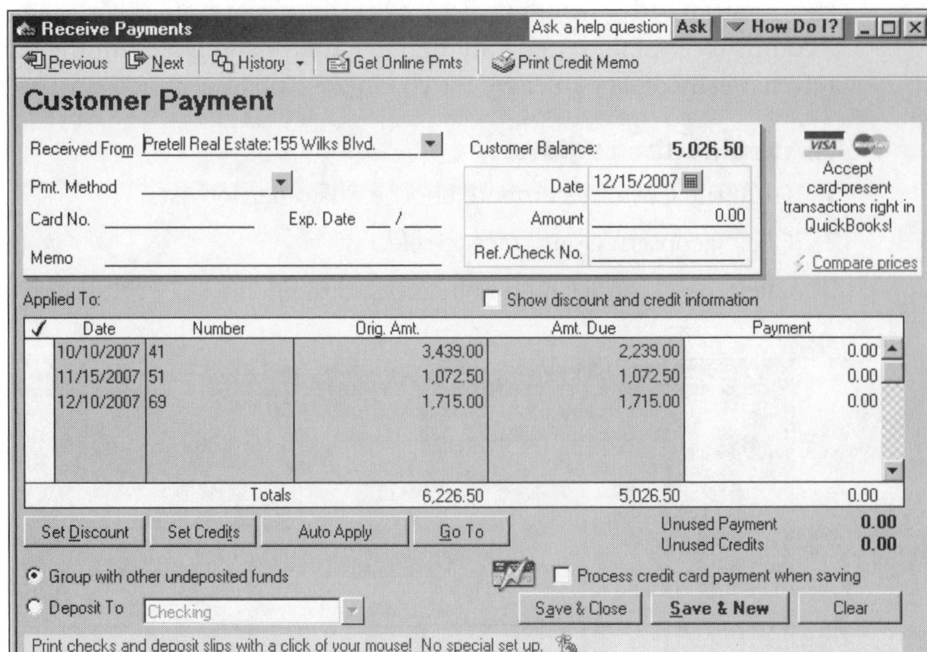

3 In the Amount field, type ***2239*** and press Tab.

4 Type ***659*** in the Ref./Check No. field and press Tab.

5 In the Pmt. Method drop-down list, select Check.

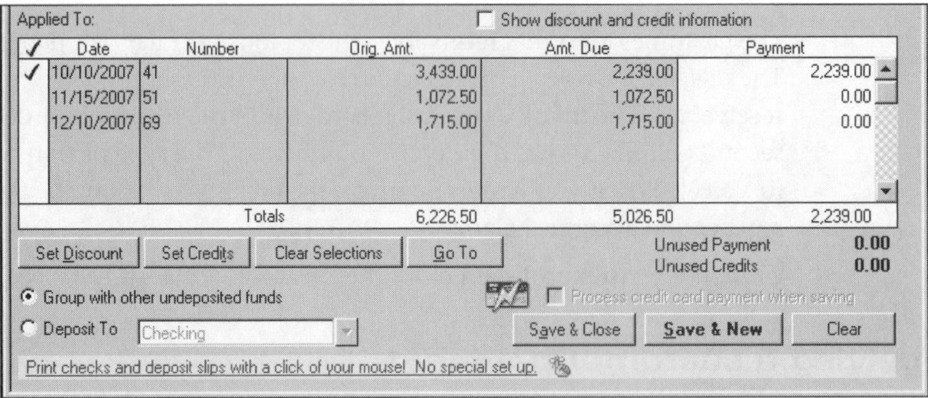

QuickBooks applies the amount to the oldest outstanding invoice, followed by the next oldest invoice. If you want to apply the payment differently, QuickBooks is flexible—you can choose to apply payments to the invoices of your choice. You'll see how to do that later in the course.

6 Make sure "Group with other undeposited funds" is selected.

When you record a customer payment, you have a choice of where to put the payment.

If you want to deposit several payments at once, select "Group with other undeposited funds," and QuickBooks holds the payment in an account called Undeposited Funds until you deposit the payments in a bank account. The Undeposited Funds account is like a cash drawer.

If you are depositing this payment in a bank account by itself, you can click "Deposit to" and choose the bank account. Then QuickBooks records the deposit in the bank account automatically.

7 Click Save & Close.

Making a deposit

If you've selected "Group with other undeposited funds," QuickBooks keeps customer payments in the Undeposited Funds account until you're ready to go to the bank. Then you just tell QuickBooks you're ready to make a deposit.

To record a deposit:

1 From the Banking menu, choose Make Deposits.

The Payments to Deposit window shows all the payments you have in Undeposited Funds waiting to be deposited.

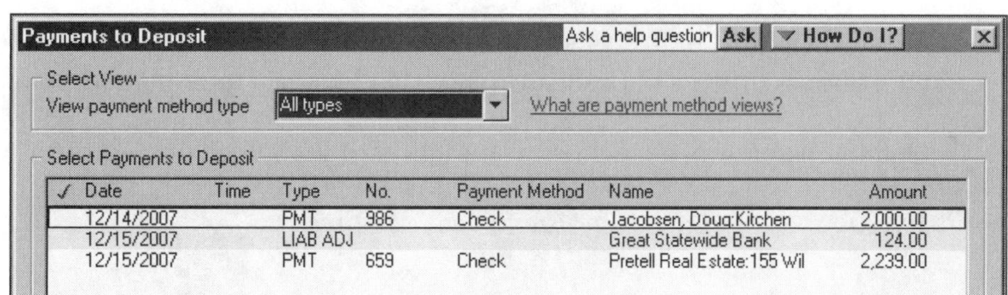

2 Click Select All to place a checkmark next to all the undeposited payments, and click OK.

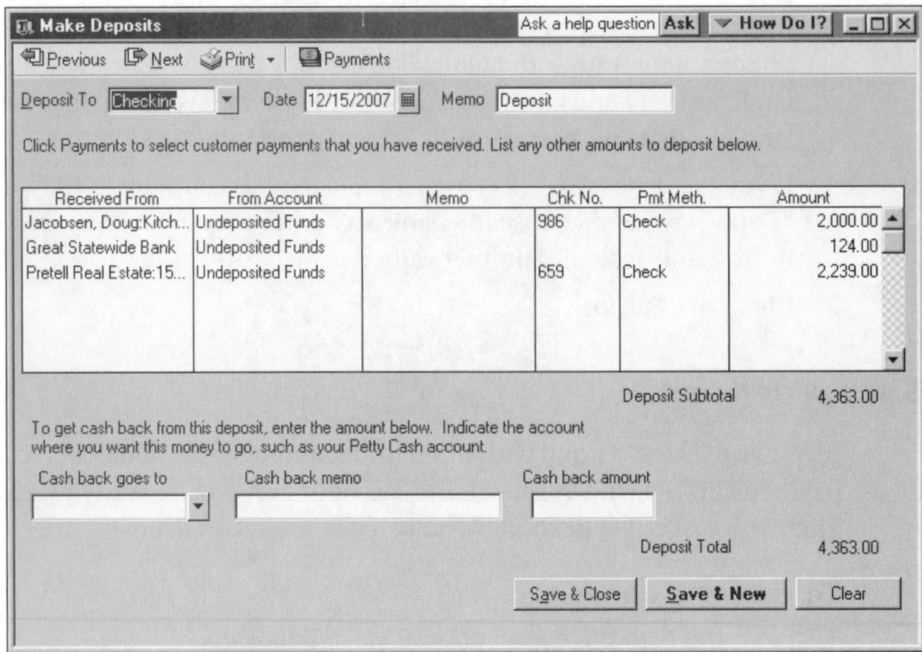

3 In the Make Deposits window, be sure you are set to record the deposit in the checking account, and click Save & Close.

If you click Print in the Make Deposits window before recording the deposit, QuickBooks prints a deposit summary that lists each payment you are depositing.

QuickBooks enters the deposit transaction in your checking account.

You can show students the register if you have time.

Entering and paying bills

Accounts payable is the record of outstanding bills your business owes. By tracking your account payable, you'll know exactly how much you owe and when. This is the only way you can get an accurate picture of your business's finances.

Using accounts payable in QuickBooks is easy: When you're billed for an expense, just enter the bill in QuickBooks when it arrives. This lets QuickBooks track the money you owe vendors in the accounts payable account.

Entering a bill

Suppose you receive a bill from Sergeant Insurance for an insurance premium and want to enter it in QuickBooks but pay it later.

To enter a bill:

1. From the Vendors menu, choose Enter Bills.
2. In the Vendor field, type ***se*** for Sergeant Insurance and press Tab.

   QuickBooks fills in the full name, using the feature called QuickFill, since Sergeant Insurance is the only vendor name that begins with "se."

   QuickBooks assigns a due date for the bill based on the payment terms you've entered for this vendor. If you don't have specific payment terms assigned, QuickBooks assumes bills are due 10 days from the date of receipt. You can change the due date if you wish.
3. In the Amount Due field, enter ***2000***.
4. Click in the Account column of the Expenses tab, and then click the arrow to display the list of expense accounts.

   This part of the form lets you track exactly what you spend your money on. The Expenses tab lets you assign the bill amount to one of your expense accounts; the Items tab is for entering details about service or product items you are purchasing. When you assign a bill to one of your expense accounts, you can later create reports that show how much you've spent in specific areas.
5. Choose Liability Insurance (under Insurance) from the list.

   You can also assign expenses to a particular customer or job, in the Customer:Job field. This lets you keep track of your costs for a specific project.

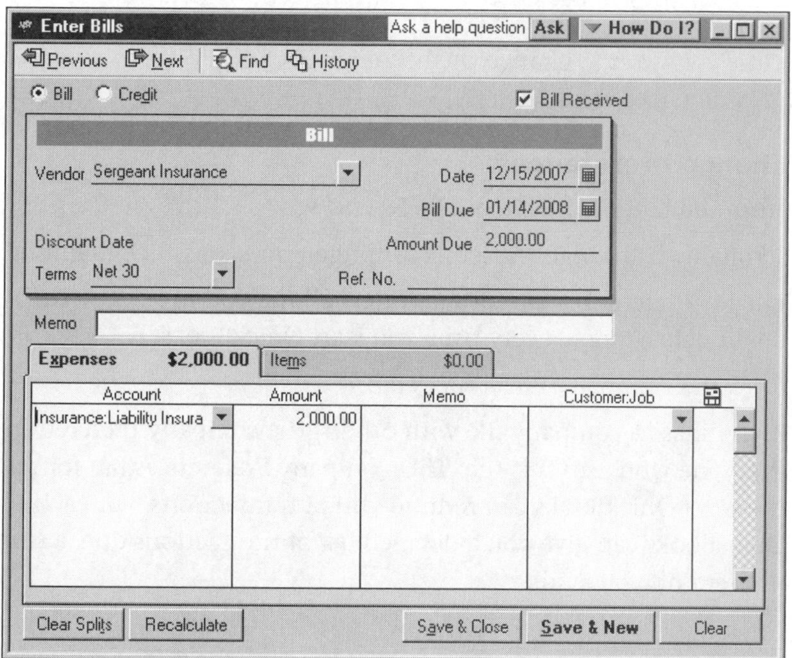

6. Click Save & Close.

   When you record a bill, QuickBooks automatically adds the amount due to the vendor's balance.

7 From the Lists menu, choose Vendor List.

QuickBooks displays the Vendor list, which shows outstanding balances for all your vendors.

8 Type "*S*" to go to Sergeant Insurance. Notice the balance is 2000.

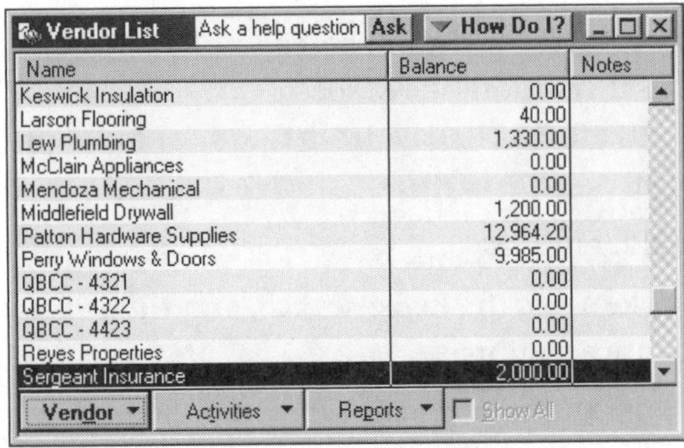

9 Close the Vendor list.

Using QuickBooks to remind you when to pay

QuickBooks has a reminder system that can tell you when you have transactions due. You can set up QuickBooks to display a Reminders window that lists the due dates for each transaction coming due. You can decide whether you want QuickBooks to remind you, and choose exactly which transactions you want to be reminded of.

Any time you want to change the behavior of QuickBooks in a particular area, you go to the Preferences window.

To change preferences:

1 From the Edit menu, choose Preferences.

2 Scroll down through the icons for preferences and click Reminders.

The My Preferences tab for reminders allows you to select whether to display the Reminders window every time you start QuickBooks.

3 Click the Company Preferences tab.

If you share a company file with others, the company preferences are in effect for everyone who uses this file. The Company Preferences tab for reminders lists all the ways QuickBooks can remind you of transactions. For each type of reminder, QuickBooks can give you a detailed list of transactions due, a summary only, or not remind you at all.

4 Click Cancel to close the window.

Any time you want to see the Reminders window, you can choose Reminders from the Company menu.

5 From the Company menu, choose Reminders.

The Reminders window gives you a summary of the transactions coming due. If you want to see a detailed list, you can click the Expand All button.

6 In the Reminders window, click Expand All.

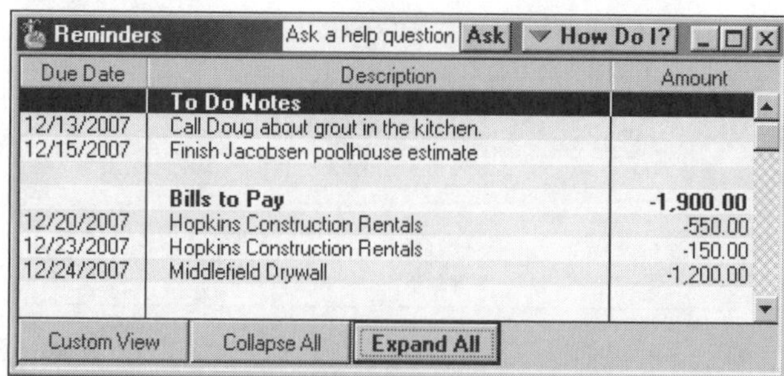

7 Double-click the Bills to Pay transaction for Middlefield Drywall.

QuickBooks displays the original bill form.

8 Close the Enter Bills window; then close the Reminders window.

The Preferences window is where you customize QuickBooks to work the way you want. You'll explore the preferences in more detail as you go through the course.

Paying bills

When QuickBooks reminds you that bill payments are due, you can decide which bills you want to pay and even have QuickBooks print the checks for you.

To record a bill:

1 From the Vendors menu, choose Pay Bills.

QuickBooks displays a list of all bills due on or before 12/25/2007 (which is 10 days after "today"). Just click to select the ones you want to pay, or click Pay All Bills to select all the bills in the window.

Suppose you want to pay by check from your Checking account.

2 Under Payment Method, choose Check and select "To be printed" (that is, be sure there is a checkmark in the box). Be sure that "Checking" is selected as the account under Payment Account.

3 Select the first two bills on the list. To select a bill, click in the left-hand column.

QuickBooks writes the checks for you automatically. It also enters a transaction for them in your checking account. At the same time, it enters a transaction in your accounts payable register, to reduce the total of your amounts payable by the amount of your checks.

If you select "To be printed," you can print the checks from QuickBooks. If you clear the checkbox, QuickBooks enters the checks in your register with numbers. (You can edit the numbers if they are incorrect.)

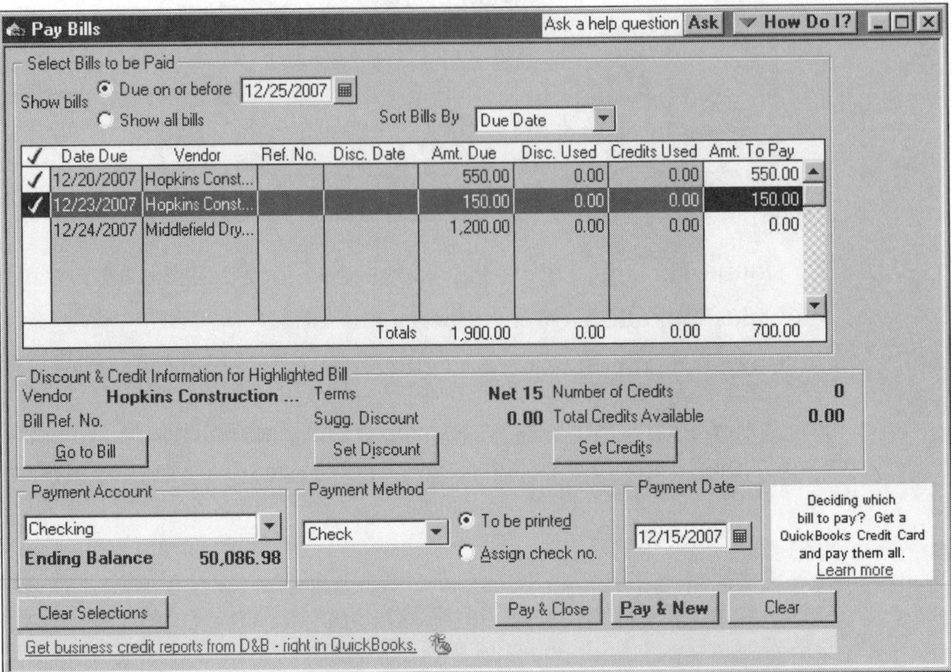

4 Click Pay & Close.

Now look at the checks QuickBooks wrote for you.

5 From the Banking menu, choose Write Checks.

6 In the Write Checks window, be sure the Checking account is in the Bank Account field.

7 Click Previous twice to see the check dated 12/15/2007 that QuickBooks wrote to Hopkins Construction for $700.00. (Notice that QuickBooks wrote one check to cover both bills—one for $550 and $150.)

The window now says Bill Payments (Check) instead of Write Checks to indicate this is a check that QuickBooks wrote to pay a bill.

The lower part of the window lists the bills that this check paid.

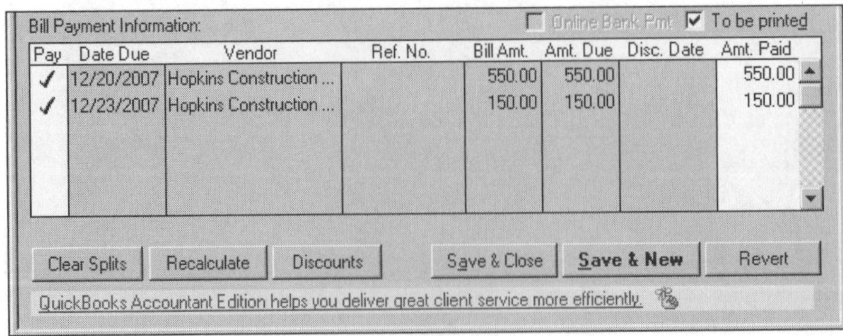

Intuit has checks you can purchase that are made to work with QuickBooks. You can have QuickBooks print all your checks at once, and save yourself from writing checks by hand. You can get Intuit checks for tractor-feed printers or single-sheet printers.

8 Close the Write Checks window.

Now, open the accounts payable register to see how the payments affect your accounts payable. You can open the register of any balance sheet account by starting from the chart of accounts.

To display the accounts payable register:

1 From the Lists menu, choose Chart of Accounts.

You could select the Accounts Payable account, click the Activities menu button at the bottom of the window, and then choose Use Register. But you can use another shortcut: Just double-click any account to open its register.

2 Double-click the Accounts Payable account.

Here's the register with the 12/15/2007 bill payment QuickBooks entered for Hopkins Construction Rentals.

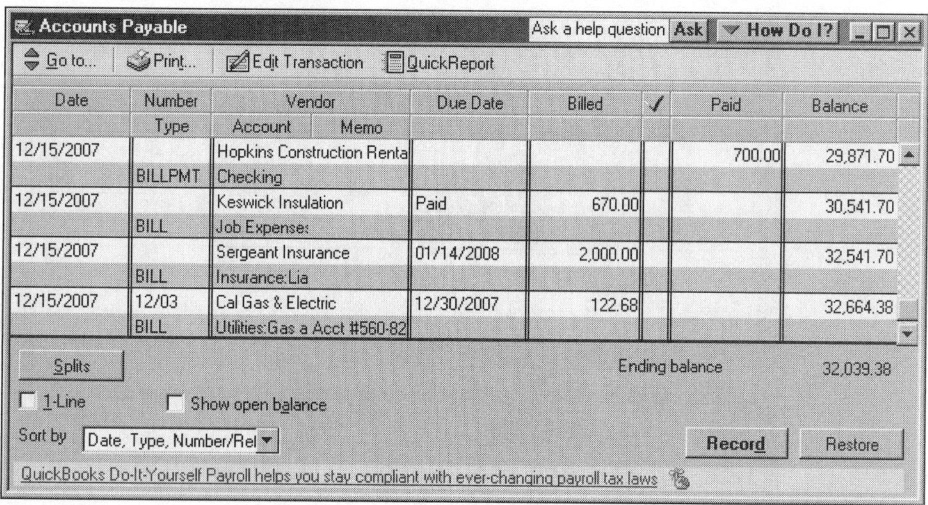

3 Close the Accounts Payable register and the chart of accounts.

Handling purchases you pay for on the spot

When you pay for a purchase on the spot, you don't need to enter a bill first. You can write a check at the Write Checks window for a manually written check or a check you want to print. (You can even set up a QuickBooks "bank" account for petty cash and record "checks" for payments made from petty cash.)

Suppose Kershaw Computer Services sends over a technician to improve the network for your office, and you want to write and print a check.

To record a check:

1. From the Banking menu, choose Write Checks.
2. In the Write Checks window, be sure the Checking account is in the Bank Account field.

   Now, fill out the check the same way you would a paper check.
3. In the "Pay to the Order of" field, select Kershaw Computer Services.
4. Type ***253.45*** as the amount, and press Tab.

   QuickBooks automatically writes the amount for you on the next line.
5. Click in the Account column of the Expenses tab and assign the check to the Office Supplies expense account.
6. To print the check right now, click Print.

   QuickBooks keeps track of two separate check numbers: the number of the last check you printed and the number of the last check you wrote by hand and recorded later. It tells you the number it expects to be the next number for a printed check.

   If you plan to print the check later, click the "To be printed" checkbox to select it.

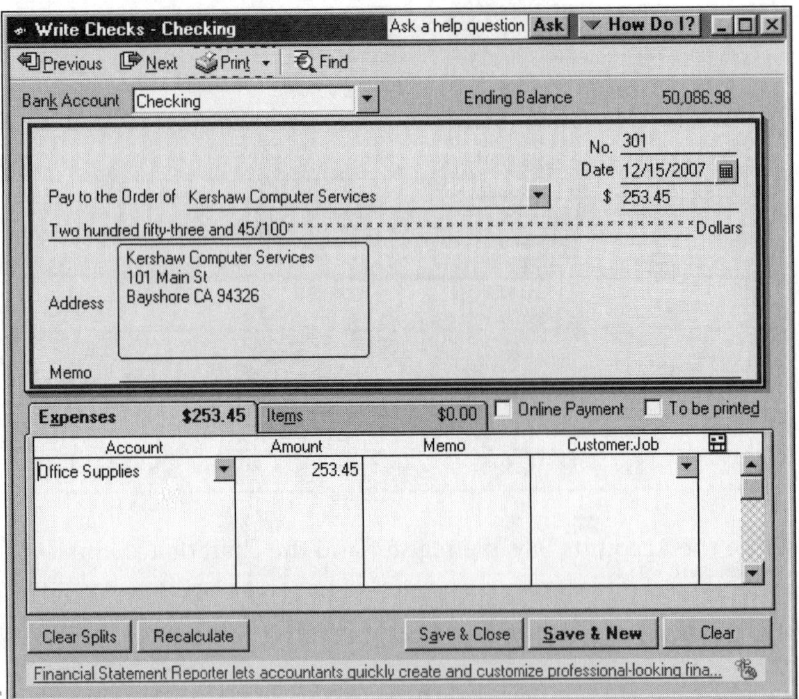

7. Click Save & Close to record the check and close the window.

   Be sure to click Save & Close or Save & New. If you click Clear or close the window, QuickBooks does not record the check.

   QuickBooks enters the check in the register of your checking account.

When you've written a handwritten check (for example, you stop at the office supply store and purchase a box of laser printer paper), just enter the transaction directly in the Write Checks window when you get back to the office.

Managing inventory

If your business has inventory items to resell, you can use QuickBooks to keep track of ordering items, receiving items, paying for items, and selling items.

Ordering inventory

The first step is to order some inventory items. Now, create a purchase order for doors from Perry Windows & Doors.

To create a purchase order:

1 From the Vendors menu, choose Create Purchase Orders.

2 In the Vendor field, start typing ***pe*** and let QuickFill fill in the rest of the vendor name. Press Tab.

3 Click in the Item column and choose Interior under Wood Door from the Item list.

4 In the Qty field, type ***35***. Then press Tab.

QuickBooks multiplies the quantity by the cost to calculate the amount.

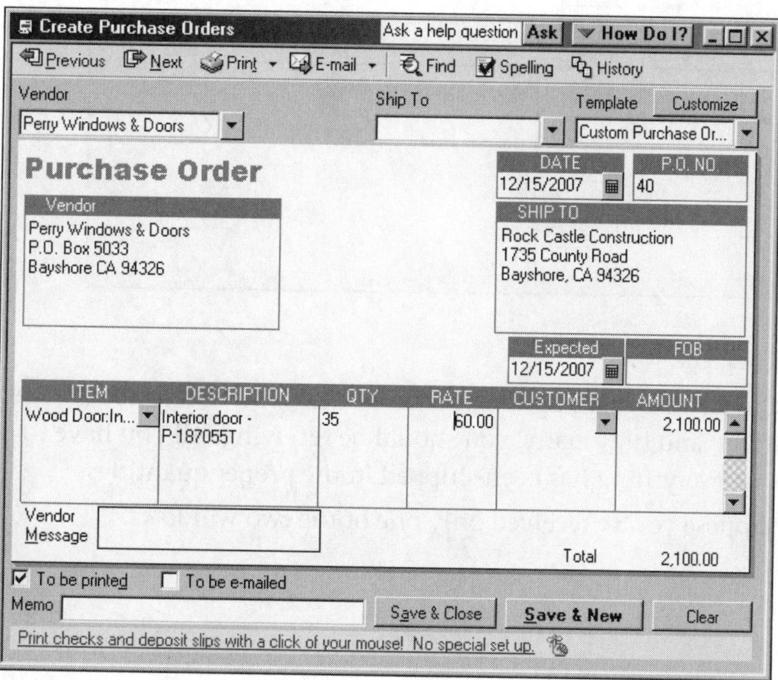

5 Click Save & Close to record the purchase order.

Receiving inventory items

Receiving items is the second step. A few days after you order the doors, they are delivered, and you want to receive the shipment to update your inventory records (the amount of the item you have on hand). Suppose you've received the inventory items, but you haven't received a bill with the items. (This is a very common occurrence.)

To record the receipt of inventory items:

1. From the Vendors menu, choose Receive Items.
2. In the Vendor field, type ***pe***. When QuickFill completes the entry for you, press Tab.

   You'll see a message letting you know that open purchase orders exist for Perry, and asking if you want to receive the items against one of the outstanding purchase orders.
3. In the Open PO's Exist window, click Yes.

   Now you need to choose the purchase orders filled by the shipment.

   QuickBooks lets you receive shipments against multiple purchase orders at one time. That's important, because it's very common for vendors to ship items from different purchase orders in the same shipment.
4. Select purchase order number 24 and number 40.

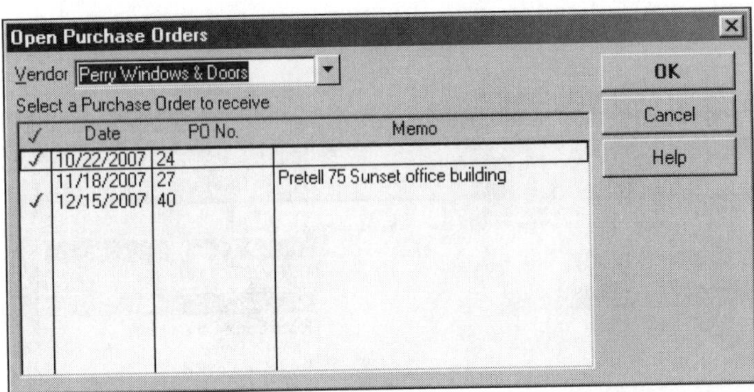

5. Click OK.

   QuickBooks looks up the purchase orders you've selected and tells you which items, and how many, you should be receiving. All you have to do is make sure that everything has been shipped in the proper quantities.

   Suppose you've received only one of the two windows.

6 Change the 2 in the Qty field for Windows to 1.

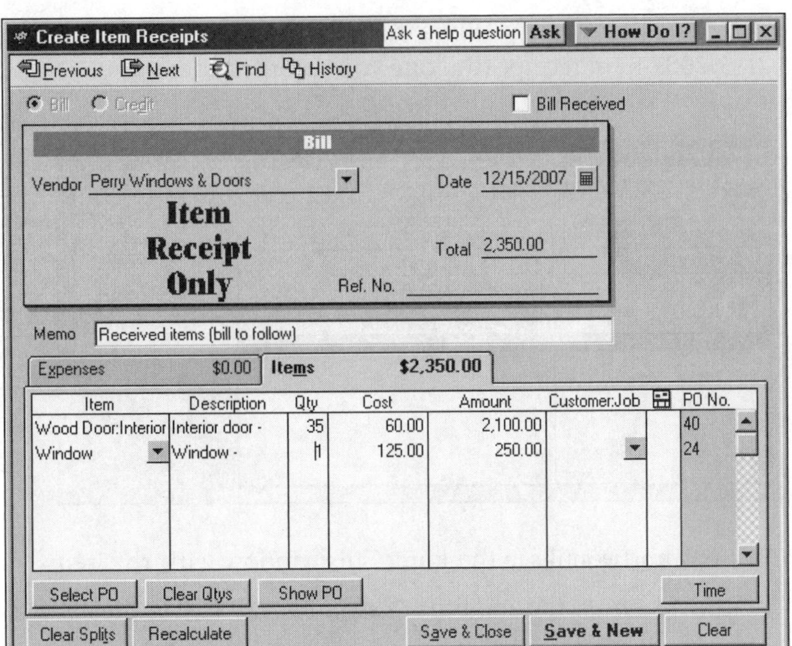

QuickBooks keeps track of the missing window, and lets you know it is still due.

7 Click Save & Close to record the item receipt.

Receiving bills after receiving items

The third step is to deal with the final bill for the items you ordered. Perhaps two weeks go by, and you get the bill from Perry. QuickBooks makes it painless to reflect any changes that appear on the final bill. As it turns out, there's one change you need to record when you pay this bill: Perry charged you $32 for shipping.

To record a bill:

1 From the Vendors menu, choose Enter Bill for Received Items.

2 Select Perry Windows & Doors from the Vendor drop-down list, and select the 12/15/2007 item receipt (the one you recorded today).

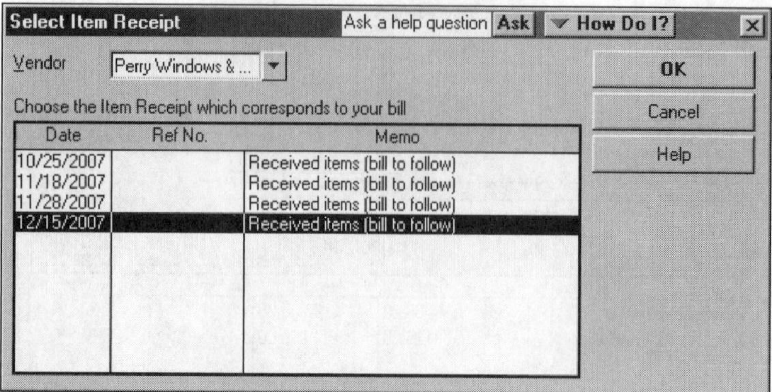

3 Click OK, and you'll see the Enter Bills window with the items already filled in.

4 Click the Expenses tab and type ***Postage and Delivery*** in the Account field and press Tab.

5 At the message telling you that QuickBooks could not find the account, click Set Up.

6 In the New Account window, make sure Expense is listed in the Type field and click OK.

7 Enter the $32 shipping charge in the Amount field to assign it to the Postage and Delivery account.

8 Press Tab.

9 Click Recalculate.

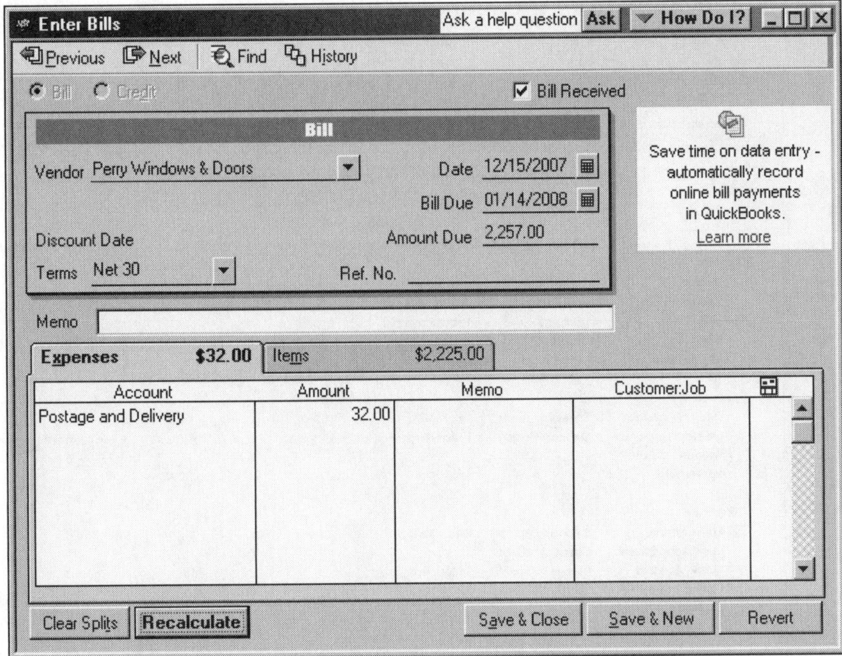

10 Click Save & Close to record the bill.

11 If QuickBooks displays a message asking if you want to change the transaction, click Yes.

Selling items

You can sell inventory items by creating an invoice the same way you did earlier. QuickBooks automatically keeps track of the items sold and updates your financial reports. If you sell three doors, QuickBooks automatically reduces the number of doors on hand by three, and adds both the revenue and the cost of goods sold associated with these doors to your financial reports.

Generating inventory reports

QuickBooks has a variety of inventory reports to tell you everything you might want to know about your inventory. Now that you've entered the bill, you can generate an inventory stock status by item report to make sure that all the items you've received are accounted for.

To generate an inventory report:

1 From the Reports menu, choose Inventory, and then choose Inventory Stock Status by Item from the submenu.

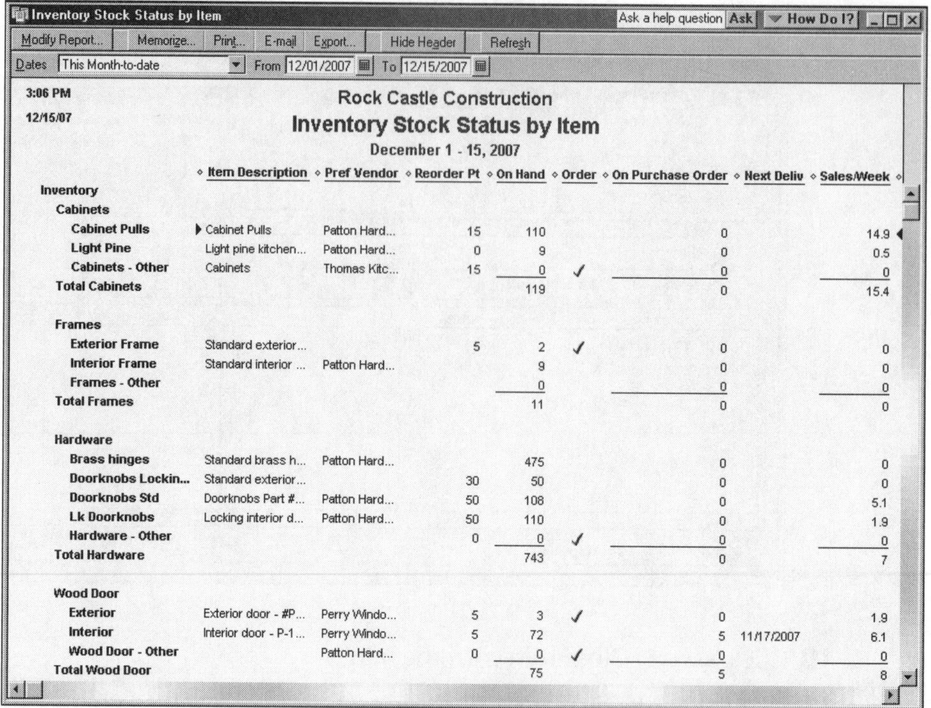

Inventory Stock Status by Item

3:06 PM
12/15/07

Rock Castle Construction
Inventory Stock Status by Item
December 1 - 15, 2007

	Item Description	Pref Vendor	Reorder Pt	On Hand	Order	On Purchase Order	Next Deliv	Sales/Week
Inventory								
Cabinets								
Cabinet Pulls	Cabinet Pulls	Patton Hard...	15	110		0		14.9
Light Pine	Light pine kitchen...	Patton Hard...	0	9		0		0.5
Cabinets - Other	Cabinets	Thomas Kitc...	15	0	✓	0		0
Total Cabinets				119		0		15.4
Frames								
Exterior Frame	Standard exterior...		5	2	✓	0		0
Interior Frame	Standard interior ...	Patton Hard...		9		0		0
Frames - Other				0		0		0
Total Frames				11		0		0
Hardware								
Brass hinges	Standard brass h...	Patton Hard...		475		0		0
Doorknobs Lockin...	Standard exterior...		30	50		0		0
Doorknobs Std	Doorknobs Part #...	Patton Hard...	50	108		0		5.1
Lk Doorknobs	Locking interior d...	Patton Hard...	50	110		0		1.9
Hardware - Other			0	0	✓	0		0
Total Hardware				743		0		7
Wood Door								
Exterior	Exterior door - #P...	Perry Windo...	5	3	✓	0		1.9
Interior	Interior door - P-1 ...	Perry Windo...	5	72		5	11/17/2007	6.1
Wood Door - Other		Patton Hard...	0	0	✓	0		0
Total Wood Door				75		5		8

For each inventory item, this report shows quantity on hand, quantity on order, date of next order receipt, and the average quantity sold per week.

If you want to see the transactions that make up any amount in a report, you can use the QuickZoom feature. Whenever you see the mouse pointer change from an arrow to a magnifying glass with a Z inside, double-click the amount you want to investigate.

2 Double-click the line for Cabinet Pulls on the report.

QuickBooks creates a QuickReport that shows more detail on that specific inventory item. You can also use QuickZoom from here.

3 On the QuickReport, double-click the Item Receipt transaction.

Now you see the Item Receipt recording the receipt of cabinet pulls.

4 From the Window menu, choose Close All to close all the windows you have open.

Creating reports and graphs

The Reports menu has a wide variety of preset reports. You can customize any of the preset reports to show the exact data you need. To create a report, you choose the report you want from the QuickBooks Reports menu.

To generate a report of overdue customers and balances:

1. From the Reports menu, choose Customers & Receivables, and then choose A/R Aging Summary.

   The report lists the jobs with open balances for each customer. The columns show which amounts are current (not yet due) and which are overdue. Notice that Brian Cook is more than 30 days overdue on his kitchen job.

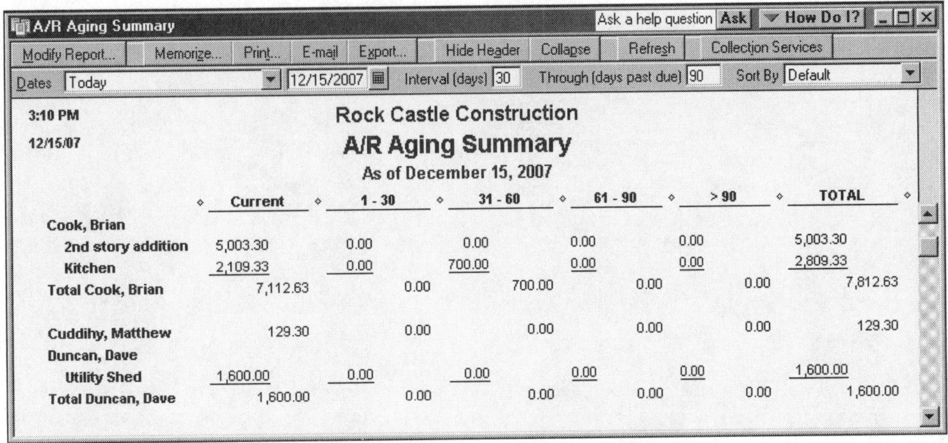

2. To see whether anyone is more than 60 days overdue, change the "Through (days past due)" field at the top of the report from 90 to 60. Press Tab.

   QuickBooks makes a column for >60. Since all the amounts in that column are 0.00, you can see that no one is more than 60 days overdue.

3. Close the report window.
4. Click No at the message asking if you would like to memorize the report.

If you want to see a visual display of how much you're owed by customers, you can create an accounts receivable graph.

To create an accounts receivable graph:

1. From the Reports menu, choose Customers & Receivables and then choose Accounts Receivable Graph.
2. When you finish viewing the graph, close the graph window.

APPENDIX C Course handouts

Using the course handouts

In this section, you'll find copies of all the handouts referenced in this course. The handout files are included on your QuickBooks exercise CD-ROM, and have been saved in Portable Document Format (PDF). You can open the file containing the handouts (handouts.pdf) using Adobe Acrobat Reader allowing you to print the handouts as desired.

Handout 1: Balance sheet accounts

The following table describes the use of each of the balance sheet account types available in QuickBooks.

This account type	Tracks
Bank	Checking, savings, and money market accounts. Add one bank account for every account your company has at a bank or other financial institution. (You should also use this account type to track petty cash.)
Accounts receivable (A/R)	Transactions related to the customers who owe you money, including invoices, payments, deposits of payments, refunds, and credit memos. Most companies have only one A/R account.
Other current asset	Assets likely to be converted to cash or used up within one year, such as notes receivable due within a year, prepaid expenses, and security deposits.
Fixed asset	Long-term notes receivable and depreciable assets your company owns that aren't likely to be converted into cash within a year, such as equipment or furniture.
Accounts payable (A/P)	Transactions related to the vendors to whom you owe money, including your company's outstanding bills, bill payments, and any credit you have with vendors.
Credit card	Credit card purchases, bills, payments, and credits.
Current liability	Liabilities scheduled to be paid within one year, such as sales tax, payroll taxes, accrued or deferred salaries, and short-term loans.
Long-term liability	Liabilities such as loans or mortgages scheduled to be paid over periods longer than one year.
Equity	Owner's equity, including capital investment, drawings, and retained earnings.

Handout 2: Accounts created automatically

The following is a list of the accounts that QuickBooks creates automatically.

- **Accounts Receivable.** QuickBooks creates this account during the EasyStep Interview, or the first time you create an invoice.
- **Inventory Asset.** When the first inventory part item is created in a company data file, QuickBooks creates the Inventory Asset account.
- **Undeposited Funds.** QuickBooks adds this account to the chart of accounts the first time you record a payment from an invoice or a sales receipt. QuickBooks uses this account to hold money you've collected until you deposit it in a bank account. To add funds to this account, select the "Group with other undeposited funds" option in the Enter Sales Receipt window or in the Receive Payments window.
- **Accounts Payable.** QuickBooks creates this account during the EasyStep Interview, or the first time you enter a bill.
- **Payroll Liabilities.** QuickBooks adds this account to the chart of accounts automatically when you turn on the payroll feature in a company file. QuickBooks initially maps all payroll items that create liabilities to this account.
- **Sales Tax Payable.** QuickBooks creates this account when you turn on the sales tax feature.
- **Opening Bal Equity.** This account is created the first time you enter the opening balance for a balance sheet account. Every time you add a new account with an opening balance, QuickBooks records the second half of the entry in the Opening Bal Equity account. This means that total equity is the net balance of the assets minus the liabilities entered into QuickBooks. Once you've entered all of the accounts and balances, you may use a journal entry to allocate Opening Balance Equity to the proper equity accounts.
- **Retained Earnings.** This account is unique because there is no register associated with it. Each time you run a balance sheet, you assign the date of the report. QuickBooks then calculates the net income from all transactions from the earliest date in the company file to the end of the fiscal year prior to the current year. QuickBooks displays the results as retained earnings. Because of this feature, you don't need to make the traditional closing entries at the end of the year.
- **Uncategorized Income.** QuickBooks creates this account when you enter an income transaction that is not assigned to any other income account.
- **COGS.** When the inventory feature is turned on and the first Inventory Part item is created in a company file, QuickBooks automatically creates a Cost of Good Sold (COGS) account.
- **Payroll Expenses.** This account is created when you turn on payroll in a company data file. All payroll expense items are initially mapped to this account.
- **Uncategorized Expenses.** QuickBooks creates this account when an expense transaction is entered that is not assigned to an expense account.

Handout 3: Registers associated with QuickBooks windows

You can open the register associated with a window by choosing Use Register from the Edit menu when the window is displayed.

While you have this window displayed...	You can display the register for this account...
Create Invoices	Accounts Receivable
Enter Bills	Accounts Payable
Write Checks	The account you have displayed in the Bank Account field on the check form.
Receive Payments	Accounts Receivable
Make Deposits	The account you have displayed in the Deposit To field, or Undeposited Funds if that option is selected.
Enter Sales Receipts	The account you have displayed in the Deposit To field.
Create Credit Memos/Refunds	Accounts Receivable
Enter Credit Card Charges	The account you have displayed in the Credit Card field.

You can also open the register for any balance sheet account (except Retained Earnings) by double-clicking the account name in the chart of accounts.

Handout 4: QuickBooks item types

Items for things you buy and sell

Type	Use to enter
Service	Services you charge for or services you purchase. EXAMPLES: Professional fees, labor
Inventory Part	Items you purchase, track as inventory, and then resell. EXAMPLES: Electrical outlets, t-shirts
Inventory Assembly (Premier)	Items you produce or buy, track as inventory, and then resell. EXAMPLES: Pre-assembled door kits, custom bicycles
Non-Inventory Part	Items you sell but do not purchase; items you purchase but do not resell; items you purchase and resell, but do not track as inventory. EXAMPLES: Custom-made slipcovers, pizza, office supplies
Other Charge	Other charges on a sale or purchase. EXAMPLES: Shipping charges, delivery charges
Group	A group of individual items already on the item list. EXAMPLES: A group of services and lab fees for office visits, a group of services and food items provided by a caterer

Items that calculate

Type	Use to
Subtotal	Calculate a subtotal before calculating a discount or charge that covers several items.
Discount	Calculate an amount to be subtracted from the total. (To discount several items, use a subtotal item before the discount item.)
Payment	Record a payment received at the time of invoicing so that the amount owed on the invoice is reduced.
Sales tax	Calculate a single sales tax for a sale.
Sales Tax Group	Calculate two or more sales taxes grouped together and applied to the same sale.

Handout 5: Inventory workflow

The following graphic provides an overview of how to track inventory information in QuickBooks.

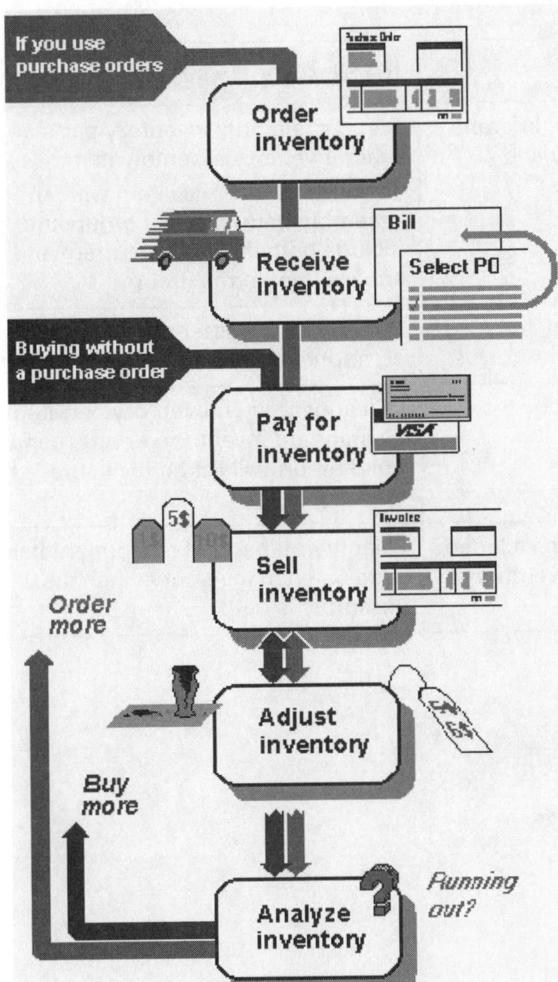

Handout 6: Group vs. inventory assembly items

The following table compares group and assembly items to help you decide which item type is appropriate for a given situation.

Group item	Inventory assembly item
Can include combinations of different item types, such as inventory and service items	Can contain only inventory parts or other inventory assembly items To combine a service item with an assembly item, create a group and include both the assembly item and the service item in the group.
Allows you to print individual items contained in the group on sales forms	Prints only the assembly name, not component part names, on sales forms
No reports available specifically for groups	Will appear after inventory part items on standard inventory reports; pending build report will list builds in the pending state
Quantity on hand of each item included in the group is adjusted in inventory at the time of sale	Quantity on hand of component items is adjusted in inventory when the assembly is built

Handout 7: Sales tax

The following graphic provides an overview of how to track sales tax information in QuickBooks.

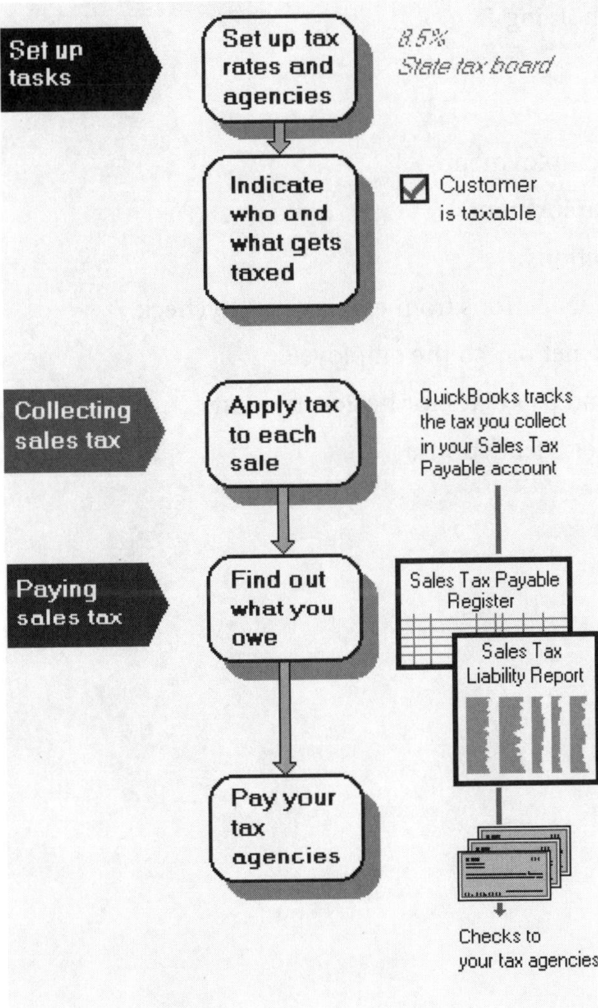

Handout 8: Employer payroll responsibilities

The following is a list of payroll activities for which the employer is responsible.

1. Calculate gross pay for employees.
2. Calculate federal withholding.
3. Calculate state withholding.
4. Calculate FICA.
5. Calculate Medicare.
6. Calculate federal unemployment.
7. Calculate state unemployment.
8. Add any other deductions.
9. Withhold taxes and deductions from employee's paycheck.
10. Write a check for the net pay to the employee.
11. Submit tax reports and pay taxes to the government.
12. Pay any other withheld deductions.

Handout 9: Payroll item types

A payroll item is anything that affects the amount on a paycheck. QuickBooks has seven types of payroll items.

The following table provides the name and description of each payroll item type.

Type	Description	Examples
Wage	Annual or hourly wage Commission	Straight time, salary, overtime Sales commission, piece rate
Addition	Addition to employee's paycheck	Employee loan, expense reimbursement
Deduction	Deduction from employee's pay	Medical insurance, employee loan repayment
Company Contribution	Company-paid payroll items	Company's contribution to 401(k)
Federal Tax	Federal taxes	Federal income taxes withheld
State Tax	State taxes	State income tax, state unemployment tax
Other Tax	Local payroll taxes	Michigan cities tax, etc.

Handout 10: List of payroll expenses and liabilities

Payroll expenses

- Employee's gross pay
- Employer payroll taxes:
    - Social Security (FICA)
    - Federal Unemployment Insurance (FUTA)
    - Medicare
    - State Unemployment Insurance (SUI)—if paid by employer
    - State Disability (SDI)—if paid by employer

Payroll liabilities

Taxes you've withheld from paychecks for the following:

- Social Security (FICA)
- Federal Unemployment Insurance (FUTA)
- Medicare
- State Unemployment Insurance (SUI)
- State Disability (SDI)
- State income tax
- Federal income tax

Index

Numerics

A

B

C

D

E

L

M

N

O

P

Q

R

S

T

U

V

W

Instructor's Guide Evaluation

QuickBooks in the Classroom 2004

____

Instructor Name

____

Organization Name

____

Date

MAIL TO:
QuickBooks in the Classroom
Intuit MS 2475
P.O. Box 7850
Mountain View, CA 94039

OR FAX TO:
1-650-944-3133

Objectives	**Success Level** 1 (low)	2	3	4	5 (high)
The guide covered all the topics and features you wanted	☐	☐	☐	☐	☐
The information was organized in a logical manner	☐	☐	☐	☐	☐
The file on the exercise disk was accurate and helpful	☐	☐	☐	☐	☐
The lessons and topics were easy to find	☐	☐	☐	☐	☐
The step-by-step format was helpful	☐	☐	☐	☐	☐
The screenshots were accurate and helpful	☐	☐	☐	☐	☐

Please indicate the class level: (circle one)

K-12 Community College University Adult Education ________________

What did you like most about the guide? What section or handouts were the least helpful?

____

____

What aspects of the guide could be improved? What topic is missing or needs more clarification for your students?

____

____

What other examples would be helpful to your students?

____

____

What other teaching materials, if any, do you use to teach this course?

____

____

What is the name of your course, and what is the course length?

____

____

Training Skill Evaluation - Before Class

This class is designed to meet the following objectives. To ensure that you receive the most effective training, rate your confidence performing each objective now, using the numbered scale on the right. Using the information you provide helps to determine whether the objectives of the course have been met.

Objectives	never attempted 0	low 1	2	3	4	high 5
Create a QuickBooks company	☐	☐	☐	☐	☐	☐
Add and edit information in company lists	☐	☐	☐	☐	☐	☐
Modify one of the QuickBooks preset chart of accounts	☐	☐	☐	☐	☐	☐
Customize QuickBooks forms	☐	☐	☐	☐	☐	☐
Create customer invoices	☐	☐	☐	☐	☐	☐
Receive payments from customers and make bank deposits	☐	☐	☐	☐	☐	☐
Write checks, assigning the amounts to specific expense or bank accounts	☐	☐	☐	☐	☐	☐
Enter and pay bills	☐	☐	☐	☐	☐	☐
Assign reimbursable expenses to customers	☐	☐	☐	☐	☐	☐
Open/use registers for QuickBooks balance sheet accounts	☐	☐	☐	☐	☐	☐
Reconcile a QuickBooks checking account	☐	☐	☐	☐	☐	☐
Track credit card transactions	☐	☐	☐	☐	☐	☐
Work with QuickBooks asset and liability accounts	☐	☐	☐	☐	☐	☐
Create and customize QuickBooks reports and graphs	☐	☐	☐	☐	☐	☐
Track and pay sales tax	☐	☐	☐	☐	☐	☐
Manage inventory with QuickBooks	☐	☐	☐	☐	☐	☐
Run payroll with QuickBooks	☐	☐	☐	☐	☐	☐
Create estimates, track time and do advanced job costing	☐	☐	☐	☐	☐	☐
Export a QuickBooks report to Microsoft Excel	☐	☐	☐	☐	☐	☐
Write a letter using the QuickBooks Letters feature	☐	☐	☐	☐	☐	☐

Success Level

____
Your name

____
Your organization

____
Your instructor's name

____
Date

Training Skill Evaluation - After Class

This class is designed to meet the following objectives. Please rate your confidence performing each objective now, using the numbered scale on the right.

Objectives	never attempted 0	low 1	2	3	4	high 5
Create a QuickBooks company	☐	☐	☐	☐	☐	☐
Add and edit information in company lists	☐	☐	☐	☐	☐	☐
Modify one of the QuickBooks preset chart of accounts	☐	☐	☐	☐	☐	☐
Customize QuickBooks forms	☐	☐	☐	☐	☐	☐
Create customer invoices	☐	☐	☐	☐	☐	☐
Receive payments from customers and make bank deposits	☐	☐	☐	☐	☐	☐
Write checks, assigning the amounts to specific expense or bank accounts	☐	☐	☐	☐	☐	☐
Enter and pay bills	☐	☐	☐	☐	☐	☐
Assign reimbursable expenses to customers	☐	☐	☐	☐	☐	☐
Open/use registers for QuickBooks balance sheet accounts	☐	☐	☐	☐	☐	☐
Reconcile a QuickBooks checking account	☐	☐	☐	☐	☐	☐
Track credit card transactions	☐	☐	☐	☐	☐	☐
Work with QuickBooks asset and liability accounts	☐	☐	☐	☐	☐	☐
Create and customize QuickBooks reports and graphs	☐	☐	☐	☐	☐	☐
Track and pay sales tax	☐	☐	☐	☐	☐	☐
Manage inventory with QuickBooks	☐	☐	☐	☐	☐	☐
Run payroll with QuickBooks	☐	☐	☐	☐	☐	☐
Create estimates, track time do advanced job costing	☐	☐	☐	☐	☐	☐
Export a QuickBooks report to Microsoft Excel	☐	☐	☐	☐	☐	☐
Write a letter using the QuickBooks Letters feature	☐	☐	☐	☐	☐	☐

____
Your name

____
Your organization

____
Your instructor's name

____
Date

continued on the next page

Training Skill Evaluation - After Class (continued)

Please answer the questions below.

What sections or handouts were the most helpful?

____

____

____

What sections or handouts were the least helpful?

____

____

____

What did you like most about the course?

____

____

____

What aspects of the course could be improved?

____

____

____

Other comments:

____

____

____